The Social Space of the Essay

The Social Space of the Essay

2003–2023

Ian Wedde

TE HERENGA WAKA
UNIVERSITY PRESS

Te Herenga Waka University Press
Victoria University of Wellington
PO Box 600 Wellington
teherengawakapress.co.nz

First published 2024

ISBN 9781776921218

A catalogue record is available from the National Library of New Zealand

Published with the generous support of a grant from

creative nz
ARTS COUNCIL OF NEW ZEALAND TOI AOTEAROA

Printed in Singapore by Markono Print Media Pte Ltd.

Contents

The Social Space of the Essay

I value the essay as a social space – a text that records something like conversational thinking-aloud. Such conversations usually begin with a commission to write or talk about something. In the early 1980s, the art dealer and gallerist Peter McLeavey finagled an art reviewer job for me with the *Evening Post* in Wellington, which I kept up for most of a decade. This was because I was interested in art and hung out at exhibition openings, including those at Peter's gallery. I looked at and talked about art in the company of friends in the art world and when I wrote reviews for the *Evening Post* our shared social space – often argumentative – was what I occupied and what occupied me as I wrote my texts expressing opinions that expected and often remembered responses.

Over the next few decades these short early encounters expanded into longer essays for a variety of magazines and journals in New Zealand and elsewhere; into talks and lectures; into books and catalogues. They involved relationships with artists and also with curators, publishers and editors, whose argumentative company animated the social space of the essay. Similarly, exhibitions on which I worked as a curator required relationships with artists but also with co-workers, including designers, conservators, editors, publicists and others; and not least with audiences, who all contributed their thoughts and voices to the social space of the exhibition and its diverse texts, including the texts I wrote for catalogues or when asked to give talks.

I've written essays about topics other than art. I've also written fiction and poetry. There's a special, solitary pleasure involved in making and inhabiting the imaginary spaces of fiction, however allegorical they may be – however much they may articulate ideas about the societies we live in. But whatever their subjects, my essays have always needed a different social mindset from novels and poems.

From the outset, the social space of the essay is involved with the text's readers to the degree that conversation is implied – more or less intimate, even argumentative. The essay will often have originated in conversation, or the conversations of groups gathered around an event. Its long form may both contain and measure the extended time of face-to-face conversation or imply that extent; in this it will differ from social media, email and instant messages. These forms are often both dynamic and distanced, with the immediate energy of in-the-moment exchanges. The essays collected here, though, hope for the pleasure of extended conversation, both in their content and in the critical participation of their readers.

Ian Wedde
October 2023

This selection of texts responds to works and the people who made them, and to conversations in social situations such as exhibition openings. These conversations animated what I wrote. The texts are dedicated first to the makers of the works but also to the congenial, argumentative, critical company they assemble.

It is also dedicated to the editors, symposium organisers, gallery directors and curators in New Zealand and elsewhere who commissioned me to write diverse texts; and to my editor Fergus Barrowman and the team at Te Herenga Waka University Press in particular Rachel Barrowman with thanks for their sympathetic treatment of that diversity and their essential part in the conversation.

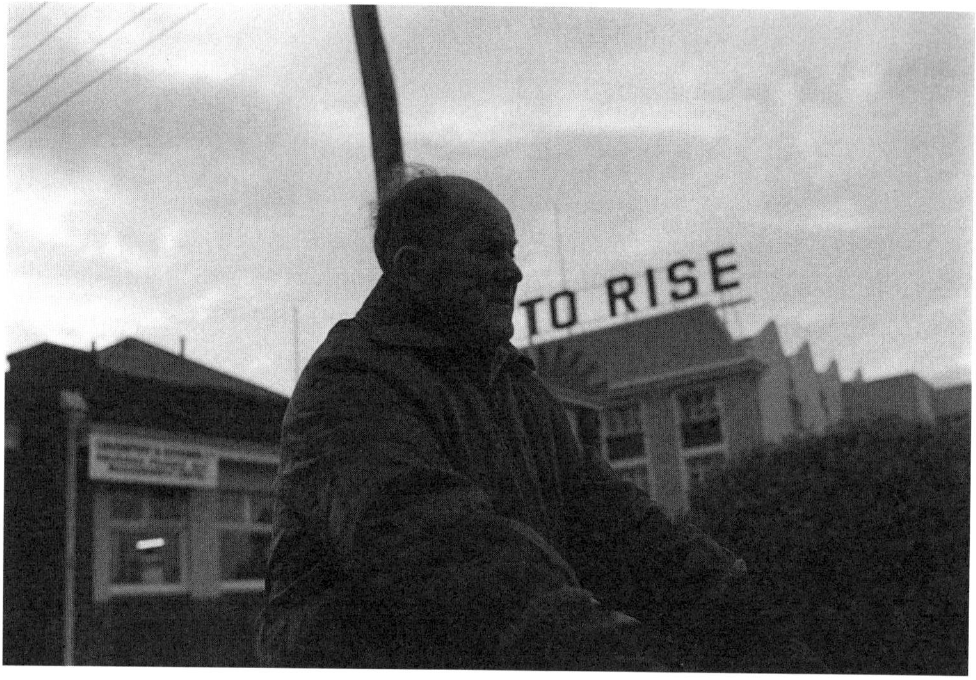

Peter Black, *Christchurch*, 1987, from
Moving Pictures series, in *Peter Black
– Real Fiction*, *Sport 30*, March 2003.
Courtesy of the artist.

At Home in the Dark

Peter Black – Real Fiction

City Gallery, Wellington, March 2003; published in *Sport 30*, edited by Gregory O'Brien and Lara Strongman (2003)

In the kitchen at our place hangs a photograph of the square in Palmerston North when the PDC department store still had the Kiwi Bacon kiwi on the roof. The flightless bird is poised in a kind of awkward plié next to the sign of its name 'in lights' (at night that would be) but in the darkness of daytime it is a black silhouette beside the black billboard stencil of its name against a washed-out sky. Though captured in a 'first position', the dumpy, earnest bird is not about to rise or jeté into an apotheosis in the sky above the provincial town whose sign it, haplessly, is.

The darkness of this image is not just found in the literally dark silhouettes of our national symbol and its name, and not just in the pooled darkness in the fore and middle ground, where car interiors are filled with shadows – in the case of the car closest to us, so dark we don't at first notice the little girl with her fingers curled over the top edge of the car's front passenger seat window-glass. The darkness of the image is also in its vocalisation, let's say, in the way it's telling its stories. The claustrophobia of the narrative, with the kid trapped in the car and seeming to strain for air at the window's open edge, the kiwi on the roof burdened with gravity and hemmed in against its own name – this is another kind of darkness. It would perhaps be 'Gothic' if it was without irony, but it is ironic: there are those craftily isolated wayfinding road-signs, arrows pointing in simultaneously contradictory directions: Where are we? Where are we going? Is there a way out (let alone a way in)?

In a sense, the darkness of this image is a simple sign of gloom – a simile that places ordinary phenomenological darkness beside a kind of national condition: the entrapment of the provincial, the boredom of childhood waiting in a car, the odd desolation of a town centre with no real heart, the depressing functionality of the PDC department store façade with not even the tacky glamour of marketing or branding to enliven its peculiar version of form meeting function – as though shopping had to be contained within the grim precinct of a building like a transformer station or public works warehouse, and the only sign of consumer excitation a hobbled national emblem next to the terse utterance of edible pork. Get up, get crack(l)ing, have a decent breakfast, don't fool yourself, there's no way out, make the best of it, and don't spoil the kids.

What's interesting about this phenomenally bleak image is, however, in the end, its odd tone of affectionate, forgiving levity. Its darkness is in its overarching poetry of claustrophobia and entrapment; its lightness in its little, grimacing details. Its laconic, koan-like yarns.

The image has a simple structure within which these droll details are sought out. There is a pale, almost washed-out upper band consisting of sky and the vacuous façade of the department store. Then there is a darker lower half, filled with cars themselves full of shadow, and in one of these interiors, the trapped, dark-haired child. Needless to say, this child is the free spirit in all of us, in need of a driver, a way out, someone with enough wit to transform the sardonic details of the scene into an emotional escape – a grande jeté out of the frame, the miracle of flight.

By contrast, in another photograph by Peter Black which often hangs by the stairs at our place, the dark image of a stocky, balding bicycle-rider passing the Edmonds Baking Powder factory in Christchurch (another national brand) contains few details. It might be dawn (or dusk) and the man might be cycling to (or from) work. Once again, the top half of the scene is light, a glaring sky beginning to darken (or lighten), with an overcast muffling of direct light.

The man's profile is almost totally black and seen in two-dimensional cut-out. A spindly pole seems to rise out of his shoulder into the sky, like the pole in a merry-go-round. On close inspection, the man's expression is firm and thoughtful – he's not having a fairground kind of time, he's pedalling to (or from) work, that's immediately clear. He's just passed a window in which there's a tiny band of sentient light, a neon perhaps, and on the outside of the window a functional sign made illegible by the dark.

The big drama in this otherwise phlegmatic story is the section of the Edmonds Baking Powder sign, '[SURE] TO RISE' – the 'sure' hidden behind the man's large, sure head, the 'to rise' rising on an optimistic gradient, in dark, clear-cut silhouette against the dawn (evening) sky, from the man's mouth.

He is sure, he's swallowed the word, and the 'to rise' rises from the front of his serious face like breath, like a miraculous utterance, like a call to prayer. He seems to be incanting it across the receding rooftop of the factory, into the pale sky, as he rides his marvellous carousel through the dark.

The Facts of Life

Ian Wedde talks to New York essayist Eliot Weinberger

New Zealand Listener (2 April 2004)

Eliot Weinberger is a really great essayist and translator of poetry. He says he's happy with these choices because he discovered he was a rotten poet. This is way too modest. Some of his essays are better poems than a lot of what passes for poetry. What's more, while discussing translations of Pablo Neruda by Alastair Reid, Weinberger suggested that some translations are better poems than their originals. The man's a poet all right, if by that we mean someone who demands his work must be an exacting, transformative, daring and interesting quest into the paradoxical facts of life, whose writing survives the acid baths of close reading, and whose approach to structure and form has more to do with the performance of language on the page, and in the mind, than with the minor rhetoric of communication.

He has also got a shrewd sense of humour, revealed by a hooded look of bored apprehension if the talk meanders into polite inanity, and by an appreciative chortle when it goes the other way, somewhere interesting. 'Interesting': key word. He uses it a lot.

We begin the interview on the balcony of his hotel room, and continue it informally at a couple of dinners. The balcony's too noisy: the tape recorder plays back traffic, a mighty wind, and the tiny sound of Weinberger's voice. We move inside – as his readers know (and also those who heard his sessions at the NZ Post Writers and Readers Week), this voice speaks fluently and sardonically from the metropolitan racket of cities and the glossalalia of history, especially history that is written and sung as poetry, recounted in dreams, captured in the sometimes farcical tragedies of scholarship (Aryanism in the essay 'The Falls'), or in the pernicious farces of political spin (the essay '9/12').

It's a voice that speaks the texts of shamanism, the surreal and the absurd, in a tone of reasonable wonder. It recounts the loony factuality of racist ethnographic practices such as cranial measurement with as much equanimity as it documents the relationship between poetry and spying. The equanimity's deceptive: Weinberger is an indignant political witness, an uncompromising critic, and a merciless student of truth. But he knows that bad information will hang itself. The tone of his essays is based on a remarkable peer agreement with the reader: we trust his account, he trusts us to figure it out.

A big reader himself, he extends his trust to the writers of esoteric texts – especially poets. In 'The Modernists in the Basement & the Stars Above', he asks for 'interesting poetry'. And what might that be?

'There are many paths of knowledge into the world, and the one that I have always enjoyed following is poetry,' he says. 'I became involved with Mexico through the poetry of Octavio Paz, I went to Machu Picchu because I'd read Neruda, because of Ezra Pound I studied Chinese, because of *The Waste Land* I studied grail stories, and so forth.'

The 'and so forth' modestly camouflages an amazing range of enquiry: many literatures and their languages, politics, the blind mole rat, anthropology, the philosophy of ideas, Atlantis, Baghdad, genocides . . . He believes literature's healthier when poets are out in the world. Some of his own experience came from writing magazine travelogues: 'They take a couple of hours, you get to travel for a month.' Weinberger is sceptical of American writing school culture – 'the university creative writing school diaspora' – poets graduating as poets and becoming teachers of poetry, poems about 'changing the storm windows'.

This isn't dislike of the commonplace, but impatience with mundanity: Weinberger's own writing's full of the vivacity of concrete facts.

'You have these very dull, middle-class lives, and they don't have much to write about except changing the storm windows and things like that. I think it was much healthier for poetry in general when people had to make a living doing something else. They knew about something else. One of the greatnesses of American poetry has been that very concrete perception of the real – William Carlos Williams's "No ideas but in things" – the problem is that the reality people are perceiving has become so limited.'

Translation is one of Weinberger's favourite antidotes to introverted mundanity. In a neat comment, which like many of his aphorisms contains a creative paradox, he says that 'translation feeds a national literature'.

'Translation is where you get the ideas that you collectively hadn't thought of before, and new ways of expressing those ideas, and that refreshes the cultural gene pool. Historically, the great periods of national literatures have also been great periods of translation. There are some exceptions, like Tang China, etc, but generally speaking this is true. The other thing that revitalises the national literature is when you have new people writing in the language. They bring new forms, new ideas and new stories. It takes a few generations before you have the critical mass and new people can enter into the national literature – but these entries are absolutely essential, otherwise the literature ends up repeating itself.'

What about the emergence of a regional pan-Pacific literature informed by Māori tikanga, by translation and by new Polynesian and Asian voices in English? New concepts of time, new structures?

'That would be tremendous. My limited knowledge of New Zealand literature in English tells me it began naturally enough as an outpost of British literature, moved through a self-absorbed nationalist phase, and turned its attention to America in the 1960s. It seems inevitable that the next phase should grow out of the region, and out of a society forming from new immigrants from Asia and the Pacific.

'There's an interesting parallel with what's going on in Mexico. Now, for the first time, there's a number of poets writing in the indigenous languages – Mexico is a country of many, many languages, with traditional oral literatures, but you haven't really had writers before. These are educated people, who've gone to universities, and are choosing to write in their indigenous languages. They are simultaneously bringing something new into Mexican literature, and bringing modernism into traditional literatures. Both are being transformed; it's really interesting.'

Is this a process of outgrowing both provincial nationalism and its close cousin, the insecurity of internationalists living far from the ordained metropolitan centres?

'Yes, it comes from a realisation that you are a centre also. And of course the way you become a centre involves a total revision of your own history, you see the precursors of what is happening right now, you see that they weren't just the outreaches of the old centres, but the beginnings of the new centre – the centre everywhere.'

Later in the interview, talking about American patriotism and the different meanings of the American flag, Weinberger uses an interesting phrase to describe America beyond New York City. He calls it 'America out there', as though it's a different country . . . as though New York City survives either as one of the old centres of modernism, or as 'a centre everywhere'.

'Fifty percent of New Yorkers,' he says, 'were born somewhere else. The other 50 percent are their children.' Weinberger's kind of place. At a dinner one night during the week, a guest asks if he doesn't find New York a dangerous place to bring up kids. Weinberger is scornful and incredulous. It's far too interesting to be dangerous. 'Out in America' is where kids get bored, into drugs, and where they shoot up schools.

Iceland is also Weinberger's kind of place: 'an extremely modern Scandinavian, cradle-to-grave welfare state' in an unpopulated landscape, where the roads avoid rocks containing 'the hidden people'. 'You know, the hidden people live here, take the road around this rock here, and now let's do the human genome project . . .' – the supernatural treated as factually as Transit New Zealand might have treated the Huntly taniwha.

How to reconcile the New Yorker at home in the modern, polylingual, teeming city, and the guy who likes his modern wilderness populated by talking rocks? What about these paradoxes in Weinberger's work, its persistent dialectic: the brilliance and banality of facts; the daring, liberating qualities of modernism, and its authoritarian, fascist undertow; the need for truth, and the dreadful places belief in truth can take you; the importance of scepticism and the value of dreams? Is this a kind of poetic 'Falsificationism' after Karl Popper, whose idea of conjecture and refutation is orchestrated as though he were composing music, which he also did?

'I guess there's a kind of scepticism in everything I do, but that extends as much to factuality as to the supernatural. I don't know – can a writer have that kind of critical distance on his work? I mean, it's absolutely true, I'll have to think about this for a while. I was very heavily influenced by the poet Charles Reznikoff. Reznikoff was trained as a lawyer but never practised law, and he said that a poem has to be as tight as a legal brief, every time you put a case you have to see if the opposite is also true. I think there's always that tension between what I've said and the opposite of what I've said.

'Also, most of what I write I've perceived imagistically – that sense of concentrated, vivid images – and the readers themselves have to decide what it all adds up to. Increasingly I try to have fewer conclusions.'

Weinberger has had a career-long interest in the surreal. Does this sense of paradox come from a perception of the world as absurd? As in, 'George W. Bush has exactly the same relationship to the policies of his government as Britney Spears does to the operations of the Pepsi Corporation'?

'The aspect of surrealism that appeals to me a lot is the found object, taking the collage of ordinary things and making something out of that. I've written a lot of things that are totally factual which are extremely weird, you know. And in the 1920s there wasn't that much difference between surrealism and anthropology, the interest in 'the primitive' as a way of liberating parts of the human psyche that had been repressed by bourgeois rationality.'

And back to Iceland. 'One of the main reasons I love Iceland is that it's one of the last places the middle class still remembers.' Implying that, elsewhere, they don't? 'Well, they certainly don't have any memory of the archaic . . . or of the taniwha, exactly. And, of course, it's also about respect for the land, quite simply, which has disappeared in most parts of the world. Whether one believes in the taniwha literally or not, it's still extremely healthy to do so.'

Just as it's healthy – and interesting – to ask, as Weinberger does in the chilling essay 'The Falls', why on earth did Nazis think they were 'Aryans'? 'After all, the Aryans were these people in India, why did these blond Teutonic types think they were Aryans? This coincided with another question, when I read about what was going on in Rwanda, the fact that they thought the Tutsis were Hamites, people who needed to be sent back to Abyssinia where they came from. How did you get from the children of Noah in the Bible to the Rwandans? It's both weird and obvious.

'And of course these two things keep intersecting: Aryanism, and the children of Noah, in the invention of "scientific racism". And so I did this collage, this DNA strand, following the children of Noah to Rwanda. What's happening in America right now doesn't yet have that depth of history . . .'

But don't forget: if Plymouth Rock could talk (and it can), it would remind us (as Weinberger does in 'A Clarion for the Quincentenary') that the *Mayflower*, on its next voyage after 1620, sailed to Africa to pick up slaves. Very, very interesting.

Thanks, Eliot.

The Next Big Thing
The Pacific's 'sea of islands'

New Zealand Listener (17 September 2004)

In the Pacific's 'sea of islands', diverse cultures are reinventing themselves and their traditions, trying to produce futures rather than memories.

Old joke: 3000 years ago some people with sailing canoes are looking at a big horizon from a beach east of Taiwan or New Guinea. Says one, 'This could be the next big thing.' These wild surmisers were the ancestors of navigators dubbed 'Argonauts of the Western Pacific' in 1922 by Bronisław Malinowski. They explored and settled what Epeli Hau'ofa, since 1997 the director of the Oceania Centre for Arts and Culture in Fiji, would in 1993 call the 'Sea of Islands'. In 1536, Hernándo Cortés 'and all his men' stared at the Pacific from their peak in Baja California; their 'wild surmise', to borrow from John Keats's ode, survives in the wistful trace of longing for fabulous continental mineral wealth in 'The Isles of Solomon', so named by Álvaro de Mendaña in 1568.

In Melbourne in July, two more sets of eagle eyes were looking at the Pacific and seeing the next big thing all over again. At Craft Victoria, its director, Kevin Murray, has been marshalling support around the *South Project* – 'A cultural highway linking the countries of the south'. The *South Project* is 'a five-year program designed to develop networks for cultural exchange between countries of the south, including southern Africa, Australia, the Pacific and Latin America'. *South 1*, the intensive, exuberant, and often weird colloquium convened by Murray at Melbourne University, was 'the initial gathering of representatives from participating countries to develop the parameters for future south–south exchange'.

Murray is an astonishingly agile wild surmiser and administrator whose board must be wondering how to manage the forces he's unleashing around the concept of a rearticulated geocultural hemisphere. The following week, James Clifford, 'historical critic of anthropology', professor in the wild surmisers' utopia known as the History of Consciousness Department at the University of California, Santa Cruz, and author of the influential *The Predicament of Culture* (1988), provided a link from *South 1* to another conference, *The Rebirth of the Museum?*, also at Melbourne University. It's a pity Clifford didn't attend both: the map he drew opened up opportunities for traffic between cultural practice and activism, and academic theory and analysis.

Unlike *South 1*, which was more focused on performance and gregariousness, the *Rebirth* conference set fairly rigorous academic standards. But it shared that sense of wild surmise. Clifford has a mind like a spring-cleaned windowpane: everything looks fresh and focused. Despite this intellectual precision, his talk hesitated modestly before the scale of 'the next big thing'. This might be described as a sea of islands of diverse culture, all of them energised and complicated by postcolonial situations in which they're reinventing themselves and their institutions, finding new ways to make traditions and custom (kastom, coutume) produce futures rather than memories.

For Murray, the *South Project* is part aspirational and part descriptive. It intends to make a difference to the ways in which power and resources are deployed in a region that chooses to disarticulate itself from a modernist, Euro-American cultural axis: to actively promote what Clifford calls 'newly articulated sites of indigeneity'. But the project also sees that the metropolitan centres of culture in Europe and America no longer exert the same hegemonic influence in a globalised world in which 'centers' have been broken up, 're-spatialised' and localised. In this sea of cultural islands, global capital flows encounter cross-currents and whirlpools of regional narrative, and the local becomes the global that the local then reprocesses (as with Pacific hip-hop).

In this big view, 'traditional' is no longer the pre-modern condition of the 'primitive', the 'before' or 'prehistory' of modernity, what

Clifford describes as the 'special object' of cultural anthropology: 'those folks out there or down there and back then: exotic societies, folklore, rural society, lower classes etc' – immobile culture trapped outside the perimeter fences of modern, metropolitan centres. Instead, tradition is also what mobilises culture to transgress those borders, to move restlessly among the centres, breaking them up and redistributing them.

One early transgressor, and ally of ethnology's wildly surmising surrealist cadre, was the Martiniquan poet Aime Césaire, who coined the term 'negritude' in Paris in 1939. The term would come to legitimise black liberationist culture based in 'roots', but Césaire meant it to describe something different: a mobile, activist, contemporary culture, acutely aware of its present and of the complex colonial histories that flowed through it.

Its successor, now – despite a provocative distinction between the 'routes' of the black slave diaspora and the 'roots' of indwelling – might be 'indigeneity'. Like Césaire's 'negritude', 'indigeneity' is a slippery word, capable of being co-opted to vague, uncritically accommodating liberalism, as well as to essentialist, roots-based definitions of tradition. Like Césaire's invention, however, 'indigenous' is also capable of activating complex understandings of cultural belonging.

The *South Project* is primarily about contemporary neighbourliness. South neighbours share cultural trading, exchange and border-crossing, colonial and postcolonial histories, complex indigeneities and connections to land and place, social diversity and a strong sense of living in a rich, culturally diverse present. The project also, as many speakers insisted, understands the complex ways in which culture, politics, ecology and economics mix, match and contest in the region.

If the ways in which some participants spoke at *South 1* was performative rather than carefully scripted, and if some presentations were haltingly translated (for example, from the indigenous Mapuche of the poet Elicura Chihuailaf), that enriched rather than diminished the occasion. So did the frightening contortions of the Brazilian Candomble-rite dancer Simone Reis, the Argentinian human rights activist Marcelo Brodsky's devastating 'Buena Memoria' project, and the New Zealand artist Maureen Lander's intricate knotting of traditional Māori string games, Marcel Duchamp and algorithms.

There was little knee-jerk resentment of generalised, north-oriented 'world orders' such as the bogey of American capital/cultural expansionism. Where anger was expressed, its situations were locally specific: the disgrace of government-supported rainforest clearance in Tasmania, the top-down co-option of culture by national identity politics in Brazil, the emergence of a plutocratic political elite in South Africa. From the point of view of the *South Project* itself, the key challenge may have come from Greg Lehman, an Australian writer descended from the Trawulwuy nation in the north-east of Tasmania. He challenged the project to confront what he called 'the nonconformity of mainstream Australia . . . with the culture of respect that is due to land and to its original people'. He also challenged the conference 'to carry along with it every expression of humanity, including that of coloniser'.

Lehman's strategic inversion of nonconformity and the inclusiveness of his sense of historical narrative would have appealed to James Clifford. Clifford's version of a 'South Project' began when, as a graduate history student, he read the Marxist historians Raymond Williams (*Culture and Society*, 1958) and E.P. Thompson (*The Making of the English Working Class,* 1963), and decided to do for ethnographic and anthropological history what Williams and Thompson had done for social and cultural history. In Paris in the mid-1970s to research French anthropology, Clifford encountered the work of the French missionary-ethnographer Maurice Leenhardt. It was Leenhardt's letters written in New Caledonia between 1902 and 1926 that were the basis of Clifford's first book, *Person and Myth: Maurice Leenhardt in the Melanesian World* (1982). In this book, Clifford began to assemble what he now calls his 'toolkit', a set of ideas with which to organise the critical study of Western ethnology and anthropology as sciences – or pseudo-sciences – of human culture.

His study soon became focused by the institutions to which culture had been seconded by ethnology: the museums. This in turn has led him to practise a kind of second-remove ethnographic fieldwork of his own, in which he researches what's going on in museums and cultural centres as they go about reinventing themselves, their governances in respect of national identity politics, and their relations with the communities they represent and whose treasures and narratives they retain.

The sciences of ethnology and anthropology were under attack in the liberationist, postcolonial era following the post-World War II break-up of the colonial estate. The former objects of ethnographic and anthropological research had become activists in liberation movements. They resisted and rejected the fieldwork and narratives of anthropologists, whom they regarded as instruments of colonial oppression. Clifford's work on Leenhardt, and his study of the French 'surrealist' anthropologist Michel Leiris among others, together with his own research in New Caledonia and his contact with the Kanak independence leader Jean-Marie Tjibaou, led him to empathise with indigenous resistance.

With this empathy, however, also came the acknowledgement that postcolonial cultures were being revitalised and rearticulated in complex ways. These included the processing of Christianity (as the missionary Leenhardt had recognised), the co-option of anthropology, the control and management of tourism, land claims, repatriation struggles, and other reversals and take-overs of 'nonconformity'. These cultures were now vigorously negotiating and renegotiating borders, not retrenching around 'authentic' interiors.

At the *Rebirth of the Museum?* conference, Koori writer and curator Tony Birch made a similar point. Birch was an important leader in the development of the Melbourne Museum Bungilaka Aboriginal Centre's Koori Voices exhibition in which a life-size model of the anthropologist Baldwin Spencer is displayed in a museum case. This was not, Birch insisted, about pushing a black version of history in the faces of white visitors. Nor were the displays documenting kidnapped Aboriginal children and massacres intended as 'black armband', white-guilt history and museology.

'Black armband' is a term that the Australian political right used to attack museum workers, including the senior Aboriginal public servant

Dawn Casey, former director of the National Museum of Australia in Canberra. Casey left the position in December 2003 under pressure from what Professor Mick Dodson, Chair of Indigenous Studies at the Australian National University, described as 'the history wars'. Tony Birch put it succinctly: 'This is white history, too.' There aren't separate black and white histories. You can't look at one without seeing the other. Indigeneity now incorporates and carries along with it the 'expression' of the coloniser. Settler history and culture embody indigenous narrative. What Birch was calling for wasn't wishy-washy liberal political homogeneity, nor a variety-night cultural sampler, but willingness to confront and accept cultural difference within shared historical contexts. The museum, in this challenge, becomes a place to encounter, understand and process difference and relation. In time, it may become a place for reconciliation.

Clifford describes the theatres where these cultural performances are being acted out – museums or cultural centres – as 'contact zones'. This is not least because such institutions contain the spoils of anthropological fieldwork, and need themselves to participate in new articulations of power, research, knowledge and cultural formation. Ideally, this will happen in partnerships that return the historical benefits of anthropological and ethnological scholarship to indigenous owners – as is happening in the Vanuatu Cultural Centre in Port Vila. Clifford's ideal 'contact zone' is, therefore, dynamic, performative, process-oriented rather than material-oriented, and interested in social rather than institutional capital. The influential Australian curator and media theorist Ross Gibson describes such places as 'cultural laboratories'.

Those who work in larger, metropolitan museums know that there's often a clash between mobile cultures and the immobilising operational constraints that prevail in museums. Big museums almost inevitably over-capitalise culture and orient their assets towards nationalist cultural branding. As a consequence, they'll tend to reinvoke a reactionary, over-simplified terminology of 'authenticity', 'tradition' and 'the iconic', while cultures at large are untidily generating new, polysemic forms, new modes of storytelling, new cultural agencies such as MTV, and new audiences.

There's much to learn from the discussion that spills from initiatives such as the *South Project* and the *Rebirth of the Museum?* forum – and from the low-key visit of Clifford to New Zealand after the conference. The theme that linked these talkfests was that wild surmises always serve the culture better than risk-averse retrenchments, and that you'll never find the next big thing if you turn your back on it while you worry about the 100 percent purity of the national brand.

Action Man

Max Gimblett's paintings have come home. But where exactly is 'home'?

New Zealand Listener (10 December 2004)

Max Gimblett's in good shape. Yes, that's a bad pun, and no, it's not. Hale and hearty, nearly 70 years of age, Max works out, plays squash, hasn't touched a drop in decades, is full of mirth and easy tears, and the shaped canvasses that have characterised his work since the 'crisis' of 1982 (see later) are looking great, too.

I ask him if he's happy about the exhibition, *The Brush of All Things*, curated by Wystan Curnow for Auckland Art Gallery, and opening at City Gallery Wellington this week. Max's eyes fill with tears – that's a yes. Some of the emotion comes from a sense of rightness: there have been many dealer shows in New Zealand and the US where he and his wife Barbara Kirshenblatt-Gimblett live, but this is the first time that a sample with the emotional outline of a personal journey has come home.

'Home'? What's this about? Max has been a contented denizen of New York City for more than 30 years. Let's talk about this 'home', and while we're at it, let's talk about some other big words: wisdom, beauty and self, for starters. 'Okay,' says Max optimistically, as is his way. 'Sounds good.'

Are you an expatriate, Max? Is that what's meant by 'home', even after all these productive years somewhere else? Now Max gets angry. Home is where your sense of self is deeply stirred. It's where your sense of yourself is strong enough for you to let it go unprotected in your work and when you work. It's wherever Barbara is – when she and Max were young, home became so when Barbara placed a piece of fine fabric in whatever accommodation their love was passing through. Besides, the word has such a feeble purchase on the robust, satisfying complexities of living in a geocultural space tensioned by locations, histories and art, rather than merely by subway stations. Home isn't a place, it's a situation. Home is a trampoline for the spirit.

I've seen the sculptor Bill Culbert, who lives in Provence and London and visits New Zealand yearly during the Bluff oyster and whitebait seasons, react with similar angry scorn to the idea that he's 'ex' anything simply because he chooses to live somewhere 'else'. Even the term 'belonging' seems insipid in the context of a discussion of 'home', if the teeming contemporary traffic and landings of people and cultures all over the place are to make better than small-talk sense or generate more than third-drink passion.

Before you can say 'Venice', 'belonging' will transform perfectly good art into national identity. 'Belonging' sags in a hammock between 'roots' and 'routes', suburbanising a prime site of cultural toing and froing. It sedates the hearty appetites most of us have for different ideas nurtured in other places by foreign cultures and cooked up in the globalising kitchens of media fusion.

If you don't agree with that statement, then you won't be able to think of any good reason why other people somewhere 'else' (like Venice) might be even a bit interested in what we do here aside from grow meat and make monocultural assertions on Fonterra's 'Milk' website. We need to embrace the likelihood that traffic might both enrich local culture and sharpen the definitions of its differences, while simultaneously advancing its global playtime. Think Pacific hip-hop.

Zen rapper Max was born in Auckland in 1935, and has been resident in North America, and mostly in New York City, for more than 40 years – that's part of what makes home. He and Barbara have come back to New Zealand regularly, in ways both businesslike and emotional, for years – that's another part. Max's painting has often reached into a sense of Oceanic space and brilliance, learnt also on the Pacific coast of the US, where he used to maintain a second studio in LA – that's another part. I visited Max's western outpost once with a couple of my kids – they were impressed by the steel fortress of the studio's security system: this Pacific had gangs and guns in it. And the work also reaches into Asia, into a mix of philosophies, practices and places sampled in 1994 by Dianne and Peter Beatson's exhibition at the Manawatu Art Gallery, *The Crane and the Kotuku – Artistic Bridges Between New Zealand and Japan* – home is also back and forth along these Asian bridges, and where they disclose friends like the Chinese American poet John Yau in New York.

What about wisdom? It comes with great mentors, says Max – with great traditions of discipline. If you don't 'get it', you don't get it. But if you think you're wise, you're not (and if you don't think you are, it doesn't follow that you might be). Being wise is remaining open to learning: it's valuing ignorance. It's not wanting to finish.

As Thomas McEvilley reminds us in a shrewd essay for the *Brush of All Things* catalogue, Max retro-entered the moment of high modernism in America as one born 20 years after and far away from the great American abstract expressionists Pollock, Kline and Motherwell; also de Kooning, who introduces a narrative pressure to Max's influences. His mentored American practice began as the baton of high art was being passed to the pop artists of the 1960s who wanted to be rid of the heroic and the transcendental, and as American modernism's huge confidence began to break up on the Coney Island beach of the postmodern.

Seventeen years ago, at the height of neo-expressionist frenzies (not least around Max's 'hood), McEvilley's famous *Artforum* essay about the artist Agnes Martin, 'Grey Geese Descending', drew a careful line under the moment when the postmodern began to spin out, and suggested that it might be time to look again at the thoughtfulness, the mentoring, of modernism's rested wisdom. It seems easy, now, to say blithely that Max Gimblett is an unabashed modernist from way back, with all the transcendentalism and heroics intact.

But his persistence wasn't just stubborn, or dumb; nor was it just a consequence of the time-lapse noticed by McEvilley. Max processed the disciplines of modernism, he stayed with them while finding ways to change his practice and take on new learning. He didn't finish. From 1982, his monochromatic and colour-saturated paintings began to be shaped, most memorably as quatrefoils. They became physical –

signs of action appeared that owed as much or more to Zen learning and traditions of bold brush ink calligraphy as to the 'action painting' of the great abstract expressionists, with the possible exception of Franz Kline, though the gestures weren't exclusively calligraphic – there were also pours, throws, pools, jabs and spatters.

In *The Brush of All Things* there's a big quatrefoil painting from 1995 called 'Action Painting'. Yes, that's a bad pun, and no, it's not. The title's a homage to the physicality of Jackson Pollock and the heyday of American abstract expressionism in the 1940s and 50s. But it's also a way of measuring the distance Max Gimblett's use of that teaching has enabled him to travel from it. The title's a historical artefact, and the disciplines that have directed the work's astonishingly fluent calligraphic choreography are now Rinzai Zen ones of 'all mind/no mind'.

They disclose a self unrestrained by distinction between body and consciousness: the impacts, swirls and halts of paint beautifully within the container of the shaped canvas seem as thoughtless as they are perfectly articulated. There's a sense of freedom that's captured in something Max says in a lovely interview with Barbara ('How do you know when a work is finished?') published in the *Brush* catalogue: 'You can beat the mental thought process with your body movement. Get ahead of it. A lot of sport does that.' He also says, '. . . you might beat the personal identity, you might beat the narcissism, you might beat being caught up in any self-consciousness.'

Max says at one point in the same interview that Jackson Pollock was 'a master of completion', and a bit later that 'there's something unpleasant about the two words "completion" and "finished"'. In 'Action Painting', Max seems to be saying that it's possible and necessary for him to admire Pollock's bloody-minded heroic staying-in-the-painting till it was done, while also developing strategies to escape that material lock-down and its attendant anguish.

And in another terrific, lucid interview from 2002 with Anne Kirker, the curator of the *Language of Drawing* exhibition at the Queensland Art Gallery, Max says of ink drawing that 'it is a form of meditation'. As such, the drawing and, on occasion, the painting can't be 'finished' – rather, perhaps, the work comes to or wakes up in the world where the artist is putting his brush down, turning his back and going through to the kitchen for caffeine and sugar and, with luck, a smooch.

Well, we seem to have done 'home', 'wisdom' and 'self' without finishing any of them. That's all right. Time for a story. 'Beauty' might make an appearance.

As a staunch modernist, Max is also a staunch internationalist, whose passion for his art is matched by his passion for damn-nuisance causes. Max's frequent email spams with anti-Republican chain letters, alternative website connections and rabble-rousing blasts have probably got him on some National Security database down at FBI Central – along with half the population of the remnants of New York's Bowery, Soho and Lower East Side art-loft community that have survived the gentrifying urban renewal processes of the 1990s. The members of this cotton-top community of internationalist lefties, crazy artists and Zen radicals, if they didn't self-destruct, might recognise a familiar spirit abroad in the polyvocal internationalism of hip-hop. And I'd even have to say, watching Max whirl into big kung-fu action at one of his canvasses, the guy can get down. In the Kirker interview he says, 'The language of modern dance is a parallel sensation in my studio when I'm painting.' The words 'action' and 'gesture' slide away from art towards bodies in motion.

On September 11, 2001, all suited up on a cultural mission, I found myself shut out of the New York hotel I'd left shortly before the catastrophe of the twin towers. Max and Barbara took me in, hooked up an email connection I could talk to home on, fed me and let me tear around the TV channels looking for a way out. They let me make a grand mess in their kitchen while attempting to get home to the Pacific by cooking seafoods from it. The air outside their Bowery loft was full of dust, and there was no way of getting past the security lines at 14th St, even if there'd been somewhere better to go, which there wasn't, except home. There was nowhere better to go partly because they made it easy to be at home with them.

A couple of days went by. I made the occasional foray out. They indulged me with the Chinese wet markets. Barbara worked away within an immense catacomb of books under a cone of light, like a Talmud scholar. Max's studio looked fresh and empty and ready for some action. But how could anyone achieve the lucid state of mind required to make art as a 'form of meditation' when huge trucks were still tearing up and down outside through the smoky dust day and night?

One morning, I woke to the sound of music and emphatic thumps on the floor of the studio. There were occasional yells. It sounded as though a substantial dance workout was under way. It was. 'At every step the pure wind rises,' asserts Rinzai. It sounded more like a hurricane. The days were long, with lunchbreaks. Max was back at work. The studio filled with an astonishing daily quota. We invented a grandiose new-work naming ritual. The paintings seemed to be simultaneously somewhere the racket outside wasn't, and filled with what was outside: whirling destruction, light and colour through dust, phoenixes of hope rising, bones, reincarnations.

Max showed me his 'Spirit Box' cabinet of drawers, which has now become his twin towers memorial. It was made to Max's direction in close collaboration with the jeweller Warwick Freeman, former studio manager Todd Strothers, cabinetmaker Jim Cooper and Max's closest ally and studio soulmate, his manager and assistant of 11 years, Anthony Fodero. The drawers are full of exquisite skull death-heads. Signs of mortality but not, in Max's scheme of things, macabre or morbid, they nonetheless seemed in the context of the enormous catastrophe outside the studio to be fearsome warnings about pride and confidence.

In the figurative drawing from four years earlier, *F---in' Charmer* (1997), a grimacing raver with wild tongue rants from the surface of the paper, partially obscuring the serenely smiling profile of . . . a woman? There are narratives reaching for the surfaces of many of the works in this exhibition, as Curnow observes in his canny notes.

You might expect the narrative of 9/11, the bones and skulls of mortality, the political rage, to now break those surfaces. Max used to look at the towers from the window of his studio, where 'Spirit Box'

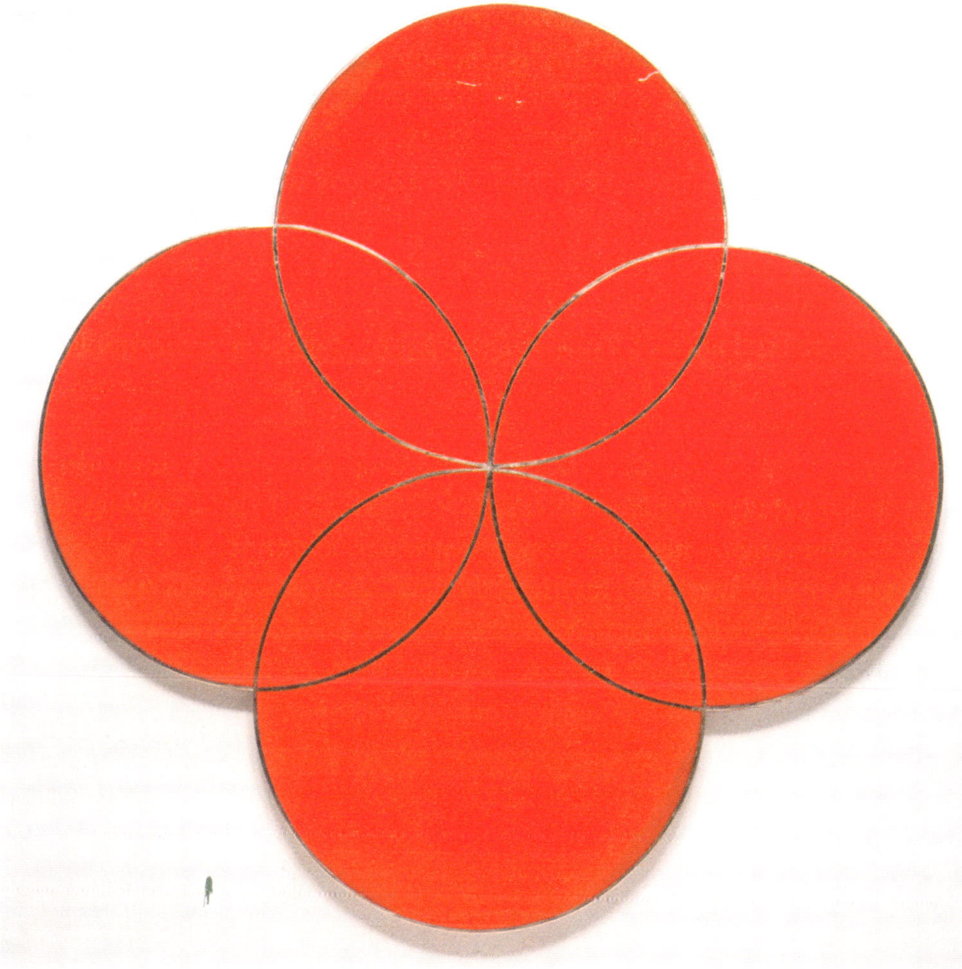

Max Gimblett, *Sky Gate*, 2003 – gesso, polyurethane and acrylic polymer on wood panel, 152.5 x 152.5 cm. Private collection, New Zealand.

resides. But the circular *Jade*, *Tiger* and *Onyx* paintings of 2003 are among the most serene that he has ever made. Their splendid shiny surfaces throw back light – it would be easy to say 'illumination' – not fire and smoke. They make it necessary to think again about responsible ways to use words like 'beauty'. The simple diagrammatic internal intersections of the four circle components of the red and gold quatrefoil painting *Sky Gate* (2003) form the shape of a lotus or frangipani – it now seems to have been sweetly implicit in all the hundreds of quatrefoils.

More violent – 'distressing' is Curnow's good word – are earlier, pre-9/11 works such as *Crucifixion – after Peter Gabriel* (1989–91). It's as though another 'crisis' has enabled Max to move his learning along, and the path it's found for him is a radical purpose for beauty, a beauty that interpolates itself like grey geese calmly descending into blindly reactive situations whose enraged oppositions are cranking each other up towards apocalypse.

Reflecting on his collaborations with Max, and the fact of having not seen him since 9/11, his friend the poet John Yau wrote in October 2001, 'I know I will go to Max's studio soon. Something unexpected always happens when we work together.' I don't know, these old modernists. There's no stopping them, thank God.

Where Everyone Gets a Buddha

Serious fun with artist Yuk King Tan

New Zealand Listener (30 December 2005)

The interview with Yuk King Tan, two days before her show *Overflow* opens at City Gallery, Wellington, is one of the more casual I've done, but I get the feeling it's pretty normal for Yuk. We sit at the edge of the installation space upstairs in the north project gallery and watch Tobias Berger and Richard Maloy beaver away laying out Yuk's major work in this exhibition, the commissioned installation *Overflow*.

Berger is Yuk's husband, formerly director of Artspace in Auckland and currently curator at the Para/Site Art Space in Hong Kong, and Maloy is one of the newer stars in Sue Crockford's stable of younger 'World Famous in New Zealand' artists, who's made his mark with engagingly incompetent constructions such as his now famous *Kissing Booth* at the Canberra Contemporary Art Space last June and July. This is some serious assistance.

We're joined by City Gallery's curator Sarah Farrar and Yuk chats to her while I eavesdrop, take notes and occasionally interfere with a question. The interview's sense of casual fun underpinned with thought captures the impact of Yuk King Tan's work. I first encountered this in 1995 when the Auckland Art Gallery installed her *The New Temple* assemblage as one of its window projects in Wellesley St.

The work featured a witty miscellany of objects collected from the artist's friends – masks, guns, dark glasses, binoculars, sandals, basins, car jacks, table-tennis bats, etc. The objects were reproduced as red wax casts and displayed a bit like a symmetrical quasi-ethnographic cabinet of curiosities. It established a number of qualities we now expect in Yuk's work. It was exquisitely elegant, both in its appearance and its thought. It conveyed a sense of cultural strangeness or estrangeness without being abject. It translated mostly familiar objects to an 'exotic' oriental cultural space and toyed with the idea of commodities and low-level commerce as the trade and exchange zone of cultures.

It addressed what reviewer Tessa Laird has called the 'two-to-tango fact of exchange', how capital's effects and products must be both produced and acquired before there's much to say about them. Yuk's adroit conceptual skills – what Laird has called an 'ideas-trader' – are in this zone. It's never been a zone where sonorous questions about identity were going to get a lot of purchase, so to speak. The work's always deflected such enquiries back into the bourse of ideas-trading, where the flightier trash emporium or disposable products of global capitalism are given the job of representing the serious issues of cultural trade and exchange.

I leave this entertaining interview a couple of hours later with the gift of a trashy toy gun made of paper – a flammable facsimile of a weapon that can be burnt as part of customary Festival of Hungry Ghosts funerary rites. The theory is, you may need a piece on the other side. The thought's at once amusing and sinister, as if the afterlife isn't going to be different from this one, just more disposable. Also available for vaporising to the next world are paper cans of coke, paper money and bullion and paper cellphones – among other essentials.

One of two 'snowflake' works included in the exhibition, *Sunset Industries* (2005), a crisply printed LED print, organises images of flammable paper objects (including the gun) used in such Chinese funerary rites. The patterning of *Sunset Industries* is modelled on the structures of snowflakes. It's also based on a kaleidoscopic, 12–sided dodecahedron structure within which each unit mirrors (and therefore reverses) its neighbour. The effect is simultaneously precise and arbitrary. It represents an order that seems more the result of chaos than design, or an idea of order as ephemeral, about to go up in smoke – a kind of temporary paralysis.

This is what happens to the more incendiary of Yuk's works, such as her 'Flightpatterns' piece, *The Floating World*, commissioned by Connie Butler for the Geffen Contemporary in Los Angeles. This work was developed from a 1997 commission *The Picturesque*, at the

Govett-Brewster in New Plymouth. Yuk enjoys remembering the compliance dramas and 'lovely firemen' involved in setting off these works, whose sputtering pyrotechnics traced the scorched ghosts of their passage to the next world on the pristine gallery walls of this one.

There are no fires lit in Wellington's City Gallery when the exhibition opens, though the wine is an icky colour from something squirted out of eyedroppers. After the speeches, Yuk makes presents of child-sized military caps and cheap, imitation Gucci handbags. The effect's anarchic – deflating the seriousness of the event, but serious about the ephemeral brand chaos of cheap global commodities. I'm tempted to make a connection between works of art that have to explode in order to be realised and art-world dignitaries who have to look ridiculous in order to be taken seriously.

The market that Yuk has ransacked for the flammable paper objects photographed in *Sunset Industries* is an Asian one. The image market from which the objects in the second 'snowflake' work in the exhibition, *Shock and Awe* (2005), have been sampled is a combination of *Time* magazine and the Al-Jazeera website. Within the temporary paralysis of *Shock and Awe*'s mirror images, George Bush Jnr and Osama bin Laden are cheek to cheek. The work's pristine, LED moment of arbitrary order freezes a narrative explosion outwards from a core of September 11, 2001, to the London underground and bus bombings of July 7, 2005. These two 'flake' works are carefully chosen in the complete context of the *Overflow* exhibition – as Yuk suggests, they're templates for the big floor piece.

The global market from which the astonishing assortment of objects in the installation *Overflow* has been drawn includes the Warehouse in Wellington. The red shed, with a kind of weirdly appropriate brand consistency, given Yuk's fondness for the colour of firecrackers, lamp tassels, animal-astrology masks and shrine candle wax, has been the source of the installation's Buddha figures. Other sources have been markets and junk emporia in Shenzhen, Australia, Germany and Hong Kong, where Yuk currently lives. If the Buddhas come from Kiwi red sheds, where do the Bruce Lee figurines come from? The toy tanks, cellphone covers, wristwatches and plastic model aeroplanes splattered with white candle wax like Judy Darragh's ejaculate-festooned *Wild Thing* (1999)? What about the crude wooden crucifixes, the fans, the artillery shells, electronic calculators, police truncheons, toy helicopters and microphones? The Chinese Buried Army statuettes, passports, Transformer figures like the ones subsumed by Japanese neo-pop out of graphic artists like Katsutaka Miyatake and robot anime, the film-set clapperboards, charging Taurus miniatures and much more?

The point is, you can't really know and Yuk's not telling (red-shed Buddha aside). The fact that it doesn't matter is what matters. The point here's the anywhereness of things, despite their air of cultural, even geocultural, specificity. But Yuk's conversation isn't the product of vapid globalism. Far from it.

The initial concept for *Overflow* was called 'Power Systems' and she set out to take a look at 'desire, status, money, aggression, luck and control'. The smallness and cheapness of the items was intended to highlight the paradoxical 'domesticity of these objects connoted with "power"'. The organisation of 'Power Systems' (and the final patterning of *Overflow*) was intended to suggest power operating also at the microscopic, viral level. The two-to-tango principle of commercial and cultural exchange goes all the way down to seething, microbiological activity. Are we having fun yet?

'The collection will have pieces that suggest status, control and power – designer goods next to copies of designer goods – toys of violent roleplay such as guns, tanks and shells – paper tokens of symbols of wealth. [The work] obeys rules and strategies involving underlying systems of need and desire or trade and value. There's also a type of wealth in aesthetic mass. The work's about different systems that relate to the order/disorder of our wider environment.'

There's one question we have to get to sooner or later, but its obviousness makes it best approached indirectly. I tell Yuk a story told by the Australian cultural theorist Meaghan Morris. Morris left Australia because she was fed up with Australian politics and took a job as head of the Kwan Fong Cultural Research and Development

Programme at Lingnan University in Hong Kong. There, one of her first PhD candidate dissertations was written by a young Chinese scholar on the subject of Hong Kong's wet markets. The external examiners were all from the US, Britain and Australia – and all had cultural reactions to the wet markets that, Morris believed, prejudiced their assessment of the PhD candidate's research. They were incapable of reading the dissertation without feeling disgust for the subject matter. To Morris, there seemed no escaping the 'intellectual colonialism' of the international academic community.

This is good, an interesting story, thinks Yuk. She can also see where it's headed.

So, how does it feel to be a 34–year-old woman of Asian ancestry, born in Australia and raised in New Zealand, a veteran of artist residencies in Australia, Germany and London, with international shows under her belt in Germany, Australia, the UK, US, Hong Kong, the Netherlands, Brazil and Lithuania – to be now, for the first time, living in an Asian city?

'The thing is, there's so much pre-literature. Hong Kong's layers and layers of colonisation and recolonisation and all its records and products. And it's full of global citizens from Shanghai, New York and London. Its friendships are transitory. Now, it lives in the shadow of China, which is bigger and more powerful. Is it even an "Asian" city? There are really no fixed heritage points any more. Heritage is now about change, about moving markers, about relationships to global capital, reverse colonisation, migrancy, commerce.'

Yuk says she feels freer in Hong Kong. There are good artists there, though they're overshadowed by the huge resources available to artists in China and also by the huge challenges to freedom that some Chinese artists confront. Artists in Hong Kong are freer of the 'art industry'. Yuk says she has more time to think – to reflect on and plan her work.

'As for the place of order and feeling culturally at home – how do you organise a market? A wet market with trussed livestock or a supermarket with use-by dates on labels? Who do you trust? Objects in markets are organised according to priorities of seductive experience – combinations of strategy and chaos – like a truly great city, at once seductive and repellent.'

And the familiarity, the homeliness of order? 'There are kinds of belief and order that are shared equally by stock markets and astrologers using numerology. They don't differ much.'

There are two other works in *Overflow*. One is a collaborative photographic work with Neil Pardington, *Loudspeaker #1–#6* (2005), in which Yuk's face is obscured six times by a loudhailer as she stands in locations in Hong Kong. The work appears to echo the Korean artist Kimsooja's *Needle Woman* (2005), in which the artist was videoed standing facing six more or less hostile city streets. But the Pardington–Tan work isn't uneasy in this way. Nor is the video work *Meeting* (2005), a whimsical and touching 11 minute and 15 second DVD loop in which couples encounter each other (or don't) in Hong Kong locations.

Both these works might be most obviously about communication – how to do it across interpersonal, cultural and geographic space. Hello – can you hear me loud hailing from Hong Kong? Can you hear me calling from 5 cm away? Can you hear me thanking my helpers at an exhibition opening? How to listen, how to hear, how to look and see? How to look-see-hear those amazing temporary paralyses that can become art, those seductive marketplaces where chaos has stopped for just a moment?

Little Creatures

Babies, toddlers and other monsters: Australian artist Patricia Piccinini and the 'birthing pains of our new millennium'

New Zealand Listener (24 February 2006)

My interview with the Australian artist Patricia Piccinini takes place by phone from Melbourne and is orchestrated by Hector, the artist's nine-month-old son. Piccinini rings me an hour later than planned on the first day – Hector's resumed the full-alert position after being driven around in the car for a while. I'm familiar with this, having done a fair bit of it in my time. My favourite child-director story concerns a budding genius who'd only open his mouth to receive fresh flakes of flounder from his mother's poised spoon at the precise moment his father went past the kitchen window on a bicycle. Repeatedly. And waving.

On day two, the interview's delayed not by Hector but by the artist's work schedule. She phones from her car on the way home from the workshop and asks if we can delay a bit. Fine with me – I'm no longer dealing with the brain fatigue of getting up to small children during the night (or synchronised bike-riding) and I clearly don't have the kind of work schedule (or ethic) that's generated Piccinini's staggering exhibition history since 1991 (in excess of 40 solo exhibitions). When we get to our second phone talk an hour later, Piccinini apologises for being 'vague' and blames Hector. Piccinini's 'vague' is somewhere up around A+ on most people's on-to-it registers, so I don't imagine Hector's going to be held responsible for any obvious decline in the conceptual quality of his mother's work over the next year or so.

And in any case, Hector's interventions and his mother's rueful delight in being put through her maternal paces are appropriate in the context of what we're talking about. Maternal love – or, more broadly, the love of parents for their offspring – may be the most important and most contentious overarching theme of Piccinini's work. For most new viewers, it won't be apparent at first sight.

Much of Piccinini's work is characterised by the sleek surfaces of high-end product design or the kind of hyper-detailed and pixilated appearance we've come to expect of realism factories such as Wētā Workshop. The art's impeccable 'realism' – for example, the believability of the 3D animatronic *SO2* or *Siren Mole* or *Excellocephala Parthenopta* she had 'living' in the wombat enclosure at Melbourne Zoo during her Federation Festival *Superevolution* project in 2001 – is what causes the first of several audience double takes. How can something that looks so believably real be made up, the product of the artist's thought and imagination and of a workshop production team?

The second double take occurs across the axis of the word 'natural'. We're familiar in a New Zealand repetitively branded as 'pure and natural', '100% Pure' and the like, with the inherent contradictions of signage such as *Wilderness Road* and brand names like *Untouched World*. Piccinini's work plays with this ambiguity and takes it into the territory of stem cells, genetic engineering and biotechnology.

New Zealanders may be impervious to the oxymoronic nature of their unspoilt reality, happy to ingest fresh salmon coloured orange by its fish-food dyes and to gulp pure spring water bottled from taps in light-industrial suburbs, but our natural credulity may be challenged by Piccinini's uncanny creations. This is because the origins of her species tend to be in the Petri dishes of laboratories, the digital data of computer animation, the intelligent agents of Artificial Life, or in mass-production factories of robotised industry. This world of science and industry, and especially the world of the new biotechnologies, rather than the video-game park of Animal Planet or the TV-primitivism of *Survivor* in media Guatemala, is what strikes most of us as unnatural – or more unnatural, on the lovable-to-repellant scale.

Here are some of the other questions the conversation was orchestrated around. At a time when the Human Genome Project is telling us that we're mostly the same, how are we to understand and accept our differences? How are we to understand and accept definitions of life that are generated outside of sexually reproductive biology? What's normal? How can we be responsible for the life we make when it happens by means many people continue to find 'unnatural'? How can we relish, let alone love, the Flavr Savr gene-engineered tomato, genetically spliced with a cold-sea-bottom-living flounder? The moth-gened potato? What would we be willing to do to eradicate human autism? Down's syndrome? These serious questions segue into the grotesque territory of cultural cosmetics. Can whole nations eradicate crooked teeth? What prices will we be willing to pay to become a species of Ken-and-Barbies?

More simply, what biotechnological solutions would we embrace if they could prevent our mother dying of cancer? What life forms would we create if they could protect endangered species? What feral companion species – Nature's Little Helpers – could we generate that wouldn't wreak the innocent havoc of their 'natural' cousins, the cane toad, rabbit and feral cat?

How can we love our own went-wrong creations as we insist we should love nature's mutant blunders? How can we develop an ethics capable of compassion towards and acceptance of the products of both lab and womb? How do – do? – they differ?

The history within which Piccinini discussed these questions isn't a new one. It reaches back as far as Mary Shelley's novel *Frankenstein* of 1818, whose plot was driven by the writer's fascination with the new-fangled force of electricity and the possibility that this energy could make life. Piccinini's a kind of contemporary, antipodean 'Mary-Victor Frankenstein', with the difference that she insists, when talking about Dr Frankenstein, that his only mistake was to not love the creature he'd created. The only real monster in her natural world is maternal – parental – discrimination. Far from being warm and fluffy, though it may be understandably Hector-centric at present, this attitude is a rigorous challenge to our ideas about family, community, nation and even species. Implicitly, it challenges the we-are-all-pretty-much-the-same baseline of the Human Genome Project to produce an ethics capable of resisting the fascist (or fundamentalist) eugenics of yes-but-only-if-your-kids-look/think-like-our-kids (and have nice, straight teeth).

Piccinini's memorable contribution at the 50th Venice Biennale in 2003 was called *We Are Family*. In her catalogue essay for this much-discussed installation, the Australian curator Linda Michael included two astute quotes. One was from the writer Bryan Appleyard, who's the uncle of a severely disabled girl: '. . . at birth we want a normal baby. We value adults for their difference, their idiosyncrasies.' The other was from Daniel Harris, author of the 2001 *Cute, Quaint, Hungry and Romantic: The Aesthetics of Consumerism*. Writing about the child-imaging world of toyshops and movies, Harris noted that it's become an image battleground 'in which the image of the child as the unnatural spawn of Satan . . . has locked horns with that of the child as the inanimate stuffed animal'. Michael also quoted Piccinini herself from a statement she wrote at the time of her 1999 project *Truck Babies*: 'like most newborns they will be both cute and repulsive, resembling their parents from beneath a thick slime of packing-grease'. The truck babies in question were two beautifully finished, embryonic 18–wheeler trucks painted 'baby blue' and 'baby pink'. Ironic she may not be, but Piccinini isn't humourless. Other titles in her career are funny and provocative: *Nature's Little Helpers* (2005, ongoing), *Love Me Love My Lump* (2003 and 1995) – where LUMP is an acronym for Life-form with Unevolved Mutant Properties – *Call of the Wild, Game Boys Advanced* and *Still Life with Stem Cells* (all 2002), *Car Nuggets* (1998, the precursor of *Truck Babies*) and *Cyclepups* (2005), to name a few.

What she doesn't find funny is one consequence of a component of the Venice installation, *Leather Landscape*. In this, the viewer confronts a life-size tableau of creatures that look like crosses between meerkats and humans congregated on a white-leather hillock, and a human toddler dressed in pink overalls. The toddler and one of the meerkat-humans are looking at each other with friendly curiosity. In April 2005, an image of the meerkat-human appeared in locations within the Islamic world, first on a Sudanese Arabic-language website. The story the image illustrated was about a girl from Oman who threw a copy of the Koran to the ground following an argument with her

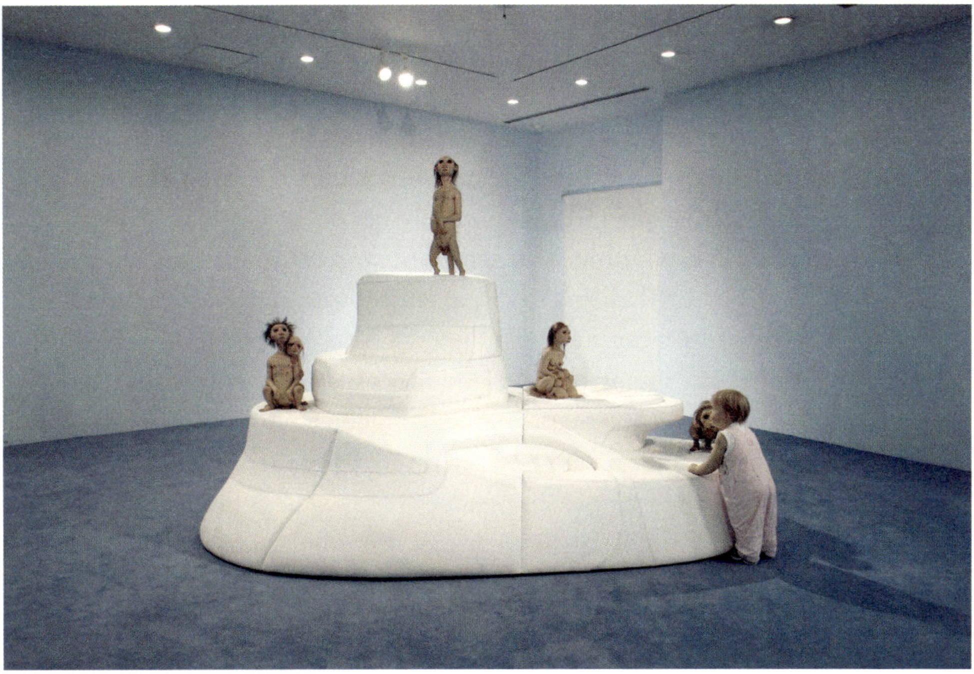

Patricia Piccinini, *Leather Landscape*, 2003 – silicone, polyurethane, leather, mdf, human hair, 290 x 175 x 165 cm. Courtesy Roslyn Oxley9 Gallery, Sydney, and the artist.

mother. As a consequence, the website and its successors proclaimed, Allah transformed the disobedient child into a monster – a little, leathery subhuman.

The story upsets Piccinini for several reasons. The most obvious involves an officially punitive and repressive attitude to the girl. The next most obvious involves the misappropriation and misrepresentation of her own work. A third reason she's upset is more surprising and interesting. It's that the girl and probably her society as a whole had no access to the kinds of movies, television and consumer goods that would have nurtured their critical, sceptical and indeed humorous immunity to superstition and ignorant prejudice. Now there's a riposte to technophobes convinced that humanity's doomed by PlayStation. I'll bet Hector gets a PlayStation when he's old enough.

Piccinini insists often, as she has also in a number of lucid artist statements, that she isn't preaching, doesn't know better, doesn't have answers, isn't interested in the high moral ground and is not in the least ironic. She keeps it simple and she keeps it real. The art's there to extend processes of encounter and discussion into the world it came from. It's a world Linda Michael has suggested involves a 'shift from modernist to suburban', picking up panel-van painting, beach culture, brand sensationalism and the gloss of high-tech finishes along the way. Piccinini isn't a scientist or a moral philosopher. She's not interested in the art world's tendency to self-regarding irony. At first, she says, her work wasn't easy for the art world to identify or accept. Although she'd studied painting between 1989 and 1991 at the Victorian College of the Arts and was good at video and computer processes, her work fitted neither in the world of fine art nor in the world of 'multimedia' art that had flourished with Australian government support during the 80s.

Prior to studying art, she had completed a degree in economic history at ANU in Canberra. Although she insists she only did it because her family thought the degree might get her a job and because 'economic history' was preferable to accounting, she learnt about the economic forces that underpin material history – and she heightened her awareness of the importance of branding as the colourist of cultural values, the shaper of the look and feel of surfaces within and behind which life-and-death questions are found.

Sandman was the panel-van beach-culture name of Piccinini's Federation Square work in Melbourne in 2002. It's also the name of the scary, cannibalistic, 19th-century horror, who throws sand in the eyes of disobedient children and takes them off to the crook of the moon. Offenbach included this ghoul in *Tales of Hoffmann*, along with the bleeding-eyed living doll Olympia. They're in Freud's 'The Uncanny' (1925). Piccinini knows this parallel, but says the foreground story is the panel van one. The other Sandman's a kind of Gothic spook who's there, a lot of the time, in the peripheral vision of her uncanny art.

Piccinini says she hopes her work engenders joy and humour. Writing in *Artlink* in 2001, Jacqueline Millner suggested that her work 'seeks to engender love'. In the same year, discussing *The Breathing Room*, Juliana Engberg thought that 'these are the birthing pains of our new millennium'. Peter Hennessey, a key collaborator with Piccinini and, in addition, her husband and the father of Hector, wrote in the 2002 *Call of the Wild* catalogue that Piccinini displays 'an extraordinary faith in human nature'.

This is all good. But it doesn't mean Piccinini's work is tritely feel-good. And now Hector's awake again. There's a lot to do and to think about. Patricia Piccinini's a bit tired.

Listen, Hector: you look after your mum, okay? She's something else. And eat up your nice, fresh fish.

A River Ran Through It

A writer takes an emotion-packed trip on the huge, brown river of his childhood in East Pakistan

New Zealand Listener (10 March 2006)

In front of me in a hotel room in Chittagong, Bangladesh, were five objects. I felt emotional – not for the first time that day I sponged up tears with Bangladesh's rose-scented tissues. Earlier in the day, I was handed some in the archive of the ruinous paper mill at Chandraghona. There, in a dim, mouldy archive room, I'd seen a faded photograph of my father on the banks of the Karnaphuli River, in what was then East Pakistan, in 1954.

Chandraghona had been our family's improbable home for four years. Mostly, I remember going feral with my twin brother David along the banks of the big, brown Karnaphuli River, where vultures tugged the guts of drowned cattle out via their anuses and where immense bamboo rafts floated down to the chipper at the mill.

Last year, I went back to find our old home on the jungly hill above the river. Later, I rearranged the objects on the Chittagong hotel table and took a picture. The result's a peculiar kind of still-life. Equally peculiar is a photograph of a narrow doorway obscured by a grubby rayon curtain with the sign Room No.1 above it. Room No.1 had been David's and my bedroom.

Room No.1 was also the site of a labour union accommodation scam. Notwithstanding its rich secret life, the door sign's odd precision (there was only one other door) is typical of a Bengali art form: neatness. Even demonstrations can be neat. On 9 February 2005, some 30,000 male jute mill workers from eight mills in the Kulna-Jessore industrial belt formed a human chain in bare feet and sleeveless undershirts, and all carrying empty earthenware plates. A similar human chain had been formed the day before at Rajghat in

Jessore's Abhoynagar upazila (administrative zone). A line of 60,000 empty earthenware plates over two days.

Such demonstrations don't rule out rioting. The ordinariness of violent unrest was captured in a *Daily Star* newspaper headline following the first day of the two-day hartal (general strike with demonstrations) on 14 and 15 February 2005: 'Street show-off ends without confrontation.' In fact, armed clashes took place all over the country. On the second day of this hartal non-event, a crowd at Dhaka University was hit by four bombs left in potato-chip packets.

The neatness extends to loony bureaucracy. I went through various processes to gain access to the Rangamati region where the old paper mill is located, to the mill itself and to the Chittagong Hill Tracts. I forked out extra cash to the local upazila official in Chandraghona. At the army checkpoint on the road to Bandarban in the Hill Tracts, I handwrote my missing name into the army's typed ledger of the day's quota of authorised travellers (having previously purchased an 'official' permission in Dhaka).

Everywhere, things are sorted: bamboo graded by diameter, new-season bricks, stooks of thatch, cowpats. Chaotic in motion, rickshaws always end up parked with their front wheels aligned. Things are bundled, basketed and bagged. The baskets are patterned and stacked or arranged in rows. The bags are endlessly rewashed: from trains, you see jute and synthetic sacks drying in rows by village ponds. The kids selling freshly sliced carrots by traffic roundabouts have arranged them in circular patterns on wide bamboo trays. There are elaborately symmetrical flower arrangements being taken home in rickshaws on Valentine's Day, marigolds and zinnias on the Saraswati puja, which combined rites for the Hindu goddess of knowledge with the traditional Bangladeshi spring festival; the immense arrangements of flowers at Dhaka's Shaheed Minar memorial for Ekushy Language Martyrs Day. The beautifully patterned spatial and communal orderliness of the rice paddies; the frugal symmetry and serial construction of my airy, creaking, all-bamboo house-on-stilts high above the Sangu River in the smoky Chittagong Hill Tracts.

'We must clean the path,' said Rubana Huq, a forceful Bangla businesswoman. 'Clean the path' is a brilliantly apt exhortation to a culture whose genius is to do that every day in a million small ways. It's a clever appeal to Bengal's history as 'Shonar Bangla' – golden Bengal, once the richest and most fertile country in the world. Once the world's leader in textiles and weaving, always the world's only supplier of jute, it was consigned to the ranks of 'Least Developed Nations' by 19th-century British textile tariffs and now by the globalisation mantras of the Washington Accord neoliberal economic fundamentalists.

The still-life objects on the table in the Chittagong hotel room included four plums from the 50–year-old tree planted by my mother outside Dave's and my bedroom window. They'd been collected by Humayunkabir Huron, a cook at a Thai restaurant in Chittagong. He'd agreed to come with me to Chandraghona and when we got back to the hotel he gave me the plums, washed and wrapped in a tissue (of course).

The other objects were a letter from the secretary of the Bangladesh Chemical Industries Corporation that carefully skirted around giving me permission to actually enter the mill. It was good enough to get us past one army and two police check-points and through the mill gate. The third object was a multi-stamped and signed permission in Bangla that Huron procured from an official of Rangamati upazila in Chandraghona. For Tk100 ($4), this impressive piece of paper gave me permission to be there and to have lunch on the hilltop where our old house was crumbling away. The guest-house manager, a union guy, required a piece of paper exonerating him from cooking for journalists sniffing after the housing scam that had transformed our old bedroom into Room No.1. The fourth item was a receipt for the lunch. There were three of us: me, Huron and Jahangir Alam, the personnel manager at the mill. We had curry potato and dhal soup, curried river fish, curried goat, mixed vegetable bhaji and sweet mushti dhoy, with chai to finish.

I saw Mr Alam being harangued by the mill's union rep outside the general manager's offices, but he was making the man laugh and everybody greeted him as we did the rounds of the mill's crumbling

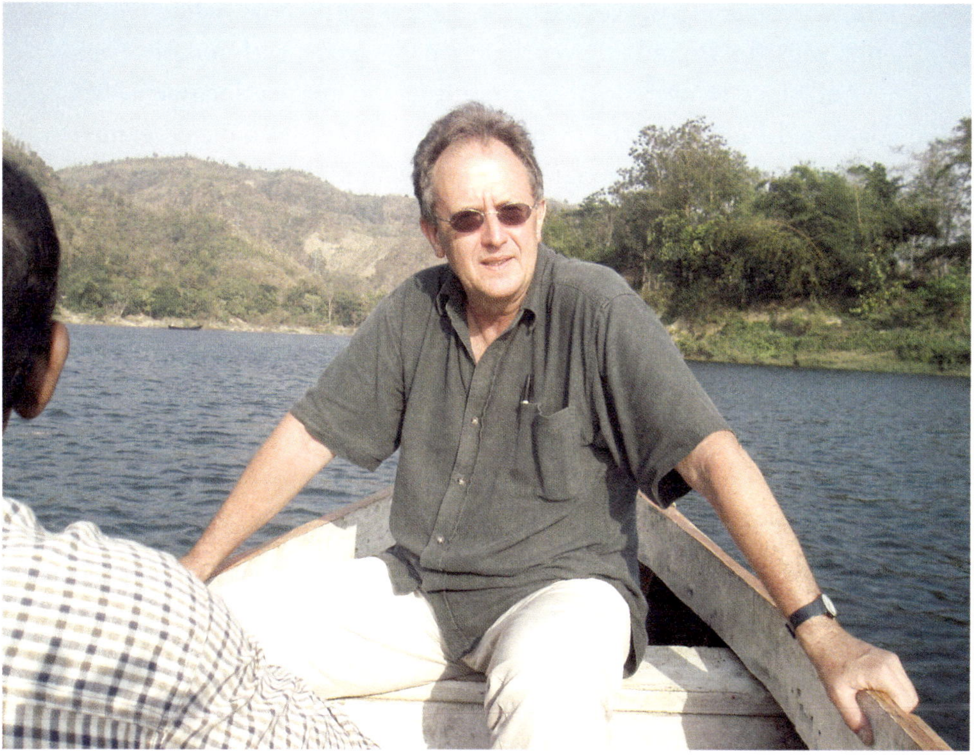

Ian Wedde on the Karnaphuli River,
Bangladesh, February 2005
– photograph by Humayunkabir Huron.

buildings. He introduced me to some very old men who claimed to remember my father. My father was an energetic man who liked to talk to people. He walked fast. He had two little boys, white-haired ones, who ran around all over the place like goats, with no shirts on.

And since we were legal as a result of the upazila document, Mr Alam and I obtained the fifth item, three tickets to a picnic garden between Chandraghona and the Kaptai Dam. Here we drank sweet tea and then went on the river in the same kind of beautifully curved double-ender boat with a creaking scull-oar at the stern that had plied the huge, brown river of my childhood.

'This is your Karnaphuli,' said Huron and took a photo of me in the bow of the boat with Alam's jug ear sticking in from the left. I have a look on my face halfway between sooky and bewildered, as if I'd like to ask Huron to pass the tissues again, but can't quite work out why, specifically, this time, I feel the way I do.

How to Outrun Jet Lag

In Bombay and Wellington with Suketu Mehta, the pre-cynical traveller

New Zealand Listener (7 April 2006)

I didn't have sex with Mona Lisa, says Suketu Mehta. We'll get back to that.

Suketu Mehta's outrunning jet lag. He reckons that if you keep ahead of your biological clock you don't get tired, you just sleep when you get into a bed. His run has paused in Wellington for Writers and Readers Week, but how he got here and where he goes next, before he heads home to Brooklyn later in April, makes his enthusiasm for a trip over the hill to the Wairarapa vineyards seem perverse. But then, Chris Price is explaining to him that there's only one road out of Wellington. Those of us who live here understand how this stands for something about the place, how our little city's critical mass becomes dense, an agreeable sting in the tail of Te Ika. Mehta's eyes light up as if at a view of a simple cosmos. 'Only one road,' he repeats, visualising a pure dharma. In an incomprehensibly complex universe that devolves into the chaos of mega-cities like Bombay/Mumbai, just being in a place with one road out of it might feel as good as the kind of sleep that realigns you with phenomena like sunrise and sunset.

But that trip's tomorrow. We repair to his hotel room, where there's a laptop that looks all too ready to stay awake and a bed that doesn't look all that slept in. *Maximum City: Bombay Lost and Found*, Mehta's first and so far only book, is substantial: 595 pages long; it was, at one stage, a thousand pages longer, he told the audience at his Writers and Readers Week session. The surviving pages are packed with information and incident, but you don't get jet-lagged reading them. Mehta's trick for outrunning jet lag may be to just keep on doing what he does so tirelessly in his book: stay consciously observant.

What he observes as an ethnologist or urban historian he processes as a novelist. The layers of narrative that simultaneously tear, amble and meditate their way through the book aren't fictionalisations of documentary material so much as the tracks of a consciousness seeing, analysing and describing social and cultural patterns. The research, and we'll have to come back to that term, is phenomenal. So is the record of it. The stories and characters are all there: their shapes just had to be seen. Mehta had to be awake to them.

The book's three large section headings – 'Power', 'Pleasure' and 'Passages' – are the first obvious signs of this wakeful seeing. Like Dickens in 19th-century London, like Zola in Paris, a tirelessly conscious power of observation is able to extract narrative sense from the city's piled-up profusions of detail.

The book has won Mehta extraordinary acclaim and, according to the blog of Sonia Faleiro, which I visited in preparation for the interview, the opprobrium of the Bollywood film director Vidhu Vinod Chopra. '*Maximum City* should be banned!' Faleiro reported Chopra as saying somewhat vehemently, among other things. Mehta has written adoringly of Bollywood movies, and in the course of our interview speaks with regret of the falling-out with Chopra. He says that the stories the movies tell are 'pre-cynical' and that 'Bombay is a city whose contrasts are so extreme that only movies that make no claim to represent reality could do justice to it'.

It makes sense to say that Mehta's view of Bombay is 'pre-cynical' as well. His disenchantment isn't world-weary. His outrage at the plight of street kids has led him to donate his Indian royalties to a children's rights agency and he tells me he's involved in taking the BJP (Bharatiya Janata Party) government to the High Court over its failure to protect children. At the same time he's sanguine about the power of gangsters and the brutal interrogation tactics of police. No one in Bombay is going to be surprised to read about the behaviour of the police officer 'Ajay Lal' in *Maximum City* and, when a news magazine outed the real 'Ajay' and named him, nothing happened. In fact, 'Ajay' was promoted, and he didn't send his enforcers to wring

Mehta's neck in Brooklyn.

This explains what sounds like a contradiction – why 'only movies that make no claim to represent reality' can do justice to Bombay, and why *Maximum City*, a book that plunges its readers into reality much as Ajay Lal's goons dunk the heads of suspects, does justice to the complete failure of a justice system in India whose most sensational consequences may play out in Bombay, where money, gangsters and entertainment ferment equally in the slums and in the mansions of millionaire crooks. The reality is already so lurid, and its overarching themes of power, pleasure and passage so simple, that *Maximum City* can be read like a frantic melodrama. Mehta talks with the fluent enjoyment and uncynical affection of someone who'll never get tired of end-to-end double bills at the multiplex. What's more, like the movies that provide the book's subconscious soundtrack, the song-and-dance routines of its mobsters, slum-dwellers and bent politicians, the raucous street theatre of its demonstrations, it keeps returning to other simple, 'pre-cynical' themes: family, love for mothers, reconciliation.

Mehta reckons that the huge international success of Bollywood movies is because of these qualities, these themes that elsewhere can't any longer escape the cynicism of the American industry. Once, India used to trade Soviet weapons for Bollywood movies – the stories were good currency and they weren't degenerate. They've always been effective nation-building tools: *Sujata* (1959) was a Nehruvian saga of caste liberation based on blood transfusion; *Amar Akbar Anthony* (1977) was the secularising tale of Hindu, Muslim and Christian brothers being reconciled. In a pre-cynical way, Mehta is proud of India's process of democratisation, assisted by the movies. In India, the poor vote the rich out of office. The poor vote, period. India has a Sikh prime minister, Dr Manmohan Singh; a Muslim president, Dr A.P.J. Abdul Kalam; and the former president of the Indian National Congress is a Catholic Italian woman, Sonia Gandhi, widow of the assassinated Rajiv Gandhi. Compared to the US? No contest, says Mehta. You saw it first at the movies.

We will have to get back to why Chopra vented on Sonia Faleiro's blog, I suspect. But first, let's make it simple. I ask Mehta what question he gets asked most often that he least wants to answer – just so we can get it out of the way. He answers it there and then, but he also answers it implicitly at his final session in the week. Here, he participates in a panel reading with the theme of travel, destinations and place. By now, on a slightly miserable Sunday afternoon that has dampened the pavement café brio of Wellington's Courtenay Place and brought the West Indies' dismal second innings to an early close at the Basin Reserve, you might have expected the jet lag of the festival audience to have caught up with them. But Mehta reads the crowd the story of a lovelorn young Bombay gangster and tired audience minds are made frantic again with the wing-beats of songbirds trapped inside a taxi cab, with the humid panting of the gangster and his beer-bar dancer, the accidental back-seat patting and petting that can happen under the pretence of catching the birds. The last sentence, a gem of succinct melodrama, has the corpses of songbirds being chucked from the steamed-up interior of the cab, while the few survivors fly free into the thick smog of the city.

As well as being a cinematic image to die for, it's a story about what happens to you if you enter the usual narrative of bar-girl infatuation: you get fleeced, you become an unrequited love slave, and if you do get laid, you become just another mark. Sex gets you barred from the kind of intimacy that might open doors of trust – might open up the great city to your pre-cynical curiosity. Getting laid will cost you the kind of intimacy that can transform the urban ethnologist into a novelist able to dream his subject as well as observe it, without allowing him the luxury of normal sleep. Even the normal Mumbai luxury of sleeping with Mona Lisa.

Mona Lisa was a beer-bar dancer that Suketu Mehta didn't sleep with. That answers the question he least wants to be asked. It also provides a perfect Bombay allegory for why his relationship with the maximum city could sustain its pre-cynical quality of observation. Mehta couldn't sleep with Mona Lisa, even if he'd wanted to, because then he'd have woken up one morning with his jet lag gone, aligned with some kind of diurnal rhythm, sunrise and sunset, or the rhythm of beer-bar hours. He'd have lost the unsleeping ability to watch the melodramatic movie of himself watching Bombay. He'd have lost the kind of research access that transformed the ethnologist into the novelist, that allowed him to fill the interior of his book with the hectic wing-beats of the city's stories without getting trapped in there and without becoming cynical.

The blurbs about *Maximum City* refer often to Mehta's statement in the book's opening paragraphs that, 'I went back to look for that city with a simple question: can you go home again?' Not many go on to ponder the second part of his statement: 'In the looking, I found the cities within me.' It's a clue not just to the restless, diasporic condition of our global age, but to another, simpler truth for Mehta – a pre-cynical one, again.

Born in Calcutta in 1963, raised in Bombay, migrated with his family to New York in 1977, at home in London and Paris, went back to what had become Mumbai in 1998: Mehta calls himself a 'city boy'. What he also wonders about during the interview is how Mumbai and New York may be like each other: socially jammed, culturally diverse, usually tolerant. He also wonders about an old democratic history that links India and the US, despite flare-ups like the sectarian Gujarat riots in Godhra in 2002, the Los Angeles riots of 1992, the post-9/11 vengeance. It was the *Mahābhārata* that Thoreau read on the banks of Walden Pond. It was Thoreau on civil disobedience that the young Indian lawyer immigrant to South Africa, Gandhi, had in his bag the day in 1893 when he took the train from Durban to Pretoria and was thrown out of his first-class carriage at Maritzburg. It was Gandhi's writings that inspired the non-violent strategies of Martin Luther King. Right now, it's looking pretty bad out there. Religious fundamentalism and sectarianism are driving the tolerance of both democracies underground. The Bush wars do little for global good faith, tolerance or respect. And yet . . .

Mehta suggested that when we define ourselves by who we believe our enemies are, religious and sectarian violence enter the play. In *Maximum City*, he describes the theatrical pandemonium of Mumbai's Hindu processions, with their ritualised, firecracker threatenings of

Muslims in the vicinities of mosques. 'It was not always so,' he writes. Before the 1993 religious riots, the Hindu processions would pass the mosques in respectful silence. Then things got really bad. Now, however, although theatrically disrespectful, the Hindu processions don't often break out into riots. Maybe the city's beginning to live with its internal differences again. Maybe it's in cities like Mumbai and New York that we'll learn how to do this. Maybe the futures they predict for us aren't all bad. Maybe it's their futures that we should cherish within ourselves.

Not a bad place to stop the tape, at this moment of pre-cynical optimism. Suketu Mehta does look a bit peaky at this point. A wee lie-down before the next publisher's party might be a good idea. But not for too long. Just long enough to stay ahead of world-weariness.

Nature's Volume

Elizabeth Thomson and the organisation of the world

New Zealand Listener (16 June 2006)

The last time I was anywhere near Mansfield St down the zoo end of Wellington was at the annual SPCA sponsor night. Donna and I went along because she supports an adopted dog cared for at the centre. On sponsor night, the SPCA foster parents have a drink and a snack, listen to an ancient but sprightly jazz combo and then visit their adopted animal. The dogs sniff finger food on their patrons and grin at them hopefully and their patrons wonder how this relationship might have gone.

The cats have a balcony above the SPCA courtyard. Looking up, their human foster parents can see the animals looking down through their balusters at the spectacle of snacking humans. What kind of seismic pattern do the jazzy, chatting patrons form, these specimens viewed from above? Are there olfactory isobars forming across the crowd? What kind of volume – sound and mass – does the sponsors' topography coalesce into? Does the courtyard the cats peer into resemble a tray of writhing specimens? What and where are the borders between life-forms and arrangements of them, between negative spaces and material masses, between individual components and their composite texture? How natural is the orderliness of nature? What does a natural pattern become when it's viewed abstractly? At what point and in what way is cultivated nature wild? What about topographical scale and perspective, the illusions of depth and distance created by arrangements of smaller and larger, of shorter and taller, of wider and thinner?

These are straightforward questions in the company of Elizabeth Thomson's work. Also sensible is the challenge to wonder what patterns of humans might look like when viewed through non-human consciousness. It's not frivolous to imagine how our own taken-for-granted modes of perception might be altered so that we see the natural world differently; so that we even see it at all, or see it as more than usual, more complex, more surprising, more bizarre, more unexpected, even more wonderful in some precise sense of the word.

Thomson's large industrial studio is right near the SPCA and the Wellington Zoo – the sound of grinders occasionally mingles with the hooting of gibbons. Thomson's dog Skip needs his fringe cut – he's not seeing too well. Everything about the location seems right for an artist whose fastidious attention to detail is what opens up such uncertainties and ambiguities in our perceptions of the natural world.

I first encountered Thomson's work in 1986 at Greg Flint's Southern Cross Gallery in Wellington. This was Flint's first exhibition in the new gallery and as such something of a launch statement. At the time, Thomson was still a student at Elam, specialising in printmaking but with an interest in sculpture. She was a scholarship student and would graduate in 1988 with first-class honours, but it was still a brave move on Flint's part to open with such a new artist and especially with an exhibition of prints – a low-key, unsensational medium.

What was striking about the prints, apart from their wit, was the way they suggested the possibility of sculptural mass, three-dimensionality, negative volume. They drew the eye in, played with perspectives and scales, made you want to walk around the back to see how things looked from there. These volumes weren't naturalistic – they were like museum dioramas, illusionistic and surreal. Thomson had an early interest in dioramas and wrote her MFA thesis on them. Her first sculptures used their plays with scale and dimension to create illusions of perspective. I remember thinking what a short distance it would be from the modest surface of the print to the mass of sculpture, how the printmaking process seemed to want to go there.

In 1987, Thomson had another show with Southern Cross, *New Work, Etchings and Bronze*. This time, the connection with sculpture was explicit, but the division between prints and bronze castings was deliberately unclear. One print, *Triggerfish*, grounded the creature in photo-etched newspaper. 'The fish becomes a newspaper story,' I

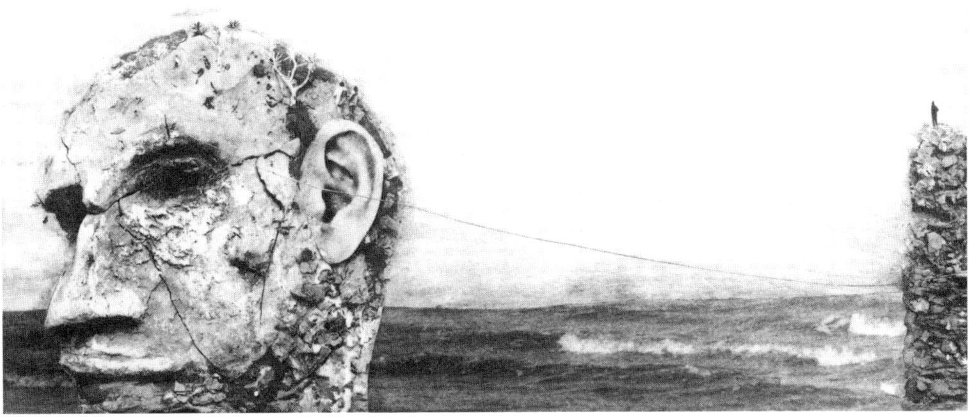

Elizabeth Thomson, *Mānukau Heads*, 1987 – photo etching and aquatint, approx. 490 x 670 mm. Courtesy of the artist.

wrote in a review back then, 'while language has transformed itself into an image. The whole thing seems capable, at any moment, of molecular reorganisation into cast metal.'

I also remember a print called *Mānukau Heads*. Showing a giant, craggy, eroding head in profile, and another 'headland' with a tiny human figure on top, it established a key feature of the artist's work, a tension between Gothic or uncanny weirdness and a sense of order, control and patterning. The effect is to make the organisation of nature seem shape-shifting or temporary, while its disorderly or fantastic aspects appear 'natural'. The little human figure on its headland seems to be gazing at the grotesque head that dwarfs it. A line like a telephone cable or a flying fox connects the two headlands – a diagram of the tension between them as well as of the possibility of traffic, the sense that everything is always changing anyway across some gap charged with uncertainty.

Thomson finds a print of *Mānukau Heads* in a plan drawer. It will be included in *My Hi-Fi My Sci-Fi*, the big survey exhibition at Wellington's City Gallery. But she locates the beginning of the transition from image to volume a step back from printmaking, in photography. It's the photograph's uncanny ability to make the apparently empirical look weird – that 'you're-not-going-to-believe-this-but' sensation – that begins the process of warping the natural into other dimensions. That sense of an exactly observed and recorded reality, for example the reality of the natural world, is moved across to a place where the representation of physical volume will look like the graphic representation of sound – like *Sonic Panorama* (2002), the large work commissioned by Auckland University, or the also large (1.8 x 3.6 metre) *Sonic Sisters* (2002), in which painted bronze mature lancewood leaves are stacked in what look like digitally rendered impacts of jarring sound. *Sonic Sisters* will be exhibited at the National Library in Wellington during *My Hi-Fi My Sci-Fi*.

Pinned on the studio wall is a photographic panorama of an olive-grove landscape south of Madrid. The view is nearly topographical and the ranks of distant olive trees make wavy patterns across the contours of the terrain. This could be the source of *North by North-*

West (2004), in which perfectly rendered individual painted bronze leaves fill a 1.7 x 2.4 metre viewfinder rectangle or diorama with wavy lines. This work was in Thomson's *Aerial* exhibition at Mark Hutchins Gallery in Wellington in 2005. The title of the exhibition suggested a viewpoint like the elevated one of the Spanish olive-trees panorama. It rationalises but doesn't take the magic away from the aerial mapping suggested by the wavy leaf patterns, which might equally be cartographic relief lines or the isobars of weather maps. The same photograph is the source for the enormous (2.5 x 14 m) *Flight Test* in *My Hi-Fi My Sci-Fi.*

In assembling the works, each individual component has to be numbered and located on an installation template. The studio process is meticulous and resembles the patient work of taxonomising, preparing, cataloguing and mounting natural history specimens. In the studio are many drawers of specimens – real as well as bronze lancewood leaves awaiting paint, for example. There is a large fume-extractor ventilation system, a sealable spray-paint shop, rows of safety coveralls hung up on pegs, a functional tea-room. Thomson's studio assistants, Belinda and Lana, and her husband Warwick are hard at work. The place might be a natural-history laboratory.

There's a persistent line in New Zealand's art history that discloses an origin somewhere in the practice of early European artists who came to the Pacific on Enlightenment voyages of discovery, such as Sydney Parkinson, Sir Joseph Banks's artist on James Cook's first voyage. Parkinson's botanical drawings became the immense *Banks' Florilegium* in 1985. The 200–year history marked by *Florilegium* seems to be entered unself-consciously and even 'naturally' by the early cut-out works of Richard Killeen, with gentle irony in the case of *Georg Forster, Naturalist* (1980). The fact that Killeen's works were presented or stored in Solander boxes, the specimen containers named after Banks's naturalist sidekick Daniel Solander on the first Cook voyage, seems deft somehow. A relationship with the specimening and taxonomising by natural-history artists seems also to have informed the work of Christine Hellyar. Peter Robinson's 1993 *Painting*, in which mocking percentage figures are organised like ethnographic trophy panels, belongs with the specimened artefact side of the history. Theo Schoon's interest in silica formations, Don Binney's ornithology and Bill Hammond's dark anthems to 'Buller the bird-stuffer', Vivian Lynn's samplings, McCahon's interest in geomorphology – the list goes on.

Thomson has an unhesitating response to the suggestion of an art-historical relationship with natural-history specimening. 'But they're dead,' she says. Meaning hers are alive? But of course – nothing has been captured, ethered, stuffed, mounted or collected, here. Nothing has died or been killed. These 'specimens' live in quotation marks. They won't be inert. 'Specimens lack animation,' says Thomson. 'They have no atmosphere.' The liveliness of her works comes from the agitation they set up between pattern and chance, from the ways in which material volumes and masses become graphics of sound or topography, from the weirdness of perspectives, the sense of perceptions warped through reorganised consciousness. You have the uncanny sense of looking at your own human perceptions with a non-human consciousness – like the cats on the balcony at the SPCA.

Or if that's too fanciful (something Thomson isn't), then perhaps with a sense of biological awareness at a cellular level, the kind of deep-wired awareness that allowed Jim Watson and Francis Crick to draw a picture of, make a model of, the spiral DNA shape in 1953. How do we know this is real? That it really represents something? It allows us to see an idea of organisation, to sense the material shape of a theory, to imagine the appearance of a phenomenon. The title of Thomson's recent exhibition at Anna Bibby Gallery in Auckland was *Interference*. The word wants to 'infer', as science does from probability, and it also wants to interfere with that reductiveness.

Thomson's life has been venturesome – motorbike trips through Mexico, sojourns on crab-infested Christmas Island, the physical life of a talented athlete, time in Spain (those Moorish patterns), flights in topdressing planes, encounters with giant New Caledonian cockroaches. The desire to interfere seems restless, even unsatisfied in the studio context. And yet one of the coordinates suggested by her habit of playing with language, including the graphic languages of cartography, is that of calligraphy. And like the large-scale calligraphic scrolls of Chinese caoshu script, the writing of Thomson's work often achieves a sense of reconciliation. 'Consider the shapes of facing danger and holding on to rotten wood, which are sometimes heavy like threatening clouds and sometimes light like cicada wings,' wrote Sun Qianli in his *Treatise on Calligraphy* in 687. 'Consider that when the brush moves, water flows from a spring, and when the brush stops, a mountain stands firm . . . these are the same as the subtle mysteries of nature: they cannot be forced.'

The restless interference that enlivens the making of Thomson's work also produces results that seem unforced, even inevitable. The unforced appearance of *A Hundred Songs for Skiffs over Mandarin Duck Lake* was possible in the Ming dynasty because the animated calmness of methodical calligraphy was able to contain the multiple sounds of singing, the sight of 100 skiffs rippling a lake and the chevron movements of flocks of ducks. In the Year of the Dog, in Mansfield St, Wellington, in consciousness range of the SPCA's optimistic orphans, Elizabeth Thomson is managing a similar kind of wonderful reordering of our headlands.

Making Light

Conviviality and the art of Bill Culbert

New Zealand Listener (18 August 2006)

Given the miserable winter that friends back in New Zealand were enduring at the time, it's probably an unsympathetic idea to start writing something about Bill Culbert with a sentence like the following. There we were, having lunch in La Chevalerie restaurant in Malaucène in the Vaucluse region of Provence on a hot, thundery day that would later unleash crashing lightning and rain squalls that tore the leaves off the plane trees and flattened them against the windscreens of parked cars. But it's where a story about Bill Culbert has to start, and that it wasn't in New Zealand and that the sky would be giving a display of spectacular argon-blue flashes are both significant facts.

At lunch, as well as Culbert and his wife, the artist Pip Culbert, were their son Clay, also an artist, who lives in Marseilles; the gallerist Michel Barjol, who runs the small, tenacious Galerie Martagon in Malaucène; his wife Pascale, who might have been the model for countless formidable statues of La République; and the essayist Guy Scarpetta and his wife, the artist Rachel Laurent. What was interesting about this moment, as well as the distance between the spectacular weather there and in New Zealand, was the way it shed light on a number of factors in the lives, the situations, of Bill and Pip Culbert.

Both have successful international careers that involve extremely hard work, a lot of travel and a lot of frugally managed time. Culbert has begun to assemble an increasingly visible public profile with substantial public commissions. In New Zealand, major public-space commissions can be found in Auckland, Nelson and Christchurch and most recently in Wellington, with the Wellington Sculpture Trust commission, *Sky Blues*, in Post Office Square. On a chilly, rainy evening in winter, the little frenzies of argon-blue neon atop their stainless-steel poles appear cool, elegant and debonair. Well known now for more than a decade, the laconic *Fault* in the facade of City Gallery Wellington was a collaboration with Culbert's old friend Ralph Hotere.

Recently, Culbert has completed commissions for Canary Wharf in London and for the United Bank of Switzerland in Melbourne. A new commission in the City of London is in development. In mid-July, Culbert was back in New Zealand to check the maquette for a major new commission with Ralph Hotere at the Museum of New Zealand Te Papa Tongarewa. This work, *Void*, due to open in September 2006, has been five years in development and Culbert regards it as the most perfectly integrated of his collaborations with Hotere.

Back to La Chevalerie. The table's conviviality is repeated in neatly kept photo albums in which Culbert documents his projects and their social and working conditions. In many of these, Culbert and Hotere can be seen ('Look! Two jokers!' exclaims Culbert affectionately) beavering away, or enjoying glasses of wine. The glass of wine appears in conceptual drawings and lithographs associated with *Pathway to the Sea – Aramoana* (1991). It's a crucial image and indeed a central concept in Culbert's work: the *Small Glass Pouring Light* of 1979 is one of those works around which a whole conceptual trajectory seems to turn, making for a broad new direction and a rush of invention and variation in the work.

The conviviality of the social space of art is central to Culbert's practice but also to the art world in which he circulates, especially in France. Small, highly professional galleries of contemporary art like Barjol's Galerie Martagon or Catherine Issert's in St Paul near Vence, where Culbert also exhibits, are linked within social, professional and infrastructural networks that sustain substantial activity outside the metropolitan centres of larger cities.

Guy Scarpetta writes for *Le Monde Diplomatique*, France's major metropolitan monthly of in-depth commentary. He and Rachel Laurent divide their time between Paris and the little town. Laurent isn't the kind of artist you might expect to opt for small-town life. Her work *Autoportrait, Molinier-cigare* shows the artist smoking a cigar and assuming an acrobatic posture of a woman disguised as a man disguised as a woman. The la-couture.com website also lists her exquisitely composed cannibal feasts where dismembered plastic dolls swim in ketchup and pasta and inflatable sex dolls are encrusted in garbage or disguised as homeless handicapped beggars styled in thrift-shop clothes.

We're redefining the straight provinces here, and in the process encountering the legacy of the socialist minister of culture Jack Lang, who, from 1981 to 2002, held ministerial warrants for culture and/or education in the governments of Pierre Mauroy, Laurent Fabius, Michel Rocard, Edith Cresson, Pierre Bérégovoy and Lionel Jospin. You can read his legacy of devolving significant artistic resources from the metropolitan centres in the public service acronyms FRAC (regional funds for contemporary art) and DRAC (regional disbursements) and in the many other associations that support communal initiatives whereby artists can get government support for venues that deliver two or more exhibitions a year.

At a stretch, you could trace this state support for the public sphere back to the French Revolution. It's an environment in which the guests at lunch in the little town of Malaucène can flourish, in which the conviviality they enjoy is shared by local winemakers, townspeople, local hospitality industry, tourists, regional art schools. It feels right for Culbert who, from the 1960s, has preferred to earth the lightning strikes of his practice at his home in Croagnes in Provence where, until recently, he also found a bricoleur's paradise in the country rubbish dumps of the region.

Bill Culbert (born in Port Chalmers, Otago, in 1935) began his professional career as a painter with exhibitions in 1961 at the Commonwealth Institute Art Gallery in London. By 1968, while also teaching at the Fine Art Department, Hornsey (subsequently at Reading University), he had made an important shift in his work – perhaps the most crucial of several that allowed him to extend his reach into the chaos of objects in the world. In that year, he exhibited at the Camden Arts Centre with the English artist Stuart Brisley. Their sculpture investigated light and made use of neon tubes.

Culbert has subsequently become celebrated for works that play with the diffusions, reflections, energy exchanges, shadows, masses and absences, volumes and peripheries of light. Sometimes these works have directly deployed the energies of light sources, not least the sun. Sometimes the material objects associated with light – its shades, bulbs, flexes and switches – have been assembled to cause a kind of freeze-frame on chaos or to map the journey of electricity to its destination.

Sometimes it has been an apparently simple aperçu involving the casting of a shadow, the appearance of light as volume and mass, the capture or spillage of light as a kind of liquid, that has installed luminosity as the familiar mystery in our world of appearances.

Culbert's use of photographic processes dates back to the 50s. Especially since 1979, photo-works (as he prefers to call them) have extended the play of light – the 'light touch' as Justin Paton has described it – in his work. He does not see these photo-works as a practice distinct from installations and sculpture, but rather another way of realising sculpture: a 'convenience'. Such photo-works ask what we're looking at here – is it the photograph, the object in it, the process that unites them, or an event that has suspended both the photograph and its object in a moment that astonishes us with this nifty eddy in the chaotic flow of time?

It's a flow along which the ordinary material world rushes, its predictability paused by the pleasure of an unexpected association, such as the one that occurs in *Small Glass Pouring Light* (1979; other versions were made subsequently). In this photo-work, a bistro glass of red wine outside in the sunshine casts a shadow in the shape of a lightbulb filled both with darkness and a brightly glowing filament.

The visual pun in *Small Glass Pouring Light* was expanded by Culbert in 1983 into an installation in which a white formica table, lit from above by three hanging lamps, had 25 bistro glasses of red vin de table laid out on it, each casting its dark-bulb-with-bright-filament shadow. As well as the table's added pun, of course, the wine

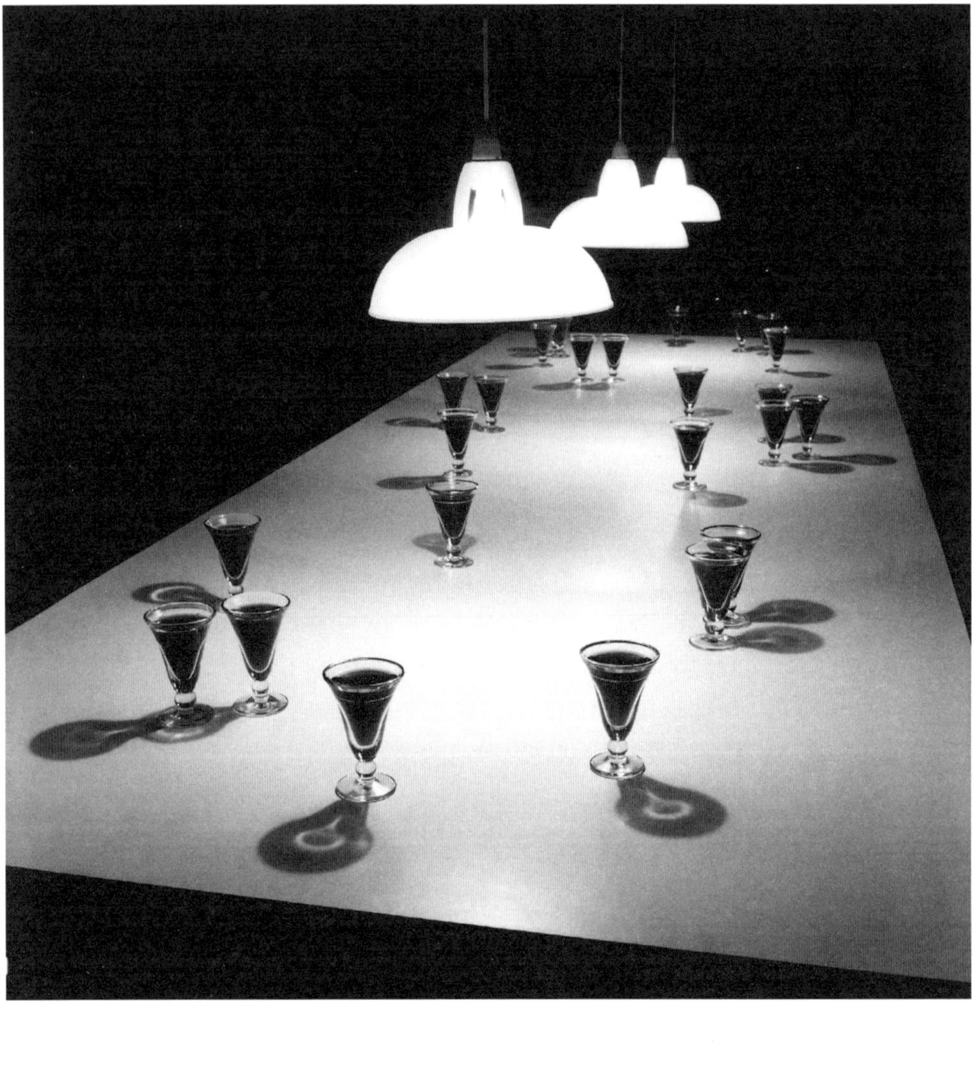

Bill Culbert, *Small Glass Pouring Light*, 1983, Serpentine Gallery, London 1983 – 25 verres bistrot, wine, Formica table, lampshades, 3660 x 1220 mm (surface dimensions). Collection FNAC, Château d'Oiron. Photograph Bill Culbert. Image courtesy of the Bill and Pip Culbert Family Trust.

could be drunk, making actual the congenial, social space of the art. And it's in this social space of art, this space in which perceptions, phenomena and artworks circulate together, in which the historical fraternity of artists enjoy each other's company, size up each other's work and engage their audiences, that any appreciation of Culbert's art has to be congenial as well as informative.

Culbert's work has been characterised by a kind of witty legerdemain that is well captured in pieces such as *Flat White Light* (2000), a wall-mounted lightbulb surrounded by an exactly spaced expanding spiral of its flex. The work poses the old question 'How long is a piece of string?', and answers it by suggesting, with a deadpan expression, 'as long as the radius of a spiral'. The work enshrines a practical solution, a piece of string tethered to a nail driven through a cork with a pencil loosely attached at its free end, the pencil inscribing an expanding spiral as it unwinds the string wound around the cork on its circular journey to the spiral's limit. The spacing of the spiral's revolutions is, of course, equivalent to the cork's circumference. It's at the fixed centre of the spiral that the lightbulb will next be installed while its flex is pinned to the wall along the track of the pencil line's diminishing vortex.

'Presto!' the work seems to say, its bulb lit up like the sign of an inspiration, its flex documenting the journey of electricity to the lighting device at the centre of its universe. And yet the work deflects any transcendental implication: this flash of inspiration doesn't need to be the sign of anything more than its moment of practical revelation, its aperçu of a simply wonderful phenomenon.

Culbert's immensely productive career has been divided between England, France and New Zealand. For many years, he's returned at least once a year to New Zealand. Besides *Sky Blues* in Wellington and a vineyard installation in Nelson, this year also sees the installation of *Void* at Te Papa.

Void – through the brash, busy core of the building a shaft of emptiness will be installed. But this won't be negative space: with typically paradoxical optimism, Culbert sees this shaft of volume as a positive. Its earth end will become a neon-ringed disk of matt black set in the floor of the museum. From above, it will produce the illusion of a bottomless pit. In the barrel-vaulted ceiling four floors above will be a corresponding disc of black, this one intersected by a line of white neon tilted off horizontal. The shaft will extend infinitely upwards and its axis to the level planes of the building's architecture will shift as you ascend towards it. Like the dark light poured into the wine glass's shadow in *Small Glass Pouring Light*, like the rich darkness in Ralph Hotere's *Black Windows*, the void through the centre of the museum will gain a kind of tangibility: the building will be pierced, poured through, by a shaft of emptiness with no floor and no ceiling.

Figure It Out

Ralph Hotere's figurative works

The Desire of the Line: Ralph Hotere Figurative Works, by Kriselle Baker (Auckland University Press, 2005)

Writing about Ralph Hotere's work has often been prefaced by disclaimers. It's said that not much has been written, the ur-text being Mark Young's piece in *Ascent*, Vol. I, No. 3, 1969, 'Love plus Zero/no Limit'. Hotere's unwillingness to discuss his work has become mythical and this reticence is often elided with the sparseness of writing, as though the artist's silence explains and amplifies the absence of critical record. Added to these disclaimers is the one that alleges a lack of catalogue information. These silences have sometimes been applauded as unpretentious integrity and this has, in turn, been elided with an oversimplified modernist dictum that expects works of art to speak for themselves.

Hotere cited a comment by the arch minimalist Ad Reinhardt in the catalogue to his, Hotere's, 1967 exhibition of 'Zero' paintings at Barry Lett Galleries in Auckland: 'The freeest and purest aesthetic statements of the 20th century have been made in abstract painting.' This laconic fingerpost remark points at a reality that belies the disclaiming myths of silence and virtue with which writers on Hotere's work have apologised for their own temerity. For a start, Barry Lett Galleries did produce a catalogue of Hotere's work in this exhibition (and the artist recorded a comment in it), as did other dealer galleries both before and subsequently. These may often have been simple checklists that, for the researcher, will complement dealer stock-book and other records. But they do exist. Secondly, the artist's reference to Reinhardt, whom, in 1964, he'd just missed hearing lecture at the ICA in London, opens up a substantial discursive territory. And thirdly, Reinhardt himself, whose 'black paintings' of 1955–66 were his ultimate statement of the freedom and purity of abstraction, engaged in the discussions his paintings seemed to banish.

Hotere may never have been as forthcoming as his mentor Reinhardt, but his use of quotation and citation would complicate and made paradoxical his apparent reticence. His incorporation of poetry often spills out of the silencing frame: inevitably discursive, the words point away from the art at worldly references or even representations, and they direct the world's traffic of meanings back into the art. By incorporating the poetry of others in his art, Hotere may seem to have remained silent himself, but the effect has often been a discursive one. The political and religious content of much of Hotere's art, overt or implicit, also sets up a paradoxical traffic between what isn't in the art and what is beyond it. The combined myths of reticence and absence of documentation begin to look self-serving (though not on the artist's part), deployed to bolster a high modernist distaste for content and especially for content narrativised along storylines provided by landscape, religion and portraiture.

It's close to 40 years since 1969 when the Govett-Brewster Art Gallery, under John Maynard, acquired one of the 1968 suites of black paintings from the now famous exhibition *Black Paintings 68* at Barry Lett Galleries – the exhibition Mark Young wrote about in the *Ascent* essay. The Govett-Brewster acquisition happened when modernist mistrust of content and interpretation was running high, and Maynard's disinclination to comment on the works hasn't wavered since – he declined, politely but tersely, to discuss the works for the 2000 publication *Ralph Hotere: Black Light*. Elsewhere, the volume of commentary on and documentation of Hotere's work has increased steadily and this increase has been accompanied by less anxiety about content and representation (especially figurative) and by increased acknowledgement of the diverse ways in which commentary about the work – including its internal indicators such as quotation and inscription – has taken place.

We can now add up a sparse but consistent service of reviewing since his exhibition *Ralph Hotere: Recent Work* at Municipal Art Gallery in Middlesborough, England, in 1964, was reviewed in the

Guardian, where the drawing series 'entitled simply "Woman"' was described by W.E. Johnson as including 'a handful of square, chunky art brut figures reminiscent of Dubuffet and one or two linear nudes that would not have shamed Picasso'. Sparse but regular commentary appeared in various professional bulletins, such as the *Waikato Art Gallery Bulletin,* No. 4, 1973, and in the art press. Beginning with Rodney Wilson's round-up of Dunedin exhibitions in *Art New Zealand,* No. 2, 1976, Hotere's work was reviewed and discussed regularly through the 1980s and 90s. As well as modest dealer gallery checklists such as Barry Lett Galleries' *Hotere: New Paintings* in 1965 and museum catalogues such as Peter Smith's 1974 *Ralph Hotere: A Survey 1963–73*, Hotere's work has been documented in substantial group catalogues since 1971 (*Ten Big Paintings* at Auckland Art Gallery), including (among others) major catalogues for the *Fifth Biennale of Sydney* in 1984, *Three from New Zealand* at the Long Beach Museum of Art, California, 1990, *Pacific Parallels: Artists and the Landscape in New Zealand*, which toured in the USA, 1991–93, *Headlands: Thinking through New Zealand Art*, Sydney, 1991, *Korurangi: New Māori Art,* 1996, *Dream Collectors: One Hundred Years of Art in New Zealand*, 1998, and *Toi Toi Toi*: *Three Generations of Artists from New Zealand* at the Museum Fridericianum, Kassel, Germany, in 1999. Hotere's work is discussed in books including Jim and Mary Barr's 1980 *Contemporary New Zealand Painters (A–M)*, Elva Bett's 1986 *New Zealand Art: a Modern Perspective*, the standard histories including Michael Dunn's of both painting and sculpture, and in Priscilla Pitts (1998). There are now substantial book catalogues devoted to Hotere's work, including Greg O'Brien's groundbreaking *Hotere: Out the Black Window* (1997) and the Te Papa/Dunedin Public Art Gallery collaboration *Ralph Hotere: Black Light* (2000).

This is the environment, a more expansive, accepting and disenchanted one than its anxious modernist antecedents admitted, into which Kriselle Baker's book catalogue of Ralph Hotere's 'figurative works' has been introduced. This accepting environment has immediate consequences for Baker's timely scholarship.

The first is that Baker's catalogue appears to join rather than presume or commence – it contributes to an expanding effort to bring together what had until O'Brien's 1997 book been a steady but piecemeal accumulation of information about Ralph Hotere's oeuvre. Another consequence is that the book's bridging of the spaces between figuration and abstraction, using the clear margin of Hotere's woman drawings, now seems to raise fewer Reinhardtian concerns about the purity and freedom of abstract art. There has been enough discussion of the variously paradoxical degrees of content in even the most austere of Hotere's paintings for Baker's exploration of the shared effects of the drawn line in both figurative and abstract works to seem straightforward – not threatening the autonomy of the Reinhardtian sublime. We now see Hotere's work operating across a continuum from the figurative to the abstract, with a subtle zone of exchange linking and informing both.

To some extent, this has the effect of defusing anxiety about what may be considered minor in Hotere's body of work – though it was the figure drawings that were noticed by the *Guardian* in 1964, reflecting not just conservatism in that critical judgement but acknowledgement of Hotere's engagement with early moderns such as Dubuffet and Picasso. Baker's book admits a less judgemental history than the one encapsulated in the Govett-Brewster's *ultimate ground* exhibition (2003) of Hotere's *Black Paintings* (1968) together with the large *Round Midnight II* (2000) and the collaboration with Bill Culbert, *P.R.O.P.* (1991). The curatorial premise of the Govett-Brewster show was both rigorous and logical: it traced an austere arc from the high modernist discrimination of John Maynard's acquisition of the *Black Paintings* to Hotere's own persisting rigour 30 years later in 2000. But in conserving the apparent silence of the work, in concentrating on frugal surfaces that display minimal effort, in privileging the apparent coolness of the black 'ground' and the noiseless anti-sublime of industrial finishes, the exhibition averted its eyes from the emotion, effort and 'noise' in Hotere's work as a whole – let alone in the overtly political significance (or content) of *P.R.O.P.* and the nifty musical cue in *Round Midnight*.

The expanded field to which *The Desire of the Line* contributes its commentary also allows Baker to make some extremely useful suggestions. One is that there is a worker-oriented political dimension to Hotere's liking and respect for industrial processes and materials, such as the high-quality lacquered finish of expert car painters. Another is that the carefully drawn line and its evidence of mental focus are deployed equally in the most apparently effortless and elegant of the woman drawings and in the tensely vibrating striations of lines applied to works such as the Founders Theatre mural of 1973 or even the runnels of corrugated iron itself. Baker is able to speak about landscape references in the 'black window' paintings of the early 1980s without detracting from their rigour. In a sense, what she's able to imply is the stretch in Hotere's work between the 1964 *Guardian* reviewer's relish for the artist's figurative, Picassoesque woman drawings and his near-miss of the Ad Reinhardt lecture at the ICA in the same year. What comes frankly into view is the fact that Ralph Hotere has always lived and worked within and along a continuum where the sensual, emotional, erotic, politically engaged and 'noisy' flowed in and out of the 'purest and freeest aesthetic statements'.

The Desire of the Line has been published as part of a longer-term agenda to catalogue Ralph Hotere's complete oeuvre, on a model similar to the McCahon database. Kriselle Baker's long-term project has the backing of the Dunedin Public Art Gallery and is supported by the Hotere Foundation Trust. We would have to wish them all well in this mammoth task, which has shaped the form of this, its inaugural publication, serving also as the exhibition catalogue of Hotere's woman drawings at the Dunedin Public Art Gallery. The catalogue contains the first published evidence of an index system for the works which will get very long indeed.

Good wishes for the long haul having been offered, a couple of cautions are probably necessary. One is that the figurative margin of Ralph Hotere's work is not occupied solely by woman drawings (or figure studies such as the Nice carnival works), as this preliminary catalogue raisonné chapter might suggest. Early 'figurative' works such as the 1959 *Still Life (vase with flowers and fish)* in Te Papa's collection continue to circulate in auctions and Baker's own text (p.2) refers to the 'earliest figurative works' dating from 1953–60 when Hotere was working in Northland as an arts advisor for the Department of Education. The catalogue for Auckland Art Gallery's exhibition *Contemporary New Zealand Painting,* 1961, the year Hotere left for England, includes a painting by Hotere called *Sand Dunes, Hokianga*. Given the existence of such early *representational* work, the term 'figurative' might read evasively, skirting the issue of a wider pictorial term of reference. I hope this isn't pedantic – I only mean to suggest that the slightly protective term 'figurative' will one day, in the context of a catalogue raisonné, have to accommodate more than the figures of women.

Second caution: while Auckland University Press deserves credit for its ongoing commitment to publishing books about New Zealand art, Kriselle Baker's usually insightful essay texts come unstuck sometimes. For example, there is a lapse in concentration on page 30 where the writer suggests Hotere's painting 'has always been directed by a conscious and intensely focused emotion'. She has just posited 'motorial memory' as the means by which an artist's drawing can become 'an unconscious act of pure emotion'. This seems to reopen a divide between intuitively motorial figurative drawing and 'conscious' and 'focused' painting. I don't think that's what Baker meant to say, in which case she's left herself with a contradiction between conscious and unconscious in two adjacent statements. And if it is what she meant to say, then she's contradicted her own book's persuasive overarching thesis, which argues for a continuum of exchange between the drawings and the substantial paintings and installations.

Finally – what's to be said about the drawings themselves? Their stylistic and emotional variety is astonishing, their variations on the erotic are poignant and their simplicity discloses qualities of sophistication and refinement that are at ease among the majestic masterpieces for which Ralph Hotere is usually celebrated.

How Gothic Is It?

The Darker Side of Kiwi Culture

'Afterword', *Gothic NZ: The Darker Side of Kiwi Culture*, edited by Mischa Kavka, Jennifer Lawn and Mary Paul (University of Otago Press, 2006)

Graf Orlok: Is this your wife? What a lovely throat.

—*Nosferatu, eine Symphonie des Grauens* (F.W. Murnau, 1922)

Warden: The patient that came in yesterday is having a fit.
Van Helsing: Which one?
Warden: The one that bit the cow.

—*Nosferatu: Phantom der Nacht* (Werner Herzog, 1979)

Van Helsing: Yes, I agree using garlic seems like nonsense, but I sense something evil and I must try everything to combat it. Evil will not disappear simply because we disapprove.
Dr John Seward: But what is evil?

—*Count Dracula* (BBC TV, 1977)

Carl: Here, take this.
[he hands Van Helsing a bag, then begins to fill it]
Carl: Rings of garlic . . . holy water . . . silver stake . . . crucifix . . .
[they pass two monks test-firing a Gatling gun]
Van Helsing: Why can't I have one of those?

—*Van Helsing* (Stephen Sommers, 2004)

Not only does Sam Neill [in *Cinema of Unease*] provide interesting insights into what drives New Zealand's filmmakers, and the cultural background (or apparent lack of it!) they come from – it is also a brilliant piece of documentary film-making in its own right.

—*Review comment by 'frodolives', 4 July 2002*
IMDb online movie database.

No laughing matter

There's a question that haunts the essays collected in this book. It resembles a more disorderly one that was present at the conference which preceded the book. Back then, I sometimes found myself trying to focus the question while looking at the tranquil, green landscape surrounding the Albany campus of Massey University north of Auckland. I was trying not to be distracted by the familiarly incongruous Tex-Mex architecture of the university's buildings, the drone of the northern motorway and a suite of light industrial buildings cresting a nearby hill. The ordinariness of these surroundings and not least their random sampling of a semi-bucolic Kiwi modernity seemed at first to be a distraction from the question I was trying to hear in order to attempt an answer. The question kept stumbling back and forth across a kind of grammatical tripper: how Gothic is this? And then, how is this Gothic? Even with my eyes shut to the distracting, fragmented modernity of the environs, even looking for the question within a darkened, internal place of thought, it kept stumbling. It wanted to be in both places at once. It wanted both places to be held by a single question.

Soon, however, the surroundings, and not least the coffee break's plate of chocolate wheaten biscuits snacked upon by shoulder-to-shoulder scholars of Gothic literary classics, aficionados of Taranaki Gothic, kohl-eyed Goths, Gothic dungeon clubbers, the neo-Gothic storytellers of the movie *Scarfies*, goth fashionistas, and austere theorists of the uncanny, stopped intruding on my hunt for the phantom question and began, instead, to frame it. I reviewed the motley conference crowd, sometimes dabbing crimson jam from its lips, at home in the terracotta-roofed buildings that might, in a shape-shifted reality, have been the film set for the vampire lap-dance bar in the Quentin Tarantino/Robert Rodriguez bloodsuck romp, *From Dusk Till Dawn* (with the incomparably uncanny Juliette Lewis). I took in the unnaturally green pasture, the unsafe screech of traffic on the northern motorway, the unwholesome, blankly shuttered profile of the light industrial buildings looming on the rise. I sensed an infection seeping not into these comfortably familiar surroundings from the Gothic business of the conference, but into the conference from its homely milieu.

When, now, I read in Jennifer Lawn's introduction to these texts that it may, on their evidence, already be a given for us to speak of a New Zealand Gothic 'as a mode, not a genre', that Gothic acts on us as 'a shifting warp of the familiar', that it 'exposes the tenuity of the natural, scaled, domestic world', I remember the sense of uneasy displacement with which my stumbling questions coalesced, somehow, into a single one whose tension was between the external, defined materiality of genre taxonomies and etymologies, and an internal, uncertain, phantasmagoric unease.

It's a tension captured in Jack Ross's marginal annotation of the narrative Gothic costumery of crown, ear pendants, neck chain, breast ornaments, girdle, clasps and loincloth as, respectively, walkman, dark glasses, gold cross, tank top, black jeans, watch-strap and G-string. It's there in Sarah Shieff's chillingly accurate suggestion that an appropriate homologue for Tourism New Zealand's original '100% Pure' landscape might be *Lebensraum* – a Gothic repositioning of the sublime as awe and terror before the Unnatural (with eugenic and racist undertones). It's there in Stephen Turner's and Scott Wilson's discovery of 'viewer-pleasure' in the horror of television accident-safe advertising. It's certainly there in David Craig's identification of photography as a key medium of 'Gothic modernism' – an exploitation of the uncanny effects of a seemingly empirical, realist science made to reveal spooks and, we might add, a link to the uncanniness of science that mesmerised Mary Shelley in 1818 when electricity was weird, new, modern, the future.

The uneasiness that the conference was looking for ways to out and document now, in these texts, appears as linked stages in a circular process. It begins with a precondition of, or predisposition to, uneasiness. It then employs 'the Gothic' as an instrumentalising mode of production whose uneasy effects can be taxonomised as genres, histories, conventions, codes. These uneasy Gothic products are, next, the causes of uneasy affects. Their uneasily affected subjects are returned to, or reinforced in, the uneasy predisposition with which the process began. It's eerie, it's inevitable – we're doomed.

But this is way too deterministic, even fatalistic. Applied to Misha Kavka's mordant plumbing of the mouldy domestic, for example, it would turn all of us into abject fatalists, the victims of rising, or is it creeping, damp – rather than the cheerfully accident-prone renovators we are. We may not have crashed through glass tabletops in our own accident-safe commercials, but we've bashed our thumbs with hammers and laughed to tell the tale. As Gothic fatalists, we'd be impervious to the belittling, even parodic, aspects of architectural history that, in Ian Lochead's account, can take European cathedrals through a declension from High Gothic through Gothic Revival to the little tin shed of the Naseby Athenaeum. As Gothic determinists, or predeterminants, we'd be without humour and we'd lack the cultural confidence that laughing at yourself sometimes discloses. Even the tremulous sniggers of uneasy provincials in the haunted houses of cultural subalternism.

What was the question?

Vampire hobbits

Let's return to the quotations with which this essay began. Although the attentive credits-reader would have spotted Wētā Workshop Ltd (NZ) well down the long list of Special Effects Companies involved in Stephen Sommers' comprehensively inclusive Gothic camp spoof *Van Helsing* (2004) – Wētā was responsible for making the miniature ship – this would hardly qualify the movie for inclusion in Sam Neill's and Judy Rymer's 1995 *Cinema of Unease: A Personal Journey by Sam Neill,* even had the latter been capable of looking into a Gothic future for New Zealand film that would include the uncanny and Gothic elements of the *Lord of the Rings* trilogy and *King Kong*, not to mention Glenn Standring's hugely successful video release *The Irrefutable Truth About Demons* (2000).

The 'apparent lack of' cultural background – surmised by the Hobbit-bitten 'frodolives' after viewing Sam Neill's and Judy Rymer's biomentary – wouldn't have explained why Neill and Rymer (thought they) detected such an uneasy undertow in postcolonial New Zealand culture in general and film culture in particular. What the film might have converted the zombie Frodofanatic to, however, is the rabid belief that New Zealand film is incapable of levity, parody, self-mockery, genre-awareness, or plain, simple fun.

For several years I've walked or run most mornings through parts of Wellington's Mount Victoria green belt and it was here, during the filming of the first of Peter Jackson's *Lord of the Rings* trilogy, that I encountered Frodo and his companions cowering under the enhanced roots of old pines off to one side of the walking track. Long after all traces of the location equipment had been cleared away, I'd meet small parties of *Rings* devotees and tourists re-enacting the scene in which Frodo and his hobbit mates hide from the Gothically hooded dark riders. Many of the tourists had gone to some trouble to dress up in heavy cloaks reminiscent of *The Monk* and they were usually taking turns videoing each other. Some of the tourist hobbits were laughing and hamming it up, but there were some who took the re-enactments very, very seriously. Sometimes, I'd meet hobbit-location seekers and undead Dark Rider hunters wandering lost in the wrong parts of the green belt with their vague internet printout maps the wrong way up, and I'd have to redirect them to the dank cowering location.

Whether or not New Zealand culture in general is metonymically darkened by postcolonial unease and guilt (or whether, on the contrary, it is blinded by the 'hard, clear light' famously lampooned by Francis Pound, like Carl's vampire-blinding invention in Stephen

Sommers' *Van Helsing*), this debate isn't, in the end, as productive or interesting as one that asks for evidence of confident mockery in the cultural production of 'unease'. 'Unease', after all, can be both an affect and a consumer experience: the former the more or less involuntary condition of a psychologised subject, the latter the more or less voluntarily desired commodity of a fully conscious thrill-seeker. Most of us are both – that's how it works. An audience's awareness and confidence – its *consciousness* – are easily found in evidence of its willingness to accept the conventions, the genres, the discourse models, of cultural products at face value: to conspire with the artist in knowing willingness to role-play, to accept the mode of informed spectatorial address described by Michael Fried and exemplified in the disenchanted comment of a child recorded by the great American animator Chuck Jones, to the effect that you don't *draw* Bugs Bunny, you draw *pictures* of Bugs Bunny. New Zealand audiences are no less saturated in the long, bloody history of hardcore Gothic than audiences anywhere else and are no less susceptible to and able to play with the inevitable ironies, spoofs and camp-ups that such a sensational history of repetition and reproduction will inevitably generate. The demand-side and the supply-side feed, and feed on, each other: the culture of pastiche is vampiric by nature. The nourishment it provides has to be simultaneously familiar and fresh. It is hard, now, to look back at the folkloric founding intentions of F.W. Murnau's 'classic' *Nosferatu* and not be entertained by the historical process that has transformed Graf Orlock's 'What a lovely throat' into a joke – let alone keep a straight face at the 'one that bit the cow' dialogue in Murnau's most direct descendant, Werner Herzog's, 1979 homage, or at the muffled English common sense of Abraham Van Helsing's scepticism about the efficacy of something as trans-Channel as garlic to combat evil in the BBC's television version of 1977.

It seems highly improbable that the 'unease' detected in Sam Neill's and Judy Rymer's investigation of the dark side of New Zealand film culture could be attributed to the 'lack-of-cultural-background' idea with which the IMDb zombie hobbit's thought has been infected, though provincial cultural uncertainty has certainly been the cause of humourlessness on more than one occasion. But nothing announces cultural confidence more loudly than the sound of loud, confident laughter as culture vampires feast upon the bodies of products for which they've developed an educated taste. Though ironic tastes for the camp, kitsch, spoof, pastiche and parody can go beyond a joke, the undying loop in which vampiric supply and demand satisfy each other is one sign of a healthy, well-fed 'cultural background'.

Some mornings, watching the by-now normal hobbitic charades being enacted under dripping pines off the muddy Mount Vic track, I had to remind myself of the components and structure of this cultural sport. The dark, sopping pines were in New Zealand and originated mostly from the Monterey Peninsula in California. The hill they covered had been renamed from Māori after an English queen. The characters they were impersonating derived from an English fantasy novel which recycled elements of mostly Scandinavian but also Germanic (and Gothic) myth after processing them through the mouli of xenophobic and racist British nationalism, Anglo-Catholicism and anti-Semitism – though, to be fair, very few viewers of the movies are going to be thinking this, let alone spotting Gollum for an anti-Semitic caricature. The Gothic, too, has to live with the blithe consumption of its products by audiences who couldn't care less. The chilly, cowering Hobbit re-enactors were from many parts of the world, especially Asia, and seemed not to be locating the world of the film outside the film world in which it lived and prospered – though they were welcoming the chance to elide the supra-national and non-geocultural world of the film with one of its production locations. The hero of the film was its director and co-writer, the New Zealander Peter Jackson, and its support star was the special effects team of Wētā Workshop Ltd – the same that would subsequently provide Stephen Sommers' *Van Helsing* with its miniature boat. But the film was produced, financed and distributed by the American film industry, for which New Zealand existed only as the location preferred by its director and as the non-unionised labour force preferred by its American project managers. That notwithstanding, some of the film's spectacular mountainous scenery would be conflated at governmental level with the 2002 '100% Pure' Tourism New Zealand marketing campaign and with mountainous endorsements from Mastercard as key signifiers of New Zealand's (Pacific?) national identity – a sublime drawn uneasily between eugenic cleansing and awesomely unnatural deculturation. The Wellington City Council would co-opt the film's international success and revenue-earning clout to its 'Creative Capital' marketing campaign, adorning its airport with a gigantic facsimile of the über-Gothic creature Gollum, though the city's useful contribution to a local film industry has been confined to the marketing opportunities of red carpet celebrations and cutting some slack in respect of location scouts. It has not run to venture capital, nor to themed shelter for the dripping Hobbit-fans once they'd come down off their dark mountain, or rent-a-hood services before they got themselves up there.

But this is how it works – it's all over the place. The confidence of a cultural idea and history as global and popular as 'the Gothic', composed of equal parts of classic genres, spoofs, psychologised subjects at national and individual levels, fashions and tastes, uncanny cultural conditions and varieties of the sublime whose terrors are felt before spectacles of the awesomely unnatural rather than the majestically natural – such a confidently persisting, resourceful and undying idea is pretty much free of the provincial anxiety of the self-perceived underachiever.

Isn't it? Surely the 'unease' that might be attributed to either (or both) postcolonial malaise and guilt, and 'lack of' robust, spoofable cultural background, isn't the sort of unapologetic background that's made possible the edgy humour of *Bro'Town*? Which, surely, can only with extreme implausibility be co-opted to a 'Gothic mode' as White Fear? The sprawling geocultural audience reach, global capital flows and complexly mediated and retooled narratives of *The Lord of the Rings*, encountered in miniature in a giggling huddle of drenched Japanese hobbit role-players on the Californian hillside above my house in Wellington, New Zealand, altogether constitute a not-bad model from which to launch an enquiry into the Gothic down-under that wants to know not, uneasily, 'are we up to it', but, confidently, 'how do we get up to it?' How Gothic are we?

How Gothic is it?

How we get up to antipodean Gothic was the enquiry of the *Antipodean Gothic* conference from which this book has emerged. From time to time during the conference, while chasing my phantom question around the *From Dusk Till Dawn* setting, I thought about the German writer Walter Abish's 'detective story' *How German is It?* – not because his novel is a Gothic one or because the conference had a detective-story (or even a whodunit) shape to it, but because, embedded in the novel's crafty appropriation of the detective genre, the question '*Wie Deutsch ist es?*' appears as an unforgiving, tireless, remorseless demand for answers: the sleuth-novel that won't stop and that will stop at nothing. The answers the novel's demanding in the guise of a hard-bitten detective who won't let go of his enquiry relate to the historically sinister vibration of the book's German title, *Wie Deutsch ist es?* And they're also succinctly captured in the novel's laconic epigraph by Jean-Luc Godard: 'What is really at stake is one's image of oneself'.

The haunted self-reflexivity of the German investigation (or denial) of what it was to be German in 1979 when Abish's book was published did, of course, reach back to an uneasy past in Nazism and, past that, also to the dark forests of bad-blood mythology, redemption and expiation, and the fresh reissues of these narratives in the present. What the book's remorseless enquiry worries at is the tension between the involuntary unease of the culturally insecure or infected subject and the voluntary unease of the redemption-seeking role-player. It probes the degrees of self-consciousness and authenticity with which its subjects ask the question, 'How German is it?' It wants to know if its characters are aware of their 'spectatorial address', if they know that what they're looking at (in themselves, for instance, in 'one's image of oneself') is a 'picture of', or if it's *das Ding an sich*, the Kantian unknowable reality that haunts phenomenal experience – or if it's just the phenomenon that scares the living daylights out of them when they encounter it, when they encounter themselves. The quest of Abish's unforgiving novel is for identity – 'German' identity as well as self-image – defined in terms of its position along the continuum from haunted abject to ironic subject. Where, on that continuum, do the novel's characters locate themselves? Are the abject merely victims of history – infected by the sins of their fathers? Are the ironists cynical vampires nourishing themselves knowingly on the fresh reissues of old stories? How to be simultaneously disenchanted and ethically committed? How German is it to be abject, disenchantedly ethical, cynical? How is one to be those things in a 'German' way?

The enquiry 'how do we get up to antipodean Gothic?' might be rephrased with more nuance as 'where do we find the antipodean Gothic on a continuum from haunted abject to ironic subject?' Or, 'how Gothic are we antipodeans when we are abject or ironic down here?' Or, 'how are we antipodeans to be those things in a "Gothic" way down here?'

This has now, of course, become also a question about brand identity, a cultural tool whose influence has grown hugely since Walter Abish wrote *Wie Deutsch ist es?* in 1979. Now, in 2006, much cultural unease is generated here in New Zealand by the question, 'how excellent is it?' ('how excellent are we?') – a question that derives the authority of its enquiry from commodity marketing's version of the Jean-Luc Godard question about self-image. Excellence is attributable to products and is often best judged by brand strengths and successes – by the efficacy of brand values. Excellence is less frequently, and less smoothly, attributed to social processes and conditions. Excellence measures appearance, performance and desirability in a competitive or comparative present. It is less likely to be asked to, or be able to, measure social interiority, process and relevance within a sustainable history. Along with being reminded from time to time during the conference of the dry, precise, laconic humour with which Abish interrogated the 'values' of Germany in 1979, I was often reminded of the pseudo-seriousness with which brand values and identities are discussed a quarter-century later. This was because the conference itself, as you'd expect, represented in its registrants diverse 'brands' of the Gothic and diverse points of view about which brands had the strongest values; that is, which were the most excellent. There were several academic brands whose values were derived from scholarship and taxonomic and/or etymological rigour. There were club brands whose values depended on the excellence of the leisure experience they provided – of the architecture, art direction, music, drugs and immersive risk-taking in Gothic clubs. There were down-home brands – in New Zealand, the Ronald Hugh Morrieson version prevails – which saw value in the appropriation of luridly 'Gothic' narrative tropes by giant-shadow-casting ripping yarns. There were brands defined by gender and sexual orientation and by their politicised values in feminist and queer estimations of excellence. Some brands announced their values through dress and fashion – how could you presume to Gothic excellence if you weren't a goth? Gothic excellence manifested as a ghastly, waxy pallor on the surfaces of some artworks and as a brooding chiaroscuro in others whose noir colour-grading emphasised the carmine of lips and the impenetrable darkness of shadows. Urban camp values shared the same plate of chocolate wheaten biscuits at morning coffee time as values derived from the investigation of a rural uncanny associated with ferality.

The question 'how Gothic is it?' is by now being asked to answer to several measures of truth: 'how excellent is its brand?', 'how sustainable are its social conditions?', 'what are its cultural manifestations?', and 'what kind of ethical confidence does its self-analysis disclose?'

Smells uncanny

Carl:	Why does it smell like wet dog in here?
Van Helsing:	[*running past him*] Werewolf!

—*Van Helsing* (2004)

'The Gothic' was certainly pungently present at the conference, in all its many guises. I'd naïvely come to the conference expecting my one presupposition to be endorsed, but it wasn't. My only defining thought about the Gothic prior to being in its strongly marked presence had been that 'the Gothic' in its classic manifestations such as Matthew Gregory Lewis's *The Monk* (1796), Mary Shelley's *Frankenstein* (1818) and Bram Stoker's *Dracula* (1897) was incompatible with humour – would tissue-reject humour – but that its later, antipodean (or, more probably, postcolonial) manifestations were all about humour – were, in fact, about the liberated piss-taking by postcolonials of imperial culture's sacred cows, especially the ones that went 'Mooo!' in the night. Nice theory. But while vampiric, postcolonial irony and a relish for fresh imperial cow were manifest at the conference, so were varieties of seriousness in which I began to see that 'the Gothic' persisted as an unbroken, not-funny historical narrative from its psychoscientific frisson in Mary Shelley through Sigmund Freud's essay 'The Uncanny' of 1919 to contemporary vampirisms of blood products associated with pathogenic catastrophe, AIDS, ghoulish trafficking in human organs, the Undead of cloning, and the unnatural chimeras of transgenic mutation. It was clear that some of the serious, core questions asked by and in the Gothic narrative were not going to die.

If we stay with this dead serious spoor, we find that Mary Shelley's fascination with the life-creating energy of new-fangled electricity is decanted into the psychopathology of Freud's look at uncanny states of life such as the 'living doll' Olympia in Offenbach's *Tales of Hoffmann*, the same essay's succinct summary of 'the double' as a preservation against extinction' and its inclusion of 'suspended animation' states such as epilepsy. The same life-and-death narrative appears almost unchanged in our own times in the uncannily beating heart cells cultivated in a Petri dish from stem cells, or in the blubbing new-life-from-old sound of the uncannily onomatopoeic word 'Bellerophon', which is a contemporary 'double': at once the Greek hero who horse-whispered Pegasus and with the winged horse slew the monstrous transgenic Chimera; and the biotech software-assisted programme Bellerophon used to detect chimeric genetic sequences.

Think of Gollum as a Gothic product nurtured in the Petri dish of racialism from stem cells of anti-Semitism.

Though less Gothic in their disembodied, bloodless nature, digital Artificial Life (rather than Artificial Intelligence), or 'Alife', agents whose algorithms begin to have lives (and minds) of their own, may also be narrative descendants of Mary Shelley's prescient fascination with the unnatural science of life and the Gothic mirror in which life and death look at each other and see themselves. Then fall in love with each other/themselves. Then have sex (with each other/themselves). Then spawn. *Liebestod.* Self-perpetuating digital babies. The technological sublime. Especially if we accept the ALife researcher Christopher Langton's hypothesis that life is a property of form not matter – of organisation (so to speak), not materiality. Note to reader: this is not by any stretch of credulity an argument for Intelligent Design. God only knows what ID advocates would make of the idea that the software organisations of computers could 'come to life'.

Needless to say, the hauntings of fascist eugenics are what spook bioethics committees peering into the murky mirror of the Human Genome Project, for example. If we're all nearly the same, what's the difference and how is it marked? Branded? Let's hope it doesn't come down to competitive 'excellence' and the values of national brands – to commodified versions of the question, 'How German is it?'

Maybe (I think) what we need more of are unsettling Gothic stories, the ones about life and death and everything in between, that we can tell and listen to with varieties of Michael Fried's 'spectatorial address' from serious to camp and everything in between.

We'd benefit, too, from a Gothic impetus to put the bite on one or two other sacred, nationalist cows (and let's not forget the cannibalism, Pacific-historical and post-immunosuppressant, that public culture continues to avert its eyes from): newzealandgenetics.com, for starters, the 'livestock improvement' subsidiary of Fonterra (formerly New Zealand Milk). In its logo, as in Fonterra's, a familiar landscape appears. It's what '100% Pure' alps look like when logoised and lowered to the uncraggy horizons of pastureland. It reminds us that the sublime backcountry Nicholas and Caroline Chevalier spurred their horses towards when crossing the Taramakau River through massive forest giants in April 1866 would soon, under Nicholas's pencil and brush, become the picturesque vistas of marketable real estate – realty not reality – tufted with grassy fodder for the mossy cattle beasts the painter shrewdly imported to the scene from the Scottish Highlands. The Otago and Canterbury Provincial Councils paid his fees.

What the fees also bought – not the cheerfully enterprising Nicholas's fault – was a tradition in which the abject dissociations of a European sublime would be persistently co-opted to the pragmatic urgings of antipodean realty (the new reality). The glassy picture frame through which we view versions of the verdant vistas from Massey University's Albany campus is now, in its prime hilltop locations, usually organising our safe distance from haunted places. They are haunted by the ash of forests and the ghosts of Pacific uruk-hai. Inhabiting these hauntings and histories, as Donna Haraway proposes, rather than viewing them, might be a Gothic task – a liberating one, as Martin Edmond suggests in this book.

We could end, then, with a kind of answer to a kind of question. Leaving plenty of room for confident self-mockery of Gothic pretension and compassion for Gothic abjection, we can argue with Jacques Attali in *L'Homme nomade* (Fayard, 2003) for displacement as the foundation of culture. If Gothic is, as Jennifer Lawn suggests, more a mode than a genre, it may be more a mode of displacement than of any other condition. And as a mode of displacement it may be what jolts us, through laughter or horror or both at once, into the kind of cultural confidence that lives in its histories, not in spite of them. That chooses to be haunted as a necessary condition of consciousness. That doesn't turn up its nose at the smell of wet dog.

Tuning the Museum
The harmonics of official culture

South Pacific Museums: Experiments in Culture, edited by Chris Healy and Andrea Whitcomb (Monash University Press, 2006)

Abstract

National museums – especially national museums developed in the cultural environments created by neoliberal economics, proliferating virtuality and global social formations – are asked to mediate significantly tensioned and even conflicted remits. The state may expect them to put the best possible face on a marketable national identity within which commerce, culture and tourism converge; at the same time, they may be expected to report on and represent complex, contradictory, polysemic and polyvocal identities that resist the smoothing effects of statist emulsifiers. Museums may be asked to defer to the expectations of socially and politically influential lobbies, while remaining the custodians of minority, alternative or critical alterities. They may be expected to balance commerciality and good public programming. They will need to evolve while retaining critical success instruments. They need to be capable of taking risks without jeopardising high-level support, especially government support. The metaphors of tuning and of 'loosely coupled' systems are used in this essay to explore and critique the Museum of New Zealand Te Papa Tongarewa's management of its organisational harmonics: the combination of social listening and directorial conducting that keeps the place in tune.

Tune-up

The metaphor of 'tuning' and by implication of orchestration suggests two converging kinds of effort – as well as results that are harmonious, dissonant or even discordant. One kind of effort is the activity of social listening; the other, the organisational activity of directing or conducting. Applied to large public sector, officially national institutions such as state-supported national museums or TV broadcasters, this metaphor of 'tuning' implies a tension between polyvocal communities (citizens, consumers, audiences), who expect or hope to be left to their chosen discords or differences, and the state, which will usually prefer national harmony.

This tensioned space between polyvocal communities and the state that would prefer them to get on the same song sheet has been deemed a space of debate: a democratic 'forum for the nation', as the mission statement of the Museum of New Zealand Te Papa Tongarewa (Te Papa) has it.[1] This mission statement supposes that a state-subsidised, legislated institution may act as a mediator between the state and its citizens: a sound-proofed practice room in which citizens can make some noise without disrupting civil society or attracting the attention of the Sound Police. The political benefits of such debate are both democratic in appearance and regulatory in effect. The museum may be a place in which to *stage* debate rather than have it. The sometimes off-key vibration between regulation and democracy is also what we might expect of a centre-left, Labour-led political coalition in government, even one that has inherited much of

1 Te Papa's Mission, developed in 1992, states that:

> The Museum of New Zealand Te Papa Tongarewa (Te Papa) is a forum for the nation to present, explore, and preserve the heritage of its cultures and knowledge of the natural environment in order to better understand and treasure the past, enrich the present, and meet the challenges of the future.
>
> Ka tū Te Papa Tongarewa hei wānanga mō te motu, ki te whakaara, ki te hōpara, ki te whakapūmau i ngā tikanga maha, me ngā mōhiotanga mo te ao tūturu, kia whai mana ai ēnei mōhiotanga, mai neherā, kia mau pakari ai mō ināianei, whai ki te wā kei mua.

Available from: http://www.tepapa.govt.nz.

the radical neoliberalism of its famous predecessor, the fourth Labour government (1984–87) of David Lange.

The governance structure within which Te Papa is required to be 'a forum for the nation' is elaborately orchestrated, and the creative space it allows for the museum's executive to improvise, shift registers or defy the sound of impatient baton-tapping will depend on the extent of the government's wish to intervene – and on its levels of response to lobbies. The extent to which the state, in the form of the funding government, has oversight of and expectations for the civic outcomes – or 'civic yields', as Tony Bennett (2004) has it – is adumbrated in a summary statement above the museum's Concept.[2] The Concept (what the museum commits to being and doing) sits above the legislation that translates that commitment into a duty (what the museum is legislated to be and do).[3] Statement of Intent targets contract the duties as performance measures against which the museum's activity is measured. The museum's Mission next mirrors and summarises the Statement of Intent; its Corporate Principles then describe the organisational culture to which its employees are expected to subscribe in order to deliver the Mission to standards measured by the Statement of Intent and (re-ascending the scale) thus meet legislative duties and achieve the government's goals in respect of national identity and the Treaty of Waitangi.

There are other ways in which the tuning metaphor is apt. In New Zealand, another contentious tuning gap opens up when a broadcaster or a museum is required by its stakeholding government

2 'Te Papa makes a significant contribution toward the key government goal – *To Strengthen National Identity and Uphold the Principles of the Treaty of Waitangi.*'

3 The Museum of New Zealand Te Papa Tongarewa Act 1992 establishes a national museum with the following purpose:

[to] provide a forum in which the nation may present, explore, and preserve both the heritage of its cultures and knowledge of the natural environment in order to better –

(a) to better understand and treasure the past; and

(b) to enrich the present; and

(c) to meet the challenges of the future.

to return both a commercial dividend on the state's investment and a cultural result in terms of the public good. The double whammy of neoliberal market forces and Reithian public service expectations does not produce a democratically tensioned space in which broadcasters or museums safely mediate public debate. Instead, it produces an internal organisational tension between pragmatic programmers and 'content providers' (curators, scriptwriters, researchers – 'creatives'). Programmers take care of the institutional bottom line and look for content most likely to generate good ratings and sponsor benefits. In contrast, content providers are more interested in cultural value: the cultural value of representing low-rating, uncommercial minority interests; cultural production taking place away from or regardless of major capital flows; disreputable, casual, quirky or somehow uncoached activity; ephemeral, immaterial, transient stuff; strident, oppositional, angry stuff; the voices of the soft-spoken; alterity.

In this case, the tuning involves organisational structures, administrative delegations, management devolutions and the fit of business units within the 'forum for the nation', as well as degrees of creeping regulatory governmentality in respect of the state's strategic orchestrations of its commercial and cultural remits. A keyword, 'excellence', has emerged in this tuning gap. Its origins in the mid to late 1990s coincided with the appearance of other key words, including 'innovation', 'creative' and 'knowledge', prompted in varying degrees by Bourdieuian concepts of cultural capital. In March 1999, for example, the introduction to published proceedings of a ministerial Cultural Foresight seminar stated that, 'a nation's cultural capital bears on its ability to deploy cultural resources within a global market, creating distinctiveness and competitive advantage' (O'Brien, 1999). An involuntarily Bourdieuian note was struck by New Zealand's capital city's local authority when it branded the city as the nation's 'Cultural Capital'. On song with the rhetoric of the 'knowledge economy', the 'excellence' keyword originated with high-end marketing and advertising but it has spread with viral success through governmental agencies for research, education and culture in the later, 'fiscally responsible' stages of neoliberalism. 'Centres of excellence' are where contestable capital and competitive economic and cultural brands converge. 'Excellence' allows the policy language of public agencies and of government to target (and reward) either commercial or cultural values; of course, preferably both at once. In New Zealand, for example, the Pacific hip-hop music industry may be deemed 'excellent' in terms of its economic contribution to gross national product, but may be culturally penalised through a politicised media beat-up over hip-hop opportunity-development grants awarded through the government's Community Employment Group (CEG).[4] 'Excellence' policy may be satisfied with the national museum's production of a commercially successful exhibition about the *Lord of the Rings* films and may also find the project to be in harmony with statist agendas for economically driven national brands such as the '100% Pure' campaign featuring pristine mountain ranges. 'Excellence' was not, however, awarded to the national museum's imbrication of icons of modernist New Zealand art, industrial design, Anglo-Oriental ceramics, TV commercials and town planning in its investigation of mid-century modernism in New Zealand. In the exhibition *Parade*, one of Te Papa's opening projects in 1998, the 'excellence' of Colin

4 In March 2004, the MP Katherine Rich (National) asked a question in the House of Representatives about the award in June 2003 of a grant by the Community Employment Group (CEG – an agency of the Department of Labour) to Fuarosa and Saralia Tamati, of the Aiga Productions charitable trust in Christchurch, to 'research and explore hip hop culture as a tool for further community development with Pacific youth'. The ensuing media frenzy uncovered significant ignorance in mainstream New Zealand about the scope, quality, ubiquity and relevance of hip-hop culture globally and in the Pacific. The heritage and culture minister, Helen Clark, described the grant as 'loopy' and others made by CEG as 'stupid' and 'odd, to say the least' on the *Holmes* show (TV1) on 26 March 2004. On 20 September 2004, Steve Maharey, the minister for social development and employment, announced the closure of the CEG.

The hip-hop melody lingers on: on 21 May 2006, the *Sunday Star Times* carried a post-budget, full-page ad placed by the *Independent Financial Review* in which Prime Minister Helen Clark appeared dressed as a hip-hop rapper on a page suggesting what else her government might have done with its surplus, including 'more hip hop tours'.

McCahon's celebrated painting *The Northland Panels* was officially deemed incompatible with other contemporaneous aspects of New Zealand modernism, and the exhibition was eventually removed. Its riff on a local modernism was too dissonant for the 'excellence' terms of reference favoured by the art lobby, which was small but politically influential. In addition, the exhibition was quirky and local; it was seen to have little, if any, international brand leverage, although Colin McCahon has frequently been seen as New Zealand's one chance for an international art profile.

As well as social listening and organisational activity, a third way in which the metaphor of tuning the museum may be apt involves how the museum produces meaning; most importantly, the ways in which it produces (and is even required by the state to produce) meanings germane to national identity. These may constitute a harmonious, even celebratory, national anthem, or a polyvocal cultural cacophony, or a battle hymn of revolt. This kind of harmony – or dissonance – is projected into spaces beyond and outside the institution; beyond the hum of internal organisation, the drone of statist statement of intent and key performance indicator objectives, the clamour of contained and managed public debate. The tuning of national identity reaches out to international tourism, to the nationalist branding of economic points of difference, and it involves the ability of politicians to successfully serenade their constituents. A post-liberal and even re-regulatory New Zealand anthem to the excellence of national unity was generated by the politically expedient convergence, in 2004, of international tourism leverage applied across the considerable fulcrum of Middle-earth, of the pasteurised sublimity of '100% Pure' natural products with brand names such as Untouched World, and of the leader of the National Party, Don Brasch's Ōrewa-speech appeal to what Labour's Trevor Mallard would subsequently dub 'Pakeha indigeneity'.[5] There was little sound, in this barbershop trio of effects,

5 Don Brasch, the newly elected leader of the National Party, galvanised public opinion with his 'nationhood' speech to the Rotary Club at Ōrewa on 27 January 2004. The ruling Labour-led coalition government swiftly appointed Trevor Mallard as its minister of race relations and on 29 July 2004 he made a

of the discords inherent in viewing sublime landscapes as *Lebensraum* for ethnically purified creatures out of Euromyth, of the legislated untouchability of the world of foreshore and seabed resources,[6] or of critically led debate about what might constitute the probable histories, let alone the ontologies and epistemologies, of indigeneity.

Of course, none of these apparently dichotomous tune-ups – between the state and communities, between commercial and cultural, between programmers and creatives, between polyvocal and hegemonic national identities – involves anything like an absolute stand-off. The most important tunings of all might be described as harmonics: third-term effects (though perhaps not 'ways') are produced by the plays across and between these dichotomous elements. Keeping the tricky harmonics in play requires a good ear, patience, an ability to listen, tolerance of dissonance and even of discord, and above all a relish of and nerve for the risks of regular retuning. And the ear, the patience, the listening, the tolerance, the nerve and risk-taking all require combinations of leadership and collectivity – what biologists, software developers and systems theorists like to call 'loosely coupled' organisational structures. Think again the slidey, sly and eliding tunes, rhythms and harmonies of Pacific hip-hop – it doesn't get any looser and more coupled than this. These are anthems to supple resources not overcapitalisation, to fluidity not stasis, to the reinventions of evolving cultures rather than to the retardations of material sustainability. These are anthems to renewal, reinvention,

provocative speech in his home town of Wainuiomata on 'Pākehā indigeneity'. On 18 August 2004, Don Brasch returned this serve with an opinion piece published in the *Australian Financial Review* foreseeing a future for New Zealand as 'just another Pacific Island state'.

6 The Foreshore and Seabed Act 2004 and the Resource Management (Foreshore and Seabed) Amendment Act 2004 received royal assent on 24 November 2004. The legislation mediated complex public attitudes to 'customary rights' of Māori, commercial opportunity and the general public's 'traditional' rights of access to the beach. It generated significant Māori protest and more than any other factor was responsible for the formation of the Māori Party in 2004. The party was registered by the Electoral Commission on 9 July 2004 and currently holds four seats in Parliament following elections in September 2005.

retuning; to the ability to prosper in one sector while another is threatened; to the ability to accept and manage risk.

Loosely coupled harmonies

During the *Reinventing the Museum* conference at the University of Melbourne in 2004, a number of loosely coupled terminologies were used. They almost became thematically conspicuous, as if the conference was disclosing a commonly held unease that had not been shared or discussed previously.

Tony Bennett talked about 'the reconfiguration of social objects so that they match with appropriate social formations' – a tuning directorial and conducted, or voluntary and opportunistic, or a harmonic of both. His comment struck a warning note, though. He spoke of the museum's 'civic yield', which, likewise, might constitute a public good (such as national unity) designed by the state or produced by the actions of citizens – by the *Gesellschaft* of duty or the *Gemeinschaft* of empathy – or, again, created by a tensioned combination of both. Or this might be a warning. He made a provocative and probably crucial distinction between 'statist museums' and 'eco-museums': the fine-tuning between these might resemble that between museums representing or reporting on culture or between museums shaping or containing it – again, a loosely coupled dichotomy (Bennett, 2004).

We heard about 'the bounds of forces in the political domain' and we heard Paula Hamilton say that 'having a culture has become essential to the idea of nationhood' – not as self-evident as it might seem, given that before about 1987 and the sharemarket crisis of the deregulated economy in New Zealand, the emphasis was on having an economy rather than, or without regard to, having a culture. The conference's undertone of anxiety about the increasing volume of the state's voice in the choir, about its management of excellence and even of the terms of reference for authenticity, began to surface in a phrase, 'the teleology of the nation', and in John Macarthur noting that cultural franchise is analogous with political franchise (Hamilton, 2004; Macarthur and Stead, 2004).

A related scepticism about and wariness of the regulatory management of official culture emerged in James Clifford's comparison of the Tjibaou Cultural Centre in Nouméa, New Caledonia, and the Vanuatu Cultural Centre in Port Vila (Clifford, 2004). Clifford was careful to describe rather than judge, to analyse discourse models rather than prefer them. Nonetheless, what emerged in his account was a kind of state-channelled 'civic yield' of postcolonial *Gesellschaft* in the case of the major tourist attraction in Noumea, and a communally activist *Gemeinschaft* in the case of the off-the-beaten-track centre in Port Vila. Clifford likes a Foucauldian articulation of power as subjectivisation with attendant effects of ambivalence in respect of identity politics: complex harmonies and shifts of register rather than monadic shouting. And he likes the contingency – the attentive retuning – of Gramscian history rather than the teleology of official, received history. The conference's mood was with him. It seemed to be preferring a reinvention of the museum, a retuning of it, as more subjective than official, more contingent than teleological, more *Gemeinschaft* than *Gesellschaft*. The museum was envisaged as more loosely coupled Pacific hip-hop than state anthem, with national identity emerging somewhat subjectively from diverse, contingent histories, rather than getting configured as a national brand refined from state-administered contestations of excellence.

Retuning Te Papa

The somewhat uneasy mood of the conference, and what I intuited as its wariness of statist conductings or orchestrations of public culture, matched my own at the end of a decade's work with Te Papa. It was a privileged adventure to work there when I did, but at the time I left – the time of the conference in Melbourne, near enough – it was also clear that a tune-up was needed and should be welcomed as a reinvigorating challenge. As I suggested earlier, this process would require a good ear, patience, an ability to listen, tolerance of dissonance and even of discord, and above all a relish of and nerve for the risks of regular retuning. In 2004, in a climate of increased governmental jitters over the management of national identity, the kind of tune-up most likely at Te Papa appeared to have been determined at a high level.

What had begun to happen at the time I left, in January 2004, was a consolidation around ideological structures, a progressive simplifying or mainstreaming of cultural narratives, a reprofessionalising of records and a redisciplining of discourses. The official founding armature of biculturalism, customer focus and commercial positivity had developed the critical inflexibility of dogma, while also becoming subject to the selective evasions of 'excellence': for example, the politically powerful but minority art lobby had effectively achieved the sequestration of its collection resource to the upper storey of the museum. A self-funded architectural proposal by one wealthy patron of the arts had included an elevator up the outside of the building to the art galleries at the top: this would have allowed him to get there without wading through or sharing elevators with the crowds in the rest of the place.[7] Increasingly autonomous (rather than 'loosely coupled') business units had begun to be formed. The cross-disciplinary and cross-cultural field of research enabled by the museum's diverse collections and wide public support was being reorganised into discrete silos. The symbolic stand-off between programming pragmatists and curatorial idealists appeared to be approaching an actual crisis close to dysfunction.

What appeared to be happening was less a robust, critically strategic operational consolidation that retuned and moved ahead from the radical opening programme of the new institution, and more a reactionary retrenchment of old museum benchmarks of excellence within an increasingly ill-fitting official armature. A similarly ill-tuned (or ill-fitting) situation was simultaneously unfolding within parallel institutions of public TV, with similar priority stand-offs between

7 The noted arts patron and cultural philanthropist Denis Adam is well known for his support for chamber music and for several generous endowments, including the Adam Art Gallery at Victoria University of Wellington. In 2001 he contracted the celebrated firm Athfield Architects to draw up a plan for the relocation of a national art gallery on the top floor of Te Papa.

bottom-liners and culturists and similarly off-key management performances. In both sectors, the word 'excellence' could be heard veering promiscuously across economic and cultural bandwidths; it was consistent only in its desired target outcome of enhanced national identity. The statist desire to yolk national identity, excellence and cultural production together may have reached its crisis threshold in the government's – the prime minister's – vehement public objections to the decision to send the installation artist collective et al. to the Venice Biennale in June 2005. As was the case with the CEG fiasco in 2004, the government's reaction appears to have been stimulated by a combination of extremely poor official advice, political face-slapping in the House of Representatives and voter-critical media derision stirred principally by TV1's *Holmes* show. The curator of New Zealand's 2005 Venice Biennale presence was Natasha Conland, who was seconded – appropriately, one would think – from her position as curator of contemporary art at Te Papa, the country's national museum. The players in this public spat about the regulation and management of New Zealand's identity at the Venice Biennale could hardly be described as operating in a 'loosely coupled' harmony. The discord between government, Creative New Zealand (the administrative agency responsible for the Biennale commission) and the national museum's seconded curator was acute. It was also consistent with and symptomatic of government's interventionist predilection in respect of culture.

A word of caution at this point: increasingly, national museums are expected to generate polysemic meanings and values, and to report on and represent the conditions of diverse cultures. The museum's instrumentalities are diverse, the modes of reception it both generates and anticipates are complex, and many of its remits are conflicted or at best in tension. Contemporary communications, and data storage and retrieval technologies, complicate the situation. The leisure, sporting and consumer environments taken for granted by most museum visitors extend such complications into the everyday. Even if it wished to – or even if government wished it to, which it does not in the case of New Zealand's Te Papa – the museum cannot aspire to a monadic tuning. This is not about conspiracy theories.

What needs to be examined is the extent of tuning that might be possible: what are the limitations and what are the signs that they exist? This can be a fairly practical, disenchanted exercise. It doesn't need to be paranoid; it should, however, be critical.

The limits to a tune-up

There will be political limits to a tune-up of the national museum. There have been many examples of the politicising of culture and of its institutions, of which the most notorious include the case of the Enola Gay in the USA in 1998, and the more recent action against Dawn Casey at the Australian National Museum in Canberra. A less highly visible stream of evidence increasingly shows culture as the vehicle of political vision in the 21st century, as economics was in the 1980s and 'knowledge' in the 1990s.

In July 2004 New Zealand's Prime Minister and Minister for Arts, Culture and Heritage Helen Clark – known as a committed champion of the arts in New Zealand – had this to say about devolution and neoliberalism:

> We think that government in the 21st century needs to form partnerships beyond its ranks in order to succeed. While in many ways governments have fewer formal powers than ever before, only governments have the ability to lead at the national level. A large vacuum is left if governments fail to organise so that they can lead. (Clark, 2004)

This makes sense as a centre-left Labour critique of the neoliberal economic policies that retired government regulation from social services. However, such proactivity may be more problematic in the cultural sector. This is because culture produces signs that are easily appropriated to the expedient branding of political values, much as corporate sponsors of culture will choose to cross-brand with cultural products that affirm their brand values. Such politically expedient cultural values are often, if not usually, going to be nationalist in intention and scope. They are also likely to be the ones that will return sufficient votes to keep a political party in power, as well as the ones that will drive major revenue engines, such as repatriated or international investment and international tourism.

'Creative' cultural agencies may find it hard to resist risk-averse pressure to conform to, and produce, smoothly marketable national brands. Such brands have the additional advantage of absorbing and muffling alterity, contradiction and change within monumentally sustainable products – products such as very long-term, capital-heavy exhibitions excluding ephemeral or time-based components and focused on the major, canonical icons of cultural and social majorities. What might such an icon be? Sir Edmund Hillary – you can't argue with Ed, and why would you want to? He's a great guy and a classic example of the opportunity provided by a national icon for popular metonymy: Sir Ed is seen to embody a set of national virtues that no one wants to mess around with. Ed's with the mountains.

A striking example of expediently political national branding appeared as a backdrop in a *Dominion Post* newspaper photograph on 26 August 2002, on the eve of the New Zealand delegation's departure for the World Summit on Sustainable Development in Johannesburg. New Zealand's Prime Minister, Helen Clark, spoke before a banner depicting a sublime mountain-scape of snow-covered peaks, with no people in sight, not even Ed, and the slogan '100% Pure' emblazoned across it. The banner was part of a now-famous and award-winning national branding campaign, '100% Pure New Zealand', commissioned by Tourism New Zealand. It can be visited at www.newzealand.com where T-shirts are available.

Similarly overdetermined incongruities appeared following the success of the third of the *Lord of the Rings* films at the Academy Awards in Los Angeles in March 2004. The day after the ceremonies, Tourism New Zealand placed full-page ads in the *Los Angeles Times* and the *New York Times*, showing a sublime, mountainous landscape, again entirely empty of people, with the slogan 'Best supporting country in a motion picture', an interesting neo-colonial riff. Mastercard, 'proud partner of *The Lord of the Rings: The Return of the King*™', also ran full-page colour ads on 3 March 2004, with the familiar backdrop of vast mountains and, in the foreground, a cavalcade of fair heroes out of Euromyth. Mastercard congratulated cast and crew 'and Middle-earth itself, New Zealand'. Not an orc or uruk-hai in sight – '100% Pure New Zealand' had been cross-branded with a racially purified Middle-earth.

We may even be entertained by these instances of the expedient cross-pollination of national branding, cultural signing and political sloganeering. But then we shouldn't be surprised when 'culture' is co-opted or shaped to similarly expedient institutional ends. Nor should we be surprised at the spectacular success of an international touring exhibition about *The Lord of the Rings* originated by Te Papa at the centre of this nexus, nor by the exhibition's apparently effortless reconciliation of the museum's commercial and cultural remits within its Statement of Intent answerability to government.

There will be governance limits to retuning the museum. An example of these appeared in a newspaper article (*Capital Times*, 2004) reporting the publication by Te Papa of a large, splendid coffee-table book about its collections, *Icons Ngā Taonga: from the Museum of New Zealand Te Papa Tongarewa* (Smith, 2004). The article was based on an interview with the then chairman of the museum's board, Dr Roderick Deane. Dr Deane was also chairman of Telecom's board and as such arbiter, then, of about one third of the value of the New Zealand stock exchange, with commensurate (though, in 2006, rapidly waning) political leverage. He and his wife were well known and highly respected patrons of the arts and exerted substantial supportive influence on the activities of Wellington's City Gallery, a collection-free contemporary art gallery in Wellington's Civic Square near Te Papa. Under the influence of Roderick Deane, Telecom was also ubiquitous as a sponsor of high-profile cultural events, for example major exhibitions of contemporary art and the New Zealand International Film Festivals.

As chairman of Te Papa's board, Dr Deane's key reporting line was to the minister responsible for the Ministry for Culture and

Heritage, who is also the Prime Minister. The no-surprises clause in Dr Deane's contract aligns directly with this reporting line; his governance responsibility requires him to scrutinise the national museum executive's implementation of its Statement of Intent, which is its contract with the ministry whose officers report to the Prime Minister.

In this closely monitored environment, with its potential for both support and regulation, the newspaper article about the coffee-table book on Te Papa's collections made interesting reading. 'Even Better than the Real Thing,' read the headline. It went on: 'No tourists, no screaming kids, no rides, no sore feet – Te Papa's virtual museum, *Icons Ngā Taonga*, is better than the real thing. The newly published book is a whole museum on your coffee table, says Te Papa board chairman Roderick Deane.' (*Capital Times*, 2004) Further on in the article, Deane said, 'I've been very keen to change the balance so that [the museum] continues to be popular, but to upgrade the scholarship and research functions. In a way, it's like a university.' (*Capital Times*, 2004)

As a former advocate for research and scholarship at the museum, I'm delighted to hear of the chairman's support and I look forward to evidence that the museum's budgets and recruitment priorities now reflect his enthusiasm. But, alas, the book in question, while excellent, is an unlikely scholarly benchmark, consisting as it does of images with 250-word captions. The book may provide a less irritating and busy social environment than the museum with its tourists, screaming kids and sore feet, but it is not (let alone better than) a museum. And finally, while discussion about the nature of museum-based research and scholarship continues internationally, there is broad agreement that its terms of reference and field of dissemination differ significantly from those of the university.

If the chairman of the museum's board, who answers to the policies of an avowedly proactive and interventionist government with strong cultural agendas, whose minister for arts, culture and heritage is also the Prime Minister; if Dr Deane is able to go public with the assertion that a book about the museum's collections is better than the museum itself, and that the museum resembles, or should resemble, a university in respect of its scholarship; and if he takes seriously the no-surprises clause in his contract with the Prime Minister, then we may logically conclude that the minister for arts, culture and heritage would also prefer the national museum to be free of 'screaming kids', and to resemble a university.

There will be policy limits. In December 1993 I joined the concept team that was being assembled to move the new Museum of New Zealand across the threshold of its enabling legislation and institutional concept and into its yet-to-be-built premises. In January 2004 I left the museum to return to a life as an independent writer and curator. I did so with mixed feelings. The museum is an addictive cultural and social space.

I had joined the project on the strength of four aspirational planks in the institutional concept and I stayed because these planks remained challenging and in some respects tantalisingly unfulfilled. I left believing they remained unfulfilled, but also that they might always be so – that their instrumentality within the museum's policy and performance are more about agency and ongoing process than they are about result or closure, that they are about negotiable rather than conclusive actions. The four planks were the museum's audience, the potential for polysemic narrations of its collections, the museum's research and scholarship, and its commitment to exploring a meaningful implementation of biculturalism.

The museum made a commitment to winning a new, large, socially and culturally diverse audience and this commitment formed the base of a pyramid of values. It meant, for example, that knowledge about the significance of collection items would be conveyed in exhibition narratives that were diverse in terms of narrative position, reading age, and cultural meaning and value. It meant that varieties of epistemology would be accepted and deployed in the museum's scholarly research. And it meant that new modes of governance, new curatorial cultures, and new kinds of relationships with communities of interest would be developed within bicultural policy frameworks.

There were entry-level thresholds for these aspirations. Some would seem to fall short in the interests of getting started, as well as for reasons of operational capacity and capability. Inevitably, these commencement benchmarks would produce opportunities for strategic development and change, and especially for increased nuance – for fine tuning – in implementation. Thus, the large audience would in time become more intimately known and its different needs understood and addressed in niche rather than generalist interpretations. The amount and variety of narration, and the architectural and way-finding organisation of narrative within the museum's spaces, would become clearer as start-up confusions were analysed. The nature and variety of the museum's research and the modes and economies of its dissemination of knowledge would become better understood, while research planning, publishing and archiving activities would become more coherent, with better and more appropriate recording, reporting and peer-reviewing procedures. Understanding of the museum's bicultural and indeed multicultural responsibilities would evolve through incremental stages of external relationship-building and internal training and capability. The architectural structure of the museum and the ways in which it locked in policy frameworks would be broken out in new spatial formations.

This bedding-in process required a fundamental commitment to ongoing change and to strategic planning predicated on evolution not status quo. This was always going to be a tough call when Te Papa's most spectacular success occurred at the base of its aspirational policy pyramid: its winning of a large and diverse audience. It has become a place to just hang out. It's a default destination for young families with not much dough at the weekends. During the school holidays, sadly, it's where a lot of single working parents drop their kids for the day. It's become a cruising destination. Such real popular, rather than merely populist, success generated an 'If it ain't broke don't fix it' policy attitude. A foundational and even monumental loyalty to Day One policy and structure did emerge.

Institutional stubbornness around foundational policy inevitably clashed with a culturally proactive government and with powerful lobbies. Vision, patience and nerve are required of the museum's leadership: this leadership needs to be capable of implementing change at a considered rate. Patience and nerve are also required of stakeholder lobby groups, who will, however, be impatient with the museum's slowness to recognise their special needs – many of which will derive from a sense of disenfranchisement as a result of the museum's popular success. And patience and nerve will also be required of the interventionist government, which may, however, be vulnerable to lobbies, and especially to the kinds of lobbies represented in Te Papa's case by art patrons such as the chairman of the museum's board.

An almost inevitable scenario unfolds at the national museum at this point: Day One loyalists determined to cement the status quo of the museum's initial success, strategic revisionists determined to tune and recalibrate the museum's functions, and impatient lobbyists and stakeholders (possibly including the government) will come into conflict. I suspect that the subtext of the remarks I quoted earlier in relation to the *Icons Ngā Taonga* book of Te Papa's collections is a tiebreaker. The subtext's unconcealed impatience, uttered by the board's chair on the axis of his reporting line to the Prime Minister, appears symptomatic of a move not to retune or recalibrate the museum on the basis of its initial successes, but to place it at the disposal of a reactionary rebranding.

The impatience that wants to reconfigure the museum in this way is also the product of a fundamental confusion. The rebranders have, I suspect, confused the discords of a complex, elaborately tuned and therefore sometimes dissonant museum in the start-up stages of its development, with endemic operational and conceptual dysfunction. Those with patience, nerve and a long view will recognise the essential health and necessity of institutional dissonance, of loosely coupled harmony, of risk-taking and attendant failure, and of the empathetic learning achieved through deferring rather than forcing conclusions. But there will be governance limits to their patience, nerve and long view.

There will be epistemological and hermeneutic limits to the museum's retuning. It is useful to think about this in terms of what we mean by the 'esoteric' – partly to demonstrate that the esoteric and the popular are not binary opposites, but more importantly to suggest that only a complex, loosely coupled suite of harmonies can deal with the proliferation of knowledges within a multidisciplinary, polysemic museum, and therefore, possibly, within a complex multicultural society. In discussions within the museum, and in 'dumbing-down' critiques from without, the esoteric was frequently conflated with 'elitism'. This reflects a significant, and a significantly limiting, confusion.

The esoteric is that which is culturally opaque to those who are not initiates. At its simplest, this will include what Steven Pinker calls 'accumulated local wisdom' and in the same book 'shared arbitrary practices' (Pinker; 2002, pp.63, 64): for example, which side of the road to drive on, currency, designated days of rest, and other ordinarily 'normative' cultural practices. At its more complex, the esoteric will include highly exclusive normative business, such as Masonic handshakes, the arcana of regatta laws, cricket, Aussie Rules, the Kabala, the encrypted references to a history of quotation in art, architecture, popular music, cuisine or whatever.

The chief function of the ordinarily normative esoteric is to produce broad social conformity and a sense of belonging. However, the chief function of the exclusively normative esoteric is to signal welcome to a community of initiates, while at the same time signalling unwelcome to non-initiates. One effect of the esoteric is therefore to make people feel either welcome or shut out. Another is to make them feel tantalised, intrigued and envious.

What is not esoteric? Simple information, available with ordinary effort, not designed to produce conformity or induce exclusive feelings of belonging. Information that is not culturally coded, dependent on 'tone of voice', nuance, inflection or historical context. And socially shared information (George W. Bush is the 43rd President of the United States) and facts about the natural world (the whale is a mammal) (Searle, 1995).

Why would the museum seek to exclude such effects (and their attendant affects) from its cognitive environments? Why would it privilege one exclusively normative esoteric over another ordinarily normative one, or over simple information? Why would it wish to exclude feelings of belonging, tantalisation or envy? The cognitive displacements caused by the esoteric may be what stimulate audiences and rewire epistemologies. They will certainly confound any complacency in the museum's hermeneutics, in its wish to herd or direct audiences along narrative tracks, its wish to generate homogeneous text hierarchies and 'voices'. But in the end, the museum's epistemological limits will tend to match the limits it places on audience segmentation and therefore on different knowledges and knowledge systems.

Complex, loosely coupled case study

I will finish with a hypothetical research project whose civic yield might be tolerance, or rewired epistemologies, or rearticulated spatial practices in terms of the museum's conceptual architecture. Such outcomes will only be produced in a museum willing to engage with complex and possibly dissonant narratives and to permit different epistemologies and knowledge value systems to be discordant, harmonious or harmonic. This possible project is based on entirely available, even modest resources: it does not require a large ensemble.

In Te Papa's art collection are two watercolour paintings by Captain Richard Aldworth Oliver, who as commander of the *HMS Fly* carried out surveys in New Zealand and Pacific waters between 1847 and 1851. Both paintings are dated 1849. One is titled *Neddie, a Half-caste*; the other, *Feast at the Bay of Islands*.

There's a narrative connection between the giant hākari (feast) platform with its ostentatious loads of food, and the 'Neddie' character with his high-quality firearm. Art historical research isn't especially interested in the details of this narrative and will tend to move past it to discuss contexts of the painting's mode of production. Social historical research will linger over the narrative and tell us about the 1849 hākari, the scene of a sumptuous reconciliation between the warring Ngāpuhi factions of the tribal leaders Tāmati Wāka Nene,

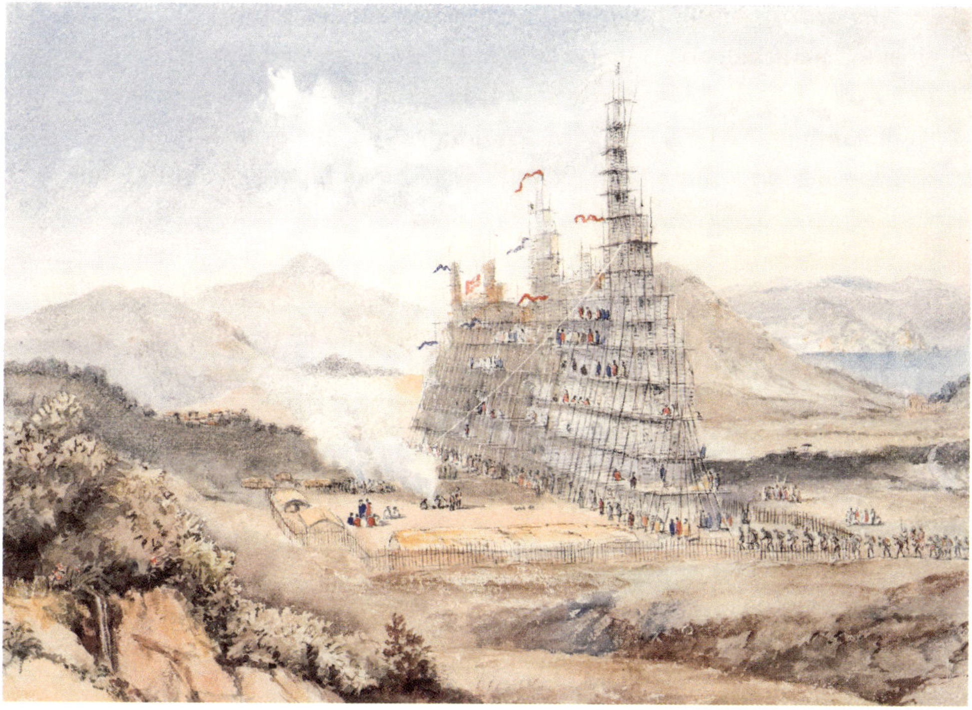

Feast at the Bay of Islands, September 1849, circa 1849, New Zealand, by Captain Richard Oliver. Purchased 1995 with New Zealand Lottery Grants Board funds. Collection Te Papa.

and Hōne Heke and Kawiti, and between Ngāpuhi and the Crown. Discussion about the artwork will focus on the historical evidence provided by it. Military history will refine that scrutiny and draw in associated evidential images of strategic positions and fortifications.

As the research moves towards whakapapa (genealogy) and mātauranga Māori (Māori knowledge), it tells us about the identities and futures of 'Neddie' and his companions and about the mana (prestige and authority) of the key players at the hākari. This information is hidden from Captain Oliver and the intended audience for his painting, but will suffuse the painting viewed through matauranga Māori. The painting will become an ancillary taonga (treasure), a gloss on the mana retained in taonga given by these men to others as marks of respect and obligation. Also in the collections at Te Papa is a Ngāti Hao taiaha kura or spear decorated with scarlet feathers that belonged to Tāmati Wāka Nene. A substantial narrative attaches to this taonga, including Wāka Nene gifting it to the Wesleyan missionary Gideon Smales.

The potent nature of this gift was conveyed by, among other signs, the red kākā or parrot feathers in the awe or decorated collar below the tongue of the taiaha. The narrative linking kaka kura (red parrot), Wāka Nene, the taiaha and Reverend Smales would extend to the customary association between kākā kura as leaders of flocks and important ariki (hereditary leaders) such as Wāka Nene as rangatira or chiefs of iwi (tribes). The rarity and significance of kākahu kura (kākā feather cloaks) would also be relevant.

Ornithological illustrations by J.G. Keulemans will show us the chiefly kākā; the taonga store will release not only rare kākahu kura, but also mutu kākā (bird snares) and kākā pōria (bird tether pendants). Now, it becomes noticeable how often red is displayed in Captain Oliver's painting. And what about those crimson pennants flying in the air above the hakiri platform?

The advantage in the war in the north, which was concluded at Tāmati Wāka Nene's hakiri in 1849, did not lie with outright military victory. It lay within the mana-sustaining contexts of manaakitanga (hospitality). The Ngāpuhi of Kawiti and Hone Heke knew that victory lay not just in the military conquest of your enemy, but in the diplomatic skill with which you were hospitable to the futures that your victory had opened. Hone Heke now claimed a derisive rhetorical victory by presenting Governor George Grey, the Crown's representative at the hākari, with a pig as a token of peace. This mocking act of manaakitanga referenced Heke's previous dismissal of Governor Fitzroy's bounty on his head of £100, which Heke had likened to the base transaction of purchasing a pig rather than winning a victory. Oliver's painting stresses the monumentality of the hākari platform, which would in fact have been burned to cook the food on it. For Māori, what was monumental was the prestige of the hospitality. Its symbolic monumentality highlighted the material insignificance of Governor Grey's presentation pig.

Diverse 'esoteric' knowledges will be found in cultural spaces that overlap the pictorial space of Captain Oliver's paintings – though they may not be *visible* there, except to viewers of the paintings for whom it becomes a mnemonic. Or except – to see the tuning metaphor through to a conclusion – to listeners whose ears have been opened to tantalising, loosely coupled harmonies.

References

Bennett, Tony. 2004. 'Civic laboratories: Museums/the fabrication of cultural objects/self-governance'. Keynote address at *The Rebirth of the Museum? An International Symposium*. July; University of Melbourne.

Capital Times. 19 May 2004. 'Even Better than the Real Thing'.

Clark, Helen. 2004. 'Paterson Oration 2004'. A speech delivered to the Executive Master of Public Administration Programme, Australia/New Zealand School of Government. 28 June 2004; Victoria University, Wellington. Accessed 2 July 2006. Available from: http://www.beehive.govt.nz/ViewDocument.aspx?DocumentID=20149.

Clifford, James. 2004. 'Pacific Museums'. Keynote address at *The Rebirth of the Museum? An International Symposium*. July; University of Melbourne. See also Clifford, James. 2004. 'Translating museums, articulating heritage: some Pacific performances', unpublished notes for keynote address at *The Rebirth of the Museum? An International Symposium*. July; University of Melbourne.

Hamilton, Paula. 2004. 'Looking away: The politics of memory at the NMA'. Paper for *The Rebirth of the Museum? An International Symposium*. July; University of Melbourne.

Macarthur, John; Stead, Naomi. 2004. 'Allegory and populism at the National Museum of Australia'. Paper for *The Rebirth of the Museum? An International Symposium*. July; University of Melbourne.

O'Brien, Louise. 1999. Introd. to 'Seizing the future: Cultural value in the knowledge economy'. Proceedings of the *Cultural Foresight Seminar Three*. 9 March; Wellington, Turnbull House.

Smith, H. 2004. *Icons Ngā Taonga From the Museum of New Zealand Te Papa Tongarewa*. Te Papa Press: Wellington.

Pinker, Steven. 2002. *The Blank Slate: The Denial of Human Nature*. London: Allen Lane.

Searle, J. R. 1995. *The Construction of Social Reality*. New York: Free Press

The Right Stuff in the Right Place

The institution of contemporary art

Museum Journal, curated by M.A. Malden (Vol. 50, No. 1, January 2007)

Abstract

A long walk in the 'world' of contemporary art gives multiple views of interlocking ecologies that, in their particularities, contradict the stereotypes suggested by language, invert 'north' and 'south', question what is 'traditional' in artistic practices, reflect on the intermix of society and art, glimpse the colonial mind in postmodern dress, and illuminate a restless subculture of profitable migrants. What does our ramble reveal about the institution of contemporary art? 'Diversity' hardly seems an adequate word.

1. An institutional mantra

I begin this essay by taking a walk around the pleasant waterfront of my home city in New Zealand and composing an institutional mantra based on the phrase 'contemporary art world'. I might be warming up an institutional branding session in which we establish our values, points of difference, target audiences and market opportunities. Or I might be asking about the place of artists in this vision, since without artists there would be no need to institutionalise their work (there may be no 'need' anyway, just an ecosystem). I should be thinking about the issues canvassed by Bruce Altshuler in his compilation of texts addressing the potential oxymoron of museums collecting contemporary art. In his introduction, Altshuler cites Gertrude Stein's observation that something could either be modern or it could be a museum, but it could not be both (Altshuler, 2005.).

On my return walk around the waterfront my view takes in the photo-op Oriental Bay fountain, whose windblown gushings are being videoed by a coach-load of Japanese tourists. Across the water on the city side is the late Len Lye's recently installed *Water Whirler*, the Wellington Sculpture Trust's most recent public sculpture pride and joy. Between me and the Museum of New Zealand Te Papa Tongarewa is the new Waitangi Park skate park, which has begun to be intricately tagged. Opposite the graffiti-adorned skate park is a new, unfinished apartment building facing the sea. Its inland wall is covered by an immense five-storey-high disaster-preparedness banner depicting a tsunami. The banner, a to-die-for object (given its location and the prospective apartment owners' awesome harbour views), perfectly articulates George Dickie's institutional theory of art (Dickie, 1974, 1997). Dickie would say that the banner would be art if accepted as such by the institutional art world; that is, by museums and collectors. (Werner would say: if transformed into museum capital.) Danto would object, sensibly and self-evidently, that such institutional endorsement only matters if invoked – activated – by an artist.

On the inland-facing wall of Te Papa, and just visible in the distance as I cross the road by the skate park, is a large and splendid commissioned artwork by the senior New Zealand artist Milan Mrkusich. It consists of three-storey-high lines of coloured glass squares organised according to the artist's scrupulous schemes of colour theory. The pride and joy of its commissioning curators (and of the artist), it is regularly mocked by the mainstream media, which is not convinced either by the institution's endorsement (as Dickie argues), nor by the artist's invocation of institutional theory (as Danto argues), nor by the possibility of informed mediation (as Freeland argues (Freeland, 2001)). For Mrkusich's glass squares to be art, then, must they also win the love of the mainstream public? Kuspit would hope not; in fact, he would say that such mainstream affection would degrade Mrkusich's contemporary masterpiece and might even disqualify it, with or without institutional approval (Kuspit, 2004). Freeland, however, would argue that broad comprehension and acceptance isn't too much to expect; what's required is the mediation of institutional advocates and the empowering of an informed, critical citizenry.

Beyond Te Papa is City Gallery Wellington, a collection-less *Kunsthalle*-type contemporary art gallery. Because I've just written about the work of Elizabeth Thompson, an artist exhibiting there, I have a clear, pleasurable sense of its gallery spaces in my mind. Is my mind, then, also an institution? What constitutes the border between the mental space in which I can map the architectural space of the gallery, and the gallery? Which of the two am I more within? Do I contain the institution, or does it contain me? And, by extension, what kinds of institutional borders characterise the spaces (mental as well as physical) where my sense of the present and what's in it converges with that of the artist?

Without sidetracking from my route home I pass a high-end contemporary art dealer's gallery and, in the same block, a commercial gallery of authenticity-trademarked *toi iho*™ Māori art. I pause to buy a take-out coffee at a small, crowded café where works of art for sale are casually displayed on the walls. The most obvious sign that these variations within the institutional art market have anything in common is their use of circular red stickers to indicate that works have sold. The café has the most red dots and its slices of aubergine tart are modestly priced as well. I buy a tart to take home and feel a sense of proximity to the act of buying a work of art.

Inside my front door are some works of art whose function is both decorative and stimulating. Their show-times are changed somewhat capriciously, and I like to get little surprises from them, even though they will always be also familiar. I like to think that they relate to museums the way household pets relate to zoos.

In my office at the top of the stairs, I first encounter a lithograph by the artist Ralph Hotere. The work protests the deranged disfiguration by the Otago Harbour Board of the headland Kōpūtai on which Ralph's studio had stood above Port Chalmers. The lithograph has chopped the 'K' off 'Koputai' and shows 'oputai' with a gashing 'cut' directed at the headland's dark bulk. It's right in the world. On the wall behind my desk there is a whimsical miniature cut-out assemblage by the artist Richard Killeen; its sophistication is worldly. To my right, a little brass wall plaque by Mary-Louise Browne reads 'Concordia vincit'. It resembles a *carte-de-visite* and might be visiting the world. On top of the bookshelf is an exhibition brochure whited out by 'Blanche Readymade' and inscribed with the signature 'P Mule' – a throwaway work by the et al. collective of artists whose installation at the Venice Biennale in 2005 caused a political firestorm in New Zealand because – according to the nation's identity scrutinisers – it failed to 'represent' 'us' to 'the world'.

2. Defining moments

In 1984, the exhibition *Te Maori: Maori Art from New Zealand Collections* travelled to the Metropolitan Museum of Art in New York and subsequently to the Saint Louis Art Museum and the Fine Arts Museums of San Francisco. The works in the exhibition were taonga or treasures of iwi Māori – of diverse Māori tribes in New Zealand. The taonga were old but the situation they approached and entered was a contemporary one. In a move that was strategically and conceptually astute, the taonga exited the institution of ethnology in their place of origin and entered the argumentatively discursive space of art on the other side of the world. They deliberately travelled a long way to one of the great metropolitan centres of art where they were in a sense purged of their ethnographic history, a history that had locked them in an institutional past sealed off from the contemporary world by the use of words like 'traditional'.

When they came back to New Zealand as the exhibition *Te Hokinga Mai (The Return Home)*, they returned as contemporary agents endowed with active mana (prestige) in the present. Their reinvigorated instrumentality owed something to the calculated strategy that had liberated them from colonial institutions of history, from categories of temporal and geocultural marginality. They were returning with refreshed epistemologies and redefined modalities of authenticity and understanding. They had changed the institutions 'over there', including institutions of contemporary art, and they would be changing the ones here on their return home.

At the Met and other venues 'over there' the taonga were accompanied by elders whose ceremonial protocols also confounded institutional categorisations of what was 'traditional' and what was 'contemporary'. For the people who accompanied the taonga, the centre of the world was wherever the taonga were and the protocols with which they protected them were neither traditional nor contemporary; they were simply what you did – then, now, next.

During a maturing phase of the postmodern discussion, the exhibition *'Primitivism' in Twentieth Century Art: Affinity of the Tribal and the Modern* opened at the Museum of Modern Art in New York, in the same year as *Te Maori* at the Met. *'Primitivism'* provoked a crucial response from Thomas McEvilley (McEvilley, 1984). The possibilities that metropolitan centres might be imperial vortexes; that definitions of art might be appropriative and discriminatory; that modernist avant-gardism and the cult of individual genius might be Eurocentric; that modernist tariff borders between art and culture might need to be opened to diverse traffics in materiality, narrative and popular commercial culture; that modernism's postindustrial progressivism might need to be reprogrammed with a sense of pre-industrial history; that acute anxiety about what constitutes 'the contemporary' might be no more than a symptom of modernism's pathology of decline; that critical modernist values of opposition might have been swept away by or rolled into capital flows; that squeamishness about brand and money associations with the global corporate world might be at best naïve and at worst disingenuous – all these possibilities were in discussion at the time *Te Maori* came to the Met.

Shortly afterwards, in 1986, the Sydney Biennale *Origins, Originality + Beyond* assembled the gurus of the postmodern critique of late, anxious modernism and its hyperanxious child, the contemporary art world. Thomas McEvilley was in the catalogue as postmodern critic *du jour*, along with Rosalind Krauss, Jean-François Lyotard, Pierre Restany, Hal Foster, Sarah Kent and others. The biennale mixed the 'signatures' of 'original' artists such as Rosemarie Trockel and Cy Twombly with the aggressively appropriative art of

Immants Tillers, Masami Teraoka, Laurie Simmons and the Russians Komar and Melamid – the 'Beyond' of the Biennale's title, one supposed. Some miscellaneous 'Origins' were also proposed in the form of Pierre Klossowski, Joseph Beuys, and others. In addition, the biennale featured paintings by the Aboriginal artist Michael Nelson Tjakamarra, as well as appropriations of the 'dot painting' technique by the Australian artist Tim Johnson. This mélange now seems very much of its time. At its core was the issue of 'the copy'.

Rosalind Krauss wrote that '. . . the discourse of originality represses and discredits the complementary discourse of the copy. Both the avant-garde and modernism depend on this repression . . . It is thus from a strange new perspective that we look back on the modernist origin and watch it splintering into endless replication' (Krauss, 1984). Hal Foster asked, in familiar style, '. . . how to retain (or restore) a radicality to art without a new foreclosure or dogmatism' (Foster, 1985). Thomas McEvilley suggested presciently that, 'Contemporary Japan also shows in various ways a respect for the autonomy of the copy' (McEvilley, 1984b, 1985). Contemporary art would then be about the performance of known tropes to a knowing audience: its mode would be primarily complicit, often ironic. Eschewing originality or moving beyond it, contemporary art would perform in a complicit world of repetition or pastiche in which there was room, also, for the 'unoriginal', de-ethnologised repetitions of traditional indigenous art forms.

I remember one non-official event during the 1986 Sydney Biennale as the benchmark, after which we did indeed enter a rearticulated sense of what 'contemporary art world' might mean. At the press opening there was a performance by the Ramingining Performance Group. Their dance took place in an architectural well in the Art Gallery of New South Wales, where they had constructed a sand sculpture. The 'sculpture' entered the uncertain discourse of a postmodern reordering of what might be admitted as contemporary art, or, perhaps, as an 'Origin' for it. The Ramingining Performance Group was present at the Biennale on equal artistic terms with the international cadre. During the performance, however, members of the press corps remained unconvinced by the Biennale's rhetorical manoeuvre; I watched them tip their free drinks down into the gallery's architectural well onto the dancers below.

This derisive gesture, shocking simply for its cynicism and racism, was also shocking in the context of a biennale of contemporary art that had sought, even if naïvely, to implement a changed way of mapping and institutionalising the 'contemporary art world'.

A few years later, in 1989, as successive versions of the remapping shifted centres, peripheries, traffics, histories, and limits – rather like the shill routine of find-the-pea-under-the-cup – I curated the small New Zealand component of a large project located in Marsala, Sicily, at the southernmost tip of Europe, the point closest to Africa (so the curatorial theory went). The exhibition project was called *Il Sud Del Mondo: L'Altra Arte Contemporanea*. Its curatorial director, Italian art historian Carmelo Strano, had assembled work from 'the south of the world' and was installing it in an ancient basilica at the edge of Europe. This was an ingenious if histrionic expression of the quest for decentred maps in the contemporary art world. But I found myself remembering the press corps insult at the Sydney Biennale in 1986 on this occasion, because Strano – having assembled a bewildering variety of contemporary art from a 'south' defined entirely in relation to his own 'north' – then set about mixing and matching his trove according to the very kind of 'new foreclosure of dogmatism' Hal Foster had dreaded three years previously. Our comical tug of war, as I attempted to power-up video works the Italian considered 'too technological' for a pre-contemporary south, was really about the demons of false consciousness that continued to torment the new, self-consciously uncertain world of postmodern contemporary art.

There were many things about Strano's rhetorical 'world' that were unclear. What was clear enough was that he'd identified an 'other' contemporary art – one that existed beyond the edge of his northern world – whose remoteness he'd made geoculturally literal by dangling it off the edge of Europe.

3. Security vs speculation

In 1993, I implemented a conference and exhibition project called *Under Capricorn: Is Art a Western Idea?* for the International Festival of the Arts in Wellington, New Zealand. The project was the brainchild of Wystan Curnow, an exceptionally astute and rigorous curator and writer. *Is Art a Western Idea?* gave some of its own game away by having Cook Island tivaevae hanging around the theatre where the conference took place. The event was branded with a photograph of Gauguin's contemporary descendants holding one of his paintings in a Pacific setting, and it was closed by a group of Samoan *a cappella* street performers.

By now, a kind of weariness had begun to infect the discourse of postmodern pea-cup-shifting. Thomas McEvilley was a keynote speaker at the *Under Capricorn* event – but the moment of his crucial intervention at the time of MoMA's *Primitivism* exhibition (and of *Te Maori*) a decade earlier seemed to have passed. His essay, 'Grey Geese Descending: The Art of Agnes Martin', had appeared in *Artforum* in the summer of 1987 and there was a sense in 1993 that he was trapped by his postmodern fame in an anachronism that he had, in 1984, initiated as a fresh start. He wasn't alone in wanting the repose, the security, of high modernism's symbolic capital, not the speculative risks of contemporary art's futures – especially when those futures seemed to want to lose the word 'art' altogether.

There were other signs of retrenchment: for example, *Bilderstreit: Widerspruch, Einheit und Fragment in der Kunst seit 1960*, curated by Carmen Giménez, Knud Jensen and Nicholas Serota for the Ludwig in Cologne in 1989 – a gargantuan exhibition that seemed intent on making a shut-up-shop inventory with substantial samples of the works of 126 artists, only one of whom (Marlene Dumas from South Africa) wasn't from the transatlantic 'north' of the world. The sensation this exhibition produced was caused by an attempt to stuff the now full-grown multicultural 'contemporary' back inside the body of 'the modern'.

René Block's *The Readymade Boomerang: Certain Relations in*

20th Century Art, the eighth Biennale of Sydney in 1990, had a similarly summarising, stocktaking character. Finding its 'Origins' in Duchamp, Man Ray and Picabia, it adopted the slogan 'Art is easy' and tracked a 75-year path of iconoclasm through the conceptualists of the 1960s to the postmodernism of the 1980s. Unlike the Ludwig's *Bilderstreit,* Block's boomerang managed to convey the elliptical, uncollectible, transmutable nature of contemporary art. But where *Bilderstreit* materialised and reinstated art as a northern, transatlantic phenomenon firmly located within the north's institutions (including its history), Block's boomerang took the north's history (and much of its art) down under. It articulated a certain flightiness in the boomerang's trajectory. Even so, it sustained a divided, antipodal sense of the world, and it restated the north's historical supremacy.

Then, through the 1990s and into the 2000s, there occurred an astonishing proliferation of biennale-type events in the 'south': the *Indian Triennial,* which has in fact been running since 1974; the *Hong Kong Art Biennale,* which started in 1975; the *Bangladesh Asian Art Biennale,* a regular since 1982 (the 2006 event deployed 532 artworks by 348 artists from 31 countries, all but three – Estonia, the Kyrgyz Republic and Lithuania – located geographically in the 'south'); the *Istanbul Biennial,* which began in 1987; the Queensland Art Gallery's influential *Asia Pacific Triennale* launched in 1993; the first *Johannesburg Biennale* in 1995, also the year of the first *Kwangju Biennale of Contemporary Art* in Korea; *Fukuoka Asian Art Triennale* (launched 1999); *Shanghai Biennale* (launched 2000); the *Auckland Triennial* (launched 2001 with Allan Smith's *Bright Paradise*); *Taipei Biennale, Busan Biennale* and *Guangzhou Triennial* (all launched in 2002); *Yokohama Triennale* (launched 2005); the first *Singapore Biennale* in 2006. In addition, there were numerous expeditions of art from Asia, Oceania, Africa and South America to the north – and McEvilley wrote about many of them in *Artforum.*

To some extent, this crazy proliferation reads off as 'art behaving like money' – as Paul Werner continues, usefully, to nag. The Asian – and especially Chinese – capital surplus in 2006 is behaving much as its northern counterparts did at the birth of 'the contemporary art world' in America in the 1960s. Then, as Bruce Altshuler reminds us and as Gertrude Stein reminded him, modern art went into museum collections and 'permanent hangs', while contemporary art kept dodging.

But 'the contemporary art world', the 'world of contemporary art', 'contemporary art in the world' and 'art in the contemporary world' have shifted along channels cut not just by capital flows symptomised by the Asian behemoths, but by something metaphorically like the resolute movement of the *Te Maori* exhibition in 1984, including its return as *Te Hokinga Mai*. It's already banal to add to this metaphor the actuality of a demographically and digitally globalised world. The hegemony of a 'northern' contemporary art world has been broached – some, like Donald Kuspit, would perhaps say that the barbarians have entered the city – and what I see at the end of my promenade looks very different from what I saw 20 years ago.

4. About now

About now, the institution of the contemporary art world looks like a number of different phenomena. It looks, rather frequently, like the kind of discussion presented by *Access All Areas – An International Symposium on Accessing Contemporary Art and Artists in Public Museums and Galleries* at the Irish Museum of Modern Art in November 2006. The symposium asked presenters to discuss their institution's 'policies relating to access and engagement with the assets of the institution and to present models of practice'.

About now, but also for some time, the institution of the contemporary art world has looked like books marketing and commemorating in equal measure the grand architectural visions of new institutions. Examples might include the architecture historian and theorist Witold Rybczynski's *Un Lieu pour l'art: L'architecture du Museé des beaux-arts du Canada,* whose preface, memorably, includes the following: 'You want to see a real panda, you go to the zoo; you want to look at a real Picasso, you go to an art museum' (Rybczynski,

1993, p.9). What then – I have to ask with pedantic irritation – is the art world equivalent of a wild bamboo forest?

Lars Nittve may have had one answer as long ago as 1996 when, writing from within the remarkable accomplishment of the Louisiana Museum of Modern Art outside Copenhagen, he suggested that: 'We are living in an era when the limits of art are constantly being tested, and when art in its turn is constantly testing the limits of "the world". The literal "nowhere" of utopia has today become what I have referred to elsewhere as "nowtopia" – *NowHere*' (Nittve, 1996, p.10).

The institution of the contemporary art world also resembles one without physical architecture. The Portuguese curator Isabel Carlos's 2004 Biennale of Sydney, *On Reason and Emotion*, took as its point of departure the neurologist António Damásio's anti-Cartesan concept of an 'emotional brain': an architecture of intelligence both affective and cognitive; a kind of 'transparency' and containment at the neural level; pandas slouching contentedly between wild bamboo thickets and performance venues.

In France, even under pressure from neoliberal trimming of the public sector, the institutional world of contemporary art resembles a congenial space whose social outcomes are underwritten by the state. A great many small, highly professional galleries of contemporary art – like Michel Barjol's Galerie Martagon in Malaucène or Catherine Issert's in the otherwise *chichi* St Paul near Venice – are linked within social, professional and infrastructural networks that sustain substantial activity outside the metropolitan centres of larger cities. Guy Scarpetta, who writes for *Le Monde Diplomatique*, and the artist Rachel Laurent divide their time between Paris and the little town of Malaucène. Rachel Laurent isn't the kind of artist you might expect to opt for small-town life. Her work *Autoportrait Molinier-cigare* was included in Galerie Martagon's 2004 group exhibition *Postérieurs* and shows the artist smoking a cigar and assuming an acrobatic posture of a woman disguised as a man disguised as a woman. Also well known are her exquisitely composed cannibal feasts in which dismembered plastic dolls swim in ketchup and pasta; and her inflatable sex dolls encrusted in garbage or disguised as homeless handicapped beggars styled in thrift-shop clothes. We're redefining the straight provinces here.

5. Retrenchment vs continuity

A final note on biennales and what they now tell us about the institution of contemporary art. While the curators Maria de Corral and Rosa Martinez, of the 2005 51st *Venice Biennale*, placed *The Experience of Art* and *Always a Little Further* in some kind of tensioned relationship between consolidation and experiment, their concept – its feminist agenda notwithstanding – was fundamentally conservative and even retrenching. There were few challenges to the status quo(s).

Despite Venice's sense that 'the contemporary' might have reached its own version of the crisis of distension that caused 'the modern' to give it birth half a century ago (at the same time as *Documenta*), the 2006 Biennale of Sydney, *Zones of Contact*, curated by Charles Merewether, suggested otherwise. Merewether's own fluid zones of contact have been in Australia initially; subsequently Mexico, California (at the Getty), Spain, China, Hong Kong and Singapore – biennales of contemporary art being events that make their locations cosmopolitan by mapping them into far-flung locales.

And finally, the world of contemporary art may sometimes even frequently resemble a very large number of small, discursive, casual, opportunist spaces like that provided in New York City by Apexart at 291 Church St. Its exhibition space is negligible and somewhat irrelevant. Its online service is brisk, economical, ecumenical, casually global and multicultural. Its social space – extended through projects that are more about talking than looking – resembles the state-supported democracy of the congenial French model more than the competitive economy of the dealer world where art behaves like money. Its geocultural and demographic reach is wide and enfranchising. It offers residencies which forbid practitioners to do projects or make work; instead, incumbents are urged to meet up with people in the city and have conversations. Entering the modest street-front offices of Apexart, I have the odd but pleasant sensation, without any sense of anachronism, of walking into (let's say) a black-and-white photograph of a 'conversation piece' such as Ben Vautier's *Tout est Art* performance in Nice in 1964, or hearing John Cage say, 'I welcome whatever happens next.' This lightly sketched institution isn't, of course, ahistorical – free of its world's archive – let alone essential. But the sense of a 'contemporary art world' that it and its many counterparts convey is a continuity without time.

The same is true of many cutting-edge cross-over media and performance clubs. In New Zealand, the sense of being in a contemporary art world whose dynamism has to do with its social engagement within a wider, somewhat anarchic world of casually networked institutions, is mostly provided by small, artist-driven organisations such as the Physics Room; by a number of project-driven online magazines and blogs; by dealers whose street-fronts are permeable to diverse, casual traffics. This multiple, dispersed, often evanescent institution centres itself where its work and its audiences place it. It has, constantly, strategised and executed its exits from ethnology and from the colonising vaults of museums. Its codes, formalities and rituals are neither 'traditional' (dating back to an originary past) nor anxiously 'contemporary' (the prisoners of the moment); they are, rather, what has to be done – then, now, next. The institution's contingency is elastic: it tests the limits of art at the same time as it tests the limitations of the world. Like the post-ethnographic taonga in the 1984 *Te Maori* exhibition, and like the post-object art with which the postmodern exited modernism, this institution feels contemporary because it has an attitude rather than an administration, prefers ritual to form, and because its most active audiences are perhaps more likely to buy an aubergine tart (or some party drugs) than works of art.

References

Altshuler, B. 2005. *Collecting the New: Museums and Contemporary Art.* Princeton: Princeton University Press.

Blais, I. and I. Ippolito, 2006. *The Edge of Art*, London: Thames and Hudson.

Brophy, P. 2005. *100 Anime*. London: British Film Institute.

Danto, A.C. 1964. The artworld. *Journal of Philosophy* 61 (19): 571–584.

—. 2005. *Unnatural Wonders: Essays from the Gap between Art and Life*. New York: Columbia University Press.

—. 1997. *Art Circle: A Theory of Art*. Chicago: Spectrum Press.

Dickie, George. 1974. *Art and the Aesthetic: An Institutional Analysis*. Ithaca: Cornell University Press.

—. 1997. *Introduction to Aesthetics: An Analytic Approach*. Oxford: Oxford University Press.

Foster, H. 1985. *Recodings*. Washington DC: Bay Press. Excerpted in *Origins Originality + Beyond: The Biennale of Sydney*. N. Waterlow, ed., 22–26. Sydney: The Biennale of Sydney: 1986.

Freeland, C. 2001. *But is it Art?* Oxford: Oxford University Press.

Krauss, R. 1984. The originality of the avant-garde: A post-modern repetition. In *Art After Modernism: Rethinking Representation*, B. Wallis ed., 13–39. New York: New Museum of Contemporary Art. Excerpted in *Origins Originality + Beyond: The Biennale of Sydney*, N. Waterlow, ed., 16–18. Sydney: The Biennale of Sydney, 1986.

Kuspit, D. 2004. *The End of Art*. New York: Cambridge University Press.

McEvilley, T. 1984a. Doctor lawyer Indian chief: 'Primitivism' in twentieth-century art at the Museum of Modern Art in 1984. *Artforum* 23 (3): 54–62.

—. 1984b. On the manner of addressing clouds. *Artforum* (Summer): 61–70. Excerpted in *Origins Originality + Beyond: The Biennale of Sydney*; N. Waterlow. ed., 27–29. Sydney: The Biennale of Sydney, 1986.

—. 1985. Marginalia. *Artforum* (October). Excerpted in *Origins Originality + Beyond: The Biennale of Sydney*; N. Waterlow. ed., 30. Sydney: The Biennale of Sydney, 1986.

—. 1987. Grey geese descending: The art of Agnes Martin. *Artforum* 25 (10) (Summer): 94–99.

Murakami, T., ed. 2005. *Little Boy: The Arts of Japan & Exploding Subculture*. New York: Japan Society and Yale University Press.

Nittve, L. 1996. Nowhere but NowHere. In *Nowhere*, A. Fuchs and L Grambye. eds., 8, 11. Humlebaek: Louisiana Museum of Modern Art.

Rubin, W., K. Varnedoe and P. Peltier. 1984. *'Primitivism' in Twentieth Century Art: Affinity of the Tribal and the Modern*. New York: Museum of Modern Art.

Rybcznski, W. 1993. *Un lieu pour l'art : L'architecture du Musée des beaux-arts du Canada*. Ottawa : National Gallery of Canada.

Werner, Paul. 2005. *Museum, Inc: Inside the Global Art World*. Chicago: Prickly Paradigm Press.

Bill Hammond

Look This Way: New Zealand Writers on New Zealand Artists, edited by Sally Blundell (Auckland University Press, 2007)

I can't remember when I first saw paintings by Bill Hammond but I do remember one of his first shows at Peter McLeavey's gallery in March 1987. At that time I was reviewing art for the *Evening Post* once or twice a week and, as any honest, hard-working newspaper reviewer will tell you, it's not always easy to sustain your enjoyment of art when you have to get around the traps, and the traps of publicity-starved dealers who think you're writing their advertising copy, a couple of times a week, scribbling away. I remember getting a boost of enjoyment and confidence from the quotation Bill had affixed to this show at McLeavey's. It was from Orson Welles' *The Lady from Shanghai* (1947) and it was the perfect, noirishly laconic set up for the paintings: 'An empty amusement park makes a great hideout.'

Glinting with criminality from the shadowy recesses of screamingly popular entertainment, the paintings had titles like *Egg + Sperm Gate 5*. Their veiny, queasily creeping floors were smeared across tacky metal surfaces of tin and copper – on these materials the paint was ill at ease, it had none of the gravitas and decorum of nicely stretched canvas or accommodating art board – it was tasteless, opportunistic, kind of disposable. The sense of a carnivalesque biology that confused the capillary systems of veins and the plumbing of testicles and ovaries with the mess of guitar leads and cable on stage at a rock concert was a sure sign that Bill had no trouble grappling with the idea that culture and nature were in each other's faces.

It was great to see T-Rex and Bobby Dylan there, in the empty amusement park. I remember King Crimson, too, from somewhere, and that particular show at McLeavey's had two paintings called *Country and Western Songbook* in it. The paintings had a lot in common with country and western music's ability (at its best) to be simultaneously parodic and serious, to stage exaggerated pastiches of itself so well you couldn't tell the difference, to enlist the banal moans of faux suffering to stories that were completely convincing at the level of – what? Cliché? The truth of cliché, as has often been pointed out, resides in our having to admit its irreducible plausibility. Like country music, like the posturings of big stage acts such as T-Rex, like the urbanised, nasal cred of Bob Dylan's countrified yarns, Bill's paintings were simultaneously piss-takes and irrefutable truths, to pinch a neat formula from Glenn Standring's later filmic variation on sincere pastiche, *The Irrefutable Truth about Demons* (2000).

The great thing about this complex mode of address is that it treats us, its audience, as grown-ups. It doesn't talk to us as if we need to be brought up to speed. It doesn't have a high moral tone. It doesn't know better. It doesn't behave like a boring drunk at a party, ramming us into a corner and prodding us in the chest with insistent fingers: 'Y'unnerstan' what I mean? Eh? Eh? Eh?' We've all done this – okay, I've done this, and looking at Bill's paintings is one excellent way of getting a wry grip on such bad behaviour.

The mutant relish that these paintings displayed allied them with confrères and lurking mentors elsewhere: writing about the show back in 1987, I hazarded guesses at the Chicago Monster School and at the grandpappy figure of post-World War II grotesque, H.C. Westermann. Was Bill a member of an international conspiracy?

I doubt it – but in the same way that the Gothic can transmute internationally from its dark origins in the likes of spooky Mary Shelley in 1815, landing us with the über-Gothic creature Gollum dangling his nasty little hands over the façade of Wellington Airport (brand tag-line: 'Wild At Heart') in 2002, certain modes seem to drift like fungal spoor across the planet without constituting anything as alarming or invasive as a flu virus or an international art movement. Such capricious drifts may be captured theoretically in the suspiciously social Darwinist and determinist nets of memetics, the idea that culture moves around in ways that resemble the movements of genes. Are Bill's paintings memes, those tight-lipped cultural fragments that know their way through *Egg + Sperm Gate 5*? In the empty amusement park of globalised culture, I think it works in more savvy ways than this – with more intelligence and *consciousness* than the zombie-like passivity of memetics, let alone the passivity of art-market zombies buying art because its prices are running with its brand values.

And it's the *consciousness* of Bill's paintings that, in the end, endear them to the audiences he has the decency to treat as intelligent adults. He knows what he's doing, he has grounded reasons for doing it – for telling the stories, performing the songs, showing the tells of his paintings. Because he was a toymaker, he understands the crazy pleasures of playthings and the liberating irresponsibility of yarn spinning. Because he was a musician, he understands performance and its combinations of hyperbole and skill. Because he's a grown-up, he understands the complex pleasures and responsibilities of communicating with his equals. Because he knows that the world's a criminal place, he knows that its denizens need hideouts. He knows that the hideouts are often best disguised as places of innocent public entertainment.

Which brings us to the chilly birdlands of the Auckland Islands, which Bill visited a couple of years after the 'empty amusement park' show at McLeavey's. The artist's biographers and the historians of his art, and not least the writers of exhibition labels and book captions (among whom I have to include myself), have got us used to accepting that this visit was the defining moment in Bill's life and particularly in his life as an artist. It was from now on that the creatures of the paintings, which had often included, as well as musicians, a yee-hawing Mr Ed-type horse who might have been advertising a teeth-whitening gel-pump, began to be almost completely replaced by the tragic, sardonic, majestic, watchful and watching birds that now most often populate Bill's paintings. These are the paintings that have brought him fame and wealth and they are the ones that collectors vie for. Do the bird paintings constitute an 'after' to the 'before' of the empty amusement park hideout? Is the 'before' somehow more innocent, less committed, than the 'after' that follows the defining moment? Was the visit to the Auckland Islands Bill's Damascus Gate? When Bill grew up? I don't think so. I mean, I don't think he wasn't grown up already. I don't think the defining-moment scenario makes for a convincing 'before and after' story.

In these paintings, the birds seem to have phased out the grinning horse and the bent musicians. The ring of fire has become the ring of a bleak coastal profile that, itself, recalls the first masthead images of European arrival, mapping, conquest, pathogenic invasion and species extinction. The squeal of smoking guitar solos, the plangent, broken-heart laments of country music, have been replaced by the moan of a sub-Antarctic wind. It's blowing in from a place that's even more remote but every bit as doomed. The spectres that haunt these pictures aren't any longer those noir agents of regret and disillusion who hang about in the shadows of ephemeral popular pleasure. Now, they're the undead taxidermist vampires spawned by Walter Lawry Buller (1838–1906), the 'Bird Stuffer' as Bill has called him, the author of *A History of the Birds of New Zealand* (1873), usually known as *Buller's Birds*, with its incomparable chromolithographs from watercolours by J.G. Keulemans. Buller was indeed a bird stuffer, as well as, ambiguously, an advocate of sorts for conservation. But it's for his role in the Victorian gentleman's pleasures of natural history specimening and collecting, the infantilising of ornithology as nursery toybox hoarding, that Buller the Bird Stuffer matters in Bill's paintings. Any kid who's grown up, let alone any grown-up toymaker, will understand that the stretch between a toy and a stuffed bird (or, say, between a teddy and a bear) is often an unbroken one. We talk about 'toys for the boys' in order to disparage immature gratification. What we should be on the lookout for, however, isn't the faintly prurient fetishising of adult toys, especially the ones that end up in 'collections', but the lack of self-critical consciousness that allows adult collectors to believe they're still innocent children.

That's why the critical, sardonic intelligence of Bill's earlier paintings matters. He may well have passed through a Damascus Gate of some sort, I wouldn't know – but it makes more sense to say he grew up and learned to look at the world with disenchanted concern and commitment, and that he was doing this long before he went down to Birdland. So what happens to the 'An empty amusement park makes a great hideout' quote once we get to the bird paintings is a kind of shift of emphasis, a re-stressing of the phrase, like a musician finding a variation within a riff.

What I began to hear when I saw the earliest bird paintings was a riff from the *Country and Western Songbook* that was at once familiar and a bit different. I heard the words 'empty amusement' moved together so that the 'park' became a place where empty amusements were found. Why were they empty? Because they lacked critical consciousness, because their innocence was a sham, because their pleasure was shallow, their gratifications infantile. Maybe because, like specimens (or teddy bears), they had to be emptied before they could be stuffed. The 'hideout' was now less the tree hut of game-playing kids or the thrilling lair of a noir crim, and more the place where psychopaths lurked or their victims hid. The watchful birds hiding out in the park were waiting for Buller the Bird Stuffer to arrive to gratify his empty amusements. Or perhaps the Stuffer was already hidden among them, and they would soon be emptied and their island home turned into a park.

This would be the kind of park you can see on Animal Planet, whose electrified fences have replaced its coastal profiles which, anyway, are edited from the frames of virtual safaris. The safari lands are traversed by collectors in sports utility vehicles whose speeding flanks are emblazoned with the logo 'Back in the Jungle' (W.D. Hammond, *Meanwhile Back in the Jungle*, 1986).

Meanwhile, back in the Safari Bar at Park HQ, the birds are waiting for Buller. It's his round. The birds've had a few. They may have a deal for the Stuffer – one he can't refuse. They've learned a thing or two. The barman, a guy called Bill, reaches high for a special bottle. It's the Stuffer's personal formaldehyde.

'He's back.'

Billy Apple: *Less Is Moore*

Online essay for One Day Sculpture series, onedaysculpture.org (23 March 2009)

The plan

My plan is to visit Henry Moore's *Inner Form* (1985–86) on its grassy slope above Wellington's Lady Norwood Rose Garden, have a think about Billy Apple's *One Day Sculpture* project to admonish the city to scrape the 'protective coating' off it, and then return on the one day itself and see Apple's promised billboard: a before, meanwhile, and after narrative structure.

The first visit

On a crisp autumn day, the walk from the Kelburn cable car terminus through the park and down to Moore's *Form* is a pleasant fusion of nature and culture: birds twitter, Mary-Louise Browne's elegant word-stairs ascend into damp shadows; and there it is – the large bronze form, looking somewhat like a dully gleaming Easter Island statue, gazing across at the stubbled zone of Tinakori Hill where pines have been felled to be replaced by indigenous plants. An implacable stare-down: 'Fell *me* if you dare!' Or a kind of Ozymandias monument – not just an historically inscrutable figure, but an actor in an artistic competition, in which Billy Apple is playing Horace Smith to Henry Moore's Percy Bysshe Shelley in their famous sonnet joust of 1817: 'Look on my works, ye mighty, and despair!'

But I am losing the plot, or inventing one. Paying real attention, what do I notice? I have seen this work at the Henry Moore Foundation, Perry Green, Hertfordshire, as a component of the much larger sculpture *Large Figure in a Shelter* (which visitors to Te Papa's

Moore show in 2002 will remember a smaller version of). Now, on its own, I see that it may be called 'inner form' not just because it (elsewhere) is inside an outer form, but also because it accomplishes one of Moore's characteristic (or even 'signature') spatial effects. Walking around *Inner Form*, approaching it from above on the slope of the hill, then from below walking up to it, looking at the different ways it presses itself out into space (a horn-like form here, a sharp profile there, a hollow, a flat plane, a swelling), it is clear that the form's 'innerness' is as much about describing or filling a negative space as it is about articulating a solid mass.

What else? That it is not as shiny as I remember the outdoor sculpture at Perry Green was; hardly covered in verdigris and tūī shit but a bit mottled, dullish. Nearby, on the other side of the path down the hill, is a housing with an aperture: a video surveillance camera. Further away near the tennis courts off Salamanca Rd is another housing, an electricity transformer. This is covered in the kinds of tagging the video camera is on the lookout for over at *Inner Form*.

The plaque adjacent to the work contains an important item of information, a reference to Wellington City Council's Arts Bonus Scheme. Under this scheme, developers (such as Fletcher Challenge Ltd) were able to win plot easements on building plans in proportion to the value of a commissioned artwork. Moore was not commissioned, but I guess the outcome was the same: Fletcher Challenge would have been able (say) to add a floor to a building on the strength of the purchase price of *Inner Form*. The negative space the *Form* fills, then (Fletchers having filled in the forms), may seem to resemble that of Rachel Whiteread's *Ghost* (1990) or her notorious Turner Prize-winning *House* (1993) – casts of the spaces inside buildings, negative space given mass, or – in the Arts Bonus case of *Inner Form* – the vacant or potential architectural space of a plot easement given the substance of capital realised as mass. At the same time, just to complicate things, the *Form*'s somewhat shiny appearance tilts our perception of it (and its value) towards surface. Whatever its latent mass and meaning may consist of, its manifest significance is in, or on, the surface you admire for the way it *appears*.

The work's splendour is, at first sight, more bling than thing; it's with the pay-and-display crowd over at evolutionary psychology.

What else do I know? That, contrary to an easily made assumption, there are more Moores inside than out; that the standard patinas of both inside and outside works are usually *applied* rather than accreted, and that these applications are often refreshed by conservators from Perry Green; that the weathering of outside sculptures allegedly favoured by Moore was often, in fact, a less than completely 'natural' process; even so, that more recent administrators of the Moore Foundation's assets (including the brand) have possibly been more zealous than the artist in their conservation policies.

Having a think

It is not easy to hear the tone of Billy Apple's title – *Less is Moore* – because, given Apple's deliberate, reductive, and sometimes sardonic concision, one would have to assume either that its naffness is intentional and implies irony; or that we are meant to hear it literally and therefore, as it were, tonelessly.

This space between the tonelessly literal and the ironically naff (at a stretch, between the 'natural' and the 'cultural') is, of course, where Apple likes to play. Getting strung out across the space is what is likely to happen to us, and this consequence may, too, be a calculated one. His well-known *I.O.U.* and *N.F.S.* works are just what they say they are: in the first case, a token of redeemable value lodged against capital; in the second, a work that is not for sale lodged nonetheless within the security of a collection's insurance and conservation resources. But this toneless or deadpan stare-down then has consequences on a scale from mildly ironic to agent provocateur. The brand relationship of art to capital, the transaction relationship of art value to commodity value, and the signification relationship of gesture to material are brought sharply into focus. Again, at this stage, the focus is at once literal and provocative: at once a toneless 'This is just how it is,' and a provocative 'And what are you going to do about it?'

Likewise – to bring the various terminologies devolving from 'natural' into play – Apple's plan for a ceramic apple pie dish divided into serving segments according to exact Fibonacci or golden section proportions, or the real *organic* Billy apple that might make its way into school lunch boxes with the assistance of Saatchi & Saatchi's marketing clout. The apple pie will be just that – a tasty, wholesome dessert divided into segments that are in some measure convenient. But who can utter the words 'apple pie' without suspecting that their natural 'whole-some-ness' has been infiltrated by the mordant (albeit anachronistic) pragmatism of the 33⅓ percent dealer's cut? No *whole* pie for you, kid, you have to give up a slice, that's how the unnatural world works. And this juicy organic Billy apple: someone persuaded your mum to buy it for you, and while you thank her for your healthy bite of the apple you should also be thanking the marketing guy who put the whole-some idea in her head.

If the invitation of Apple's work is to enter the space of play between the tonelessly literal and the subversively ironic, what kind of event are we being invited to by *Less is Moore*, Apple's billboard project associated with Henry Moore's *Inner Form* (1985–86) on the Salamanca Lawn in Wellington's Botanic Garden? At the most literal (and toneless) level, Apple's billboard is promised to demand simple respect for Henry Moore's alleged injunction against 'protecting' his work from the effects of weathering and patina out in the 'natural world'. That Moore preferred and intended his outdoors sculpture to be affected by the elements and atmosphere of its surroundings was endorsed in the case of *Inner Form* by no less an advisor than Professor Bernard Meadows, the chief administrator of the Moore Estate, on 20 April 1988, in a memo sent to John Baldwin, Director of Corporate Affairs for the work's principal sponsor, Fletcher Challenge. So, please, suggests Apple straightforwardly (tonelessly) in 2009, can we remove the 'protective coating' from this work and return it to the condition preferred by Moore himself?

Sounds reasonable. But why should Apple care? Moore, after all, represents modernist sculptors not just one but at least two generations back from the students Apple shared digs with while studying design at the Royal College of Art in London at the dawn of the 1960s.

Moore's narrative references to form, especially the found forms of the natural world such as the human figure, bleached bones, etc., his use of materials and processes that retained the hallmarks of hands-on modelling, and not least his characteristic publicity shots wearing a splattered apron, had already been declared redundant in the 1960s by his former assistant Anthony Caro in a classic Oedipal or sorcerer's apprentice move. Caro himself was somewhat the older guy at the party by the time the natural Kiwi Barrie Bates bleached his hair unnaturally with Lady Clairol Instant Cream Whip and rebranded as Billy Apple in 1962. Apple went to New York a couple of years later, an even more emphatic distance from the grand master of Perry Green contemplating an elephant's skull and getting modelling clay on his bib.

The reasons why Apple should (or does) care may be what tip the *Less is Moore* injunction past simple common sense (please just do what we are told Moore wanted) in the direction of irony and subversion. For a start, 'less is more' might be a general slogan for the stringent economies of means and ends with which modernism was frequently preoccupied in Moore's early days. Modified by Apple, this pithy line of advertising copy folds together a modernist icon, a catchphrase for a key modernist value-set, and 1960s urban pop art's romance with Madison Avenue. It also takes up the challenge to move modernism's reductive impulse a whole lot further: in fact, to move art well away from art. And it deploys this combination of references on a billboard (or billyboard, perhaps), an object whose value is signalled emphatically by its impeccable, impervious, glossy, well-protected surface. No verdigris, water stains or weathering permitted here! Sharply executed design replaces handicraft, brand identity replaces signature, surface replaces presence, and production values replace creative genius.

And then, by the time Fletcher Challenge Ltd, the Wellington Sculpture Trust and the city fathers had decided that a work by Henry Moore was desirable for Wellington in the 1980s, the Moore Foundation was already a global enterprise of large appeal (one might guess) to Billy Apple. At Perry Green, Moore made small clay maquettes which a team of assistants scaled up in plaster on wire armatures. These were subsequently turned into moulds and bronze casts were made from them, most of which came in editions. These editions were marketed to an international clientele, the great big ones to great big cities, corporations, and museums; the middle-sized ones to small cities like Wellington; and the little ones to collectors with no doubt spacious but nonetheless domestic room for them. This was an efficient and extremely profitable industrial enterprise which made the Moore brand ubiquitous on a global scale. Not surprisingly, that brand was carefully guarded and managed. Decisions about which works went where were not made by clients on the basis that they had shown they could afford to choose what they wanted, but by an advisory and consulting process that involved Moore himself in diminishing degrees until his death in 1986, and subsequently by the Foundation's loyal staff. The work continues: 'Henry Moores' are still shipping.

In their zeal to protect Wellington's 'Henry Moore' and, by implication, to protect the value of the Moore brand and its associated brand value to the city, the protectionists have, however, stepped into the very trap that has made Billy Apple's eyes light up like Bengal flares. By keeping the product of a scrupulously managed commercial process bright and shiny, by denying the 'less is more', organicist modernist ethos of the work, by enhancing its industrial, urban character at the expense of its natural inclination to weathering and patina, they have shifted it affrontingly, inappropriately, into Billy Apple's neighbourhood. No longer looking anything like the natural, elemental product of beach walks, bone collecting, clay squeezing, and (eventually) being kept shiny only if sheep rub up against it, *Inner Form* has lumbered across a couple of art generations, has pursued Billy Apple from rural Hertfordshire via New York to New Zealand, and here confronts him with a pallid, glistening, pancake makeup, surface-privileging, fashion-spread travesty of the pop art scene in which he thought he had found a safe haven from handcrafted modernism all those years ago – a haven where billboards, signwriters and concept gurus such as Saatchi's CEO Worldwide Kevin 'Lovebite'

Roberts rule supreme. No wonder Apple wants *Inner Form* vanishing-creamed back to where it belongs, on a green hillside somewhere off the beaten track in the Bronze Age of modernism.

But, thinking this through in advance of the actual encounter (and bearing in mind Apple's demonstrated commitment to natural products such as organic apple pies), one soon discovers an intriguing final twist: Billy Apple's own zeal in respect of natural products, including organic apples, is entirely sincere and non-ironic, and thus the tone of *Less is Moore*, strung across the space between literal (just clean the damn thing!) and provocative (get off of my patch!), has a subwoofer in it, which grumbles, with a hint of impatience, something like, 'Just do the right, the *natural* thing – how would you feel standing there in public season after season with that blonded, Lady Clairol Instant Cream Whip look?'

Visiting *Less Is Moore*

When sighted on another perfect day, the billboard – as you would expect – has been crisply executed in Apple's familiar and preferred fonts and colours. It looks like 'an Apple' in the same way that *Inner Form* looks like 'a Moore'. A fairly strident admonition to the city council and the people of Wellington is accompanied by a large facsimile of the famous Fletcher Challenge memo incorporating the advice of Professor Bernard Meadows. Some people have left real apples on the pediment of the Moore; another (Pacific Rose) lodges inside the billboard's cross-bracing. People come and go; they take photos. Having read the billboard text, most of them get up close to the Moore and scrutinise its surface; many have a covert scratch at it. No one riots, sets fire to the Apple, takes to the Moore with a rasp. Then (like me) they wander down the hill to the Begonia House. Here, the lineaments of the stretch between natural and artificial are made simple: allusions to Monet's *nymphéa* float on a pond, the arcade structure of the building recalls Walter Benjamin's famous analysis of commercial passages in 19th-century Paris (and their counter-relationship to the impressionist garden), and I hear a delighted woman describe an outrageous, can't-be-real pink-rimmed begonia as 'a work of art'.

I'm with Billy Apple in the end. Though I believe, on the strength of what I know about procedures at the Moore Foundation, that he has overcooked his case for the natural-look *Inner Form*, and though I know it to be a work of art not a bone (or begonia), still, its appearance or manifest is a tad . . . shrill for my liking. But this is a matter of taste, not very interesting. What is interesting – what has been interesting, as one might expect from the circumstances of the project – has been its ability to touch those flinching, sensitive points of contact between civic and public space, latent and manifest value, surface and substance. What has also been touching in another sense has been to see that Billy Apple cares about what has happened to Henry Moore's work.

Antic

Paintings by Robert McLeod

Dandini Comes Clean: Paintings by Robert McLeod, edited by Aaron Lister (PaulNache Gallery, 2011)

When I look at Robert McLeod's painting as a whole, from when I first encountered his *Grids and Tartans* at Elva Bett's gallery in Wellington in 1977 to his recent figurative cut-outs, it's the word 'antic' that I want to put to work. The word carries a double charge. It suggests 'antique' and its etymology sustains this suggestion since the Italian 'antico' was used to describe grotesque designs on Roman artefacts; this historicising function has carried over to English. The content of these grotesque designs or friezes has subsequently fed back into the word 'antic', emphasising its references to jokes or clowning. As a theoretical tool, then, the word suggests a mode of practice aware of and referencing a grotesque lineage in art history; it may also suggest a practice pitted against or mocking art, cultural or social conventions.

Robert McLeod told me that during his childhood and art school years in Glasgow, a cartoon character called Lobey Dosser was popular. I looked him up. The creation of cartoonist Bud Neill, Lobey Dosser's name derived from the tramps who dossed on the city's tenement landings. This rough and ready character, with his broad Glaswegian accent and huge bestubbled jaw, might seem to be an amiably subversive affront to genteel society in much the same way that popular comics and cartoon strips were to academic inheritors of the Glasgow School early moderns such as Charles Rennie Mackintosh, the city's painterly tradition inherited from the impressionist Glasgow Boys, and even the modernist, improvisatory abstraction of Alan Davey – a Scottish painter McLeod has admired. In this, the cartoon or comic strip's popular and subversive character as a low form of art might seem to resemble pantomime's as a low form of opera, or stand-up comedy's as debased theatre. But perhaps it's not that simple anywhere, and least of all in Glasgow.

In Glasgow, the Industrial Revolution's economic boom produced a large skilled working class and a cosmopolitan middle class. The Glasgow School's 'Group of Four', also known as the Spook School, were influential in Europe through the 1890s for their syncretising of Celtic and Japanese influences – they, too, were subversive of the time's existing academic canon. The School's 'Glasgow Boys' George Henry and E.A. Hornel spent time in Japan; Thomas Millie Dow painted his best-known work on the Hudson River in upstate New York. The same economic forces that cosmopolitanised Glasgow's vigorous art and design world also distributed its Clyde-side engineers and builders, and a surplus of workers, out along the trans-Atlantic trade routes to the Americas and to the far corners of the British Empire. And it wasn't just the Industrial Revolution's skilled workforce and cosmopolitan artist class that sought their fortunes at the frontiers of the expanding world, it was also the Lobey Dossers – the urban poor squeezed out or marginalised by Clyde-side success as their rural forebears had been by enclosure or the potato famine of the 1840s.

No surprise, then, that Bud Neill's Lobey Dosser should turn up on the American Wild West's frontier as the sheriff of Calton Creek. In this, Neill's model was as much the Shakespearean actor turned silent movie cowboy William S. Hart as the emigrant Scots who joined the wagon trains heading west through 'Indian territory'. In one of Sheriff Lobey Dosser's adventures ('A Surprise', from *Lobey Dosser – His Life Story*) he meets up with a wagon train of Glaswegians '. . . fae the Calton', Dosser's home patch. 'Imagine that!' exclaims the sheriff. 'I'm fae the Calton masel but was brung up by ma auntie in Springburn.' In the background, inked in Neill's emphatic style, are the Arizona desert and what might be ominous smoke signals. In another strip from *His Life Story,* 'The Bunnet', a 'cannibal king' in darkest Africa also turns out to be 'fae Glesca': 'Whit pert o Glesca are ye from, Mac?' asks the cannibal king. 'The Calton, how?' replies Lobey Dosser. 'We're fae Clydebank,' says the cannibal king, 'pleased tae meet ye.'

This running gag, in which Glaswegians keep turning up in most parts of the world, takes a sardonic turn when one of Sheriff Dosser's posse notices the kilt-wearing squaw whom chief Toffee Teeth has sent out for hot fish suppers. 'That squaw the chief sent out for fish suppers wore a kilt – who would *she* be?' asks the perplexed cowpoke. 'Probably Pawnee Mary o' Argyll,' answers a missionary. The strip has now arrived at another kind of frontier, one of cultural identity. Here, the internationalist Glasgow School with its fondness for Japanoiserie and Bud Neill with his taste in silent Westerns meet the tartan as worn by Nepalese bagpipe-playing Gurkas, Prince Charles, fifth-generation New Zealanders of mixed Māori and Scottish descent, and Japanese kogyaru schoolgirls.

In the Lobey Dosser strips, this sardonic cultural cosmopolitanism also meets the identity politics of pantomime. Filled with craftily scripted puns, double entendres and gags, many following an audience-prompt-and-response formula, the pantomimic Lobey Dosser plots also feature an anthropomorphic two-legged horse (El Fidelio), an obvious villain (Rank Bajin), a tapdancing fairy (Fairy Nuff), and a ba-boum joke-cracking Indian chief (Toffee Teeth), whose Pawnee tribe appears to have originated somewhere in Govan on the south bank of the River Clyde in, you guessed it, south-western Glasgow.

Pantomime itself is an old, antic frontier-crosser descended from popular erotic and gender-bending song-and-dance performances by travelling troupes in ancient Greece and, later, Rome. Infused with Italian commedia dell'arte narrative conventions and characters, pantomime developed in England during the 18th century, spurred by competition between rival theatrical entrepreneurs in London, where it transformed from a travelling entertainment to a seasonal Christmas fixture. The plots, based on well-known children's stories, had certain fixed conventions, most of them to do with gender, class and taste: a girl dressed as a boy in costumes that emphasise her real gender (the 'principal boy') wins the heart of another girl (dressed as a girl) with the assistance of a human or humans masquerading as an animal such as the front-and-back pantomime horse, and an old dame, usually the principal boy's mother, played by a man. There is usually a good fairy who enters from stage right, and an obvious villain who enters from stage left: in the commedia, Heaven was always on the right of the stage and Hell on the left. Such traces of ritual or superstition reached back past Christianity to old mid-winter feasts and ceremonies during which the natural orders of things were reversed, such as the Celtic Samhain, which was both a harvest festival and a festival of the dead. Pantomime thus has associations with the grotesque, carnivalesque aspects of Saturnalia, an important characteristic of which was the reversal of social roles: in Rome, masters and slaves changed places. The Saturnalia ended on or about what is now Christmas Day, the 25th of December, also the high season for pantomime. Gender-bending; role, class and identity reversal; raucous sexual humour and satire; harvest festivals, rites for the dead and for the winter solstice, all converge in one way or another around the broad comedy and slapstick of pantomime. This could be a not uncomprehensive description of Robert McLeod's figurative cut-out paintings.

Though pantomime's set-piece stories themselves may not easily be detected in recent entertainments such as television's 1990s cartoon series *The Ren and Stimpy Show*, aspects of a broad antic tradition of disenchanted, subversive, culturally mobile, often violent, and deliberately lowbrow mimicry flourish there. The *Ren and Stimpy* animator, John Kricfalusi, based the character of Ren on the 1946 photograph by Eliott Irwitt of a cosmopolitan New York chihuahua in a sweater; the dim-witted cat Stimpy clearly has a dipsomaniacal Jimmy Durante nose. Like pantomime – and like Robert McLeod – Krikfalusi took what was fit for his purpose from the broad cultural stream of the antic.

In Robert McLeod's figurative paintings, this antic instinct and knowingness are declared, even flaunted, in many ways. Earlier work, such as abstract paintings based on tartans, thick impasto minimalist paintings, and the large folded cardboard *Lanark* drawings, might seem remote from the antic extravagance of the figurative cut-outs. But here too, traces of Lobey Dosser's mordant Glaswegian spirit can

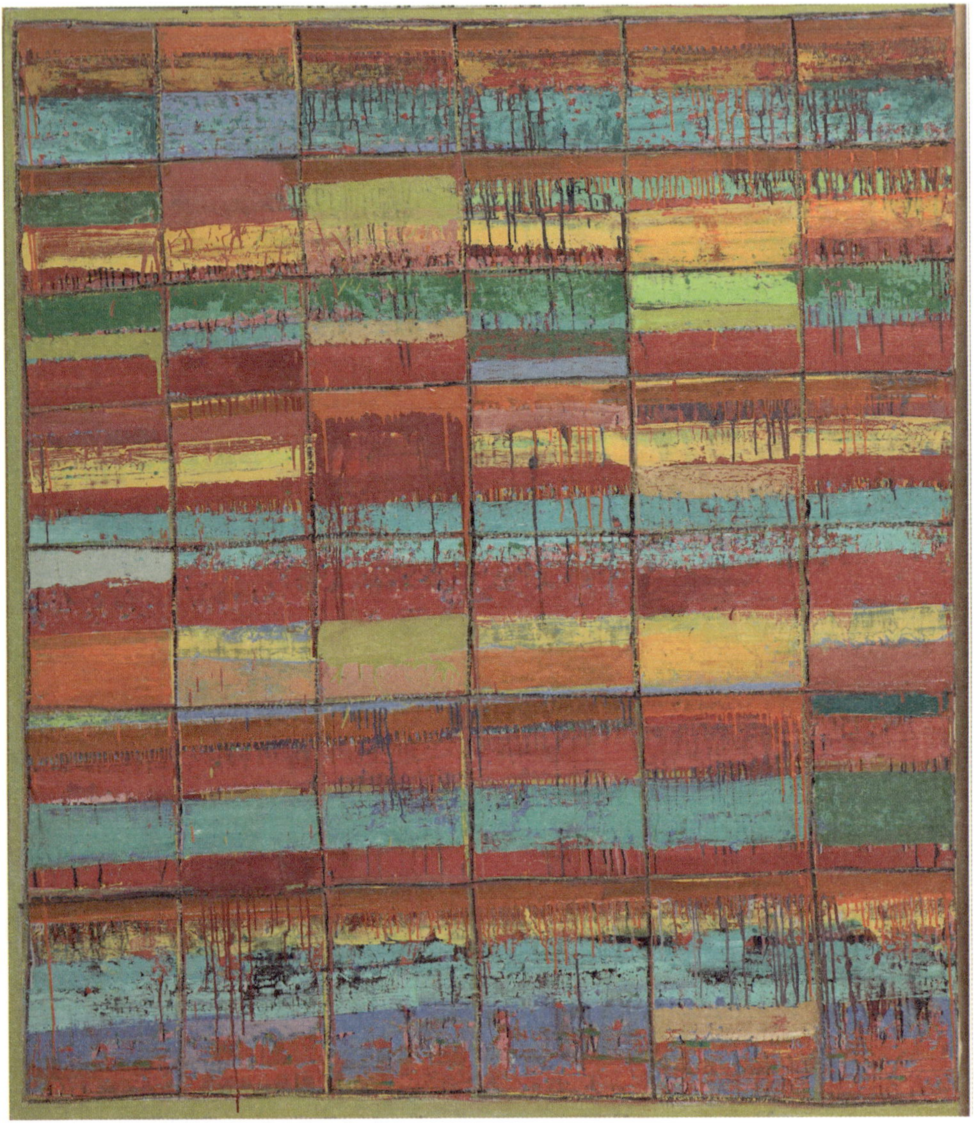

Rob McLeod, *Lots of Little Landscapes*, 1977, Wellington. Purchased 1985 with New Zealand Lottery Grants Board funds. Collection Te Papa.

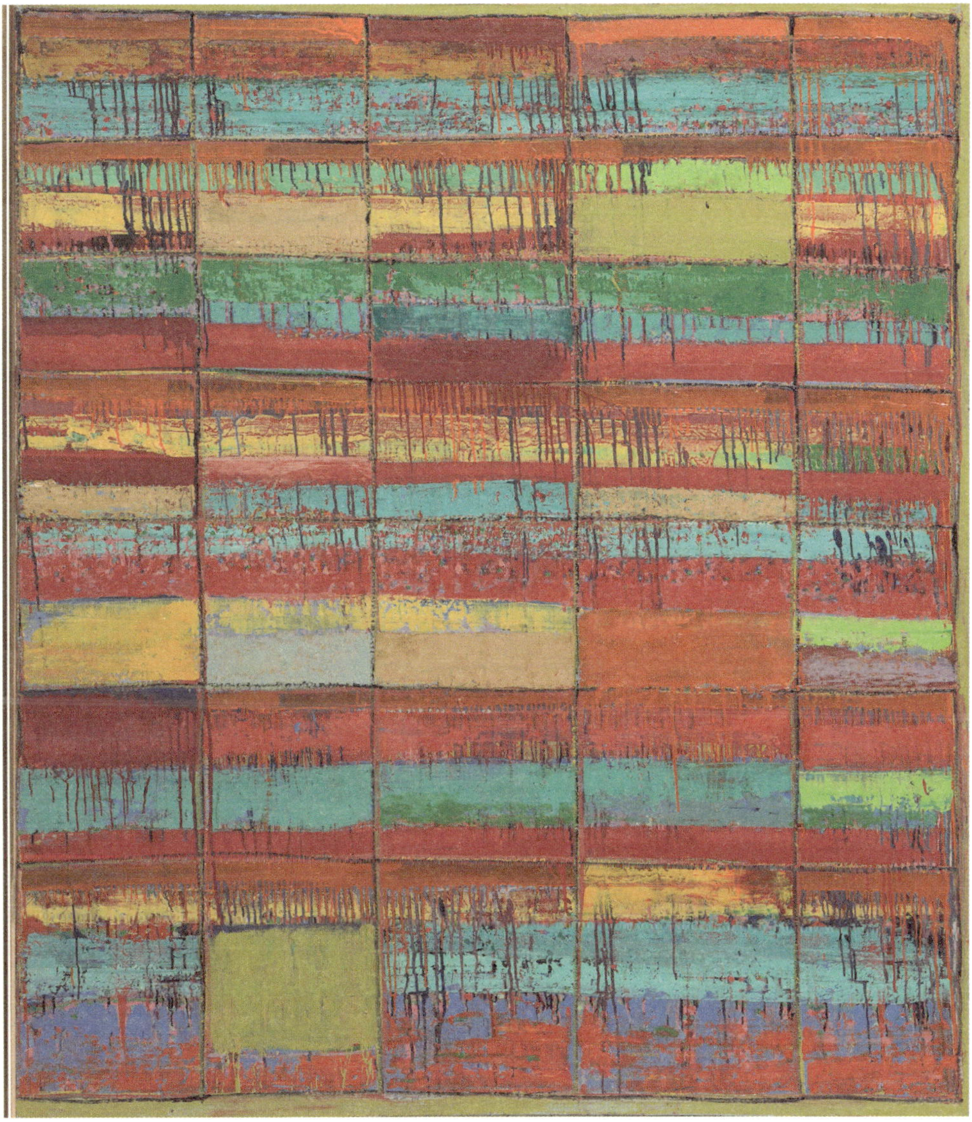

be found. Though a clear rupture or distinction between abstract works and the figurative ones is practical – and Robert McLeod might prefer to mark his practice with such a distinction – nonetheless, there are continuities, strategies of resistance, and even themes that traverse the early and the later work. In fact, the earliest work of McLeod's that I'm familiar with, *Crying through the Keyhole* (1972) contains jigsaw-like shapes that, while abstract, hint at figuration and even narrative in ways we might now be tempted to see anticipating his recent cut-outs.

The grids and tartans that McLeod painted in the 1970s, for example, were simultaneously aware of the grid as one of modernism's key organising strategies, and of its 'antique' use as a perspective plotting device in early Renaissance paintings approximating architecture. It subverted both by pushing paint-pies in their faces; McLeod's vigorous, shoulder-through-wrist painting technique and the take-that attack of his colours were also affronts to the identity traditions of the tartan. A painting like *Snow Job (for A.M. ateurs*, 1978), also asked to be read as an antic comment on the legacy of Jackson Pollock; the title of the grid/tartan work *Learning to Count* (1976–77) had a similarly mordant tone; it was hard to see *Lots of Little Landscapes* (1977) as anything other than a piss-take (via tartans and grids) on New Zealand art's preoccupation with landscape as a way of representing identity.

The antic tone and even intention of these paintings is fairly aggressive. What pushes back against this tone is the paint – in fact the *painting* – itself. McLeod is an exceptionally good painter in terms of both what he can do with paint and how he can think with it. It's the fact that he does painting as a serious way of making art and of thinking that stops his 'antic disposition' from being merely flippant or throw-away. In many respects he is a deeply traditional, craftsman-like painter. And the fact that he *paints* is also what pushes back against the possibility that the thick, shaped minimalist paintings or the long series of shaped and folded *Lanark* works of the early 1980s could be read as sculpture. They are not – they are paintings, but paintings that exert antic pressure on three-dimensional mass. In the thick, paste-brushed monochrome works of the 1980s (for example the *Shaped Minimalist Paintings*), the heavy brush-loads of paint seemed to press out into the work's foreground, denying both 'pure' surface and hierarchical perspective. These days, it's still painting that pushes against the temptation to see the cut-out figurative works as three-dimensional or even sculptural. In a sense, McLeod's antic instinct is turned against itself (or against himself), as well as against the more available targets of identity, convention and history.

For me, the clearest sign of this double-edged 'antic disposition' is found in relatively low-key works such as *Red Grid Over Blue* (1981–82), in which a confidently textured weave of thick red brush-dabs is fissured here and there to reveal what might almost be a secret blue painting – not, at any rate, merely a blue underpainting or ground. Many of the thick, apparently simple, shaped minimalist paintings that preceded the complex *Lanark* works also carried the suggestion that there was more to them than met the eye: what the paint concealed was as important as what its surface consisted of; around the edges of the stretchers, breaking through the impervious surfaces here and there, was something else, possibly something subversive.

Such complex antic qualities are also in the cut-out, post-*Mutant Mickey* paintings that have developed a wide range of references over nearly ten years. As well as a cast of mutated 'toon characters such as Tweety Bird and Mickey Mouse, there are references to a dark, spooky Northern Renaissance tradition of painting almost in antic opposition to a sunny Southern Renaissance one. The distorted sinews and gaping mouths of McLeod's melodramatic groupings are out of Matthias Grünewald, his elongated female figures from Lucas Cranach. He prefers the north's weird, flattened perspective to the South's deep, light-filled one. In some instances, this flattening even extends to reversible figures which can be lifted free from the plywood group, flipped around and reinserted. He likes the North's repertoire of nasty surprises, not just the 'Death and the Maiden' variety but also inter-species action reminiscent equally of nightmarish creatures from the scary right-hand panel of Hieronymous Bosch's *The Garden of Earthly Delights* (1503–04) and of Robert Zemeckis's feature film

Who Framed Roger Rabbit (1988), in which 'toons and humans coexist in a state of violent anarchy.

There's another way in which the *painting* as act and thought constitutes the central antic quality of McLeod's work. Though their graphic, 'toonish aspect might suggest they have been drawn initially in outline, this is not so. McLeod begins and ends by moving paint around, not by prearranging or sketching cartoon-like groups or narratives. The paint itself, then, is what resists narrative – what pushes the groups towards the surreal, accidental or arbitrary. In this, the works recall the figurative qualities in paintings by Philip Guston following his shift away from abstract expressionism in 1970. Guston's use of the word 'impure' to describe painting, and his belief that we are 'image-ridden', move him close to an antic mode like McLeod's. So do his capricious, anti-hierarchical perspectives. In this, he joins another American painter to whom McLeod has made admiring references, Willem de Kooning, whose *Woman* series of paintings during the 1950s were antic rebukes to the increasingly reductive and restricting formalism of modernist abstraction.

Though Robert McLeod's pantomimic cut-outs may be filled with riotous (or rioting) clusters of mixed 'toons, Cranach-like nudes, dog-critics pissing on the paintings from within, trashy sci-fi images and whatnot, their antic core retains the depth and complexity of rites reaching back to the Saturnalia, Samhain, and other old business. They also continue to demonstrate the anarchic, surreal ability of painting to push ideas past the narrative limits of cartoonists like George Herriman or Robert Crumb in the case of Philip Guston, or Bud Neill's Lobey Dosser in the case of McLeod – while taking much of the cartoonist's antic resource along with them.

Michael Parekōwhai: *Yes We Are*

Online essay for One Day Sculpture series, onedaysculpture.org (28 May 2009)

I saw the sign some time between 6.30 and 7 am at the ferry terminal. However I was going the 'wrong way', north on the motorway prior to turning around at Petone and coming back for a proper look, trying not to crash. I didn't see it on the way back but did a U-ie under the Westpac stadium, where parking wardens threatened me, and returned to the ferry terminal. Here I optimistically entered the vehicle lane in the direction of the sign only to realise I was about to get marshalled on to the ferry, so did another U-ie, this time menaced by men in orange coats waving light sticks. Are we having fun so far? Yes we are.

Had I been able to see the sign heading south I'd probably have read it as a promise that the city was OPEN – but for what and in what sense? More on this soon.

As it was, my first glimpse of the sign seemed to be saying that what I was leaving behind was OPEN, and this little puzzle was typical of how the day would proceed. And probably of Michael's destabilising or even subversive method.

After a cup of coffee I walked from my place up to Massey and saw the sign in daylight outside the war memorial. Its flashing arrow was directed away from the memorial into a vacant lot on the other side of the road.

Exactly what was OPEN here? I thought of it as an OPEN question.

There was a guy photographing the sign for the School of Art – we had a chat and I watched the drivers heading west for the motorway tunnel lose their bearings and do some lane-jive when they saw the sign – some of them seemed to read it as a warning that they would have to merge lanes. There was a small 'native' plant in a pot on the tray of the truck but I didn't know if this was intentional or not – maybe a sly reference to Shane Cotton? People walking along were all looking at the sign. A little girl was calling out 'Look, Mum!' and walked slap bang into one of the wrought iron tree protectors on the footpath. This was around 8.30 I think.

Then I had some other stuff to take care of, but around 2 pm I phoned the One Day Sculpture HQ to check that the sign was on Oriental Parade, where I'd had a tip-off it might be parked early in the afternoon. I thought I'd pay it another visit and stretch my legs at the same time. No, I was told, it was at Parliament, could I leave my cellphone number, they'd text me the next secret destination.

I guessed they'd parked the sign there to keep an eye on Bill English's budget. It was an OPEN secret that there wouldn't be any tax cuts.

While waiting for the text from One Day Sculpture HQ, I pondered the significance of the sign, its look and feel, and the seductive word 'OPEN'.

There's a fair bit of neon around Wellington, but nothing quite like Michael's sign. Bill Culbert's argon calligraphy-on-a-stick down at Post Office Square, some modest bar signs, a bit of corporate stuff downtown, a few motel signs around the perimeter of the city.

Michael's sign looks big and American, and kind of retro. It reminds me of the big, confident, casino or bar neons that American proto pop artists like Robert Indiana appropriated in the 1950s and 60s, though not in neon. There's an art historical arc that vaults from Indiana's graphic art, signage, and decal influenced shapes to the deadpan neo-modernism of, say, Julian Dashper. The space between Indiana's open-shirted American populism and Dashper's neo-modernist cool is very large and very interesting, and one day someone should spend some time with it – but not me and not now.

Indiana's words were all big American promises – EAT, for example, and most famously LOVE – but Michael's OPEN is an uncertain word. Though the sculpture has a name – *Yes We Are* – this isn't of course visible to the punters going past in cars etc, so let's have a think about OPEN and keep *Yes We Are* in the back of our minds.

What's OPEN?

Is 'OPEN' a description or a command?

If it's a description, does it describe an OPEN physical entity like a shop, or a non-physical condition like a state of mind (as in 'an OPEN mind')?

If it describes a physical entity, like a shop, could that description be applied also to a city? A country? What about applying 'OPEN' to a nation; that's to say, to the combination of a country, an economy, and an assortment of human cultures? Are we in New Zealand an OPEN nation and is Michael justified in pointing to us like that? Or does his pointing to New Zealand as an OPEN nation have a kind of ironic question mark at the end: 'OPEN, us? Really?'

For that matter, will the Auckland super city be an OPEN entity? 'Super city' sounds like some kind of supermarket – will anyone be able to shop there, will its super council be OPEN to that?

If Michael's 'OPEN' describes an OPEN mind, then what does the sign intend when it's pointing at Wellington harbour? At a vacant lot? At Parliament buildings? In what sense does Cuba St have an OPEN mind? Is Cuba St where you'd go to find them? OPEN minds?

As you'd expect with a work by Michael Parekōwhai, there's a political itch in this set of questions. There's trouble.

If the word 'OPEN' is a command or suggestion, then what is it that we're being asked or told to open? The city? The House of Representatives? Oriental Bay? Is 'OPEN' a shortened version of the police-style yell, 'OPEN up in the name of the law!'?

My phone rang. It was ODS HQ. The OPEN sign was on its way to Oriental Bay, near the Fryberg Pool. The pool is usually OPEN around 2.30 pm; what other suggestions might we find along there?

I walked down to the Bay. When I arrived at the Fryberg site about half an hour later there was no sign of the sign. I had a coffee and looked out the window of the Parade Cafe. Then I went to buy some fish – I was confident that Moore Wilson's Fresh would be there and that it would be OPEN, and OPEN to the possibility of providing me with the fish I wanted.

Then a text arrived from ODS HQ: the sign would be at Oriental

Bay in about half an hour. Too late – my last chance to sign on for the experience of the sign would have to be at night, on the summit of Mount Victoria.

You'll have noticed that I've been avoiding the science of signs, or semiotics. But of course this is what Michael's sign is all about.

The non-arrival of the sign down at the Bay was a sign in itself. One of its absent signifieds was a schedule – or schedules as a class or category of object. It occurred to me that the schedule for the sign was OPEN-ended – that struck me as appropriate. Not that ODS HQ was trying to mess with me, but that it would have been anomalous for the sign's schedule to have been locked down for my benefit. That wouldn't have been OPEN, it would have been closed. And privileging the future commentator on the sign by providing him (me) with a closed schedule – moreover a schedule that wasn't available to anyone else – would have been unfair.

I was pretty happy with this piece of sophistry. The more I thought about it, the more it seemed to propose an historiography – that is, a model of a way to structure how to think about history.

The sign is historical, in that by looking at it we can see something of its cultural and indeed art historical provenance. But like most history, even history that gestures vigorously in a certain direction like the arrow in Michael's sign (for example, towards the vacant lot opposite the war memorial), it's an uncertain and unreliable diagnostic or predictive tool. You may get a good idea from it about where it's come from, and where it is, but you may learn very little – or get very unreliable hints or, so to speak, text messages – about where it's going. Where it's going to be next.

You could erect a sign like Michael's next to Rodney Hide, or North Korea's Kim Jong-il, and think that you could read their historical trajectory like an OPEN book – but you'd be wrong. The past only exists in the present's memory of it, and only in phantom fragments, and the future OPENs up bit by bit from there, but don't go thinking you've got the future schedule nailed, that 'signs of the times' give you clairvoyant powers, because they don't.

At this point I cooked the fish I'd bought from the reliably OPEN fish counter at Moore Wilson's Fresh and ate it in the company of my family and a friend who is staying with us. Meanwhile we watched John Campbell interview Bill English on TV. The government's books were OPEN but what we saw there were a number of closed-off options.

Around 9.30 in the evening I jumped in the car again and drove to the top of Mount Victoria. On the way there I thought a bit about Michael's way with monuments.

Monuments are usually monumental – that is, both big in themselves and the markers of some big/important event, person or place: memorials. Monuments do big memory.

Quite a lot of Michael's work has been monumental in the sense of being big. What's interesting about its relation to the second part of 'monumental' – the memorial part – is that Michael's memorials usually OPEN up a whole lot of issues about what, why and how we remember.

One of my favourite Parekōwhai works, *Ten Guitars*, remembers a much-loved song while at the same time remembering a musical term embedded in our culture, 'Māori guitar'. The first and major installation of *Ten Guitars* also remembered a bunch of great guitar players, and got them along to play.

Then the big monument got broken up into smaller parts: the guitars were sold. But here's the catch. What *Ten Guitars* remembers most of all is the singalong. It's a song that gets sung by a whole bunch of people, usually with more than one guitarist. So if you want to have Michael Parekowhai's *Ten Guitars* in its true monumental and memorialising form, you have to organise a get-together. All those art collectors – and Te Papa – have to get in touch with each other and organise a singalong.

Atarangi II outside Te Tuhi in Pakuranga – another favourite of mine – looks in many ways like a monumental industrial sign. It fits right in with the light industrial neighbourhood. A bit like the Telecom brand, it seems to be remembering the cool design qualities of neo-modernist abstraction à la Richard Thompson or even the classic colour theory modernism of Milan Mrkusich.

But no – what *Atarangi II* remembers and memorialises is the Cuisenaire rods developed by the Belgian child-educationist Georges Cuisenaire to teach kids how to understand numbers and relationships. It's a monument to relationship and to kids learning to count.

I arrived at Michael's OPEN sign on top of the lookout on Mount Victoria. ODS HQ were there and so was Michael. Everyone was having a beer. Down below the city looked great, and pretty OPEN.

What kind of monument is Michael Parekōwhai's OPEN sign?

This is where I OPEN the question up for discussion.

('Are we OPEN?' Yes we are!)

Michael Parekōwhai, *Yes We Are*, 2009 – aluminium, automotive paint, neon signs, 6350 x 1720 x 285 mm. As seen in the One Day Sculpture series, Wellington, Aotearoa New Zealand. Courtesy of the artist and Michael Lett.

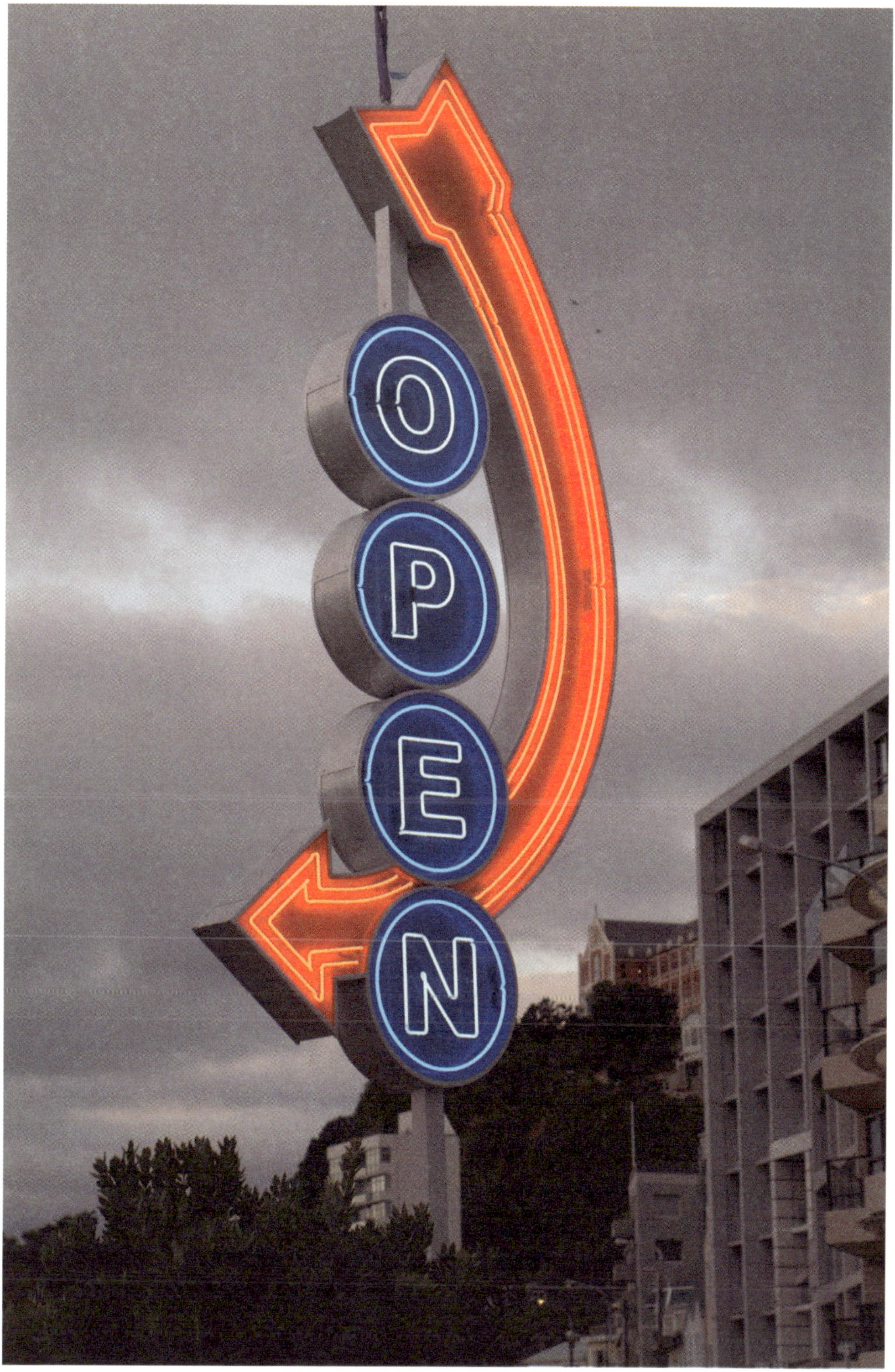
OPEN

Does Poetry Matter?

Talk given on 21 October 2009 as part of the University of Auckland and Michael King Writers Centre residency, published in *Ka Mate Ka Ora* (New Zealand Electronic Poetry Centre, 9 March 2010)

Dedicated to Leigh Davis, and to his wife Susan and their children Greer, Henry, India and Betty

I ran into Murray Edmond the day before yesterday and he suggested some alternative titles for this talk, such as 'Does poetry metre', 'Does poetry mutter,' and a German one, 'Does poetry Mutter', but I'm afraid we're stuck with the rather unprepossessing question, 'Does poetry matter?' For which I take complete responsibility, it was my idea.

Some time back the *Dominion Post* columnist Karl du Fresne, who writes under the faux-ominous byline 'Curmudgeon', wrote an opinion piece about the uselessness of poetry, or more specifically of poets, in the course of which he asserted that if he wanted to get his plumbing fixed he wouldn't be asking a bloody poet would he, so what good were they?

There are quite a few possible responses to this statement, one of them being to point out the collapse of logic within his sentence; and another that I, and no doubt other poets, have often attended to the plumbing in our homes, with about as much success, or failure, as any other non-professional plumber, probably including du Fresne himself.

Is it a waste of time responding defensively to statements of this sort, which might be described as the practical handyman's reply to the question 'Does poetry matter?' Maybe it's not a waste of time. The 'No, it doesn't' answer might equally, on the basis of du Fresne's logic, be extended to nuclear physicists, professional basketball players, or the council employees who blow leaves off the road with motorised puffers, since none of them has any professional connection with plumbing either. But of course, inside du Fresne's illogical statement lurks another a-logical rather than illogical premise, which is that poetry and poets are useless in a more comprehensive or pernicious way than nuclear scientists or leaf-blowers. In a little while I want to argue that this comprehensive rather than pragmatic uselessness is one of poetry's great virtues, and one of the reasons it does matter – so thanks, Karl, for helping me get on track with this aspect. But more on this soon.

Some of you will have read another columnist recently, in last weekend's *Sunday Star Times*, where the mayor of Whanganui, Michael Laws, pulled out all the stops in a tirade against 'arties, writers, and culture vultures' and, a paragraph or two later, against 'arties, feminists, and way too many academics' who, Laws asserted, 'perceive rugby as an oafish display of mindless macho'. Leaving aside the fact that I and a number of friends who are writers of various stripes, including my wife Donna Malane, who is the author of a rather successful book called *The Girl's Guide to Rugby,* regularly gather around television screens to watch sport of many kinds – leaving aside these mundane responses to the mayor of Whanganui, it's worth noting the counterintuitive ubiquity of references to poetry in the language of sports commentators, not least the husky-voiced bard of television rugby coverage, the louche Murray Mexted, who frequently draws the viewer's attention to the 'pure poetry' of a well-executed line break, or the 'poetry in motion' of an audacious play by Cory Jane. Again, I'll return in a little while to this incorporation of references to poetry in such vernaculars as sports commentaries. Little-known marginal fact: Pierre de Frédy, Baron de Coubertin (1 January 1863–2 September 1937), the founder of the International Olympic Committee, proposed poetry as a contest (which it was, and is, in many cultures) in the Olympics.

The point here, surely, is not so much the obvious one that it's banal and pointless to respond defensively or even derisively (which amounts to the same thing) to the curmudgeon's or the mayor's responses of 'No, it doesn't', but rather to see the opportunities that their negative responses open up.

These will often be opportunities that neither the naysayers nor their opposing yeasayers will want to engage with – any more than will publishers, for example, contemplating their print runs in literary markets such as our English-language one here in New Zealand where the artefact of the poetry book is in general not widely sought.

On the part of those who think, for various reasons, that poetry does matter, this disinclination to engage with discussion opportunities opened up by the likes of the curmudgeon and the mayor will often take the form of a sorting or prioritising process – a categorising of what's judged to be worthy of consideration and what's merely trivial. This categorising process is one of canon building and as such is a complex cultural phenomenon in which judgements of 'excellence' have an inescapably political tincture.

Those of us who do enjoy poetry and consider ourselves serious about it – who will want to answer 'Yes' to the question 'Does poetry matter?' – will have varieties of motives for being affirmative, and we may wish to distinguish *our* affirmative motives from those of other affirmers. The ways in which we categorise what we believe to be significant or trivial in our responses to the question 'Does poetry matter?' will also be ways in which we distinguish our positions not only from the naysaying curmudgeon and mayor, but also from other, let's call them 'poetry lovers' – though I suspect that term itself may already make some members of this audience flinch.

The point is, though, that by categorising what we consider time-wasting, or boring, or banal, or trivial, or intellectually or aesthetically minor, or dated, we are also identifying social and professional markers of distinction – *distinguishing* brands of cultural capital, if you like, with which we'd rather not be associated. Teams not wearing our preferred team colours. Furthermore, by identifying these things that we wish to exclude from our discussion, we'll be identifying not only those aspects of poetry that we consider minor in some way, but also identifying *ourselves,* because, as ethnographers and sociologists of culture have been fond of pointing out to us for some years, cultural artefacts of all kinds, including language artefacts such as poems and novels, are not only material *objects* – which is to say *matter* – they are also *subjects*: they are actors who perform their societies, and they are agents which link up and network their societies – if you subscribe to the actor-network theory associated with the French sociologist Bruno Latour. We can also say, following the cultural fetish and related social distinction theories of Durkheim or the later materialist analyses of Bourdieu, that cultural artefacts – cultural *matter* or stuff – brands its consumers as socially distinct. That 'shoe-of-the-week' thing.

Here, we have to include some by now well-rehearsed links to evolutionary psychology that suggest uselessness and excess in cultural artefacts are sexual selection indicators – in other words, our displayed or flaunted preferences for what kinds of poetry (or shoe) we think matter are really about mate selection; and the fairly common avant-gardist anxiety about being *au courant* with recent developments arises from the fear of falling behind in the evolutionary foot race. Argument continues over the evolutionary psychologists' position; my view is that it's relevant in a common-sense kind of way.

The contradictory behaviour involved in denying the significance of categories or positions in respect of poetry – that is, naming a category in order to exclude it from consideration, uttering something in order to silence it, asserting one thing but doing another – also draws us deeper into the mesh of one of poetry's more exquisite and inescapable traps, the very one that the curmudgeon of the *Dominion Post* and the mayor of Whanganui got tangled up in when they drew attention to the ubiquity of poetry by asserting that it didn't matter.

One of the most enjoyable ways in which *poems* can be useless involves disobedience, the trap of expecting the poem to do or mean what it's told to. Often half the pleasure of reading poems involves a kind of somatic or language nervous-system malfunction in which the poet may be more or less complicit. Often we seem to be in a situation where the poet is asserting one thing while the poem appears to be doing another, or where the poet is ordering language to mean one thing while the language has a contrary mind of its own about what it wants the poem to mean.

When Shakespeare asked, 'Shall I compare thee to a summer's day?' he was writing as much about this critical unreliability in the rhetorical apparatus and language of poetry – in this case the artifice of metaphor – as about the person addressed in his sonnet. He was disclosing his awareness of the metaphor's tendency to disobey its master's or mistress's wishes – even to make those wishes appear ridiculous. The booby trap of the word 'like'. He was turning the whole of his sonnet's rhetorical structure around the issue of the poem's unreliability, its potential for disobedience, the possibility of its uselessness in performing the metaphorical task its master wanted to accomplish. It is Shakespeare's rhetorical hesitation, his critical awareness of the instability of language, that makes his poem matter – more, I would suggest, than its apparent task of courting and flattering a lover. Does this poem matter? We don't know if it did the pragmatic job of successfully courting a lover – if it fixed a dripping tap, so to speak, *pace* Karl du Fresne – and really, who cares whether it mattered or matters in that pragmatic sense? Whether it was *successful* or effective as an act of courtship? But it still does matter – and I would say matters more – because of the way it identifies and plays with one of poetry's oldest traps, its potentially subversive uselessness as the docile tradesperson of the commanding poet.

A reverse kind of disobedience may occur in poems that seem highly refined and effortless as artefacts, when in fact they have been made to appear that way at the expense of huge effort on the part of the poet. The poet Virgil famously only managed to write a couple of lines a day and on his deathbed pleaded for his *Aeneid* to be burned because he was sick to death of it, yet over some 10,000 lines of craftily compacted hexameters in the *Aeneid* there is little sense of the *poet's* struggle, only of an internal struggle *in the language itself* between its natural stresses as a kind of speech, and the length of syllables in the prosody. This tension has been noted recently by the scholar-poet Sarah Ruden in the Preface to her extraordinary, to-weep-for translation of Virgil's great poem.

Poetry can also be very good at wasting time and subverting intentions, just as it can be good at making something out of the banal and the trivial, or launching itself into a series of digressions. The veteran artificer John Ashbery is one of my treasured digressors, as in his poem 'The Leopard and the Lemur', which begins with a kind of droll classical echo or pastiche, perhaps of Ovid in the story of Pyramus and Thisbe in the *Metamorphoses*:

> The voice is stilled, that once
> Spoke out of a crack in the wall:
> The origins of the earth are eroded;
> We don't know at what point history begins
> And the speech of the sky is clouded.

And so on, very charmingly, with quite a few of those elbow-slipping-off-the-edge-of-the-bar slapstick rhymes, making inconsequentiality appear just as effortless as Virgil's rigorous consequentiality does.

Meanwhile, of course, in the midst of all this talk of uselessness, excess and inconsequentiality, we need to remember that a great deal of poetry gets written to be effective; for example, to be a call to arms, a focus for meditation, a way of retaining and transmitting knowledge, and so on. More on this later.

Let's push this discussion in the direction of the word 'poetry' itself.

What might be a use of the word 'poetry' that people who are 'serious' about it would prcfcr to bc distanccd from? 'Poctry' is a word that's used widely in the vernacular; for example' when Johnny Tillotson in 1961 sang of a girl that she was 'poetry in motion / walking by my side'. Here, 'poetry' conveniently describes the indescribable, it's the word the lyricist falls back on when he's at a loss for words or when events render him speechless. It's the word for an ineffable phenomenon, for a kind of beauty or loveliness too classy to describe in terms of actual body parts, for a fine aesthetic that idealises without getting specific. 'Poetry' here describes or rather signifies a quality, in fact a 'quality' quality. Poetry flatters by association.

Used in this way, 'poetry' also has a certain air of wistfulness – the implication is that the girl may now be a little out of reach, that the singer's admiration for and pride in the poetry of his girl's motion is also the measure of a certain distance: a girl with such classy poetry of motion may be by his side, but is she within reach? He can be touched by her poetry, but can he be touched by her – can he ever be closer than by her side?

'I, too, dislike it', Marianne Moore's famous opening line in her poem 'Poetry', seems by implication at least to be directed also against the kind of poetry that merely flatters its object or occasion – an outflanking of du Fresne and Laws. Moore's line has been appropriated by the online blog and comment site *Slate* for its series (headed up by Robert Pinsky) on 'poets who don't like poetry'. The famous final line in Sylvia Plath's poem 'Daddy' – 'Daddy, daddy, you bastard, I'm through' – reads not only like an enraged assault on a fascist vampire patriarchy, but also perhaps on the kind of overbearing male poet by whose side Plath felt lock-stepped into minor compliance.

A slightly different set of speculations emerge when we listen to the husky-voiced rugby commentator Murray Mexted, a poet of the television sports channels, who is famous for what's referred to as his 'poetic' turn of phrase. I've often heard him use the word 'poetry' to describe an otherwise indescribable event in a game of rugby, usually, like the Johnny Tillotson song, involving motion. In fact, on several occasions I've heard him refer to Carlos Spencer as 'poetry in motion'. Most often, though, I've heard Murray use the familiar phrase 'pure poetry'. In the case of a gigantic South African lock forward being lifted high in the air at line-out, the work being done by the phrase 'pure poetry' isn't quite the same as Johnny Tillotson's. 'Pure', here, describes exemplary physical rather than aesthetic qualities, but in doing so it associates exemplary physical action with moral quality. It allows us to read physical prowess through a filter of higher being.

I'm not suggesting that Murray Mexted is subscribing to the kind of Nazification of physical prowess associated with higher moral being, but there is a hint of awe in his commentary when he enthuses warmly about the 'pure poetry' of a particularly bone-shattering tackle, and this awe, which is familiar to us in combination with terror, is of course the sign of the sublime. The 'pure poetry' that

Murray is huskily invoking is in fact the sublime, that inspirer of awe and terror so often associated also with Romantic poetry (and excoriated by Sylvia Plath).

In these contexts, where the word 'poetry' does the job of expressing some otherwise inarticulate feelings of awe, its companion term 'poetic' is also likely to make an appearance. By 'poetic' here I mean the adjective used to describe a condition or affect, not the noun used for the practice and theory of writing poetry. Rather like the word 'artistic' uttered as a pejorative by artists, the adjective 'poetic' is frequently used ironically by 'poets who don't like poetry' to describe minor or sentimental qualities they dislike or don't want to be associated with – Marianne Moore again. The word 'poetic' has come to be seen as devalued or even degraded, to belong in the languages of caption writers in travel magazines or marketing copywriters describing new lines in Laura Ashley home furnishing fabrics. And unlike the neo-fascist moral superiority undertones of 'pure poetry' used to describe exemplary physical action, 'a poetic turn of phrase' often hints at deviousness, at a faintly immoral way with the truth. The word 'poetic' is uttered with a shudder or a sneer by poets wishing to dissociate themselves from sentimentality or amateurism, or from the language of marketing copywriters; but it is also uttered somewhat sceptically by non-poets who want to suggest that someone is lying. Or if not exactly lying, then coming up with some unusually creative kinds of truth. Hence the term 'poetic licence'.

Movement and truth-telling; or walking and knowledge of the world: I find it interesting that the vernaculars of 'poetry' and 'poetic' so often sheet back to these fundamental and probably archaic concepts of movement and knowledge. I think it's also likely that there's a connection between the two, that there's a cognitive link or bridge between movement and knowledge, or between physical movement and the recognition of kinds of truth. Poetry somehow reminds us of this connection, and almost certainly articulates it. I suspect, partly on the basis of my own experience, that many of us think best when we have settled into a rhythm of walking, that the bridge created between walking and thinking is built with language, and that what crosses that language bridge between walking and thinking is knowledge or understanding. Sounds like poetry to me, at a complex level most often associated with oral traditions such as the spatial geographies and genealogies of Aboriginal 'songlines', or the combinations of whakapapa and rāhui in Māori tauparapara, whose rhythms may often be those of canoe voyaging and portage. This is not to deny that we may accomplish something similar by dancing, swimming, driving the car or, in the case of John Ashbery and his fluid digressions, by consuming excellent cocktails. Nor does it rule out the kinds of cognitive patterning produced by the visual rhythms of the printed page, the typewriter or computer keyboard, or the interconnections and cross-currents of diverse digital domains. I recently travelled on the London underground with a rush-hour crowd most of whom were listening to iPods while reading or texting, and there was one strap-hanging woman who involuntarily uttered ethereal fragments of the song she was listening to, with a slightly unnerving, off-key, trance-like timbre to her voice – another kind of 'poetry in motion'. Nor should we overlook the obvious importance of rhythm and performance in hip-hop and rap, something the fast-talking PI Selena Tusitala Marsh and the 'fast talker' David Eggleton have brought to the poetry scene here in New Zealand.

But to return to the older model of walking: it's no accident that our word for the basic measure of prosody, of poetic structure, is 'foot'. I don't think it's fanciful to suggest that the rocking motion as we move our weight forward from the heel of one of our feet to its toes is one basic measure of articulated thought. The rhythms of our thought are, after all, residually or if you like *primitively* the rhythms of on-foot nomads. We may associate the evolved forms of human culture, including poetry, with post-nomadic settlement and the life of cities – with the *polis* and with metropolitan sophistication – but *how we know stuff*, how we access and structure our knowledge and understanding of *what matters*, may very well involve archaic modes of cognition activated and produced through complex interactions of walking, perceiving, thinking and talking. While you are walking, perceiving, thinking and talking, you are also breathing – in fact, you may be measuring your breaths with some regularity and care, and fitting your talking into their interstices. The 'foot', then, in poetry, is not just a measure of length or extent, but also of duration or time measured by how long it takes to breathe in and out, how long to swing one leg forward while the foot on the other rocks your body's weight forward.

Dante Alighieri famously composed his vernacular masterpiece *La Divina Commedia* while walking in the hills of Umbria during the bitter years of his exile. The *terza rima* form that he used may have derived from the *sirventes* genre of Occitan poetry used by the troubadours, notably Bertran de Born, the favourite of Ezra Pound. But it is also, in its pace and in the way in which its rhymes catch breath, the simple rhythm of walking, thinking and talking:

> Nel mezzo del cammin di nostra vita
> mi ritrovai per una selva oscura
> ché la diritta via era smarrita.

Another famous walking poet, Robert Frost, used *terza rima* in his poem 'Acquainted with the Night':

> I have been one acquainted with the night.
> I have walked out in rain – and back in rain.
> I have outwalked the furthest city light.

And yet another *terza rima*-ist and obsessive walker, Shelley, in 'Ode to the West Wind':

> O wild West Wind, thou breath of Autumn's being,
> Thou, from whose unseen presence the leaves dead
> Are driven, like ghosts from an enchanter fleeing,

And so on. And then of course there's Wordsworth, who didn't use *terza rima,* walking all over the Lake District off his face on laudanum, and his succinct Japanese counterpart Matsuo Basho walking along the route of his 'Narrow Road to the Interior'.

Yes, this is a very simplistic and reductive account of poetry. And I don't want to promote a hokey prescription for poetry as language-got-rhythm; the complex cognitive rhythms or patterns we are talking about here are not, or are not just, of the tum-ti-tum variety. But I hope I've been able to make the point that our vernacular expressions, such as 'poetry in motion', 'pure poetry' and 'poetic licence', are evidence of just how saturated everyday language and usage are in some of the archaic fundamentals of poetry – such as its cognitive and language links between movement and knowledge, its tendency to perform competitive evolutionary cultural categories and canons, and its connection to truth-telling (or lying) – and how, on this evidence, poetry demonstrably does matter, whether the nay-sayers or the variously squeamish yeasayers like it (or dislike it) or not.

It's possible, of course, that these traces in our English-language culture are merely fossils and represent a time when poetry *did* matter, rather than evidence that it *does.* I personally doubt this, though to have any weight my doubt would need to be tested by substantial comparative research into historical and contemporary conditions. However, it seems to me that cultures are rich and diverse ecologies made up of many interconnected components both small and large, which grow and diminish in cycles over time according to the equivalents of natural laws involving economies of production and distribution, the permeability or not of specialist enclaves and environments, the enrichment or depletion of food chains, and the shifting tastes of consumers. For example, to return to a couple of the examples already cited, Dryden's 1697 translation of Virgil's *Aeneid* made it a durable component of the English-language poetic canon, and did so initially by putting it into circulation beyond the walled scholarly enclave where fluency in Greek and Latin was a basic access requirement. Dante's decision to write his *Commedia* in a vernacular that would come to be known as 'Italian', rather than in Latin, was a political act whose significance was subsequently obscured or repositioned by the work's apotheosis to the higher canon of modernism, what T.S. Eliot called the 'mind of Europe' with its attendant condescension of individual subjectivity and its elevation of an 'ideal order'.

There is a kind of cyclic eco-rhythm in such examples, whereby poetry and its 'legitimising discourses' seem to move back and forth across variously 'popular' and 'privileged' domains whose relationships are of course more dialectical than antithetical, however hard their champions try to defend their perceived points of difference, significance or value.

There *are* cultures where poetry obviously does have a dominant or overarching role in cultural ecologies, and I want to finish this talk by looking briefly at three of these under the heading 'Does poetry matter?' The question, after all, can only have comparative, not absolute, answers.

In India, the *Mahābhārata* began to be composed in Sanskrit some time before 300BCE or about 2,300-odd years ago, with multiple tributaries of vernacular dialect as well as additional Sanskrit being added over the next 600 or so years. The poem contains about three million words and is about seven times the length of the *Odyssey* and the *Iliad* combined. In the late 1980s it was televised in 94 episodes based on a comic book version – towns and cities practically shut down during broadcast hours on Sunday mornings. There are numerous Bollywood versions, and, most recently, as reported in the *London Review of Books*, Chindu Sreedharan has begun to post a Twitter version called 'Epicretold' at the rate of one 140-character tweet at a time. The *Mahābhārata*'s vast scale of episode and theme in a sense boils down to the issue of dharma, how to do the right thing, and what happens when you don't. It's inconceivable that the *Mahābhārata* could ever cease to be contemporary; it's impossible to imagine that Hindu society in all its complexity could cease to be performed by the *Mahābhārata*, that it could cease to be the agent that networks that society, or that it could cease to *matter* as an artefact.

In 2005 I spent a month in Bangladesh looking for traces of my childhood there between 1954 and 1958. I was also interested in the Baul poets of Bengal. The national anthem of Bangladesh is based on lyrics by Rabindranath Tagore, a Hindu, and a melody by the Bangladeshi Baul poet Lalon Shah (Tagore also wrote the national anthem of India). Bangladeshi nationalism is deeply rooted in language – Bangla – and the founding moment of Bangladeshi independence from Pakistan was the student revolt of 21 February 1952, during which five 'language martyrs' were killed by police near the Dhaka Medical College hospital. The students were demonstrating against the decree by the central Pakistan government that minority Urdu would be the official language of both East and West Pakistan. I attended Language Martyrs' Day demonstrations at the Shaheed Minar memorial in Dhaka on 21 February 2005, during which a couple of bombs concealed in empty potato chip packets went off; these did not deter the enormous crowd of perhaps a million people that brought flowers to the monument, or quell their enthusiasm for the poets who became the voices of the people in the lead-up to the war of liberation in 1971: Rabindranath Tagore, Kazi Nazrul Islam and Mohammed Iqbal. Each of these came to represent a political faction, less because of their own beliefs as because without poets and the legitimisation of their language no political leader could expect to win credibility. When I went from the guest house where I was staying down to the nearby traffic island to get a rickshaw across to the demonstrations, I passed a guy with a little bicycle-tyre repair shop. He'd made a *papier-mâché* model of the Shaheed Minar memorial using a copy of the newspaper with Kazi Nazrul Islam's famous poem 'Rebel' on it, a rallying-cry in the 1971 war of liberation – this was partly out of respect for the language martyrs, but also as insurance against the Awami League enforcers who were policing the general strike. As the Bangladeshi historian Rafiuddin Ahmed put it, Bangladesh never believes anything until there is a poet to articulate it.

An analogous claim can be made for the roles of Arab poets such as the Palestinian Mahmoud Darwish, or the late Fadwa Tuqan, whom he addressed as 'Sister' in his famous poem 'Diary of a Palestinian Wound'. When I lived in Amman, Jordan, in 1969 and 1970, I used to walk down to the central souk in the mornings to go to a job in an outlying town called Russeifeh. I often noticed groups of early morning breakfasters clustered around radios in the coffee shops, listening to broadcasts. I found out that these were broadcasts of new poems by poets such as Fadwa Tuqan, Darwish, Samir al Qasim, and others.

Mahmoud Darwish died on Saturday 9 August 2008. News of his death was widely reported in the international media, but sadly not here in New Zealand. The great Egyptian novelist Ahdaf Soueif said Darwish was the last poet who could fill a football stadium for a poetry reading. This was literally true: 25,000 people filled a stadium in Beirut early in 2008 to listen to him; many more attended his funeral ceremonies in Amman and Ramallah. At his funeral in Ramallah, tens of thousands of black-clad mourners held aloft portraits of Darwish in streets draped with 5,000 flags printed with images of the poet and one word in Arabic: 'Farewell'.

Darwish's poetry doesn't contain a marked divide between the popular outcries of resistance broadcast on the radio and the metaphysical poems, love poems and poems about history that he also wrote. One of the clear signs of the continuum within which he wrote was that its cultural extent and continuities were recognised by a sophisticated metropolitan elite including Palestinian intellectuals such as Edward Said, as well as by the mass of dispossessed living in refugee camps. The great Egyptian diva Oum Kalthoum transposed Darwish's poems into songs whose many reprises often lasted up to an hour; performed to huge, delirious audiences, they recalled the intricately linked rubaiyat of classical Arabic poetry, the high-coloured rhetoric of political harangue, and the sounds of the prayer-caller or imam (Oum Kalthoum's father was the imam of a Nile Delta mosque).

This complex public role distinguishes what Darwish's audiences expected of him from the expectations of the small, literary audience that reads poetry in New Zealand. In 1985, after researching a bi-lingual anthology of New Zealand poetry, I encountered, in the arguments that broke out over the inclusion of Māori texts in the *Penguin Book of New Zealand Verse*, a comparable disjunction between poetry as public rhetoric and the conventions of a primarily literary, salon or academic culture. What seemed interesting to me and my co-editor Harvey McQueen was that there were, indeed, different modalities involved: it was the *differences* between the English-language and the Māori that made their inclusion together in a book worthwhile, not any similar claims they might have had to be included in such an anthology, such as the hegemonising agency of a shared definition of 'poetry'. No more fluent in Māori than I had been in the Arabic with which Darwish spoke to radio listeners in the souk in Amman, I could still figure out that the modes of address and reception for a composition by Ngoi Pēwhairangi or Pita Sharples before a large audience at the Tōmoana Showgrounds in Hastings were more like those I encountered in Amman than, even, in my own experience, the modest theatrics of 'Young New Zealand Poets' reading to enlarged audiences for poetry during the 1970s.

I raise these issues not in order to take the moral high ground, but because I have been lucky to have had encounters that have allowed me to measure the distance between the expectations of my own literary culture, and other, different ones.

At any rate, I can hardly finish without stating my position. I do believe that poetry matters in complex and contradictory ways across diverse cultural situations and in response to diverse and sometimes incompatible or even incomprehensible expectations. It matters that there isn't a simple 'yes' or 'no' answer to the question, 'Does poetry matter?' Elation – that poetic condition in which thought, emotion and perception are fused – is about immersion rather than the dissociation of sensibility – or, as Donna Haraway memorably quipped in *When Species Meet*, 'My endorphins are at high tide.'

Pleasing Everybody – or Not

Museums and civic responsibility

Text edited from notes for the Stephen Weil memorial lecture at the Intercom conference on Museums, Tourism and the Visitor Experience, Rotorua, 26 November 2008, published in *Te Ara: Journal of Museums Aotearoa* (Vol. 33 (1&2), November 2009)

Cheryll Sotheran has suggested that enterprise and crisis (such as the world's current financial crisis) may generate opportunities for focused thought and close value-driven engagement with particular rather than mass-market conditions. Another kind of challenge has been provided by Michael Gondwe from Malawi. Looking for an ethical bottom line in his museum's engagement with tourism, he asks a simple question: 'How does the museum use culture to stop people from dying?'

Keeping Cheryll's challenge and Michael's question in view, I will begin with some tourist stories that do not lay out clear propositions or come to obvious conclusions. But they contain information that more conventional openings do not.

Ownership of culture exchange

In 1968 and 1969 I spent some time in Jordan and Syria. These were times of conflict, as they still are in that region, and at an impressionable age I learned at close quarters how closely linked culture and politics could be. One example involved the late Palestinian poet Mahmoud Darwish. In the mornings on my way to work, I used to walk through a busy part of the souk in Amman to the central bus station. On the way I passed groups of men listening to radio broadcasts in the coffee shops. I found out that they were sometimes listening to broadcasts by Palestinian poets, including Mahmoud Darwish. The poems would soon begin to circulate in written form. These written versions were seldom provided by the poet, who was said to be under house arrest in Haifa at the time. They were provided by people who transcribed the poems from radio broadcasts. The status of these transcriptions – their authenticity, if you like – was *not* in question, though several variants might exist. What mattered was that they were in circulation, that they were discussed, that they were critical agents within the culture. What did not matter at this stage was whether they were officially mandated, managed, published, and authorised in some way. If anything, and in the spirit of the poet himself, it was important that these objects were *not* authorised, that the early morning coffee shop radio listeners had taken ownership of them and redistributed them freely in accordance with the wishes of the people who needed them.

Another important encounter for me around the same time was with a seller of carpets in the souk in Damascus. Here I learned at close quarters how closely linked culture and commerce could be. This man was a merchant who made a living for his extended family by selling carpets, many of which were sold to him in the first place by pilgrims making the haj to Mecca. His fabulous shop was also a kind of museum: a museum of carpets, stories and pilgrimages. One after another, carpets would be thrown down in front of you, and out of clouds of dust the merchant would tell you where they came from, what were the contexts of their manufacture, what conflicts and triumphs they had been silent witnesses to – and even, sometimes, the stories of the haji who had passed through and traded them. Many of the carpets had crossed borders illegally in contravention of export bans on heritage treasures. This was also a museum of crime.

As well as being a trader, shopkeeper and possibly a smuggler, the merchant was also a distinguished scholar. What was normal in the context of the souk was that he spoke several languages: Arabic, Aramaic, French, Hebrew and Farsi as a matter of course, but also English, Italian and German. He could recite the classics of Arabic poetry at length by heart. What was only slightly less normal was that the merchant was also one of Syria's most esteemed archaeologists. He added an ability to read texts in Greek and Latin to his linguistic span. Being an archaeologist and scholar of ancient sites throughout the wider region, he was also a tour guide and entrepreneur. He drove hard bargains as a merchant and organiser of site visits, but the satisfaction of his customers was secure.

Despite Syria's long history of scholarship, there was insufficient institutional infrastructure to support him as a scholar, but there was, and is, an old tradition of scholarship associated with his businesses. There was, specifically, no museum infrastructure in Syria capable of replicating the rich experience of hospitality, treasure, knowledge and entertainment the visitor enjoyed while spending a day in the merchant's shop. Much of the entertainment came from listening to him talk about history and tell stories of indigent pilgrims as the cups of tea were replenished. Much of it also came from the bargaining over carpets and his offers of excursions to old Greek and Roman sites in the region. If no sale occurred, the merchant would express ritual disgust, but would then slip you a present and say how much he looked forward to seeing you next time.

Encounter and context

A cynic trained in the encounter strategies of museums and 'cultural tourism' alike might want to invoke Dean McCannell's usefully sceptical phrase 'staged authenticity' at this point. However, though I am no longer as naïve as I was in 1969, I would still insist that my encounters with the Syrian carpet merchant were candid about the key facts of the situation. I was a customer, he was a merchant, and yet a substantial part of the value in our transactions was social and involved exchanges of courtesies and knowledge as well as (though seldom) of money.

Also at an impressionable age, I had an encounter with a great work of art – one of those encounters that make you go back again and again to art museums hoping the lightning will strike. This encounter took place in the wonderful Kunstmuseum in Basel, Switzerland. I walked into a small room and saw *Still Life with Oysters* (1940) by Henri Matisse. The painting seemed to extract most of my life force in a kind of outrush of astonishment and bliss, a gasp of consciousness, which it then poured back in. The effect was intensely emotional, but it was also extremely cerebral – it was one of the most complexly satisfying intellectual and emotional experiences I have ever had. The experience was an aesthetic one, but – and this 'but' does not imply something separate from aesthetics, which is the point I think – the painting also spoke clearly to me about how I thought life should be lived. It was sharp, alert, crisply beautiful, but also full of pleasure and sensory celebration. Ah, I exclaimed inwardly at the age of 22, this is exactly what life is about!

At the time I was visiting a friend who had gone to live in Rudolf Steiner's Goetheanum in nearby Dornach. I used to catch the train with a feeling of dread, as if I were going to visit someone in a lunatic asylum. Of course the Steiner Institute was not a lunatic asylum, but it was a serious place of carrot salad and special underwear. After each visit I fled back to the camping ground where my girlfriend and I were staying, and we would drink beer and eat sausages in the company of singing German tourists. Ah, I exclaimed, aloud this time, while singing with the Germans, this is what life is about!

Now, 40 years later, I am still unable to separate my experience of Matisse's lovely painting from either the Goetheanum up the hill at Dornach, or from the beer and sausages down the hill in the camping ground. Nor can I think of the art museum itself as entirely separate from these places and their contrasting tastes and sounds. And whenever I see works by Henri Matisse, I have become accustomed to being unable to separate either them or the art history in which they are embedded from the contest between the beer and sausages at the campground barbecue and the Birchermüesli up the hill at Dornach. These are wildly inappropriate baggages, perhaps – or perhaps not.

What do I now learn from this seemingly incompatible confluence of encounters? It is that museum experiences are never autonomous; that we are misguided at best and dishonest at worst if we claim (or expect) the authenticity of the museum encounter to be sealed off somehow from the circumstances, itineraries and narratives of our visit.

Emotional meaning

In 2005 I spent some time in Bangladesh, where I hoped to find traces of my childhood with my family there in the 1950s. I did reawaken many emotional memories. Out of a sense of duty, as well as in the hope that it might be an emotionally tranquil place, I visited the National Museum in Dhaka. There I saw relics commemorating the language martyrs of 1952 and the war of liberation in 1971. In a dusty vitrine, poorly lit and with a faded, handwritten cardboard label, was a torn shirt with bullet holes surrounded by faded brown bloodstains. To the astonishment of the polite Bangladeshi visitors who had joined me on my tour, I burst into tears at the sight of the shirt, which had belonged to one of the students shot while demonstrating for the retention of Bangla as the official language of his Bengali people. I do not know if my tears were caused by the poignancy of this exhibit, which did not seem like an exhibit at all, but like the forensic evidence of a crime scene; or by the accumulated weeks of re-encountering the ghosts of my mother and father. What I do know is that it was the unexpected meeting with something of huge emotional significance to *other* people, but rationally not to me, that triggered what clearly seemed to my companions to be an inappropriate reaction. Though they were too polite to suggest it, my response to the shirt with its half-century-old bloodstains must have seemed deeply inauthentic; or at best to have been an example of staged authenticity.

What else did I learn? That however hard their interpreters try, museums are not places where rational encounters can be assumed or safeguarded. They are, rather, places where irrational, unpredictable, and even wildly inappropriate affects will occur; where the emotional meanings of encounters within the museum will be impossible to disentangle from conditions outside it; where a kind of transgenic exchange of alterity, back and forth between one other and another, is entirely plausible and even likely; where, for example, my old grief for my long dead parents could suddenly gush out in front of a dirty vitrine containing the bloodstained shirt of a Bangla language martyr.

Relayed meaning

In the early 1980s I spent a few weeks hitchhiking around the East Coast of the North Island of New Zealand. I was researching the practices of Māori beach whalers in the early part of the 20th century. I went to talk to Pāora Delamere at the Whānau-ā-Apanui marae at Te Kaha. Pāora was a Bishop of Ringatū, a vigorous old man. He told me some great stories, and then said that I must not on any account go and talk to Paddy Brown down the coast at Hicks Bay. Of course I went straight to Paddy Brown on the strength of this, and Paddy told me a whole lot more great stories. He then admonished me to avoid a certain other person a bit further along at Tolaga Bay, whom I immediately sought out . . . and so it went, all the way around the coast.

The factual information I learned from each of them was not that different. What I learned was that their community's ownership of the stories mattered more than the stories' veracity, and that the *hospitality* of each of these individuals was more important than their authority. What I also suspected was that they all knew their warnings not to go and talk to so-and-so were the best way to make sure I would do so. On their marae and in their homes I saw amazing things – objects, documents, photographs – and at Paddy's place a tin of dry, rendered whale blubber which he gave me a piece of to chew on. And then, at the end of the journey, under the eave of the museum on the other side of the Cape at Gisborne, I saw the most beautiful boat ever built on the coast, a double-ended whale chaser, the *Greyhound*, which had been transported there when whaling stopped in the Bay of Plenty. Everyone I had listened to on the way there had talked about this boat. They all knew I would find it. It had gone to a place separate from all of them where all the stories about it, and all the contests for ownership of the stories, could safely converge.

We all have stories like these. Mine come into museums with me. They are inescapable components of the critical apparatus with which I experience museums. I demand that museums live up to the expectations created in me by the radio listener redistributors of

Mahmoud Darwish's poems, by the scholar businessman in his shop of smuggled carpets, by the perfect art museum haplessly entangled in an unresolvable argument about how to live life to the fullest, by the emotional ambush in Bangladesh that called into question any glib categorisation of authenticity, by the competitive manaakitanga of the old whalers who all knew that I would eventually find their beloved *Greyhound* in a place where they could not argue about it any more.

Questions of honesty

There is a more formal way of approaching the question of the museum's civic responsibility. In contrast to my stories, which have tended to endorse the museum as a place of paradox, anarchic participation and unpredictable affect, this approach assumes that the museum is also a rational place where various kinds of responsibility are expected and enacted. I have in mind Stephen Weil's vision for museums that declare their respect for audiences by welcoming active participation. To this I add my belief that enjoyment can be critical, that a democracy of knowledge within culture is what active citizens require of their public institutions. Citizens who expect museums to provide them with opportunities for critical enjoyment will keep those institutions honest. Perhaps institutions that act in good faith to meet the expectations of participating citizens will, in turn, help to keep the state honest.

The question here is: Can museums be safe places for debate in times of crisis? Museums hope to sustain a balance between commercial and cultural value: between revenue in, and enjoyment and knowledge out. Tourism hopes to transform cultural value (including landscape) into gross domestic product (GDP). National identity programmes administered by the state hope to unify citizens and transform cultural value into political capital and international brand values. These agendas often conflict with each other. They often conflict with the wishes of local communities.

The questions here are: Can museums mediate these tensions? Is conflict mediation an appropriate role for museums? Where museums are the drivers of tourism agendas and where tourism agendas match those of state-supported national branding (for example, the 100% Pure New Zealand brand), alliances may form that are careless – or untruthful – about the sustainable use of natural and cultural resources.

The questions here are: Can museums establish useful critical positions within such alliances without jeopardising their funding bases, sponsors and marketing networks? For example, can they critique state-sponsored formations of national identity without alienating the government or local authority that may be their principal funder, or indeed their employer? Can they tell the truth about agriculture's pollution of fresh water without angering the giant dairy company that may be one of their principal sponsors, for example? Can they afford to promote strategies of audience distribution outside the main centres without annoying the tourism advocates and marketers in those metropolitan centres? Can they afford to discuss poor water quality in areas where the main tourist attractions are lakes and rivers?

Big overarching question: What is the strategic task of museums in a time of crisis – for example, the current global crisis whose symptom is climate change, not to mention the financial crisis? Can museums address such issues while remaining attractive destinations?

These are serious questions and they tend to run across the strategic battle lines within institutions. And this largely rhetorical exercise – asking theoretical strategic questions – tends to generate a number of oppositional models (such as commercial versus cultural) which the Syrian carpet merchant (and Cheryll Sotheran) would consider counterproductive.

Personal questions

We can raise similar but less rhetorical questions by considering the natures and expectations of people who participate in museums – including museum professionals, others like myself who vacillate between being contract professionals and visitors, and non-professional audiences in all their diversity.

Museum professionals embody in themselves – in their natures and motivations – many of the questions asked above. For example, they embody the commercial driver of making a living and the cultural one of being expert in and passionate about the culture, objects, narrative, and knowledges that museums are custodians of.

They may well from time to time embody a tension between the commercial and the cultural, between making a living in museums and being passionate about what they do. But this tension will not be an irreconcilable conflict, or they would not be there. In fact, more often than not, their embodiment of commercial and cultural motives will be a productive one, in that they are making a living doing what they know and love. And they take this model of productive dialogue, and its rewards and satisfactions, into the museum, where they join their colleagues on a daily basis.

A complex collective of such people – the professional cultural body of the museum – *is*, in a sense that goes beyond metaphor, the museum itself. The dialogues and debates the collective embodies, not to mention its irrational and at times perverse behaviour, *are* the museum. In this professional collective, the museum embodies in various ways questions such as, 'Can museums contribute to democratic processes that keep the state honest?' This way of asking the question is more productive, and indeed more interesting, than the objectifying rhetoric of strategic questions asked at various removes from that collective body.

In the same way, it is more productive to think of the museum's collections as being part of that collective body, alive and integral to it, natured and narrativised, squabbled over and contested by diverse claimants, rather than archives of taxonomic conditions and uncontested truths.

Continuum of engagement

But, of course, the museum is not *just* the collective of those who work there. The natures and motivations of those who participate in museums include the natures and motivations of semi-professional contractors like me, who are both in and out of museums, not as committed professionally, but probably more engaged in other ways than the professionals are in their daily work. I will come in less often, I may come in a bit fresher, with my expectations, curiosity, and sometimes scepticism, more focused on what I am going to experience than on what tasks I am going to do.

But semi-professional contractors are not separate from the museum professionals who come in every day to do work. They are joined at the hip, and the ways in which the semi-professionals might embody the strategic questions I have been asking will differ only in nuance and degree, along a stretch between museum professionals and museum audiences. What occasional contractors bring to museums is not the nature and motivation – call it the consciousness – of being inside most of the time, with an inward focus, but the consciousness of transients who are also outside much of the time, who tend to mash up distinctions between inside and outside.

Nor, of course, are the museum's diverse audiences who come in only occasionally separate either from the semi-professional transient who comes and goes regularly, or from the museum professional who is in the museum most of the time. All are parts of the complex collective body of the museum, which will also, therefore, incorporate their different kinds of relationships to the collections – relationships that are not distinct or separate, but linked: the relationship of the museum kaitiaki or curator to the collections, that of the semi-regular researcher or contract curator, that of the occasionally visiting member of the public. All linked and all capable of being unpredictable and irrational.

In praise of productive imbalance

Along the stretch from professionals mostly inside the museum to the audience mostly outside it – along this continuum of the museum body – the strategic questions being considered here will generate a continuum of answers and varieties of dialogue. It is probably fair to say that that part of the museum's collective body characterised as professional and predominantly within the museum on a regular basis will tend to produce inwardly directed responses to those questions. The strategies that arise from them asking the questions will tend to produce solutions internal to the museum's requirements.

Cultural and social anthropologists, as well as their close relatives the management and systems theorists, know that over time settled institutional cultures become resistant to change. Their social structures, practices and language become codified. Clear demarcations are established between those who are encompassed by and privy to the codes and those who are not. There are insiders and outsiders. There is a theologising of what were once fresh new ideas – they become dogma.

In such an established and settled museum culture, the internal part of the museum's collective body tends to perceive the audience part of that body as existing *only when it is also inside the museum* – or perhaps, in terms of marketing, when it is *potentially* inside the museum. Archaeologists and archaeo-historians discuss this kind of settlement consolidation process in terms of human societies and how they do, or do not, change and develop. They tell us that settled societies with well-regulated codes and impermeable cultural frontiers have great difficulty changing and adapting, whereas societies whose ecologies, cultures and economies are diverse and mobile, which are subject to 'imbalances productive of change', to use Fernand Braudel's wonderfully pithy term, are going to be more resilient, innovative and able to live with, and make something of, difference.

In this context, I see my variously irrational and inappropriate responses to museum encounters, my transgenic exchanges of alterity between one other and another, as contributing to the health of the museum as a collective consciousness constantly washed in and out of by the anarchic tides of the world 'outside', where, as Michael Gondwe reminded us, people are dying. There are many examples of deliberate strategies for producing 'imbalances productive of change' that work to keep the museum open to the world. With these, I will try to come to some conclusions.

First, an example of how an inward-looking, settled, frontier-secured museum paradigm might rather be exploited and subverted. The veteran Paraguayan curator Ticio Escobar persisted for many years in his work with indigenous and contemporary art in the face of political repression. Escobar's curatorial projects include the *2007 Bienale de Valencia*, which had the wonderful Escobarian subtitle *Other Versions of the Contemporary: The Trials of Living Together*. In 2006, the Paraguayan Government enacted the Escobar Law (drafted by Ticio) for the protection of Indigenous Arts and Heritage in Paraguay – nonexistent up until then but the result, in large part, of his strategic activism. His Museo del Barro (Museum of Mud) in Asunción preserves Paraguayan vernacular culture, which he sees as an inalienable expression of resistance. His Museum of Indigenous Art is one aspect of his support for indigenous land rights. He deliberately exhibits both vernacular and indigenous art in close contact with prestigious international contemporary art, and does so in metropolitan contexts. In doing this, Escobar is publicly denying that popular and indigenous cultures are marginal.

The South African artist and curator Khwezi Gule proposed an opposite but equally subversive strategy in thinking about *Cape 2006*, the pan-African contemporary biennale project. He looked at infrastructure and movement in the Cape; for example, the ways in which public transport, especially rail transport, separated the townships from each other by routing transport through a metropolitan terminus. The directions of infrastructure had been, and continued to be, determined by the movements of labour from the townships to the city terminus and back to the townships. These flows in effect kept the townships apart as disconnected satellites of a hub. His question was, 'How could these infrastructural flows be rearticulated so that a pan-African biennale *linked* townships and empowered their audiences?' He saw the key strategic issue for the biennale as movement and dispersal rather than metropolitan convergence. The key questions were not about which artists to select from the international biennale carousel, but rather who could get where, how could townships connect away from the terminus, what audiences were disenfranchised by distance and infrastructure, which artists were rendered peripheral by the capital flows of international art as these replicated the metropolitanising infrastructural shape of the Cape's rail system on a global scale; which 'art turkeys', as he called them, needed to fly back against those flows in order to participate in Africa, how did funding move around?

In France, the Centres d'Action Culturelle established after the Second World War through the vision of André Malraux and developed by Jack Lang through successive Socialist administrations are a model of state-sponsored cultural devolution. The national and regional funds for collecting contemporary art, and the distribution of the national collections through an enormous variety of venues throughout France, are heavily bureaucratised. But the distributed infrastructure and culture they have grown over the course of half a century will not be dismantled easily by Nicolas Sarkozy. They are now integral to how people live their lives, to the regionalisation of national heritage, the celebration of regional genius and distinction.

Here we have three models of intervention in the museum as a collective public consciousness rather than a hermetic archive: first, the deliberate and provocative metropolitanising of politically marginalised culture; second, rethinking what would conventionally have been a metropolitan biennale in terms of the ability of disenfranchised participants to move and connect away from the centre; third, the socialised, state-sponsored devolution of cultural opportunity and participation. What we also have, in the form of museum encounter stories such as those with which I began this talk, is evidence that museums make meaning as much in spite as because of their rational, organising systems; and that they may be greatly enriched by these subversions if they admit them.

What my stories, not less than these strategic case studies, are telling us is that museums as complex collective bodies can be agents of radical social change and critical consciousness: that we will also find it coming and going from museums, and sometimes, paradoxically, we will find the museum's most significant agents of change somewhere else entirely.

References

Gondwe, Michael. 'Museums and Tourism', *Museums, Tourism and the Visitor Experience*, Intercom 2008 conference, Rotorua, 25 November 2008.

MacCannell, D. 1999. *The Tourist – A New Theory of the Leisure Class*. Berkeley: University of California Press.

Sotheran, Cheryll. Keynote address to *Museums, Tourism and Visitor Experience*. Intercom 2008 conference, Rotorua, 25 November 2008.

He Korowai o te Wai

The mantle of water

Reading Room: A Journal of Art and Culture (Issue 04, 2010)

In 2007 the Rotorua Museum of Art and History commissioned me to organise an exhibition and related events for its centennial in 2008. An aspect of the museum's centennial project was the completion of the building's north wing following the original architectural plan, which had remained unfinished when the building opened in 1908. This would provide substantial additional gallery space and, in order to give the opening the kind of profile the local authority wanted, I was asked to incorporate a significant loan of art works from the national collection at the Museum of New Zealand Te Papa Tongarewa in my proposal.

That was the only requirement spelled out in my brief. However there were other practical considerations implicit in the museum's operational identity and context; and what might be termed thematic factors which had to do with the history, geoculture and social formations of the place.

Practical considerations included the fact that the museum is a multi-purpose institution – in part a museum of itself as a former spa bathhouse; in part an art and visual culture museum with a modest collection at its disposal; in part a social history museum, especially in respect of Te Arawa iwi and hapū, with significant stories such as the Māori Battalion; and a natural history museum, especially given its location in the unstable geothermal environment of a giant caldera, notorious for the Tarawera eruption in 1886. Largely because of this spectacular location, the museum is the centrepiece of international tourism in the region, with tour buses disgorging their passengers several times a day in the summer season. Such tours, rather than a local or national art constituency, would be any exhibition's core audience, especially if staged across the high summer season as my project would be. In addition, at this time, schools would be on holiday for most of the exhibition's term – family visits rather than curriculum-based school groups would be the norm. But whatever their origins, most people visiting the museum between late November and early April would be in the region for the waters, including performances of their historical use by Māori.

Some thematic factors were obvious. The most obvious was the museum's historical and ongoing relationship to its natural environment of lakes and hot pools – it was there because of water, both hot and cold. Implicit but somewhat hidden in this relationship is an issue of tikanga Māori, which prohibits the association of taonga with bodily practices such as eating or bathing – which is why the museum can no longer be called 'The Bath House' and why certain kinds of pollution of the lakes' water have become highly political. Also obvious was the fact that human settlement in the region was a consequence of its watery environment. Historically, the lakes and their surrounding forests provided abundant food and building resources for Te Arawa iwi and hapū, including Ngāti Tūwharetoa further south at Taupō; though not gardens, which had to be located away from acidic volcanic soils. In the late 19th century this economy began to be augmented by tourism, especially therapeutic spa-based tourism, for which there were historical precedents, as well as the view-based tourism of natural wonders and, once exotic fish species had been introduced, the tourism of fishing and water sports. Not surprisingly, most of the art made in the region has tended to represent or derive from this thematic environment.

Less obvious themes had to do with the ways in which the social structures, lifeways, economies and material cultures of the region have also been shaped by water – its resources, flows and narratives – both before and since tourism. The settlers from Rarotonga who came ashore from the Arawa canoe in Te Moana a Toi or Bay of Plenty north-east of Whakatāne near what is now called Cape Runaway would have found eight major rivers emptying into estuaries or harbours in the region of their beachhead. From Maketū, named for a homeland kūmara pit, they were able to make their way inland along the waterways formed by the Kaituna River to the 12 lakes in the Rotorua region and, further south, to Taupō. As well as providing transportation networks and freshwater resources, the region, extremely inhospitable in winter, also provided abundant hot thermal water. This environment was interpreted in landmarked narratives involving its major volcanic features and their turbulent relationships; its topography and the waterways from the sea at Maketū inland to Taupō came to be closely mirrored in social networks, in the flows and tributaries of whakapapa, and in the cartographic narrative of a collective entity whose tail was at Maketū, belly and heart at Rotorua, and head at Taupō.

Latourian actor-network (ANT) approaches to sociology suggest that artefacts and technics are agents that perform and link up their societies. The same may be said of substantially narrativised and represented environments: they become agent subjects. The intricately braided waterways, artesian springs and thermals of the Rotorua region as it extends to the sea have in a sense acted their inhabiting human societies into existence. The cultural practices of those societies in turn re-enact their watery subject templates through material culture, language, belief systems and storytelling. It's all about water and how water sustains life, not least how it sustains social life through the provision of physical linking networks and the mirrored provision of a metonymic concept of fluid relationship.

Perhaps the best known Te Arawa narrative is that of Hinemoa and Tūtānekai, sometimes characterised as a Hero and Leander story with a happy ending. Enchanted by Tūtānekai's physical prowess in sporting contests and by the liquid sound of his flute-playing on Mokoia Island, the beautiful Hinemoa swam there from Ōwhata on the mainland and warmed herself in the hot pool Waikimihia. Here Tūtānekai found her. Their relationship, which had been forbidden, became instead a cause for celebration, uniting their warring hapū. The story landmarks Mokoia as a significant juncture in ngeri and tauparapara mapping both the Kaituna waterway to Maketū and, in terms of relationship, that between disaffected hapu, as well, perhaps, as between Ngāti Tūwharetoa at Taupō and Te Arawa hapū around Rotorua.

No great conceptual stretch is required to locate this model of fluid relationship within the human body itself, whose constituent parts are linked and related by life-bearing flows of fluid; and to extrapolate this embodied fluid model to the earth itself, warmed and cooled by intricately linked surface water and by precipitation from a water-laden atmosphere, but also the container of vast aquifers of fresh water. One hundred and ten times more fresh water is stored underground in aquifers than above ground in natural lakes; 5000 times more underground than in rivers. It is at this level of incorporation and embodiment that the phenomenal and the metaphorical or representational flow together into the political. In dealing with the body politic of Te Arawa, one will be dealing with water – with a watery body in which social and natural worlds mingle as subjects. On 31 May 2001, the Te Arawa Lakes settlement offer was made by the minister in charge of Treaty of Waitangi negotiations. Though couched in the formal bureaucratic language of such documents, its subtext of embodied water – of a resource, even a life-force, inseparable from the social body of its guardians – was entirely apparent. The Te Arawa Lakes Settlement Act that came into force on 25 September 2006 translated this symbolic understanding into practical terms, but the symbolic theme remained clear. The history of degraded water quality in the Rotorua lakes, catchments, groundwater aquifers, and rivers and streams is intensely political – indeed, the work of Te Arawa Lakes Trust is built around a confluence of commercial and cultural issues brought about by such ecologically catastrophic and culturally repugnant practices as spraying human sewage onto surrounding forests, whence it rapidly seeped into lake-feeding groundwaters.

Nor is it a significant stretch from this political acknowledgement of the locally embodied value of clean water to the global equivalent that, in 2007, was increasingly in the international news as well as in discussions around Rotorua. How much fresh water is there, who owns it, who should be looking after it, and how do these questions unite us in responsibility? 2003 was the United Nations' International Year of Freshwater, and 2005–15 is its proclaimed International Decade for Action on 'Water for Life'. The theme of fresh water for a centennial exhibition at the Rotorua Museum of Art and History seemed, in 2007, to be not only timely but obvious, at once local and international in significance, practical and literal as well as thematic and indexical, and capable of bridging the diverse cultural, operational and constituency requirements of the museum.

The curatorial task of researching and selecting works for the exhibition, as well as commissioning new work and establishing a public programme, was mostly complete by mid-2008, before the overarching concept had generated either a name for the exhibition or the kind of pithy thematic statement that would encapsulate the core idea of fluid embodiment. Then, in August, on a flight to Rotorua, I was seated near a group of people who had been in Wellington for legal consultations over the lakes settlement process. It was a beautiful clear winter's day and we were flying over the Kaimanawa forest south-east of Taupō. The densely forested mountainous country of the Kaweka Range was threaded with a multitude of glittering streams of water. A woman in the seat behind me exclaimed, 'He korowai o te wai!' – the woven cloak of water. I was travelling to Rotorua to meet with kaumātua of Ngāti Whakaue, the tangatawhenua of the land on which the museum stands. When I told them what the woman on the plane had said, Mitai Rolleston recited the tauparapara or ngeri that describes the view, the route, and the key salients of relationship for Te Arawa between Ngongotahā and Maketū – including the reference to Hinemoa and Tūtānekai.

The exhibition now had a title – 'He Korowai o te Wai – the Mantle of Water' – and a key text grounding the total project in a locally specific social topography that, however, spoke comprehensively to a global situation. The elision of human agency and the natural world in the image of a woven cloak of water also, at the level of an overarching concept, mediated the relationships of exhibition artefacts to the natural environment without discursive strain. In the exhibition a sub-theme of bathing, for example, including works by Mark Adams,

Raoul Dufy, Paul Gauguin, Colin McCahon, James Nerli, Edward Payton, Pierre-August Renoir, Thomas Ryan and Warren Viscoe, merely stated the obvious – that artists had long made bathing the subject matter of their work; that this was ubiquitous both historically, with an art historical thread back to Claude in 17th-century Europe (represented elsewhere in the exhibition), and geographically, in, for example, Mark Adams' photographs of Rotorua's Blue Baths in the 1980s or the lakeside photographs of Edward Payton in the late 19th and early 20th centuries.

The human cultures that flow with the patterns of the Rotorua lakes catchment and its many streams and rivers flow also with those cultures' complex elisions of the social and the environmental, of the artefactual and the natural, and of wayfinding and genealogy. We may suppose that these flows and patterns disclose an epistemology reaching back to the oceanic knowledges associated with island cultures and the connective, not divisive, qualities of water. In the case of historical Arawa voyagers, such knowledge was embodied in the Pacific Ocean; navigation lore linked mnemonic narratives and landmarking names with the currents, wave patterns, wind directions and astronomical figurations of an environment characterised by the late Epeli Hau'ofa as a 'sea of islands'. Hau'ofa's famous figure of speech was a rebuke to the imperial cartographies that had mapped the Pacific as a watery *terra nullius* sparsely dotted with small, separate islands physically and culturally remote from one another. Hau'ofa challenged readers of this watery terrain to see how it embodied social relations. Not only did Pacific voyagers navigate with great accuracy between landfalls, but inter-island trade, intermarriage, power-brokering, and inter-territorial dynastic bloodlines mapped a densely interwoven Oceanic construct, at once a natural world and a vast artefact, a complex suite of phenomena and an agent in the performance of a widely distributed, diverse human society.

Hau'ofa's last book, a compilation of his well-known essays, was called simply *We Are the Ocean* (2008); as well as 'Our Sea of Islands' (1993) the book included his essay 'The Ocean in Us' (1998). These succinct formulations echo the embodiment implied in 'he korowai o te wai'; like it, they are in no way symptoms of a nostalgic ethnography. The woman who likened the forest waterways of the Kaweka Range to a woven cloak was flying in an aeroplane with her laptop in the luggage compartment above her seat; for much of the trip, she had been using a cellphone in flight mode; she and her companions were returning from negotiations with Crown lawyers. Hau'ofa's essays are as much about contemporary linkages – fluidities – along air travel and electronic media corridors as they are about historical ocean voyaging. The reach of historical voyaging and social fluidity is in no way diminished by comparison with contemporary networks and flows linking Pacific homelands with Auckland, Sydney and Los Angeles. It is worth remembering the significance of the Tahitian navigator Tupaia on James Cook's first voyage, in its time the most global enterprise imaginable – a role recently documented in detail by Anne Salmond (*Aphrodite's Island: the European Discovery of Tahiti*, 2009). Such combinations of embodiment and fluidity, of social networks and environmental constructs, with emphases on links, flow, and agents rather than autonomies, hegemonies and objects, recall the kinds of liquid states articulated by theories of loosely coupled systems (for example, of software and management), the principles of Latourian ANT sociology, the 'relational aesthetics' or 'altermodernity' of Nicolas Bourriaud and others investigating the global conditions for art, and perhaps also the 'liquid modernity' critiques of 'solid' modernity deployed by Zygmunt Bauman over the past 20 years.

There are evident concordances between the 'liquidities' of the historical and contemporary social/phenomenal/political environment of Te Arawa, Hau'ofa's 'sea of islands' and Bauman's 'liquid modernity'. These will not surprise anyone in touch with the global politics and internationally networked activism around fresh water. Such global networks, and the 'solid', nationally territorialised resource borders they dispute, constitute ethical identity formations similar to those argued for by Bauman in *Modernity and Ambivalence* (1991). In a sense, 'the stranger' of Bauman's allegory of indeterminacy can be identified with both historical models of fluid social organisation at odds with modernity's control systems and taxonomies, and with the contemporary environmental activist.

The exhibition sought to incorporate such activist interventions and liquid contexts in a variety of ways – not all of which can be covered here. Natalie Robertson's three-channel video installation, *Uncle Tasman – The Trembling Current That Scars the Earth* (2007) addresses the environmental degradation to waterways brought about by the Norske Skog/Carter Holt Harvey paper mill at Kawerau; its location in the water catchment of two mountains, Pūtauaki and Tarawera, allows Robertson to structure the work around the narrative of their unhappy love-triangle relationship with Whakaari (the active offshore volcano also known as White Island) and Tarawera's tears that formed the Tarawera Falls. The sound track of the installation includes songs of mourning, haka challenging the 'solid' technology of the mill, and recorded accounts by locals of the degradation of their freshwater resources. In the exhibition, Robertson's work was shown in association with photographs of water utilities by the Burton Brothers (1880s) and C.P. Parkerson (1908); etchings and lithographs of the commercial Thames basin by James Whistler (1850s–90s); and paintings and etchings of canals and windmills by Frances Hodgkins (1907–8), Wenceslas Hollar (1650) and Petrus van der Velden (1880s). A commissioned three-track video work by the Australian artist Tim Gruchy, *Memory Floods* (2008), flooded the front windows of the museum at night deploying footage from a now defunct water organ in Rotorua's Government Gardens – a work that was at once playful and ominous. A selection of photographs from Brian Brake's *New Zealand Scenery* was installed as a slide show of rivers, glaciers and waterfalls; images from his 'Monsoon' series were also included, and both were implicitly juxtaposed with photographs by the Indian anti-Coca-Cola activist Amit Srivastava of protests against ground-water degradation by The Coca Cola company in Balia, Mehdiganj and elsewhere in India between 2004 and 2008. The tauparapara of Ngāti Whakaue was mirrored by a large topographical model of the extended Rotorua lakes system commissioned from the Centre for Biodiversity and Ecology Research at the University of Waikato in association with Environment Bay of Plenty Lake Management and Restoration. Itself constituting a topographical model of sorts, the large floor-based sculpture *Blackwater* (1998–99) by Bill Culbert and Ralph Hotere shared its room with a single-channel video work commissioned from David Cross, *Two Lines* (2008), whose small scale and intimate subject matter (human tear ducts) refocused the spectacle of the large work at the level of the vulnerable human body; a similar refocusing was provided by the Korean artist Jae Hoon Lee's single-channel video with sound, *Drool* (2006). The principle signage of the exhibition consisted of fabric 'waterfalls' background-printed with a cascade of the word 'water' in some 50 different languages and scripts. By these and other means an overall freshwater thematic was threaded – interwoven – with 'strangers': destabilising ethical challenges to the status quo represented by 'solid' technologies, histories, disciplines and narratives.

Beyond the organisational and discursive space of the exhibition itself, such liquid thematics and interweavings were ubiquitous. In the Rotorua Museum's art and photography collections, for example, self-evident themes associated with the Rotorua lakes and thermal environment predominate: significant works by Theo Schoon, Mark Adams, James Nerli and Edward Payton, among others, were included in the exhibition through a selection process that involved little or no curatorial determinism. One might even say such works flowed into the exhibition along historical channels that traversed and interwove disciplines that modernist categories had set apart – art and natural history, for example; the kinds of 'solid' categories that thinkers emerging through and since the postmodern, such as Bauman, have sought to make permeable again, porous to the indeterminacies or cross-currents of 'strangers'.

This comprehensive thematic opportunity was noted in a blog post (19 February 2009) by Jim and Mary Barr – 'Theme shows are back'. Histories within which a 'theme show' such as *He Korowai o te Wai* might appropriately embody complex epistemological interweavings have been provided by several recent scholarly works. We have already seen how Zygmunt Bauman's project to liquefy modernist morality's over-confident absolutisms enlarges the philosophical context in which Epeli Hauʻofa's *We Are the Ocean* is able to argue for a sociology of Oceanic space. Bauman also makes room, for example, for Richard Holmes's recent study of the astonishing interflows across art, science and the natural world in the period between James Cook's first voyage in the late 1760s and that of Charles Darwin in the 1830s (*The Age of Wonder: How the Romantic Generation Discovered the Beauty and Terror of Science*, HarperPress, 2009). Endorsing the case for porous thematics, the Barrs chose to illustrate their February 2009 blog post with what, since 2003, has been the most ubiquitous global image download available online: the freeze-frame splash of impact on a body of water, the ripples beginning to spread.

Marti Friedlander, *Ralph Hotere and Bill Culbert at Exhibition, Auckland Art Gallery, 19 May 1999* – black-and-white photographic print, 203 x 254 mm. E.H. McCormick Research Library, Auckland Art Gallery Toi o Tāmaki, on loan from the Gerrard and Marti Friedlander Charitable Trust, 2002. Courtesy Gerrard and Marti Friedlander Charitable Foundation.

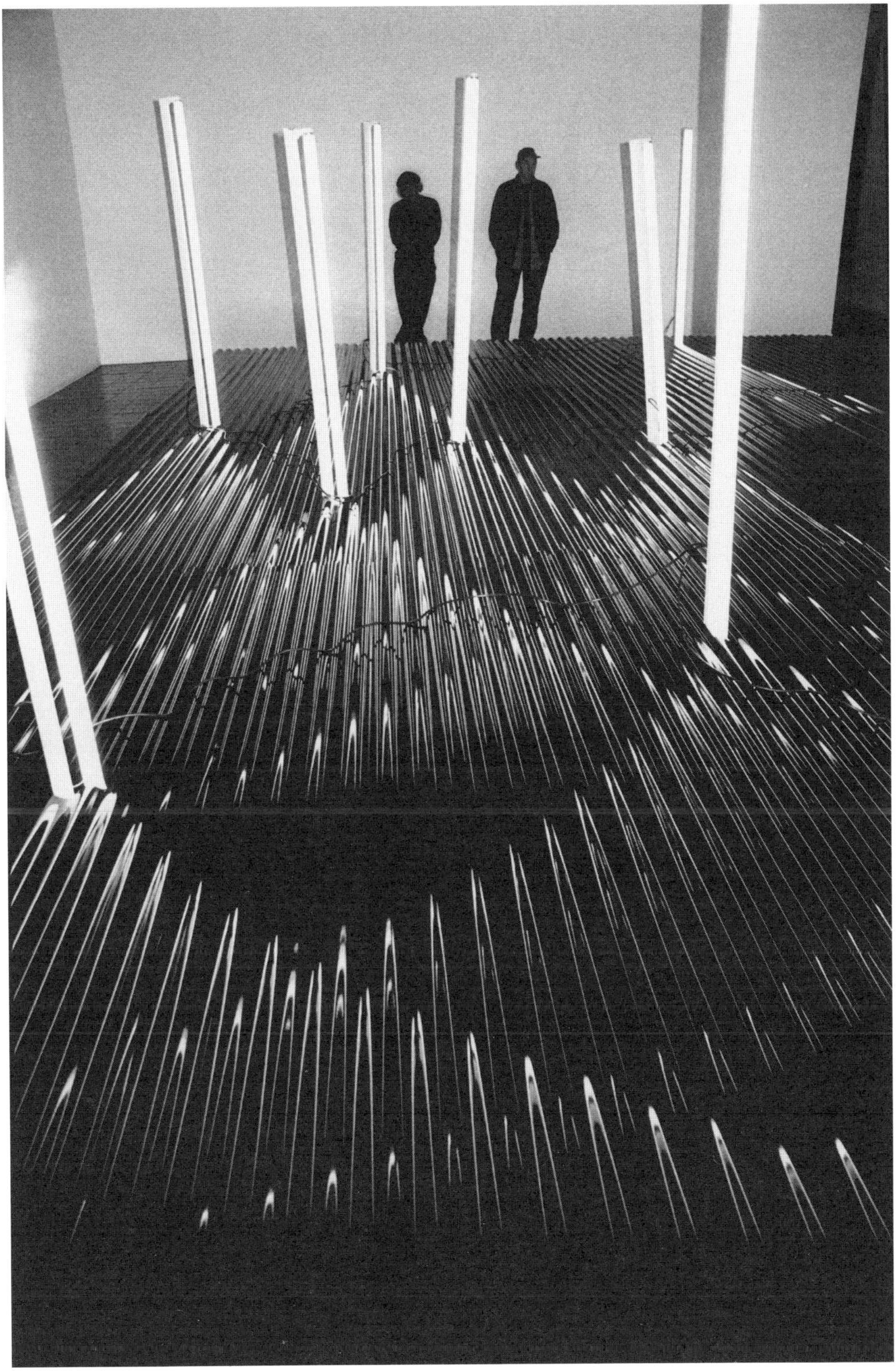

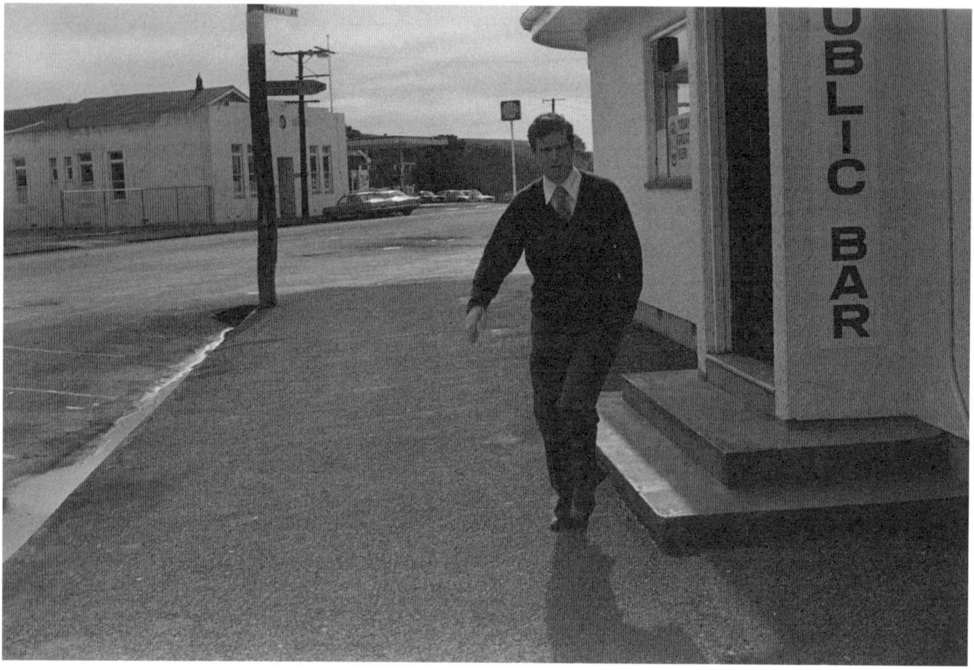

Lucien Rizos, *Eketāhuna*, 1979, in *A Man Walks Out of a Bar . . . Lucien Rizos: New Zealand Photographs, 1979–1982*. Rim Books & Photoforum.

A Man Walks Out of a Bar

Lucien Rizos

A Man Walks Out of a Bar . . . Lucien Rizos: New Zealand Photographs 1979–1982, edited by Damian Skinner (Rim Books & Photoforum) 2011)

1 Abduction

As Damian Skinner suggests in his essay in this book, the title of this portfolio immediately proposes a story: *A man walks out of a bar . . .* and then?

Even though the title of the photograph in question (*Eketāhuna*) is more succinct, offering merely the name of a small town passed through on a road trip, it inevitably attracts the kind of subheading that is this book's title; and the accumulation of a speculative narrative. The image is of a man stepping purposefully from a public bar into what (by the length of his shadow) must be early evening in (by his jersey) autumn or spring. He has been there for a few beers after work, probably. By his shirt and tie, knitted jersey but no jacket, and his black leather shoes, he looks like someone in small rural town business: a farm-supply dealership, real-estate, insurance, banking, or perhaps the owner-manager of a local store. The man looks to be in his early 30s, and he is approaching the photographer with a slightly querulous 'Who are you?' expression, not just because someone is 'taking his picture', as we say, as if describing a thief, but as if confronting a stranger – not something he expects to happen outside the public bar of his home pub, a place where nobody else ever stops unless they do so often, where he probably knows everyone by sight at least, and many by their first names.

And it's true, he doesn't know this photographer, who is also a violinist with the New Zealand Symphony Orchestra – who clearly has a purpose with his camera, but who incidentally may be passing through on tour, perhaps; who, in any case, might as well be an alien who has arrived in this weirdly depopulated Roswellian townscape. From the familiar, comforting, garrulous intimacy of the warm bar to this eerie visual chill . . . and this unexpectedly focused stranger . . .

And where was he intending to go, the man leaving the bar, before this abduction took place? Before he'd had time to adjust his senses to the chilly light, to recalibrate his reactions to 'stranger' so soon after being with 'mates'? He's even in motion across the strongly marked threshold from the bottom step of the public bar, which is itself transected by a division of theatrical light and intimate shadow. His right arm is swinging as a counterweight to the axis of his hips and left knee, but the whole story of his golfer's or rugby player's swivel towards *the next thing* has suddenly been arrested in his expression, whose purposefulness is now marred by doubt and even by a hint of incredulity. What is happening to him is not merely banal. The life he sanguinely expected to continue with after having his beer probably involved his family, who – the story pushing us towards its predictable consequences – will soon be wondering what has happened to him. Why didn't he come home? Since he always has? In the past?

This urge to narrative, to set off on a dreamy speculation about *what's happening here?* or *what next?* is irresistibly seductive, and as often as not we enjoy being seduced – we enjoy 'letting our minds wander', as we say, as if describing the kind of freewheeling imaginative *dérive* once advocated by Situationists, and by the American Beats (and the photographer Robert Frank) on their unscripted wanderings, as a way of disrupting the plod of habitual behaviour, and freeing the mind to see what routine blinds and binds us to.

But most of the images in this book seem at first to be setting off on familiar narrative journeys, towards the familiar tropes of life as it's lived. They are almost certainly indexed in some way to the photographer's own life, although this relationship remains inscrutable. What we see is that the photographs notice – but also remember – the relations between people, their camaraderie or dissociation, their loneliness or happiness, the stuff they may buy;

pervaded at first sight by a sense of *finity*, of time measured out in limited amounts and moving inevitably towards an end.

There are many groups and little thematic sequences in this book that support a sense of time-bound narrative. Even the objects or furnishings, such as the Woolmarked knitted cardigan in *Souvenir Shop – Christchurch*, or the furnishings of the *Television Lounge, White Hart Hotel – New Plymouth*, are as full of story as they are apparently empty of people – though the cardigan, or one like it, reappears with a man in it a page later in *Wairarapa* as if it, too, has been abducted. But we know from the appearances of these objects, the hang of the garment or the disposition of chairs in the empty TV lounge (one of which still seems to bear the imprint of a large arse), that we are never entirely distinct or separate from the objects through which we clad, furnish, fetishise and materialise our occupation of time; how we use objects to make ourselves 'at home' in the time we have or have pressed ourselves into; or how we fail to do that and end up homeless in time that seems to flow past and around us, bearing away all the meaning we seem unable to attach to the lives we know to be all too finite.

But there is always a catch with these photographs by Lucien Rizos, taken on photography road trips around the country, some of them with another photographer, Peter Black, and sometimes on tour with the orchestra. Despite their apparent momentum towards the tropes of 'life as it's lived', these images also stall at the very moment when the timescales of daily life want to co-opt us to their predictable measures. In part, this has something to do with the kind of arrested motion typified in the photograph of the man walking out of a bar – that swivel of purpose across the axis of the pub's bottom step, the one that marks clearly his passage into 'the light of day'. At first, the man's lifted left knee and swinging right arm seem to suggest the kind of arrested motion that became the Cartier-Bresson Leica generation's cliché of immediacy, and eventually the cul-de-sac of their 'decisive moment' approach to time and narrative.

But then, despite its articulation across poised moment and motion, the picture slows. It seems to be every bit as lugubrious as the imprint of an arse on the vinyl of the easy chair in the White Hart's TV lounge. Unlike the 'decisive moment' image, which traps the vividness of narrative in its timeless fragment (Cartier-Bresson's man leaping over a puddle behind the Gare St Lazare isn't going anywhere), the man walking out of a bar is merely held up or delayed by an intervention more glum than dramatic.

And it is in this hesitation or hold-up, this momentary and partial slowing that is the opposite of the dramatic or poetic *instantané*, that we, the viewers, have time to let our minds wander off, away from the lazy instant of the photograph, into the seductions of what else might be possible along the margins of ordinary life – some kind of abduction into the fantasies that boredom, routine and stasis might encourage anywhere, including a small town like Eketāhuna on a chilly evening in autumn, when the streets have been stripped of life as if by some catastrophe (but probably by more mundane calls on people's time).

It is these slow contradictions or tensions between narrative and visual meaning that can drive our receptions of the images into strange psychic territories, as the film critic Lesley Chow has noted of film. And indeed, there is something filmic in the way these images proceed, not quite stopping page by page, their interstices and links giving us time both to follow and to resist the plot. The photographs resist the motionlessness of discrete images allocated a double-page spread each (the format of Robert Frank's *The Americans*). They form and then subvert or collapse sequences, and this ambiguous resistance edges the still towards the moving image.

Recently, Rizos has been making videos of street musicians which turn this effect back in the other direction, since the 'moving images' of his videos are, without exception, single-frame, fixed position takes of their objects. It seems to be his instinct, if not his method, to subvert not just his own editing strategy but his entire conceptual intention. Or to subvert or even satirise our expectations of what, at first sight, in *A Man Walks Out of a Bar . . .* might look like a downbeat panegyric to 'real life', a kind of provincial Edward Steichen-like, humanist, 'family of man' portrait of the nation's heartland. Only, it is not that

– it is emphatically not that; that least of all.

A large territory opens up here, where story, location, time and image begin to tangle themselves in issues of history and what we most often call 'national identity', supposing that a collection of photographs taken on the road between 1979 and 1982 could somehow be that definitive (and of what, exactly?). But then, we know that even Robert Frank's *The Americans* of 1958, which this book quite clearly remembers well, was a kind of fiction; and, in its sometimes bitter tone, a reproof to the hubris of Steichen's 'family' and its often patronising texts. And anyway, I lose interest at the moment the story of a man walking out of a bar heads in this direction, towards the reunion of a kind of national family, or a generational portrait in the manner of Ans Westra or Marti Friedlander. This is not because I think such enquiries as theirs are uninteresting (they are interesting) – it is because I feel the tug of another kind of story.

2 Melancholy

I find myself needing to ask a strange question: where to locate the melancholy in these images – not all of which are sad? It is not enough to assert that they *are* melancholy. All that does is put an adjective next to my response to them. Rather, their pervasive sense of the melancholy stallings of time, and of fantasies and psychic disturbances opening up around these hesitations – this sense seems to gather at the intersections of certain effects and themes.

For example, melancholy is attracted to the points where repetitions or thematic clusters of images seem to stabilise time into sequence, only to break up and disperse across a reef-like irruption of nostalgia – the 'I remember that' moment lost just as it seems to be cohering into pattern. Or melancholy congeals where the experience of immediate, familiar or mundane time (*my* daily life) intersects with and disperses into the broad reaches of epochal themes known by historians as *longue durée*, and the desolate sense that there is nothing immediate, individual or specific, that everything has already always happened like this before and will always go on doing so. Or melancholy haunts the affect of alienation when, as I look at these images, I encounter the return gazes of people noticing a voyeur among them – but not me in the first instance, so the melancholy of estrangement is caused not by an encounter as such but by the intersection of an encounter (the photographer's) and my displacement from it.

These moments and others deserve the kind of close attention Rizos gives his 64 apparently casual images. This is not least because, individually and in their complex relations to time, sequence and story, they also intersect deliberately and knowledgeably with the practices and even sometimes (I'm supposing) with the specific images of two master photographers, Robert Frank and Henri Cartier-Bresson.

In the mid-1980s, Rizos shot a number of street portraits from the corner outside McDonald's in Courtenay Place – the *McDonald's Corner* portfolio. These blatantly hit-and-miss photographs were simultaneously homages to the decisive-moment strategy associated with Cartier-Bresson, and parodies of it. The parody was double-sided. It deflated the mystique of masterful sensibility – the impeccable instinct – associated with the *instantané*; and it wryly noted the melancholy provincial bathos of relocating that sensibility from the streets of Paris to the McDonald's corner in Wellington, New Zealand.

In 1986, Rizos staged an exhibition in Wellington called *My Relationship with the Old Masters*, which included fragments of collector advice on photographers including Boubat, Steichen, Arbus, Orkin and Adams. The critical instinct revealed in these works appeared in another exhibition, subsequently published as a spiral-bound book, with the title *My Relationship with Henri Cartier-Bresson* (Rizos inscribed my copy of this with the droll note, '. . . processing issues that C.B. and I had to resolve in our relationship, in order to move on . . .').

The key image in this affectionate but mordant suite of sketches, paintings and collages was one of Cartier-Bresson's best-loved photographs, *Rue Mouffetard, 1954*, the picture of a cheekily grinning small boy heading home with two large bottles of *vin ordinaire.* In one of Rizos's watercolour and China-white sketches of this photograph, a handwritten caption reads, 'I was walking along, minding my own business when, all of a sudden . . .' One of the final double-spread images in the book relocates the boy with wine bottles in the sculptor Giacometti's studio with what appears to be the sculptor's *Walking Man* of 1960 – the suggestion being that the boy has kept on walking into adulthood, but has nonetheless remained stuck to the ground of his modernist instant in history. The facing page, and the book's final image, consists of a dozen thumbnail images of the boy on Rue Mouffetard – suggesting that his *instant* was only ever a multiple-choice option, the product of an editing or film-processing decision as much as of a quasi-mystical gift of perception.

All of this is what also ambushes our encounter with the man walking out of a bar in Eketāhuna, New Zealand, on a chilly evening around 1979 – even though a strict chronology locates this photograph almost ten years before the *My Relationship with Henri Cartier-Bresson* project. After all, Rizos was certainly thinking about Cartier-Bresson and Frank long before making his droll homage in 1986. In any case, there is for me no way to avoid the possibility that the placement of the Eketāhuna man's walking legs, his exit from a bar, even the akimbo set of his arms and elbows (which could be holding bottles) are remembering the kid on Rue Mouffetard and relocating him in a suite of photographs that in turn reprocesses that decisive-moment tradition through the disenchantment of Robert Frank's *The Americans*.

And the impact of this haunting, which fills the deserted small town street with phantoms, is also a source of weird melancholy, because, although the man is where he is, and is who he is, he is also being abducted to an archive from which he will return changed, having surrendered part of his identity to the kind of directionless time the photograph trades in. *I was walking along, minding my own business, when all of a sudden . . .'*

'Hello, honey. I'm home.'

3 Close encounters

The trajectory of Cartier-Bresson's oeuvre, and his eventual disenchantment with photography, seem to have been determined as much by his leftist politics as by his travels. Thus, his *The Great Leap Forward, China, 1958* portfolio, one of the most sanguinely documentarist of his essays, contrasts with the satirical tone of his 1960 photo-essay, *Bankers Trust, New York.* A clear implication of this contrast is that Cartier-Bresson's agendas for photo-essays were predetermined to some extent by political ideology – they were not, or were not always, purely the products of 'the split-second recognition of a fact and the organisation of its forms'. This effect of predetermination became increasingly noticeable after the surreal vividness of his early work from the 1930s, most of which consisted of stand-alone images; and the harsh photographs taken during the 1940s in the immediate aftermath of World War II. Another obvious driver of the subsequent displacement of the instinctive instant by the programmed sequence was the requirement of photojournalism, mediated by Magnum, to generate coherent photo-narratives – sequences of images that would tell a story augmented by captions.

The rise of Magnum-style narrative photojournalism was clearly a conceptual driver of Steichen's *The Family of Man* project in 1955, with its overarching narrative of a human family united in the optimism of post-war democracy. Robert Frank was initially closely involved with developing Steichen's grand project, not least because of his association with networks of European photographers, but he left before the exhibition opened to enormous popular acclaim at the Museum of Modern Art in New York. His own vision, coloured by the experiences of growing up Jewish in neutral Switzerland during the Holocaust, was dark and disenchanted compared to Steichen's. What followed were the more than 20,000 exposures that became the astringently edited 83 photographs of *The Americans.*

In the deliberate randomness of its journeys across America, its begun but then subverted thematic sets of images, its interplay of still and filmic visual narratives, *The Americans* simultaneously deployed and subverted the dramatic strategies of decisive-moment photojournalism and what had become its comfortably extended form, the photo-essay. Frank's undercover camera was also a weapon against the American heartland's political and cultural conservatism, hidden as this was by the *Harper's Bazaar* or even *Life* magazine appetite for celebrities and newsworthy events. The central image of *The Americans* may well be the tuba-player at a political rally in Chicago, his face replaced by the blowhard bell of his instrument.

Nor did Frank want the gravitas of a Walker Evans stationed behind a tripod and commanding professional respect. Often set at a five- to six-foot focal range and concealed in his overcoat, Frank's Leica did not even perform like the optical prosthetic that was Cartier-Bresson's viewfinder. It was, rather, a covert instrument of cultural espionage, operating tangentially to an immediate eye–brain link, and no doubt subverting his own intentions from time to time. What he finally edited out of the succinct selection of the published works in *The Americans* may well have included much that was *intended*, whereas what was retained may often have been the product of chance occasioned by subterfuge – of the *dérive* not the schedule.

The knowledge of all this is evident in *A Man Walks Out of a Bar* . . . One of the effects of such literate artistic knowledge is, of course, to route an informed metropolitan conversation about some of the key, and often contending, strategies of pre-digital 20th-century photography through provincial, small-town narratives. Robert Frank did something very similar in 1950s America – and, like Rizos 20 years later in New Zealand, without either patronising the objects of his photographs or risking the hubris of sentimental heartlandism.

It is worth remembering that Rizos, though a photographer first and foremost, is also a symphony orchestra violinist who tours regularly and performs to audiences the length and breadth of the country, in small towns and rural communities as well as in the regional cities. The photographic expeditions that accumulated in the portfolio *A Man Walks Out of a Bar* . . . were therefore occasionally complemented along the criss-crossing and democratising grids of the symphony orchestra's independent programme and schedule, which effectively may have contributed to randomising the sequences and innate coherence of any supposed journey specifically centred on taking photographs. One might even imagine the traces of a soundtrack under some sequences – I do – though the fragments of radio play-lists muffled by motel walls or crackling in and out of range on the car radio are perhaps more likely. In any case, we may suppose that Rizos took photographs because he was moved by the fleeting glimpses of human relationship, domicile and material culture that passed the car or the tour bus window or were visible from the window of a small-town hotel; because what he objectively saw with the camera subjectively indexed memories of his own life, including its soundtracks, so to speak – or because he found himself randomly looking at such a view as that from the hotel, and being reminded of another photographic image, so that a kind of doubling took place, something like a visual chord.

Thus, the image *View from Hotel Balcony, Hawera* recalls the Frank image *View from Motel Window, Butte, Montana, 1956,* not just because it is a view of any small town from a hotel window, but because the image has a kind of cross-grained iconic redolence. In the case of Frank's photograph, the grim coal-mining townscape with its Bill Brandt-ish lighting and desolate streets answers back to a 1950s post-war America emerging from a memory of labour as depression into an era of labour as prosperity; other icons rubbed the wrong way by Frank included the cowboy, the greasy-spoon diner, the film star, the open road, the automobile, teen romance . . . and many more.

In Rizos's hotel balcony photograph of Hawera, desultory traffic cruises a main street empty of people but presided over by the signage of The Farmers' Co-op. The storefront's dark windows hardly open onto optimistic pastoral vistas, and the cars cruising the street seem to be doing the work of keeping people from one another while going nowhere. The iconic clichés of small-town community and farming prosperity are nowhere to be seen – but we sense them as absences or unfulfilled desires, as negative icons.

Elsewhere in the portfolio, such iconic desires appear more gently and even wistfully, as transitions, improvisations, or shifts in tone rather than as counterarguments or absences. Effects involving the repositioning of points of view (or timbre), speed (or tempo), and narrative (or melody) begin to appear. They seem to be *audible* as well as visible. A *Display Window* in Waverley exhibits photographs of three generations of mothers holding their baby daughters. This at-one-remove image of historical mother–daughter photographs is followed by a street scene in *Stratford* in which what might be a grandmother and mother are walking with small children in pushchairs. Then, a grim-faced man alone in *Dunedin*, who seems to be looking across the page in the direction of the next photograph, in which someone who resembles him is walking out of the page with a woman; they seem to be ignoring each other and are facing the point of view of the photographer. Next, in *Foxton*, a young man and woman are talking intensely across the axis of that point of view. In *Napier*, a middle-aged man and a woman are ignoring each other in the back and front seats of a car; both are facing forward across the camera's axis, although the man seems to have just noticed the photographer and has begun to swivel in that direction. At *Sumner Beach, Christchurch*, a young man and woman are cuddling happily on some concrete steps, oblivious to the photographer; at the *Agricultural & Pastoral Showgrounds, Gisborne*, a man who resembles the one in the previous photograph is lying on the grass next to a woman, with a small boy clinging to his back; a roll of barrier mesh seems to have been rolled back to accommodate this intimate view of them. In *Christchurch* a woman walks with three children towards the photographer. In a *Front Yard, Christchurch*, a man is playing with two small girls who have their backs to the photographer. Four people are squashed into a car in *Sunday Afternoon, Kapiti Coast.* A single man strides out through a garden gate in *Dunedin.* Another man stands by himself outside a house in *Huntly*, looking to his left across the axis of the viewpoint and in the direction the photographer is travelling away from him.

At one level, these images are experienced as desultory variations on iconic themes of relationship – as a kind of hesitant, interrupted narrative shifted through cross-grained perspectives and points of view along or across the axis of the camera's viewfinder. In this, they are textual or even dialogic – they seduce us into 'making up stories', as indeed I was seduced when I began with the image of the man walking out of a bar in Eketāhuna.

But at another level, these variations and improvisations have (dare I say) a musical structure. It would be foolish to assume that, just because the photographer Rizos is also a musician, his approaches to photography will involve 'musical structure'. Yet the best analogy I can find for a sequence like the one described above is of a riff or chord sequence, in which a core chromatic set is sustained through a sequence of tonal shifts. This impression is enhanced by the sense of time and movement in the photographs – not just within those whose objects are sighted from the speeding window of a car or bus, where a foreground blur or a tilt of perspective tell us we are moving; but in the page-by-page sense of time passing and distances traversed.

And in either case, whether the camera is speeding past its object, or whether time and distance are being traversed page by page, we as viewers remain in the one place. We are motionlessly attending to a performance predicated absolutely on objects passing in sequences, on time both passing and retarded as the pages of this score are turned; and predicated also on recognitions, on the knowledge and familiarity that allows us to understand variations on themes and conventions because we remember something like the melody. We can almost sing along to this travelling visual radio as it picks up the regional stations on its journey.

In this respect, the composition of photographs is not textual at all, or less so. Rather than being seduced into storytelling, into the kind if diurnal or everyday time into which stories fit easily, we are taken up with abstract narrative structures whose meanings are thematic not factual, general not specific, tonal not material. They are dialogic not in the sense of speaking to us and each other, but in the sense of wordlessly addressing known and remembered forms. The time of such abstractions is not the everyday time of stories, but the *longue durée* of historical themes sweeping past and leaving behind the detailed instances of human life hesitating in these photographs – hesitations and inconclusions that are momentarily glimpsed only as they fade into abstraction.

This is the achievement of *A Man Walks Out of a Bar . . .* : to orchestrate and momentarily hold on to the vulnerable fragments of human life lived across small increments of finite time and almost cohering into stories we can understand – to *arrange* these familiar desires within a larger, abstract time and space which, though we have heard something like it before, seems to be beyond us and to be always going beyond us.

I Loved You the Moment I Saw You

Peter Black

I loved you the moment I saw you (Victoria University Press, 2011)

Since I moved to Wellington in 1975, almost everything I've written has had a template of one kind or another in this place – the houses I've lived in, the well-worn yet recursively habitual tracks around town, to the post office, through Courtenay Place, Unity Books, the Vietnamese noodle shop on Vivian Street, around Oriental Bay, Moore Wilson's produce, Regional Wines by the Basin Reserve, and so on – routes that are also neural networks or rhizomatic thought-tracks so familiar on a daily basis that I could pretty much walk them at random with my eyes shut. Which, in a sense, I do, as often as not – like anyone else. That partial sightlessness becomes the default state of the habitual urban nomad, the introspective flâneur, walking around as if blind to everything but the thoughts or tasks or wishes that occupy the idling mind and are projected there on a screen whose reflexive surface is half turned away from the familiar world outside; or half blind and deaf to anything but the inner narrative that mutters and blinks there in the mind, where language and image are shiftily overriding each other – marking time until I get back to the room I work in, where a familiar disposition of bookshelves, the askance view down across the garden to the neighbour's back yard (which I don't see, because I'm looking at and listening to something mental in-between typing) are what fix me in the place of imagination. That this place of imagination is also situated has to be relearned or acknowledged anew from time to time; or I have to be startled into that acknowledgement somehow.

Peter Black's photographs, especially those taken on his own habitual tracks around Wellington, are startling in this way. How often in *I loved you the moment I saw you* we encounter an image that is simultaneously a vivid aperçu and a startled, misaligned framing of it – waist-height views that have both noticed people and chopped their heads and feet off, a gesticulating hand inside the refractive light-maze of a café window, the nomad-camera's gaze tilted up to notice a single individual looking down from a row of industrial windows, an anguished face snatched into perception from a passing van. The strategy of these photographs is to deterritorialise their objects at the same time as situating them along the habitual tracks of the nomad-viewer.

If there is indeed a correlation or mirroring between rhizomatic neural networks and the habitual mapping of an environment, then Peter's photographs of Wellington have the effect on me of lighting up that connection. This is not just a matter of recognition – or re-cognition, to give the effect a more startling quality – but of intensity, alerting, switch-throwing. Though they reward careful looking, these are not immediately contemplative images. Rather, they are adrenalin shots to my somnolent awareness. Their thoughtfulness follows. They put me back in my place; they wake me up to it; their depth begins with awareness.

For 30 years or so there's been a Wellington nexus in the narratives I've been writing, in which that mis-sighted world of imagination has brought together vividly layered memories of place and contrapuntal encounters in the present. Most recently, that narrative has been a screenplay set in and around what Courtenay Place might be like in 2090. This narrative workplace is in effect an archaeological wiring diagram upon which layers of memory are superimposed along with imagined futures – a surface at once refractive and transparent, a shifty and shifting reality of fragments, familiar and uncanny. That view of the future is possible because I already have a layered one to the past; the present is a kind of prism between them.

What is the time of the still image? Like the plate-glass windows in many of Peter's photographs of the city, still-image time is a multi-layered laminate that simultaneously contains (and preserves) the moment of the exposure, represents that moment's anachronism, reflects the situation and point of view of the photographer, implies or partially reveals a story or sequence of events continuing through time, and – because all photographs become retrospective a nano-second after they've been taken – is or metonymises a memory. The individual still image may also be situated in a thematic sequence of images, and so contains within itself the trace or potential of a larger physical time, which is both the cumulative time of the thematic sequence, and the time it takes to turn the pages of a book, click through an on-screen file, or walk the length of a gallery wall.

One of Peter's best-known portfolios was called *Moving Pictures*. This was and wasn't a pun – it was a riff on 'movies' and 'moving image' (as well, perhaps, as on 'moving' as in emotional) and it was also a deadpan taxonomy of still photographs often taken from the window of a moving car. The images in *I loved you the moment I saw you* have embodied that pun-that-isn't. Each one is a 'frame'. Frames are stitched together in varieties of thematic and narrative sequences. The whole portfolio describes a narrative arc – or circuit perhaps, since it seems to end close to where it began, with the image of a man at a pedestrian crossing with a baby in an infant car seat. And yet the sense of complex time in these new photographs isn't primarily produced by the linear effects of sequential themes or narratives. Such linear time – the time of 'moving images' – is shallow compared to the laminated layers of time in Peter's discrete photographs. When these complex laminates are then placed in 'moving' sequences, for example on the turning pages of a book, the effect is of a time-flow slowed by its very thickness, its glassy viscosity; by its thoughtfulness.

Again, we encounter the dynamic paradox that animates and even articulates Peter's photographs: the play of awakened and even startled awareness – an acceleration or excitement – with a slowing and deepening of attention.

This is also, emphatically, digital time. The sharpness, depth of field, colour-and-light complexity, translucence, heterogeneity and multiplicity of many of these images create a moment – 'the moment I saw you' – beyond the scope of a more unitary, homogenous analogue time. Though Peter's black-and-white analogue photographs were often complex in respect of their wry detail, and subtle in respect of their print tones, they don't approach the vivid complexity of his most recent digital colour work. And though this complexity may, at first glance, appear to reside in highly defined and sharply focused layerings of light, colour and surface, it is fundamentally about the time-frames and time-depths of the photographs.

The visual narrative of a screenplay differs from my more customary writing practice. I notice this difference not so much because of its obvious craft requirements, but because, instead of my lips moving to the silent mutter of drafting words, my eyelids flutter at a mental shuttering of imagined images, and my gaze drifts upwards and often to the left, looking and thinking inwardly. When I shift to the registers of language, my gaze drifts downwards under a frown of concentration. These simple mechanics of cognition and visualisation translate into equally simple diagrams of points of view. A photograph may mirror or seek to reproduce these, as may the conventions of representation associated with art. Where is the surface of the picture? What are the effects and purposes of perspectival strategies such as repoussoir? What is the plane of exchange between the picture and the viewer? What is depth? Where is the narrative junction at which image mutates into language, and vice versa? What is the indexical ratio of inside to outside, image to world? Why are we being manoeuvred into looking down (or up) – what are the power relations of the view, its strategies for sublimity? What is the agency of the picture – what kind of society does it network; what kind of viewer socius, and what kind of viewed public? How does (or doesn't) it link these constituencies?

All these familiar questions are reflections or articulations of physical actions and effects. The picture is where effects and affects mesh: the eye-movements and perceptions of the photographer or artist are as much in the picture as the picture's object, whose awareness of being photographed is also an effect – and a subject – in the picture. The picture becomes simultaneously an imaginative construct, the site of emotions, an indexical object, and an archive of mechanical and physiological actions. As well as reproducing the world in some way, and recording (or inviting) emotional responses to it, the picture reproduces the cognitive postures of the artist; and it persuades the viewer to adopt (or react to) those postures. These are what the viewer is responding to, as much as to what the image documents; they also constitute the picture's meaning. And it's the physiological difference between writing images (as in a screenplay) and writing words (as now) that has recently startled me back into acknowledging the situation of my perceptions.

But, more particularly, it has been looking at the photographs in *I loved you the moment I saw you* that has alerted me to this: to the different ways in which perception is situated, and to the laminated or layered times it takes to take that in – to be moved, to be in love, in 'the moment'.

For ten years or so, every day began for me with a walk or run with our dog Vincent up around the slopes of Mount Victoria – inevitably the same route or a slight variation on it. Dogs are creatures of habit and I was happy to comply. The dog's and my perceptions and timing fused in some way – a rhythm of movement that was not entirely my own conducted what I saw, heard and smelled. I looked down at the familiar topography of the city through the filters of senses whose vividness had been reprogrammed briefly away from thoughts of work or the inner screenings of imagination: the colours I saw below me were, for a time, like the chromatic codes of scents, or of information diverted through a warping lens of some kind. Even after Vincent's death, I sometimes feel those filters coming into play as I walk above the abstract social pattern of the city below me; a synaesthesia that seems about to exit the realm of metaphor ('loud colour') and claim a physiological truth. Though Peter's colour photographs are complex visual constructs, I feel them warping my sensory habits into a kind of synaesthesia, as though I'm perceiving the familiar world in the company of a commanding but sympathetic cognitive change-agent.

In the 1970s, early in my time in Wellington, I worked as a postie for six years with routes around the southern suburbs and the Cook Strait coast. This was a suburban environment, and different from the city one I now criss-cross daily along familiar paths; but its six-days-a-week repetitions, and the automaton-like perceptions those engendered, where habit might be shocked to attention only by a rushing dog, also shaped the flâneur-like habits I have now. I'm used to walking around on a kind of perceptual automatic pilot. When walking the dog, it was a kind of cross-species sensory recalibration that made what was familiar vivid again. When delivering the mail, it was the extreme repetition, letterbox after letterbox, that shut alertness down.

How to put the dog back into the jaded habits of the flâneur? It's surely no accident – or at least a happy coincidence – that two of Peter's previous books, *White Horse Black Dog* and *Real Fiction*, have photographs of dogs on their covers. These are the human race's most ubiquitous companions; sometimes they are even our 'seeing eyes'; our perceptions and theirs, though mysteriously different, are joined at a cognitive hip. On the cover of *White Horse Black Dog*, the animal has thrust its primary sense organ, its nose, as close as possible to the device that is staring at it, the camera, whose gaze it meets with its own non-visual scrutiny or challenge. The dog's large, moist nostrils resemble eyes; one gleams, while the other seems dilated by the adrenalin of perception. Set back, like a secondary organ, is a small, demented eye, glaring with a kind of desperate subaltern effort; the nose has it. What this image, long one of my favourites in Peter's oeuvre, seems to be proposing is a radical rewiring or even dehierarchicalising of our responses – an alternative perceptual set, quite seductive and pleasant, congenial rather than disturbing.

On the cover of *Real Fiction* another dog, more aggressive than curious this time, appears as a cross between itself and its shadow, its bark seeming to appear as a single blazing, tooth-like flash of light within its open jaws. The plane of the photograph is deeply ambiguous: what must be the ground on which the dog is standing seems to tilt almost vertically; the dog (or its shadow) seem not so much to be standing on this ground as projected against it; and what seems to be the object of the animal's aggression, the shadow of a cruciform structure, presents the illusion of occupying the same two-dimensional plane as the dog, as if we were watching a shadow-puppet screen with only minimal distinctions between silhouette and depth. What the image seems to be proposing is a deranged view of the world, in which reprogrammed perspectives, planes, shadows and solids are wrenching our cognitive faculties into new modes of reception. Our bewilderment or disorientation might resemble the dog's; like it, disturbed and angry, we end up barking at shadows. Or like an earlier dog, the German shepherd looking out the rear window of a car at night in *Dog and Mercedes Benz* from the 1982 portfolio *Fifty Photographs*, all our senses seem to have been trapped and reprogrammed as if by the action of photography: the dog's eyes blinded, its muzzle blurring into foggy out-of-focus, its ear-pricked hearing blocked by two car stereo speakers.

The photographs in *I loved you the moment I saw you* have put the dog back in the over-habituated perceptions of the urban nomad. They bring about a derangement of senses, sometimes amiable and pleasant, sometimes making our hackles rise in fear and anger. It's not clear whether this effect is what Peter has intended should happen to us; whether it's what has happened to him; or whether (as I prefer to think) the photograph is the agent that has linked – networked – these two options in a fluid transactional space in which subject, object and spectator move in and out of each other.

This portfolio by Peter is not his first departure from the black-and-white works for which he's known and esteemed – *Made in New Zealand* (1984), *Outskirts* (2008) and the ongoing investigations of *New Colour* (2009) are strikingly coherent in their own right. But *I loved you* may be the substantial body of work that establishes Peter's carefully developed mastery of the complexity and richness of digital colour, and of the printing technologies that have grown with the medium.

The title of this new portfolio of colour photographs contains a number of clues to how he looked at what he photographed, and how we might look at the photographs he took. The title of the portfolio is an almost-correct quote of the well-known line of the George Harrison song 'For You Blue', on the B-side of the Beatles' 'Long and

Winding Road' and the 11th track on their final album, *Let It Be*. But Harrison wrote 'I loved you from the moment I saw you', which suggests a whole different focus from Peter's.

Nothing is as accidental as it may first seem in a photograph by Peter; nor, I believe, is his slight adjustment to the Harrison lyric. To say you loved someone or something from the moment you saw them puts that moment in the past and the viewer in a present that is joined to the past by continuous love over linear time. But this sentimental trajectory snaps tight in Peter's rewrite, and in his photographs. Each photograph is distinctly in its now – the attention, the emotion, the object, the photographer, utterly and sometimes painfully present, however complex the layerings of time may be in that present. The attention of each photograph is minutely observant of details, though these are not the products of a Cartier-Bresson-type *instantané* or 'decisive moment': though their impact may be startling, the detail of Peter's photographs is dense and thoughtful, and coheres into themes over the course of the portfolio. What he makes into a photograph seems to consist as much of his own intensely compacted thought and observation as of an intuitively noticed event. The photograph's mass, if you like, its density of thought, detail, emotion and thematic, slows it down, giving the present in which Peter loves what he sees an unmistakable gravity.

Not that these images lack humour. They are full of it, but it's wry and disenchanted; the love, as we have already noticed in Peter's adjustment to the Harrison lyric, is unsentimental; and the grief and sometimes anger that we sense around images of suffering or deprivation are never patronising. Even the satirical bite that marks some images of privilege or self-satisfaction is without rancour. This emotional maturity or equanimity is won against the sometimes hectic grain of the images – the complexity of their detail, their fervent colour, their narrative ambiguity and richness, their tricky surfaces. This is a paradox of sorts – emotional coherence persisting through a compounding turbulence of successive, vividly present moments.

A list of what emerges as paradoxical from Black's moments of seeing and loving will include the following: the surreal absurdity of the real; the patterned choreography of random chaos; the surface of depth – and, reflectively, the depth of surface; the incoherence of informative signage – and, conversely, the strange coherence of meaninglessly aggregated signs; the humour of gloom; the cheerlessness of a colourful world; the dignity of sad people; the clownishness of serious people.

Above all, perhaps, a sense of paradox surrounds the pervasive loneliness in these images. Among the many themes that can be found in this portfolio, loneliness may be the most prevalent. Yet it nearly always manifests itself in a vividly social environment, without the conventional props of desolation or alienation, in bustling streets, busy eateries, or places densely layered with social commodities – fashion-ware, jewellery, entertainment. What happens in these situations is a kind of random switch: the lonely individual appears self-sufficient and without need of the supports on offer; and the congenial environment takes on a melancholy, almost beseeching appearance, as if it's trying too hard to maintain a cheerful, gregarious expression. It's an expression we soon see through, not least when turning the pages of *I loved you the moment I saw you*.

In the first photograph of *I loved you the moment I saw you*, a man, perhaps a grandfather by his cautious stoop and wrinkled hand, is just putting down or is about to pick up a baby in a portable infant car seat. The baby's eyes are barely open, as if it's just at that very moment waking up and seeing the grandfather. They are at a pedestrian crossing – a potentially dangerous place, though there are no passing cars in view, and the man's gesture seems appropriately careful and solicitous. In the final, 82nd image of the portfolio, the man has picked the infant car seat up, a car is rushing past close to them, and the baby's eyes are fully open, looking up at the grandfather.

Time has passed between these two images – the time of 80 perceptions. In the blink of an eye, in the time it has taken for the baby to wake up and see (love) its grandfather, the time it has taken for him to pick the baby up and for a car to speed past them, we have criss-crossed the entire city along routes marked out by unique, random perceptions and by subtly choreographed threads and themes. The slicing hand gesture of a young woman in a graduation-day tableau is followed by the outstretched hand signal of a little girl in a fluffy pink coat that might almost be parodying academic dress, and this by the hand-to-face gesture of a well-dressed man talking on a cellphone at a café, this by the sad image of a man clutching his face in a passing van. The red interior of a busker's trumpet case segues into the red door of the up-market Logan Brown restaurant about to be entered by two men in suits, this to the shining red of an expensive sports car being admired by two men, this to the red-highlighted interior of a Burger King restaurant where a single man is stirring his coffee, and this to the red Santa hat of another busker preparing to play his banjo. Across the organised grain of such curated or narrativised images drift other themes and storylines, some to do with content, others with perception – privilege and underprivilege, the body-languages of power and abjection, street people, brown paper bag drinkers, the strut and pomp of businessmen in suits, the affectionate gestures of friends and lovers, the isolation of individuals; the shattered compositions of reflections, the emotional focus-pulls of perspective, planar switches between lateral and frontal. The apparent randomness of this nomadic wander through the streets of the city coheres over and over again into narrative meaning, sometimes by theme, sometimes by colour, sometimes by cohesive sequences of light and refraction, often by all of these at once.

Of course this is the product of the photographer's homogenising decisions about order and sequence, as also of his editing decisions – we know or intuit that much has been left out. But the rigour of this organising and composing discipline doesn't contradict the larger heterogeneous truth of *I loved you the moment I saw you* – that the moment of love, that perceptual blink of an eye, contains a multiplicity of instances, a compacted shuttering of times, a derangement of senses and perceptions, a fluid network of narratives: a world at once anarchic and disordered, and full of meaning; or perhaps a world that is disordered and therefore full of meaning.

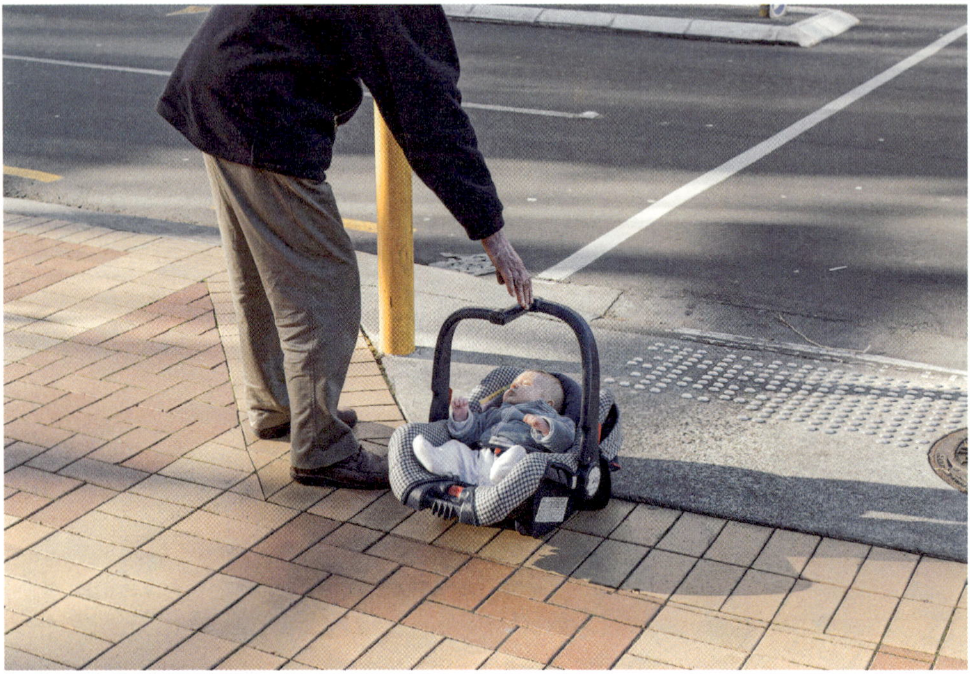

Peter Black, *Taranaki Street, Wellington, 2009 (1 and 2)* – in *I loved you the moment I saw you*, Victoria University Press, 2011. Courtesy of the artist.

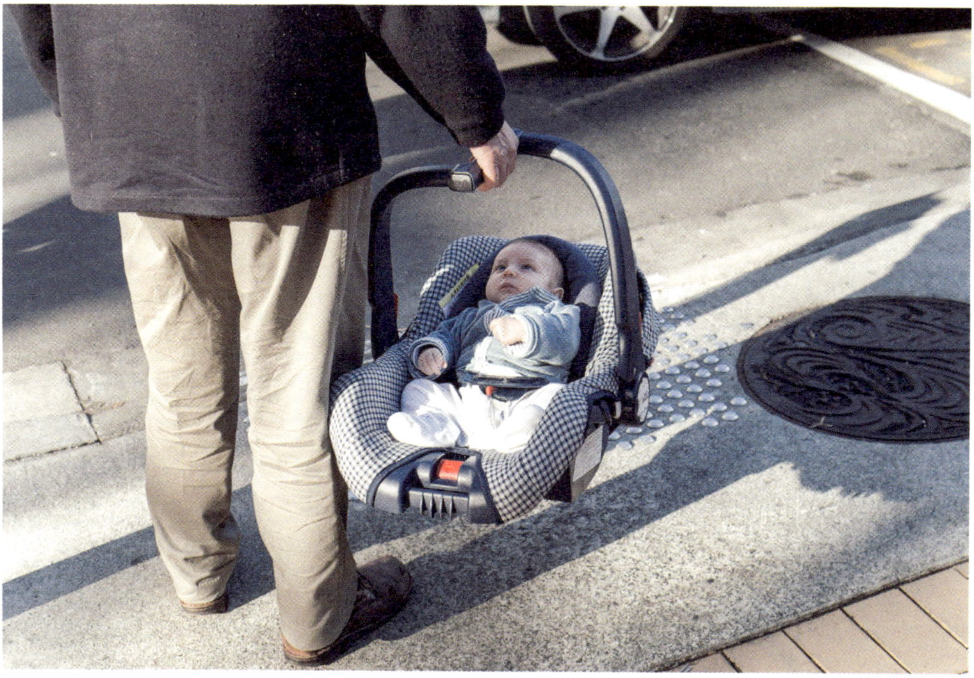

Ralph Hotere's *Godwit/Kuaka*

Auckland International Airport mural, 1977

Talk at Auckland Art Gallery, 16 October 2011

This extraordinary work asks the viewer to walk its length and was once the mural at Auckland International Airport. For many years it welcomed people arriving. It was also known to be where customs officials would detain those they thought looked a bit dodgy. The writer Martin Edmond recalls being made to wait by the mural on a couple of occasions.

Thanks to the foresight and generosity of Rob and Sue Gardiner and the Chartwell Collection, the mural can now welcome people dodgy or not to Auckland Art Gallery – for a while, at least.

I met Ralph Hotere in 1972 when I went to live in Port Chalmers out of Dunedin. He was beginning to work on the *Requiem* series, which combined varieties of prepared lacquer surfaces overlaid with fine pinstripes of colour. One of Ralph's mates out at Port Chalmers – a neighbour I think and a fellow drinker at the Port Chalmers pub – was a car painter with a workshop down on the wharf. He laid the fine spray-painted initial lacquers on the surfaces Ralph was preparing to work on. Ralph's esteem for skilled craftsmen was well known, and some were key collaborators in his work. My wife Donna's nephew Jason has a car-painting business out at Mosgiel and he too has had dealings with Ralph.

I remember Ralph laying down the long lines or pinstripes of fine colour on the lacquered panels, in his studio on Signal Hill overlooking the Back Beach at Port Chalmers. The radio would always be tuned to the Concert Programme, and Ralph would be working listening to the day's programme of classical music. The *Requiem* series was motivated by the death of Martin Luther King, who died in 1968, but more immediately by the New Zealand composer Anthony Watson, a close friend of Hotere's, who died in March 1973.

Two visual components seemed to be coming together in these *Requiem* paintings and in the numerous watercolour and ink drawings that Hotere made in preparing them.

One, stated plainly in the title *Requiem*, refers to the Catholic mass for the dead, and the sombre black ground of the painting's central panels recalled this.

The other component relates to musical settings of what are known as the *propers* of the requiem mass – compositions that are also known as requiems. The well-known lines usually sung include the Latin *Requiem aeternam dona eis, Domine* – 'Grant them eternal rest, O Lord'. One of Ralph's favourite compositions is Mozart's *Requiem Mass in D Minor,* itself a kind of requiem for Mozart himself, since he died before he could complete it. Another favourite is Verdi's *Messa da Requiem.*

Against the dark grounds of his *Requiem* paintings, which suggested the solemnity of the requiem mass, Ralph seemed to be invoking a kind of synaesthesia, a finely tuned evocation in colour and vertical line of the sounds of music. The chromatics of colour and those of music combined in these exquisitely taut, delicate lines. This basic abstract structure was sometimes complemented by words.

Godwit/Kuaka isn't a requiem – that would be a bit alarming as the key message for arriving and departing passengers. But the work is complex and does retain some of the sombreness of the *Requiem* series. The emotions of departure and arrival are themselves complex.

As you will know when you go on to a marae, the welcome also contains powerful reminders of those who have died – who have left to travel beyond the world of the living, and who have also returned to the whenua, to the place from which they first arrived in the world. So there are possible complexities in the way the mural addresses us as arriving and departing passengers. For a start, you can't arrive anywhere without having departed from somewhere else.

The poetics of arriving and departing is in itself complex, and transposed to a visual medium raises a number of questions about the direction we're looking in, what is the nature of the welcome we're receiving, where exactly are we arriving, and so on. Most of those arriving would have walked fairly obliviously past the mural, or would have taken in its immediately obvious elements (the symmetry of three central panels flanked by six on either side, the verticality of the lines and the horizontal progression of the colour, the three dark central panels with circles, and so on).

But in order to find the narrative and other complexities in the mural you have to go slow, look closely, and think about the work in relation to welcoming and farewelling, remembrance of dead, and the significance of the language incorporated in the painting.

Here I'm indebted to the marvellous research done by Kriselle Baker, whose thesis work on Ralph Hotere includes a substantial reading of the *Godwit/Kuaka* mural.

If you look closely at the first three panels of the mural, you'll discern the text 'Hau mai, Tau mai, Nau mai' – 'Enter here, Rest here, You are welcome here'. These formal words of welcome invite you into the mural as if on to a marae, or as if into the speaker's place of hospitality. They tell you that the way to proceed is from left to right, and to do so while paying attention to what's partially hidden. But, as Baker points out, you also have to look at the work from a suitable distance – far enough away to take in its overall plan, its spatial and social geography if you like.

It's not entirely fanciful to suggest that this strategy of demanding both the long view and the close inspection, the latter following a kind of welcoming route or flight-path, hints at the arrival or approach of the godwit, the mural's international visitor. A close surface viewing of the panels reveals scumbled patterns and textures like those in Hotere's ten-panelled corrugated-iron work *Aramoana* (1982) – surfaces that, without being literal, resemble a coarse mineral grain, like that of a beach. The migrating bird is invited to 'enter here', 'settle here', and told 'welcome here'.

The phrase 'hau mai' (enter here) also contains the meaning of 'hau' as wind or air – even perhaps as breath. 'Hau' appears often in mōteatea referring to the way in which the wind brings visitors to these shores, connecting this place to that and people here to people there. The word also conveys the deeper meaning of breath-of-life.

These words of welcome are complemented by the words that appear in the final verse in the text of the central panels. 'Tau atu, Tau atu, Kua tau mai', which translates as 'it [the godwit] has settled over there, it has settled over there, it has settled here'. These simple words with their complex loadings and cross-references, their combinations of welcoming and grieving, of course recall the karanga, that emotional welcome to the marae that combines the call of hospitality and protection with an outpouring of grief – a requiem – for those who have gone before.

The mural contains a karanga that both welcomes us (and international arrivals at Auckland airport) to this place, as if we were migrating godwits coming in to settle, seeing the place first from a distance, and then from close enough to make out the detail of its places of safety. But the welcome is also to a narrative. The narrative, condensed in the poetry of the central three panels, has four elements.

After the welcome, which is extended both to those arriving at Auckland International Airport and to the migrating godwits, we encounter the godwit's migration; a tribal story of Te Aupōuri, Ralph's iwi, involving their escape from danger; and the belief that the godwit's flight represents the spirit's journey after death.

The central three panels contain the text of what could be described as a tauparapara, the chant used to introduce whaikōrero or a speech on the marae. Tauparapara can also mean a canoe chant, and thus, often, an aid to navigation; it is sometimes referred to as a ngeri or challenge. The complete text of the linked verses, thought of as an aid to navigation, goes like this:

On panels one to three:
Hau mai, tau mai, nau mai – enter here, settle here, welcome here.

On panels seven, eight and nine:
Ruia ruia, opea opea, tahia tahia – scattering scattering; gathering gathering; forming a single line.

> This describes the settling activity of the godwits but also the idea of plaiting a flax rope with one hand moving over the other – a possible reference to a story of Aupōuri evading capture by enemies.
>
> On panel seven:
> Kia hemo ake, ko te kākā koakoa, kia herea mai, te kāwai korokī – death rises up (the birds rise up in fright – a reference to the escape story); it is the rope, the cry of the bird koakoa; binding you all to me here; the chattering of the flock. Again, the behaviour of the flock of godwits on a sandbank is described, but also the escape of Te Aupōuri, and – in the word 'kāwai' – the sense of reciting whakapapa, as if the cries of the godwits are a recitation of tribal history.
>
> On panel eight:
> Kia tātata mai; i roto i tana; pūkorokoro whaikaro; he kuaka; he kuaka mārangaranga – come close together; the cry of the godwit from its throat, a war party; a godwit; a godwit that hovers. This verse tells of the need to gather together for protection, the cry of the godwit as a warning, and the flight of the godwit as representing the spirit's journey.
>
> On panel nine:
> Tau atu, tau atu, kua tau mai – it has settled over there; it has settled over there; they have settled here.

Taken together, these texts and their visual grounds constitute a complex interweaving of narrative strands, like a plaited rope of flax.

Hotere has often used this motif of birds in association with poetry. A well-known example, mentioned by Kriselle Baker and installed absolutely beautifully at the Dunedin Public Art Gallery, is the great collaboration with Bill Culbert, *Pathway to the Sea – Aramoana*.

In the suite of lithographs Hotere and Culbert prepared from working drawings towards the *Pathway*, there are frequent references to the flights of birds. In one lithograph Hotere listed some 40 or more birds by their Māori and English names. He's also referred to a poem associated with his father, 'Te Tangi o te Pīpīwharauroa' – 'The Song of the Shining Cuckoo'.

Always, the voices of these birds are at once welcoming us and reminding us of the migrations we make, including the final one, that of the spirit after death. The *Godwit/Kuaka* mural is, in a sense, our equivalent of Verdi's *Requiem*, turned also in the direction of a welcome.

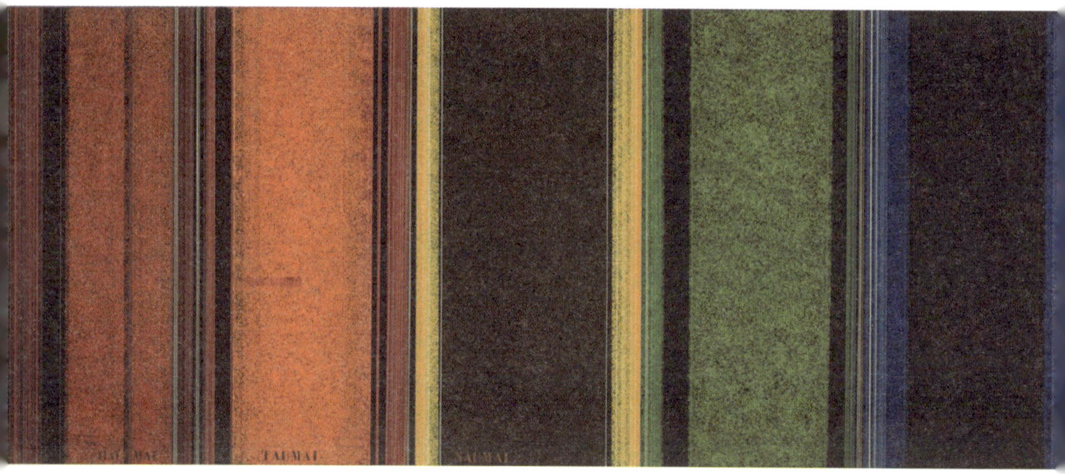

Ralph Hotere, *Godwit/Kuaka*, 1977 – enamel on board, HxW 2400 x 18000 mm. Chartwell Collection, Auckland Art Gallery Toi o Tāmaki, gift of Auckland International Airport Ltd, 1997.

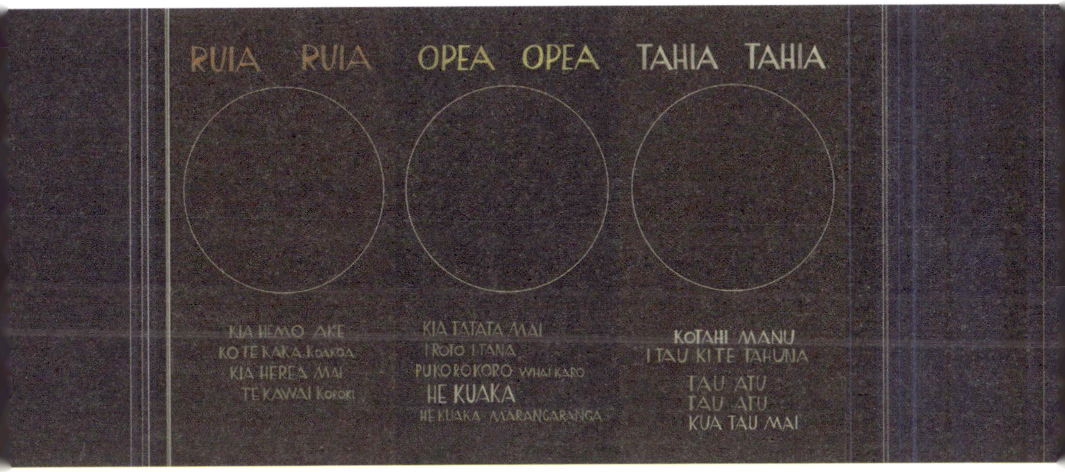
RUIA RUIA
OPEA OPEA
TAHIA TAHIA
KIA HEMO AKE
KO TE KAKA KOAKOA
KIA HEREA MAI
TE KAWAI KOROKI
KIA TATATA MAI
I ROTO I TANA
PUKOROKORO WHAI KARO
HE KUAKA
HE KUAKA MARANGARANGA
KOTAHI MANU
I TAU KI TE TAHUNA
TAU ATU
TAU ATU
KUA TAU MAI

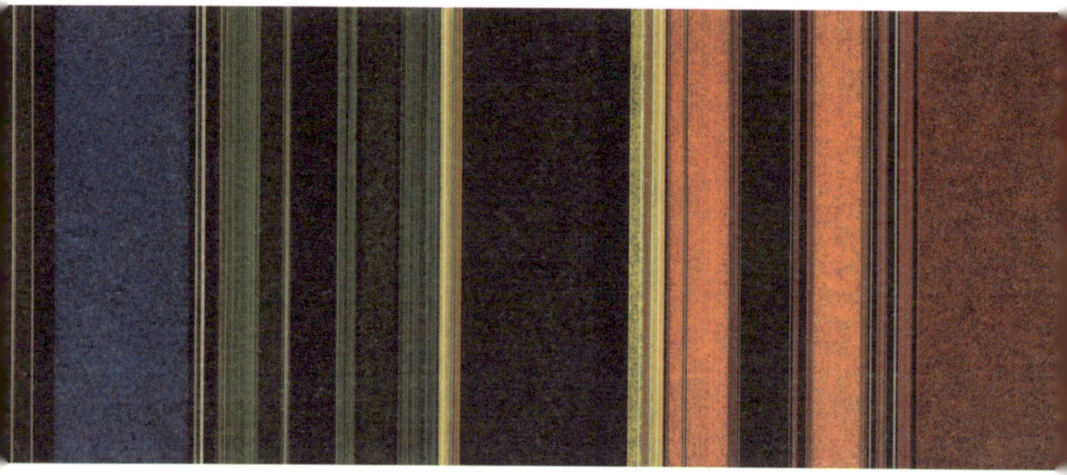

The Haunted Brand of 'Le Capne. Jacques Cook'

In *New Zealand, France, and the Pacific*, edited by Ian Conrich and Dominic Alessio (Kakapo Books, 2011)

This essay organises visual and note material presented as a keynote address at New Zealand, France and the Pacific, the 13th annual conference of the New Zealand Studies Association. That talk expanded on material presented as a short catalogue essay, 'Haunted by Cook', for the exhibition *The Captain's Ghost* at the Adam Art Gallery Te Pātaka Toi, Victoria University of Wellington, 26 May–23 July 2006

The exhibition was organised around the work of two contemporary New Zealand artists – the sculptor Christine Hellyar and the photographer Mark Adams – and a contemporary Australian artist, Debra Phillips. In different ways, these artists treated themes of site-specific memorials – some marking sites of violence – and the memories, traces or 'spoils' of Cook's Pacific encounters, especially his practical garden plantings at anchorages and the parallel scientific activity of botanising. In addition, the exhibition included historical material derived from the voyages of James Cook: a dry herbarium specimen (Elaeococarpus dentatus/hīnau) collected by Joseph Banks on the first voyage and subsequently taxonomised by Georg Forster after the second; an engraving of this plant after the artist Sydney Parkinson from the Alecto Historical Edition of *Banks' Florilegium*; an engraving of 'The Death of Captain Cook' (1785) after a painting by the third voyage artist John Webber; and, most importantly for the current essay, an engraving (1778) of James Cook by the French artist Robert Bénard (after an engraving by James Basire, after a painting by William Hodges from the second of Cook's voyages).

To the themes of memorials, violence, gardening and botany can now be added that of the internationalism of Cook's reputation and representation with Enlightenment Europe. Cults of bucolicism and sensibility associated with Jean-Jacques Rousseau found resonances in the practical gardening activities of a farmer's son turned navigator and Enlightenment explorer: the internationalism of Enlightenment science (including botany) was a ratcheting factor in Cook's transcending a nationalist brand as 'heart of oak' English hero.

This essay enters the haunted territory opened up by the artists listed above and plays on the historical stretch between (say) Christine Hellyar and Sydney Parkinson. It suggests that the 'Cook brand' was split by popular as well as scholarly forces generated within and by the Enlightenment voyages of discovery in the Pacific. To do this, the essay extrapolates a number of hints contained in the portrait of James Cook by the French artist Robert Bénard.

Ghosts

Let's start with a small portrait of the man we usually know as James Cook. This portrait of Cook is by the French master engraver Bénard (1750–1785) from an earlier engraving by Basire (1730–1802) after an original painting by Hodges, the artist on Cook's second voyage of discovery in the Pacific and Southern oceans. With only a little prompting, this particular image of the famous explorer begins to open up a number of themes.

One of the themes will be familiar to scholars of the Enlightenment. These scholars will include editors like Nicholas Thomas who have tracked the influence of the explorer–naturalist Georg Forster on European opinion-leaders such as Goethe; it will also be familiar to art history scholars like David Maskill at Victoria University of Wellington, who have studied what might be called the material residuals of Enlightenment voyages – for example, monuments erected as memorials or cenotaphs in carefully landscaped – we might say scripted – parklands. I am grateful to David for sending me a copy of his paper, 'Death in a French Garden: the Laborde and Cook Monuments at Méréville and the Landscape of Loss' (Maskill, 2006). The theme that emerges here is what might be called the

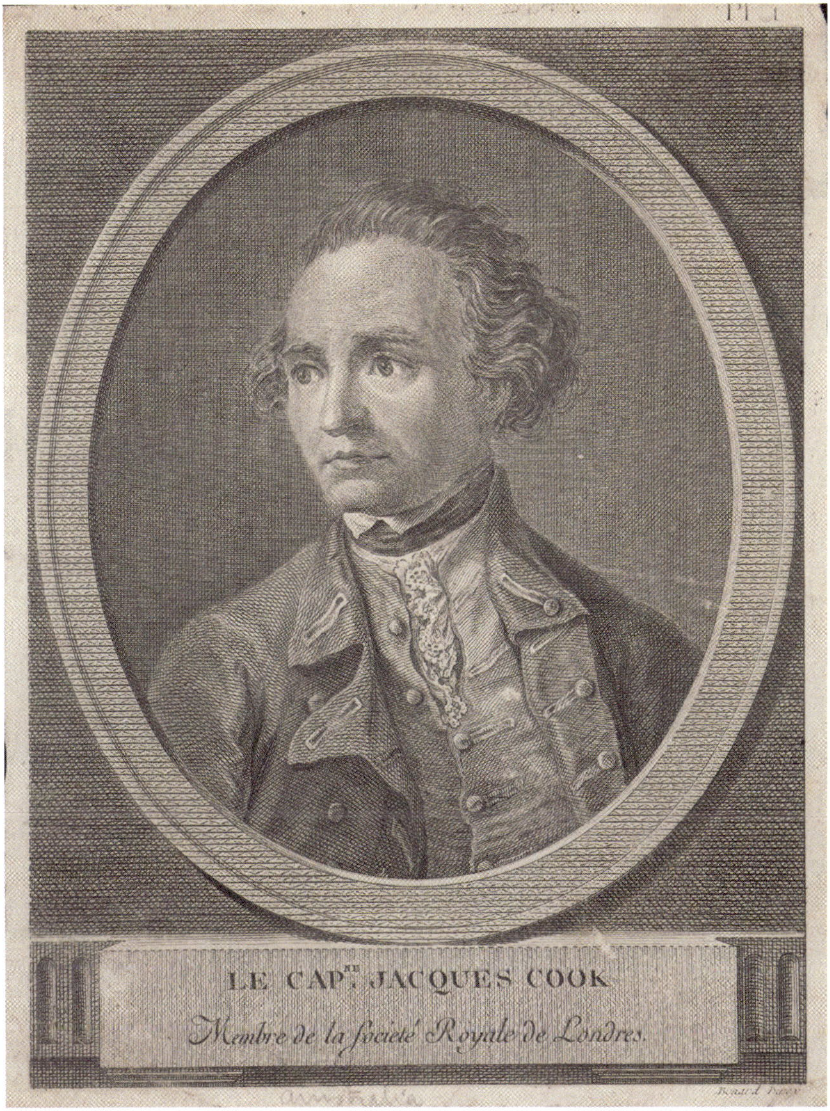

William Hodges (artist), 1744–1797, *Le Capne. Jacques Cook, Membre de la Société Royale de Londres*. Bénard, Robert (engraver), direx [18– ?]. Engraving, 220 x 165 mm. Alexander Turnbull Library, Wellington.

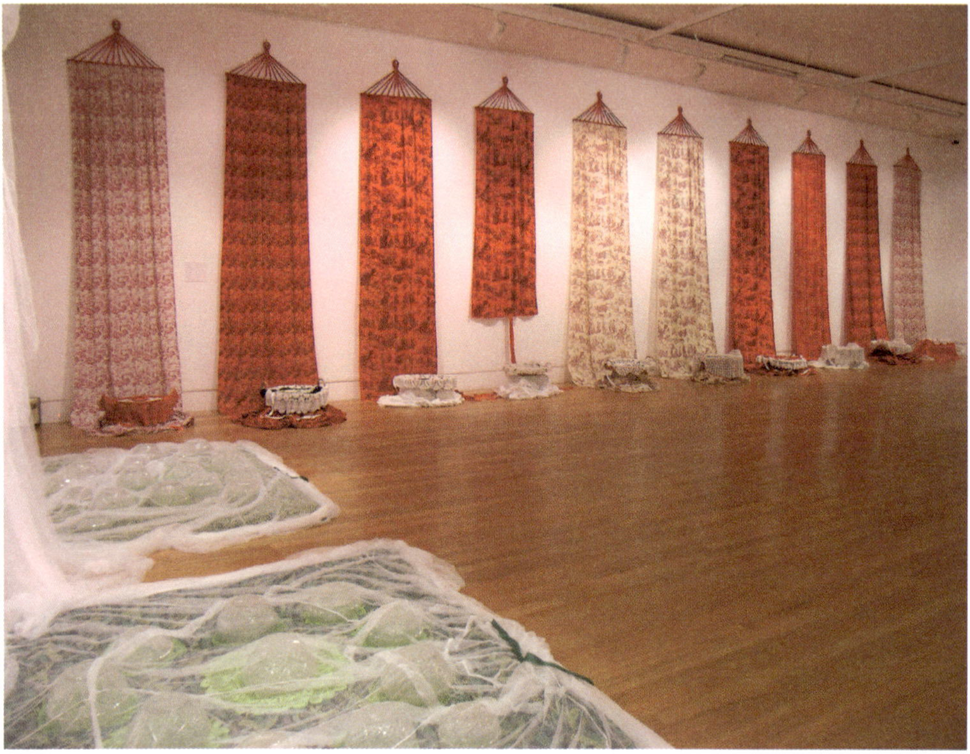

Christine Hellyar, *Cook's Gardens*, 2006 – mixed media (detail, installation view, Te Tuhi). Image courtesy of Te Tuhi, Tāmaki Makaurau Auckland and the artist.

internationalism, at least within the European geocultural arena, of figures such as Cook. While scholars are likely to be familiar with the adoption of an international Cook by non-British subscribers to Enlightenment ideas and ideals, most settler descendants probably continue to think of Captain James Cook as constituting a more or less exclusively British component in the foundational histories of New Zealand and Australia; as a central figure in varieties of indigenous contact narratives, Cook's otherness has generally come to be inscribed within larger political histories of specifically British colonisation. The 'international Cook' is one of the figures that emerges from the portrait by Bénard, and his internationalism is one of the themes I want to explore. We might call this 'the international Cook brand'.

Christine Hellyar's installation *Cook's Gardens* (2006) tells us that our Pacific gardenscape is haunted by Cook's presence. The little purple potatoes that grow wild in loamy sand behind dunes, the vestigial gardens at Motuara and Ship Cove in Queen Charlotte Sound, the 'wild' cabbage that flowers yellow in autumn, the 'wild' turnips and radishes, the broadleaf parsley – these scattered spooks may often have originated in Cook's gardens, planted to provision his crews and improve their scurvy-threatened health; and the purple potatoes that were found in cultivation in the south of the South Island of New Zealand generations later may have been traded and distributed from original plants around Tōtaranui Cook Strait in 1773–74 rather than from those in Tamatea Dusky Sound – they embody the phantoms of trade and exchange.

In *Cook's Sites*, Mark Adams has photographed the garden-haunted hillside above Meretoto Ship Cove (Adams and Thomas, 1999). Other notable ghosts recorded by Adams include the tree stumps and regenerating forest at Astronomer's Point, site of Cook's observations of the transit of Venus in 1769 in Tamatea Dusky Sound. These, too, are garden ghosts – the ghosts of an Eden imagined by the Enlightenment observers of both the 'primeval' and the cultivated utopias of the Pacific.

Such traces of practical activity align with the scientific history of botanical collecting in the Pacific and Aotearoa New Zealand by scientists aboard Cook's, and other vessels of exploration and discovery during the years of uneasy European peace between the Treaty of Paris in 1763 and the French Revolutionary Wars that broke out in 1793. This combination of practical gardening and scientific botanising embodied a key value of the 'international Cook brand'.

We should add to this history the botanical garden of John Fothergill, MD (1712–1780), Mrs Elizabeth Cook's physician – a Quaker and a brilliant botanist whose garden at Upton near Stratford rivalled that of Joseph Banks at Kew. Fothergill was a patron of Sydney Parkinson, also a Quaker, the botanical artist who accompanied Sir Joseph Banks on Cook's first voyage and died of malaria in 1771 on the voyage home. His botanical drawings provided the material that would become the great Alecto Historical Edition of *Banks Florilegium* more than 200 years later in 1985.

Mrs Cook was a Quaker, like her physician. Her husband James famously did not conduct religious service on board ship and (though this was not uncommon) refused to have a priest or chaplain as part of the crew. The plain sense of Cook's garden plantings, the scientific and more broadly Enlightenment spirit of enquiry motivating the voyages, are also, then, haunted by a kind of secularism – by a sense that the authentication of reality by divine revelation, purpose and faith was shifting to another, or differently weighted, system of belief – one that may be found somewhere in the interstices between a common-sense Quaker admiration of plain evidence, a Linnaean belief that empiricism complemented divine design, and an outright secularism.

The second theme that emerges from the Bénard engraving of Jacques Cook, is, then, one of *authenticity*: how was the significance – even the reliability – of phenomena to be measured? As teleological, that is, as revealed by God? As scientific, that is, as revealed by empirical observation? And where on the continuum from teleological to scientific do we locate the man in the portrait that Bénard made after Basire, after Hodges?

Cook's gardens haunt us in the forest textures of regeneration around old stumps in Pickersgill Sound in the South Island of New Zealand; and up the slopes behind Cook's anchorage at Ship Cove in Tōtaranui – those locations photographed by Mark Adams. They haunt us in the herbarium specimens and botanical gardens of Kew and Upton. And they haunt us with the ghosts of an emergent material, empirical, observable world which the spectre of James Cook, the farmer's son, enters energetically, often first off the boat, with the intense, patient curiosity of a restlessly unsatisfied spirit. What we also see in this record of an impatient man first ashore and first up the slope at Ship Cove is the farmer's son who wanted to weed his gardens, and did so. Such practical virtues would be fashionable among the pre-Revolutionary intelligentsia of France; they seem to spill from the little portrait of Jacques Cook by Bénard.

Hellyar's installation, *Cook's Gardens*, first seen at the Sarjeant Gallery in Whanganui in 2005, is itself in some degree haunted by an earlier collaboration with Maureen Lander, *Mrs Cook's Kete* (2002) at the Pitt Rivers Museum in Oxford. This, too, is a spooky place, the sepulchre of, among many other things, the ethnographic collections of Johann Reinhold Forster, senior member of the father–son team of botanists on Cook's second voyage. Mark Adams photographed this ghostly place on 27 November 1995. The images of it that are included in the 1999 *Cook's Sites: Revisiting History* portfolio published in book form by Otago University Press seem also to represent the crossroads where modernity's key instrument of empirical representation, the photograph, demonstrates yet again its ability to freeze frames on spooks. It is a haunted junction that also resembles the convergence and clash of teleological and empirical authenticities aboard James Cook's vessels of exploration and discovery. Like those investigations, it is the very empiricism of Mark Adams' photographs that convinces us we are in the presence of ghosts. We sense that the consequences of these observing activities and their traces, of these secular thrusts of rational curiosity into the mysterious places of a new world, have bequeathed the contemporary inhabitants of these cultivated places an unsleeping, dissatisfied, restless company of phantoms. There are also, of course, spectres of violence, rape and impregnation with unwelcome and sometimes pathogenic seed, both real and metonymic.

Hellyar's *Cook's Gardens* is explicitly a haunted place. It is a ghost ship whose hammocks – the 'Seed Beds' – are haunted by the negative volumes of absent bodies. Its 'Sad Flags' are haunted by the deaths of crew members. The 'Tall Tahitians' are spectres of dead Tahitians, but also of the 'Indians' whose confirmation dresses Hellyar appropriated as memorials, not just to the Tahitians, but to a language that made them and all native peoples 'Indians': the language-phantom of an imperial impulse to find India, or King Solomon's Mines, or a fabulously wealthy *terra incognita* – the word-ghost of the Imperial Project. These ghostly 'Indians' also haunt the 'Sad Flags' – at least two in Botany Bay and 15 in Kealakekua Bay. A sculptor, Hellyar instinctively makes work that is as much about negative space as about material volume: her work, and this work in particular, is haunted by absences. These absences include lives, what was taken from the ship, memories, the traces of personality and indeed rank that impregnated a seaman's red-and-white patterned cotton handkerchief or an officer's silk one, not to mention the pathogens that were transmitted in them.

Meanwhile, the ghostly *presences* in the installation's components are multiple, and signalled by Hellyar's multiplied or punning or portmanteau language: the hammocks that are seed beds also document the fabric designs that made picturesque the parkland conventions of botanical landscaping and of cemeteries. These kinds of landscapes, places of recreation and reflection for the pastoralised *coeurs sensibles* of Enlightenment Europe, would soon memorialise Jean-Jacques Rousseau at the Isle of Poplars within the estate of the Marquis and Marquise de Girardin at Ermenonville: a memorial, now, to the 18th-century New Age optimism that Romanticism caused to gush from the orderly findings of Cook's voyages.

What begins to emerge, here, under the watchful eye of the portrait of James – or Jacques – Cook, is the sense of a tidal surge of shifting values, of a new way of looking at the world, a spirit of change that both drove explorers into the Pacific and other new territories, and that recycled what they encountered there. The places they went to were changed forever. So was the Europe they embarked from. So the third theme – the third haunting by this spook of a James/Jacques Cook – is the post-Enlightenment, Romantic possibility of a new kind of world order represented in some way by the international or transnational idea of Cook; a possible world order that would crash and burn in a combination of Arcadian sentimentality, the Napoleonic Wars in Europe and in the Pacific's long trauma of colonialism.

Brands

This portrait of Cook by Bénard is, as noted above, from an earlier engraving by James Basire, after an original painting by Hodges. Basire's eldest son was also called James (1769–1822). Like his father before him, he became Engraver to the Society of Antiquaries. His son was, in turn, called James (1796–1869) and he, too, was a line engraver. It is speculative but not entirely fanciful to imagine the Basires cooked their whakapapa book. Not only the Basire patrilineal but a great many other English citizens swelled the numbers of sons named James in the years after the famous death of Captain James Cook. A lot of Horatios appeared after Trafalgar in October 1805. There were a lot of Elvises born after 1977, too.

The portrait of Cook by Hodges was painted between 1775 and 1777. The engravings after it suggest that it would have shown Cook's head and shoulders. He is not wearing naval uniform or displaying any of the usual naval portrait accoutrements, such as a sword, hat or telescope – unlike the 1776 John Webber portrait (at the Museum of New Zealand Te Papa Tongarewa). Also unlike the more formal but still unpretentious-looking man in the Webber oil painting, the Hodges Cook is not posed next to a view of the sea. His commands are not at anchor in the near distance, a convention of innumerable other naval portraits of the Lords of the Admiralty type. Cook's rank and fame are almost suppressed – he does not resemble one of the Lords of the Admiralty. He was not one. His appearance is rather relaxed, his hair a bit dishevelled – he has a parlour, not Portsmouth, look about him.

A reproduction of the Basire engraving after Hodges appears in

J.C. Beaglehole's 1961 edition of the *Journals of Captain Cook*, Vol. II. The Bénard engraving after Basire appeared in 1778 as the frontispiece to *Voyage dans l'Hémisphère Austral, et autour du Monde, fait sur les Vaisseaux de Roi, 'L'Aventure', & 'La Résolution', en 1772, 1773, 1774 & 1775*. The inscription on the engraving, presented in trompe l'oeil as a text cut in a stone sill, reads 'Le Capne. Jacques Cook, Membre de la Societé Royale de Londres'. A secondary inscription reads, 'Bénard Direx'. The full description of the French publication continues, 'Ecrit par Jacques Cook, Commandant de 'La Résolution': Dans lequel on a inséré la Relation du Capitaine Fournaux, & celle de MM. Forster. Traduit de l'anglais (par Suard). Ouvrage enrichi de Plans, de Cartes, de Planches, de Portraits, & de Vues de Pays, dessinés pendant l'expédition, par M. Hodges'.

It is important to fix this date of French publication and the translating or rebranding of nationalist English James into internationalist Enlightenment and pre-Revolutionary Jacques. 1778 is almost midway between the Treaty of Paris in 1763, when hostilities between France and England paused, and 1793, when they resumed for the lengthy French Revolutionary Wars, the latter interrupted by Nelson's famous naval victory at Trafalgar in 1805. It is important, too, to locate the French Revolution of 1789–99 in this schema – revolutionary Republicanism would split the James (or Jacques) Cook brand, assigning one set of values to xenophobic and paranoid anti-French-English nationalism (and a sea that separates with navies fighting each other and exchanging gunshots) and another set of values to Romantic post-Enlightenment internationalism (and a sea that joins, with explorers saluting each other and exchanging knowledge).

The nationalist Cook brand has been carefully protected and maintained for nearly two and a half centuries and we still do not expect to hear James called Jacques. An essential part of this Cook brand has been Englishness. His qualities of seamanship, fortitude and judgement did not just derive from the sea-girt national brand values associated with the invincible maritime history of Drake, Cabot, Raleigh and Nelson, they contributed to and reinforced those values. What is more, *James* Cook's name added a kind of plainness to the sea-girt, Britannia-rules-the-waves brand. Though his Christian name had been the name of English kings, here it dignified qualities unconnected to the aristocracy. James Cook was a commoner and his name said that what was good enough for a king was good enough for a seafaring Cook, a heart of oak, a true salt. *Jacques* who?

The immense popularity of the apotheosised hero Cook had a lot to do with his meritocratic, rather than aristocratic, qualities. These un-classed qualities were attached to both nationalist and internationalist Cook brands – to Rule Britannia heart-of-oakism as well as to revolutionary Republicanism. There were various hit versions of 'Cook: The Musical', one with dramatic sets by the Swiss-born artist John Webber (the artist on Cook's ill-fated third voyage and responsible for the best-known representation of Cook's death) and Philippe Jacques de Loutherbourg, the French-born English painter (1740–1812), which retain that 'French-born English'. These productions were popular in large part because they allowed English audiences to swell with national pride. Cook was English. He died for his country. He was a man of the people. His brand values became brand virtues. The *Gemeinschaft* within which popular audiences identified with Cook and admired him as an heroically meritocratic one-of-their-own fused with the *Gesellschaft* within which that same community of admirers elevated their emotion about Cook to the level of patriotic duty. The apotheosis of Cook made him a national hero at demigod level.

And then, of course, it was James not Jacques Cook who was engaged in an ambiguously territorial dance-upon-the-waters with his counterparts in the Pacific, Jean de Surville (1769) and Marc-Joseph Marion du Fresne (1772). The doughty James Cook brand prefers to be distinct not typical, and certainly not typical of Pacific explorers, including Frenchmen, even though du Fresne would come to grief and achieve popular apotheosis on a beach in the Bay of Islands, New Zealand, much as Cook did on the beach at Kealakekua Bay, Hawai'i, on 14 February 1779. And three years later, in August 1782, the self-avowed Cook fanatic Jean-François de Galaup, Comte de La Pérouse – known as La Pérouse – captured two English forts on Hudson Bay, North America, though France and England were not officially at war.

The 'French-born English painter' Philippe Jacques de Loutherbourg was elected to the French Royal Academy in 1766 and came to England – from 1771 he was designing stage sets at Drury Lane for David Garrick. By then Philippe Jacques had become Philip James and it was Philip James de Loutherbourg who was elected to the (English) Royal Academy in 1781 – not long after Cook had translated to Jacques Cook in the Bénard engraving for the 1778 French edition of the second-voyage journals.

The hugely popular and subsequently exhaustively ethnologised theatrical work designed and articulated by James de Loutherbourg and his French-trained Swiss consultant on native dress and painter of occasional scenes, John Webber, was called *Omai, or a Trip around the World*. It was presented at the Theatre Royal in Covent Garden in December 1785. The play, a combination of spectacle, mechanics, melodrama and documentary – an 'infotainment' – was a hit, with 70 performances in 1785 and 1786. In the last and most famous scene of the play, 'The Apotheosis of Captain Cook', the national martyr ascends to heaven in a mechanised cloud designed by de Loutherbourg. He has his navigator's sextant in his hand and is flanked by Britannia and a winged Fame.

Webber was a diligent artist – perhaps the most diligent of Cook's official artists. On the third voyage around the Pacific (1776–80), together with William Ellis, surgeon's second mate on the *Discovery*, Webber, under instructions from Cook to focus on people and cultural practices, created what is perhaps the first of the most accurate ethnographic records of Pacific culture – as well as the most immediate representation of Cook's death at Kealakekua Bay. Notwithstanding his plainness and empiricism, it was possibly Webber's hand that drew the image of Cook's sensational apotheosis in *Omai, or a Trip around the World* – the brand and marketing image that graces the print distributed in London in 1794 by the celebrated print seller John Thane.

It is Thane's 'Apotheosis of Cook' print from 1794 that appears on the cover of the New Zealand poet Robert Sullivan's book *Captain Cook in the Underworld* – the extended poem sequence Sullivan wrote as a libretto for a new work by composer John Psathas for the 50th birthday celebration of Wellington's Orpheus Choir in November 2002 (Sullivan, 2002). Sullivan's theatrical text reverses the heavenward direction of James Cook – it plunges him, instead, into an underworld of guilt and postcolonial expiation. The Cook brand describes an arc from demigod to demon. It also arcs from an apotheosised national authenticity that is almost teleological, to a demonised international inauthenticity grounded in postcolonial subaltern identity politics – from teleological authenticity to political inauthenticity.

But there are some other haunted stations along the way. The immense publishing success that turned James Cook into Jacques Cook – and Georg Forster into George, and Mister Hodges into Monsieur Hodges – was internationally cosmopolitan in scope, with texts, translations, editions, images and their derivatives and copies, and also ethnographic artefacts and natural history specimens trading back and forth across the whole of Europe, exciting the Enlightenment complexions of the likes of Goethe towards the hectic tones of Romanticism. Similarly, the popular theatrical entertainments based on Cook's exploits and the exotic scenarios they offered dramatists and impresarios were everywhere in the 1780s and 1790s, and continued to be popular well into the 19th century.

In Paris in October 1788, M. Jean-François Mussot-Arnould staged *La Mort du Capitaine Cook, à son troisième voyage au nouveau monde: pantomime en quatre actes.* This improbable narrative contains a phantom precursor of the crucial 20th-century argument between Marshall Sahlins and Gananath Obeyesekere (Sahlins, 1995; Obeyesekere, 1992) about Cook's ambiguous demigod status among some Hawai'ians at the time of his death. The 18th-century French narrative has the Cook brand being homicidally haggled over by the Hawai'ian king's supporters, for whom he is an almost saintly saviour (if not yet a Hawai'ian demigod), and the king's enemies, for whom he is a must-die devil. Either way, he is a martyr for the French and subsequently English audiences.

A slightly modified English version played at the Theatre Royal, Covent Garden, in 1789, as *The Death of Captain Cook: a grand serious-pantomimic-ballet, in three parts. As now exhibiting in Paris with uncommon applause with the original French music, new scenery, machinery, and other decorations.* This version of Cook's death uses internationalising impresario marketing language ('*now exhibiting in Paris*') to add value to the English brand. James's loyal English audiences can now swell with national pride because their icon is a smash hit in Paris, too. Another English version, very much based on this text, was printed in Limerick in 1790, mentioning performances in 'London, Dublin, and Paris, with universal applause'.

Now to return to the portrait with which this essay began. The loose-haired, relaxed, informal, smiling, wide-eyed and youthful Capne. Jacques Cook in Bénard's version of Basire's engraving of the Hodges oil painting is the epitome of the new Romantic, about a decade ahead of his time. He might be a poet, or a proto-revolutionary Republican. He would not be out of place meditating on Rousseau's *Nouvelle Héloïse* of 1761 on the stone bench next to the little lake with Rousseau's modest monument on the Marquis de Girardin's island at Ermenonville – the island that has become a gently accidental parody of the *sauvage* one Cook planted with practical, yellow-flowering cabbages and turnips. Did Cook really look like this vision of Bénard's?

The answer must be evasive. At this moment – the moment of the Hodges painting and the Bénard engraving – James/Jacques Cook exists at a complex historical crossroads. He is required to endorse if not symbolically represent a number of diverging or evolving sets of values. The Cook brand is stretched thinly across these competing sets. A number of Cook phantoms are now discernible within their opaque surfaces. Cook gazes out from these cloudy mirrors (such as the mirror within Bénard's *trompe l'oeil* frame) as though confronting the expectations of his branders. Cook haunts the identities and aspirations they want him to fix – to make distinct, the foci of distinct, competitive meanings. The objects and images associated with these fixings become haunted as well. Cook is a shape-shifting spook, surrounded by spooked fetishes: the sextant and map, of course, but also the botanical specimen, the painting, the drink of lemon juice or mānuka beer, the 'Captain Cooker' pig, the 'Arapawa goat', potatoes, cabbages and broadleaf parsley, the gnawed hand of Thomas Hill, Johann Forster's stewed dog, Hawai'ian cosmology, the clap, 'fatal impact', colonialism. The spooks haunt books in innumerable editions and many languages and they reside in countless museum collections around the world. The modest dry herbarium specimen of *Elaeocarpus dentatus* or hīnau collected by Banks and Solander on Cook's first voyage glows with a kind of haunted, undead energy unwarranted even by its spectacular trajectory across the short gap between Age of Reason scientific empiricism and the heightened civilising of Reason during the Enlightenment. The haunting survives intact into the hīnau's reverend repose within the exquisitely craftsmanlike pages of the *Banks' Florilegium* completed some 200 years later. We are looking at systems of signs that are spookily persistent. They persist in their wish to transmit authenticity – a serviceable definition of branding.

A short European history of authenticity would have to begin with treatments of the term's teleological origins, through which authenticity required the mark of divine design. The historiography moves on through Age of Reason scientific rationalism and empiricism to the 18th-century European Enlightenment reworking of teleology such that authenticity was established by knowledge of and about things and their purposes, and a belief that this knowledge was a civilising or enlightening force. It devolves to subsequent perceptions of cultural and indeed racial difference as determinants of authenticity within the early tourism of late 18th- and 19th-century European Romanticism (the authenticity of Rousseau's 'noble savage', for example); and of tourism's counterpart in the stay-at-home xenophobic and often racialist, if not outright racist, expectations of authenticity within nationalism (the authenticity of Rule Britannia). Most recently, the historical narrative of authenticity and the historiographic method for researching and documenting it include the perceptions of a great many market research and cultural economy analyses of the commercial and commodity hegemonies of product brands and their protected trademarks within global formations and contexts.

Spoils

The botanical scholar Patrick Brownsey has told me an exemplary story that illustrates the tensions within the complex historical moment from which Cook's haunted brands emanated. He did this while we were having lunch on a balcony above a busy street in Wellington, New Zealand – not far from the herbarium where the dry specimen of *Elaeocarpus dentatus* (hīnau) collected by Joseph Banks and Daniel Solander usually resides and not far from the Solander boxes that protect the sheets of the *Banks' Florilegium* in the collection of the Museum of New Zealand.

The post-Revolutionary French botanist Citizen Jacques-Julien Houtou de Labillardière (1755–1834) was with the expedition of Bruni d'Entrecasteaux (*Recherche* and *Espérance*) in 1792–93, exploring Tasmania and Western Australia, the north of New Zealand and the East Indies. The expedition was also looking for the lost, in fact sunk, expedition of La Pérouse – the Cook fanatic. In the course of d'Entrecasteaux's voyage the French Revolutionary Wars had broken out and in Indonesian waters Citizen Labillardière's scientific collections were seized by the Dutch as spoils of war. The Dutch were at that stage allies of the British. Shortly afterwards they became the enemies of the British and Labillardière's hapless specimens were next seized off the Shetland Islands in the Atlantic by the Royal Navy. Cook's Rule Britannia brand might seem here to have ruled the waves – but it was his naturalist from the first voyage, Joseph Banks, who petitioned for the return of these botanical spoils of war to their French owner. In 1796 Banks was able to write to William Price at the British Museum that:

> his Majesty's Ministers have thought it necessary for the honour of the British nation and for the advancement of Science that

> the right of the Captors to the Collection should be on this occasion wav'd and that the whole should be returned to M. de Billardiere, in order that he may be able to publish his Observations on Natural History in a complete manner . . . By this her Majesty will lose an acquisition to her herbarium, which I very much wish'd to see deposited there, but the national character of Great Britain will certainly gain much credit for holding a conduct towards the Science and Scientific men liberal in the highest degree.

On 9 June 1796 Banks was famously able to write:

> That the science of two nations may be at Peace while their politics are at war is an axiom we have learned from your Protection to Captain Cook & surely nothing is so likely to abate the unjustifiable Rancour that the Politicians frequently entertain against each other as to see Harmony and good will prevail among their Brethren who cultivate science.

What we make of this history may be construed as hauntings. These hauntings are also works of theatre: their representations are staged, as is Bénard's portrait of Cook. The *Cook's Gardens* of Hellyar, the phantom *Florilegium* of Debra Phillips' *52 Sidelong Glances*, the haunted *Cook's Sites* of Adams, the spooky hīnau specimen, the Romantically haunted Jacques Cook in Bénard's engraving – they whisper to us from a kind of theatrical shadow space. They are phantoms in the theatres of 18th-century entertainments in which Cook ascended to heaven, the theatre of a postcolonial Orphic underworld in which he suffers guilt, the *trompe l'oeil* theatres of representation. They generate the theatricality, as Juliana Engberg suggests in her essay on Debra Phillips' *52 Sidelong Glances*, of the spaces of representation in Diderot's *Encyclopédie* of 1751–72 (Engberg, 2001).

They haunt the dramatic tension between the authenticity of Diderot's observable world and the authenticity of Milton's teleological one in *Paradise Lost* – the same *verso* of divinely revealed truth that also haunts Phillips' Enlightenment project in her *Seven Small Forgettings*, photographs of unbound text pages ghosted with – spoiled by – the residual forms of plant specimens. As Engberg reminds us, the leaves of paper between which the leaves of Banks' botanical specimens were pressed came from Joseph Addison's *Notes upon the Twelve Books of Paradise Lost*, 'a serialised interpretation of Milton's epic poem commissioned by the *Spectacular* and published in book form in 1719' – the year Addison died.

What do we make of this haunted brand, this brand that haunts us, this persistent mark that will not be erased, this contested identity? That – as it always has – will depend on what we do with it. The good botanist Patrick Brownsey left our lunch to return to the scrupulous materiality of his herbarium at the Museum of New Zealand. I went back to my office to write about the modest portrait of James or Jacques Cook by Robert Bénard – after Basire, after Hodges; to write about the spoils of history, about a history whose impression still spoils the surface of the present.

References

Adams, Mark, and Nicholas Thomas. 1999. *Cook's Sites: Revisiting History* Dunedin: Otago University Press.

Dawson, W.R. 1958. *The Banks Letters: A Calendar of the Manuscript Correspondence*. London, British Museum. Cited in Frans A. Stafleu (ed), introduction to *J.J. Labillardière Novae Hollandiae Plantarum Specimen*. Codicote: J. Cramer.

Engberg, Juliana. 2001. '52 sidelong glances', in Debra Phillips, *52 Sidelong Glances*. Sydney: Art Gallery of New South Wales. Contemporary Projects exhibition brochure, 12 August–30 September 2001.

Maskill, David. 2006. 'Death in a French Garden: the Laborde and Cook Monuments at Méréville and the Landscape of Loss', in Martia Calder (ed), *Experiencing the Garden in the Eighteenth Century*. Bern, Oxford: Peter Lang.

Obeyesekere, Gananath. 1992. *The Apotheosis of Captain Cook*. Princeton: Princeton University Press.

Sahlins, Marshall. 1995. *How 'Natives' Think: About Captain Cook, for example*. Chicago: University of Chicago Press.

Sullivan, Robert. 2002. *Captain Cook in the Underworld*. Auckland: Auckland University Press.

Walking Down Parnell Rise and Setting Fires

Allen Curnow

Landfall 222 (Spring 2011)

I was a student at Auckland University from 1965 to 1968 when the English Department staff included the poets Allen Curnow, M.K. Joseph, Kendrick Smithyman, C.K. Stead and Ken Arvidson. The booming Sydney Musgrove was thought to dabble, though theatre was his passion and he took us at speed through Aristotle's *Poetics* as if it were a director's manual. My copy has fading but still frantic scribbles all over the margins. There were other poets lurking here and there – a full-bearded, long-haired, dungaree-wearing Wystan Curnow appeared towards the end of my time at the university, and was involved in the coterie of student writers and young staff (including Roger Horrocks) who were becoming devotees of what, risking instant anachronism, was being called 'the New American Poetry'. This was as much a brand as a practice, the sign of a distinction between us and the poet-fathers the gods required us to knock off or, if nothing else, ignore.

All of them lectured (or tutored) me at one time or another, but it was Allen Curnow who impressed me the most, though he had to do so against the sceptical grain of what 'the New American Poetry' aficionados generalised as a vein of stuffy provincial nationalism in the writing of his generation. In the end, though, Allen was the rule that proved the exception. He couldn't be ignored. His tightly strung, methodical, forensic meditations on the national condition (or malaise) may have seemed irrelevant, but his tin altars, knees of light crashing down, and those dying ejaculating their bloom bewildered me enough to win my interest – it was, after all, what was difficult in poetry that mattered then. What was he on about? Once I'd guessed that the 'tin altars' could be summer barbecues I realised that the 'difficulty' didn't arise from the obscurity or esoteric nature of the references, let alone from a distaste for what, some decades later, would be termed 'accessibility', but from a distinctly compacted way with metaphor. Much of that complexity was in the language, but it was also in the poet's powers of perception. That worked for me – the intense fusion of thought, phenomena and words was the secret ingredient that made poetry interesting, wherever it came from. The various sectarian squabbles that seemed to niggle around Allen really did seem truly irrelevant, and it has to be said his demeanour treated them that way too. His poems appeared to be scrupulously conscious of what they were doing in inverse proportion to his own benignly dissociated manner – which was, however, not something you could take as read.

I first encountered Allen in his poems, and, while struggling to reconcile my imperative to ignore them with the fact that they interested me, I soon encountered him in person. He lectured Stage 1 students on Robert Browning, a poet whose irrelevance then seemed beyond doubt (though, as a kid, I'd been weirdly fascinated by the incomprehensible 'Sordello'). At the bottom of a steeply raked lecture theatre filled with rows of semi-conscious deaf-mutes, he monologued his own way through 'My Last Duchess' as if it was the most natural thing in the world to talk to yourself in front of a crowd.

'That's my last Duchess painted on the wall,' Allen intoned, and it was hard to tell if he was quoting Browning or just riffing on his own situation. He did the same with 'Fra Lippo Lippi', talking his way through the poem while some of us overheard what he was saying to himself about the painter who saw and liked too much of the world, too much 'arms and legs' and not enough 'soul'. About then it began to dawn on me that he also knew all the poems by heart. He could quite easily have sat by himself in a pleasant location, where knees of light were crashing down near tin altars, and muttered the complete Browning to himself, or as much of Browning as it would take to fill a timetable of lectures on the subject. In a sense, this is pretty much what he was doing.

A bit later on, when he was lecturing and tutoring me on Wallace Stevens, Yeats, and Shakespeare's sonnets (and their variora), I was living in a flat in Birdwood Crescent in Parnell. I used to walk down Parnell Rise to the university, and began to meet Allen on his way down the same hill. We'd walk along, while he noticed this or that and commented on it in a Browningesque manner. I think he knew I was there, and we sometimes had a conversation, but mostly we walked along while he used me as an excuse to say aloud what was going on in his head whether I was there or not.

During his tutorials it became clear that he also knew a lot, if not most, of the poems of Yeats and Wallace Stevens by heart. It was usually close to impossible to tell when he was quoting and when he was just talking. He didn't alter his tone or mode of address. He'd sit there with the book in question open in front of him, and then ignore it. He just kept on talking or quoting, meanwhile (in the tutorials) puffing on a pipe or attempting to reignite it with matches which he struck without looking and dropped into piles in an ashtray on the table. It became clear that he not only knew the sonnets of Shakespeare by heart, but also their variora and the reasons for them. He'd talk about the difference the differences made, much as he'd generate a kind of dramatic monologue about the changes he observed while walking down Parnell Rise in the morning. He'd be dropping flaming matches into the pile in the ashtray on the tutorial table, and from time to time the pile would burst into flames – the tin altar would combust, the knees of light would crash down, and the dying would ejaculate their scarlet blooms.

In the Blink of an Eye

Anne Noble's Antarctic photographs

Ice Blink: An Antarctic Imaginary, edited by Gwynneth Porter (Clouds, 2011)

1

> 'Ice-blink' is a nautical term indicating the presence or absence of ice a long way off and refers in this exhibition also to the act of viewing photography.
> (Anne Noble, 2008)

Some fissures radiate from the compacted thought in Anne Noble's statement. For a start, it introduces uncertainty or even danger to the act of viewing. The sighting of ice at sea may be spectacular but not seeing it is potentially life-threatening. The sinking of the *Titanic* is an icon not just of industrial hubris but of a terrifying polar sublime unleashed beyond the ice sheet. The 1914–17 Shackleton Expedition's photographer Frank Hurley recorded an enormous iceberg bearing down on the ice-locked *Endurance*, and took another photograph of disconsolate huskies watching the ship being crushed after nine months in the ice. We recognise these dangers: we've seen the movie and the heroic pictures.

The danger that interests Noble is less spectacular and more insidious. 'Ice-blink' suggests vividly that seeing and not-seeing are only fractionally separated: now you see it, now you don't. What is being measured by this blink is not just perception, but cognition: the processing of information. Ice appearing in a distant view may be almost indistinguishable from the effects of light and atmosphere, especially when seen in an ambiguous melding of sea and sky. Ice, then, blinked at by the human eye or by a camera, may appear immaterial, not a 'berg' or mountain, an object to be processed into information, but only the condition – light given density by atmosphere – that makes the registration of an image possible; not an image as such, only the possibility for it to form.

It is tempting to see this radical, dangerous uncertainty – this cognitive split second between the manifest and the immanent – as a reverse analogue of the *instantané* or certainty associated with 'decisive moment' photography. In its elevation of perceptual decision making to quasi-mystical status, the concept of a 'decisive moment' implies cognitive genius matching the speed of a split-second exposure.

But Noble is not talking about the intuitive perception of an event, nor even about a subsequent viewing of that event as a photographic object. Instead, she states simply that the ice-blink 'refers . . . also to the act of viewing photography.' In this carefully phrased sentence, she steps perceptual and cognitive processes back from seeing something, distances them again from seeing that something represented indexically in the photograph, and yet again from seeing that representation as a photographic object; and arrives at 'photography', which is a practice or process, not a result.

Noble has described the photographer's pleasure as consisting of 'using light and colour and turning them against the subject viewed'. What we are really looking at, then, and either seeing or not seeing in that 'ice-blink' moment of encountering photographs by Anne Noble, is the convention of seeing photographically. You will either notice that you are doing this, or you will not. If you do not, you will see what is represented 'in' the photograph (its narrative event), and you will see the photograph itself (its artefactual surface and extent); but you will not, as it were, see the ice. And not seeing the ice puts you at risk.

What is this risk? It is perhaps first of all the risk of not understanding, or of having your understanding or your imagination disabled; for example, by conventions or expectations such as heroic and sublime tropes associated with adventure and voyages of discovery; or aesthetic tropes associated with ideals of beauty. In Antarctica, such tropes were iced in by the photographs of Frank Hurley in 1914–17, and earlier in 1910–13 by the photographer with Robert Falcon Scott's doomed *Terra Nova* expedition, Herbert Ponting. Of these tropes, Noble has said that, 'Heroic age photography is a colonising with the eye' (Noble, 2010). This addresses the impacts of ways-of-seeing on place and landscape: the image as occupier. And the impacts of such occupations or stagings on the act of looking? That we will become incapable of seeing what is there – both its indexical factuality and its visual history.

Noble has also quoted Marcel Proust: 'The real voyage of discovery consists not in seeking new landscapes, but in having new eyes.' An aspect of the risk, then, is that on our voyage to the ice we will fail to see anew. And again, welcoming the possibility of risk, Noble suggests that, 'Seeing at the boundary of cognition and perception – relishing the failure of perception – equates to the failure of language.' Apsley Cherry-Garrard, a survivor of Scott's *Terra Nova* expedition and author of *The Worst Journey in the World* (1922), wrote that 'Antarctica has beggared our language.' We are unable to visualise or imagine what is not seen. Nor can we speak of what is invisible except as a negative; a nonexistent, by definition unutterable.

The *Terra Nova* photographer, Herbert Ponting, stated that 'there was not a picture to be made' on the Antarctic plateau which Scott and his team set out to traverse to the Pole – a statement relished by Noble as a challenge, as she also relishes the challenge of working at a boundary where perception and therefore language may fail. She challenged herself to make pictures where others had thought none could exist (the *Whiteout* series) – to see the ice with new eyes – and she challenges us to transform the nonexistent into what may be understood and imagined, and therefore spoken of: 'Ice ahead!' In meditating on the collapse of language, the failure of perception and the irrelevance of representation, Noble is working with the ice-blink's tension between seeing and not seeing, understanding and not understanding, imagining or not, and she invites us to risk ourselves there and, perhaps, discover the language needed to describe our voyage of discovery. This voyage is as much into the seemingly nonexistent snow-blind world of an Antarctic sublime pushed to its limit as into the over-represented and visually colonised world of Antarctic centres and tourism.

> As a photographer and an artist I am interested not so much in re-photographing what we have seen before but asking questions about the ideas everyone has about Antarctica.
> (Anne Noble, in Jerram, 2007)

2

I want to explore this idea of the ice-blink by means of a digression. The famous white whale known as Moby-Dick was often described by his unwilling apostle Herman Melville as resembling a snowy iceberg. Sighting the elusive iceberg whale was the key task of crew aboard the *Pequod.* Uttering the cry of perception and understanding – 'There she blows!' – was a mystical act of transmutation. Because language now existed for it, the whale was made manifest. It could be uttered. In the blink of an eye, the nonexistent or immanent could be seen and believed. But what had materialised was also a kind of dream. The whale brought something previously hidden to the surface. This was a moment of terror and triumph, when something denied or unspeakable could be confronted.

Back around the end of the 1970s I began to take an interest in 19th-century whaling in the Pacific. I soon found myself enmeshed in the industry's underwriting of a potent grid comprising explorations and navigation, commerce, and an imaginary that included *Moby-Dick* and Melville's other Pacific fictions. Inevitably, I soon encountered the strange and persistent belief that the earth was hollow and that a portal to its interior existed in the frozen wastes of Antarctica. This apparently crazy notion had a distinguished list of advocates, including Jules Verne (*Journey to the Centre of the Earth*), Edgar Allan Poe (*The Narrative of Arthur Gordon Pym of Nantucket*) – and the 19th-century American army officer John Cleves Symmes, Jnr. (Rumour has it that Adolf Hitler also believed in a version of Hollow Earth.)

It is at least plausible that Symmes, a fervent public circuit lecturer on his theory of a Hollow Earth made up of interlocking shells with openings at both poles, was an indirect influence on Herman Melville. What is beyond doubt is that Symmes directly influenced the newspaper editor, entrepreneur and explorer Jeremiah N. Reynolds, who joined him on the lecture circuit; and Reynolds' article *Mocha Dick: Or The White Whale of the Pacific: A Leaf from a Manuscript Journal* was undoubtedly known to Melville, who may even have based Captain Ahab on its megalomaniacal author.

Reynolds agitated for an expedition to Antarctica to locate the entrance to the Hollow Earth. After false starts in the late 1820s, he was finally successful in motivating the Great US Exploring Expedition of 1838–42, though his own vehemence about the need for the expedition, not to mention his role as its leader, effectively denied him a place aboard it. The expedition sailed under sealed orders which, when opened out of sight of land, are believed to have contained Reynolds' instructions regarding the Hollow Earth.

Reynolds was influenced by the theories of the German naturalist and geographer Alexander von Humboldt, and can at one level be seen as contributing to the broad Humboldtian vision of early American environmentalism, at least in as much as he believed in the interconnectedness of natural forces and phenomena, and of the sciences that described them. But these beliefs also made him an advocate of commercial exploration in the interests of locating natural resources (not least whale oil) and opening up markets and trade routes.

This vision, combining a broadly environmentalist view of the natural world, and a belief in its potential commercialisation, makes Reynolds an ambiguously modern figure. What began to obsess me about him, and the persistence into the 20th century of that dual vision of environmentalist and commercial (or imperial) value, was his solution to the perceptual, psychological, and even psychic problem of denial. In order to believe simultaneously in the integrity of a coherently interlocking environment – and indeed planet – and the need to disrupt that order in the interests of commerce, Reynolds needed a powerful imaginative third term, a metaphor, one that would reconcile the inherent contradiction in his belief systems, but also one that could allow that tension to be sustained. This is because it was the active contradiction that was the productive driver of his enterprise, not its polarisation (so to speak) into either Humboldtian environmentalist 'unity of nature' science or hard-nosed 19th-century mercantile capitalism. The third term that Reynolds adopted – the one that allowed him simultaneously to deploy a holistic world view and a strategy for commercialising its material assets – was the Hollow Earth of John Cleves Symmes, Jnr. The sane but sadly marginalised object relations theory of the English paediatrician and psychoanalyst Donald Winnicott might describe the Hollow Earth as a transitional object. It mediated between interior and exterior, subject and object, self and other. I think it allowed Reynolds to comprehend a self that could be at once a hard, self-contained subject and a liqueous identity able to be drawn away towards objecthood by a kind of whirlpool or maelstrom – even towards objecthood verging on annihilation (or 'whiteout').

The Hollow Earth existed as a place that could not be found and that therefore could not be disproved. In its time, it appeared to bridge science and fiction. It was at once imaginary and plausible. It could exist as a potential, as a reconciling or cohering metaphysic, at the same time as laying claim to phenomenological provability. It was at once a compelling hypothesis and a vapour – a kind of ice-blink. In its very nature it displaced the doubts arising from Reynolds' contradictory world view. It allowed that contradiction to flourish. And it hardly needs to be pointed out that the Hollow Earth with its inaccessibly frozen access looks like an embarrassingly literal diagram of repressed consciousness, or the Freudian unconscious (not favoured by Winnicott) within which dreams are formed for the precise purpose of dealing with denial.

The narrative clients of such displacement are familiar in the Romantic lexicon: heroism, the sublime, lost paradises, lost innocence, purity, transcendence, and beauty as antithesis of or escape from mundanity (all of which could be found in, or in relation to, Antarctica). Its chief commercial clients are belief in the meritocracy of success, and the virtue of progress; here, what is beautiful is only ever what is useful (could be cities lit by burning whale oil). Thus, Romantic heroes subject themselves to awe and terror in a lost or forgotten paradise where innocence, betrayed beyond its borders, still exists; this is a pure place where the hero can access transcendent planes of experience and perceive otherworldly beauty. Commercial heroes by contrast are everyman entrepreneurs with a story of bootstrap success to tell; when we talk of their success we say that the beauty of it is that it really works.

Hollow Earthers seeking displacement are familiar to us within the value systems and representational modes of modernity, specifically as modernism, with its multiple inherent dualisms, contradictions and longings for the reconciliation of transcendence and utility, art and non-art, surface and depth. These days, Hollow Earthers are often transported to their shrines by tourism, and most often by eco-tourism, which commercialises reverence for the natural world and not seldom for its underprivileged or endangered inhabitants. Hollow Earthers returning from their pilgrimages these days bring with them not papal indulgences absolving them of sin, but digital photographs and videos that document their piety. That these images are records simultaneously of dissociated or even delusional exploitation, and of awe, is of course the point.

But to me, back in the early 1980s, beginning to construct a kind of armature for fiction from these ingredients, the most obvious inheritor of Reynolds' Hollow Earth strategy for sustaining and exploiting the denial at the conflicted centre of his belief system was the 20th century's fast food chains. In particular, I became obsessed with the vast, interconnected global network of resources, markets and indeed ideologies founded by Ray Krok, the original McDonald's hamburger man. Krok produced a tasty burger for the masses. It was cheap because its production chain epitomised an extreme rationalisation of Fordism – indeed of modernity. Its effort and resources were precisely calibrated. Its target market was the American family, and specifically American families that drove cars and were comforted by a quintessential American brand, the convenience meal of burger and shake. It mapped itself on to a geoculture networked by highways that bypassed countryside (no market there) while linking up munching suburbs. In Latourian sociology's actor-network terms, McDonald's performed America, even America putting on weight – or blubber.

But it did this also through a contradiction. Its resource hinterland was just that, a backcountry that hinted at lean American myths of cattle ranching and the prosperity frontiers of the wilderness. While emphasising American meritocracy and the material fetishes of success, not to mention the democracy of the American brand, the McDonald's experience was also fat-saturated in nostalgia – for the home-on-the-range beef cowboy, for an America as easy to understand as patty-in-a-bun, for white-picket-fence family values, for the rights to individual happiness and prosperity promised by the Statue of Liberty. But such worrying contradictions disappeared the moment your taste buds welcomed the first bite of a Big Mac. It was a dream come true; or rather, a dream mediated into complacency. There was nothing to fear. We could all have a nice day.

Perhaps I exaggerate. But blink at Reynolds' Hollow Earth and you will probably see a McDonald's. In the right place at the right time, when you blink you will see an Antarctic tourist. Ubiquitously throughout the mediascape of late capitalism, and particularly in its advertising, you will blink and see Antarctica as the backdrop to Hollow Earthers driving environmentally friendly cars while wearing Untouched World fashion-ware and the unbleached cottons of Bangladesh. The cars and the fashion-ware are often shown against pure backdrops of ice and clean blue water.

In this ubiquitously distributed and exploited image, Antarctica represents a desire, sometimes even a guilty desire, for purity and virtue; for what is 'sustainable' ethically and environmentally (Untouched World's advertising claims it as 'the first fashion company in the world to be recognised by the United Nations for sustainability'). But Antarctica also represents nostalgia, sometimes guilty, for what is lost or about to be lost: the ice and what it stands for. Desire for what is doomed is a profoundly conflicted and melancholy emotion, especially for those who feel responsible in some degree for the doom.

The denial such desire has had to repress is what generates Hollow Earth-type belief systems – and, indeed, the primitive displacement gratifications of eating. A version of Winnicott's concept of the transitional object will again come into play here – only this time the object (for example, a polar bear on an ice floe) mediates a denial or displacement rather than a disclosure. The self is extended, yes (by a kind of teddy bear), but the function of the awareness achieved is to mask a denial.

We don't expect or even want art to tell us what to think or believe (or eat). But we may be well advised to notice when art such as Noble's displays awareness of Hollow Earth strategies, and of alternative ways of looking and imagining. When Noble quotes Proust advocating the need for 'new eyes', when she confronts an image of the Antarctic sublime (pure, heroic wilderness) with its manufactured simulacrum (the Antarctic 'experience'), she is deploying such an awareness and inviting us to respond. She is asking us to recalibrate the angle at which we perceive – blink at – what is beautiful, or even understand what we mean by that. In a sense, her photographs of Antarctica are not *of* Antarctica at all; they are about consciousness. The imaginative condition we may need to find and enter will resemble a whiteout, a state of total disequilibrium, into which the materials, objects and actors of Hollow Earth will emerge as if free at last from the repressed consciousness or dream-world where they were only ever at the mercy of natures in denial.

3

Despite his protestation that 'there was not a picture to be made' on the Antarctic plateau, Herbert Ponting made a lot of them back in the environs of the expedition's base and on board the *Terra Nova*. They tend to fall into four categories. There are pictures of the expedition's men and livestock (ponies and huskies); the men are often posed heroically if nonchalantly next to their loaded toboggans, grim-faced, unshaven and haggard, with startlingly white mask-like circles around their eyes – as, for example, the photograph of Apsley Cherry-Garrard just back from the nearly catastrophic expedition to Cape Crozier in July 1911. In one photograph, men are tipping whiskey into a pony that has swum ashore after falling into freezing water. Stoic heroism in the face of deadly conditions is the theme of these images.

Then there are pictures of the expedition's activities and living conditions. These are intimate, factual, and even mundane, though sometimes heroic stoicism is hinted at, as in photographs of men crouched around the warmth of small, blubber-fired stoves.

There are photographs of the animals encountered on land and at sea – orcas, penguins, seals and gulls. These are gruff jobbing images that document in a somewhat perfunctory way the creatures of the continent – though one image anticipates the later mascotting of cute penguins ('penguins tobogganing').

Predominantly, though, and despite his 'not a picture' claim, Ponting photographed the icy landscape and what he very often called the 'effects' of light, atmosphere and weather on it. Sometimes he did so with human figures reduced to miniatures by vast distances and towering cliffs of ice – a classic sublime trope. He photographed weird and spectacular ice forms, 'effects' of light and cloud and of the auroras; grottoes and ice-caves, wind-eroded sastrugi on snow plains, and the hulking forms of Mounts Erebus and Terror. These, again, are familiar within the lexicon of the sublime.

Noble was aware that Ponting used a long lens to foreshorten and compress space; for example, in his photograph of a sled and men dwarfed by the Barne Glacier. She then photographed the Barne with a very wide lens, thus making it tiny – and implicitly coding in the term 'to pont', first coined in Antarctica to describe Ponting's composition of space, people and landscape. Frank Hurley was also famous – indeed notorious – for his arrangements and manipulations of the scenes he photographed during the Shackleton expedition.

Ponting also photographed the perilous process of navigating the expedition's ship, the *Terra Nova*, through ice fields, and, in his most famous images, the ship locked and frozen among looming pillars of ice. Hurley did the same for the more catastrophic situation of the *Endurance*. At the age of 13, the German painter Caspar David

Friedrich witnessed his younger brother Johann Christoffer fall through the ice of a frozen lake and drown. Johann may have done so while coming to the aid of his endangered older brother. It is tempting to see Friedrich's most famous painting, *Das Eismeer – The Sea of Ice* (1823–24), also known as *The Wreck of the Hope* and *The Polar Sea*, as a monument to his brother. It is certainly a monument to the artist's spectacularly grim sensibility. In the painting, vast slabs of razor-sharp ice are grinding to pieces the remains of a sailing ship. Violently pessimistic, the painting operates at the extreme terror margin of a gloomy northern sublime.

It is highly likely that both Ponting and Hurley knew about Friedrich's painting – it was hugely popular and much reproduced. It was also much emulated by more melodramatic 19th-century painters of avalanches, storms and shipwrecks, such as Francis Danby (*The Deluge*, 1840; or *Sunset at Sea after a Storm,* c. 1824) or John Martin (*The Great Day of His Wrath*, 1851–53), who pushed Friedrich's apocalyptic sublime to the margin of parody. In the age of widescreen cinema, we have Roland Emmerich, of course, and his ice apocalypse *The Day After Tomorrow* (2004) or its earlier science fiction twin, *Independence Day* (1996).

But the sublime itself is impervious to, or incapable of, irony. There is no trace of it in Ponting's photograph of the ice-locked *Terra Nova*. Rather, when we put his statement that there were no pictures to be taken on the 'featureless' Antarctic plateau together with the conventionally sublime images he did make where features and 'effects' were available to him, we have to conclude that he was remembering and photographing the convention as much as what was actually before him – what he was looking at. In a sense he was right to say there were no pictures to be taken, since they already had been. Into the vacuum of unutterable, nonexistent or negative space resembling an imaginative whiteout, rushed the almost parodic clichés of the sublime.

The effect of this is a curious kind of reversal. Ponting's factual images of working conditions and activities, the portraits of men and animals – even the perfunctory photographs of wild creatures – appear

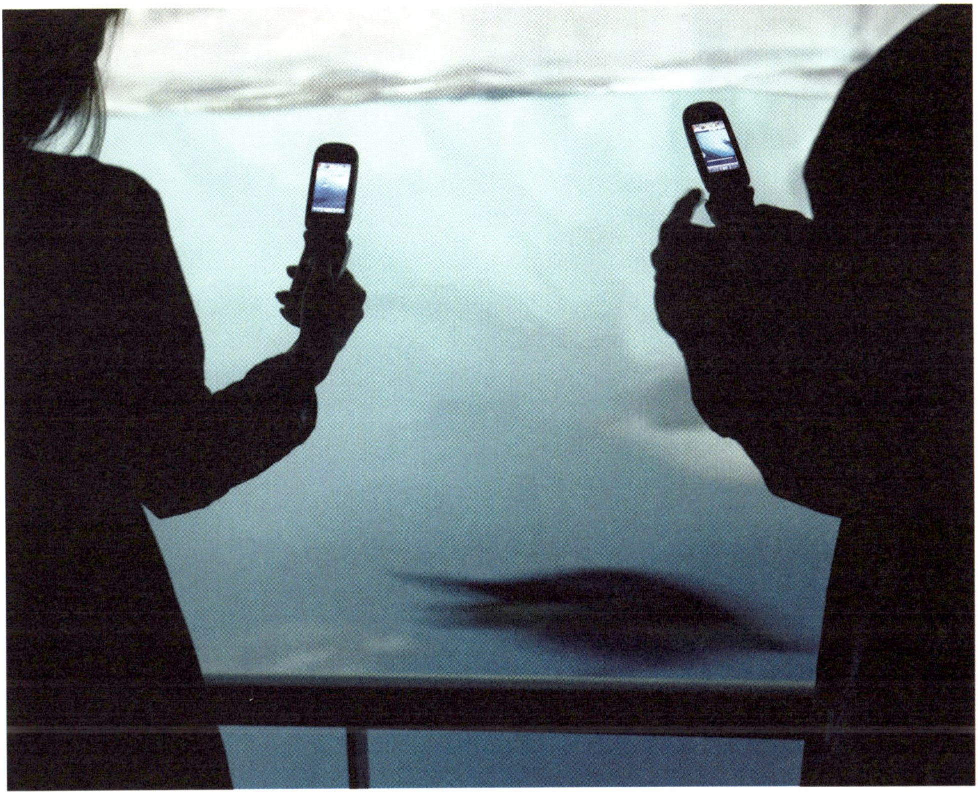

Anne Noble, *Penguin Encounter, Nagoya Aquarium, Japan, 2003—* in*Ice Blink: An Antarctic Imaginary*, Clouds, 2011.

cognisant; their objects have been understood, and so has the process of representing, documenting and indexing them. But the images of the spectacular frozen landscape, with its uncanny forms and bleak splendour, seem strangely vacuous – devoid of understanding. What they represent and index is cognition struck dumb by memory and convention; not 'new eyes' but a kind of imaginative snow blindness.

Such blindness might, however, be productive. Of her *Whiteout* photographs, Noble has written that, 'To look at whiteness – white foregrounds and white backgrounds – and in conditions where supposedly there wasn't an image to be seen, demanded something wonderful of the medium and the eye.' And also that:

> The *Whiteout* photographs aim to inspire the search for an image and the struggle to see. They also aim to evoke both the wonder of the ice and the irony that through looking at white (and all the contrasts and subtleties of that colour, tone, and hue) we can examine the act of seeing itself – the processes of creating imaginatively what is not there – and our human capacity for making that absence a presence for which we long.
> (Anne Noble, 2008)

4

Where is the terror margin of a contemporary sublime to be found? Probably in the catastrophic imaginings of climate change produced by global warming – Roland Emmerich and *The Day After Tomorrow*, again. The mascots of this sublime are, without doubt, endangered species. Of these, the most iconic are creatures of the ice, in particular the polar bear. Though not a denizen of Antarctica, the bear has come to represent the doom of the polar ice caps in general. It also, as the writer Judith Williamson has pointed out, exemplifies a key trope of denial: in its very ubiquity as an image, it represents its own eventual absence. Its icy environment represents its opposite: heat. We are urged to think of the bear as having ceased to exist by being presented with images of it existing; and of global warming by contemplating the icy poles. Ubiquitous photographs of the bear represent succinctly the denial-induced state of paralysis in which we find ourselves ice-locked in the terrifying cliché of simultaneous desire and nostalgia.

How might such a denial be reversed, or turned to imaginative purpose? By 'the processes of creating imaginatively what is not there', perhaps. By putting our blindness to work. It would be easy to assume that Noble's photographs of Antarctic Centres, aquaria, museums, and experiences (including the experiences of Antarctic tourists) are deeply ironic. But they are not – they are factual in the manner of Ponting's photographs of working conditions on the *Terra Nova* expedition. What the Antarctic Centre and Antarctic tourism photographs show us is the working condition of the popular Antarctic imaginary – the commercialised site of a compromised or even devalued sublime. Noble may be wry, and is certainly sceptical, but she does not mock either the centres or their paying audiences. What she does appear to want to do, however, is uncouple these exemplary products of (and solutions to) denial from the sublime for which they now speak. Like Hollow Earthers assuaging their bad dreams by eating Big Macs, the consumers of Antarctic Experiences are rendered incapable of 'creating imaginatively what is not there'. But if the Centres were to be seen clearly for what they are (museums of what may be lost) and the Antarctic sublime for what it is (not endlessly repeated 'effects', but an atavistic longing for redemption and virtue), then a different, critical, ice-blink-aware kind of consciousness might open up.

5

Finally, we need to remember that for all their indexical qualities, photographs do not reproduce objects, or lock them in an eternal present; photographs only ever *remember* their objects. A photograph can only ever index the past; by the time we see it, even in its split-second digital freeze-frame (or blink), its object has already gone forever. Knowing this as Noble does allows her to disarm the nostalgia which is almost the default affect of photographs.

An image of two visitors to the Antarctic Aquarium at Nagoya,

Japan, may contain the code for how she does this – and for how we might, in turn, 'see the ice'. Safe behind a barrier, two visitors stand before a glass-walled tank of water. The colours are those of purity and ice: white and blue. In the tank is the blurred torpedo shape of a penguin swimming underwater: 'in its natural element'. The surface of the water resembles a distant horizon, even a distant horizon of ice. Two visitors are cellphone-photographing the swimming penguin, whose streamlined shape is elegant, not the comical mascot form familiar in images of it on land. The photographs are visible on the twin cellphone screens of the visitors, who are looking at the screens, not the penguin – or rather, at the penguin on the screens of their cellphones. What they are looking at is, by implication, endlessly repeatable. Standing unseen behind them is another photographer, Anne Noble, who has looked at this tableau in her own viewfinder. Once blinked at by her camera's shutter, this moment becomes a memory.

Noble's photograph of *The Barne Glacier* at the Christchurch Antarctic Centre 'ponts' two tourists before a spectacular, panoramic painting of the glacier (with minute penguins on the ice sheet at its base). The participants in this experience are clad in red survival coats. The photograph explicitly references Frank Hurley's *A Blizzard at Winter Quarters*, in which one struggling figure is clutching an ice axe and leaning into the tempest.

Viewed on the page of a book, the photograph of penguins discloses a simple, lucid grammar of replacement – a putting-back-together of the sequence by which the penguin has been displaced successively from its natural environment, to an aquarium, to the screens of cellphones, to Noble's memory-chip, and finally to the pages of a book. The Antarctic Centre photograph has done the same thing to another inhabitant of Antarctica – that is to say, Hurley's iconic picture of it.

By this time we know we are looking at *photography* – a process through which consciousness can reprocess memory – rather more than at a 'penguin' or the photograph by Frank Hurley. The image is an eye-opener, as we say. And it returns us to where we began, with

Noble's succinct parsing of the nautical term 'ice-blink', and 'the act of viewing photography'. Far from offering us the self-congratulatory redemption of irony, or representing the all-too-easy clichés of the polar sublime, Noble's photographs offer opportunities for us to make something of the transition between now-you-see-it and now-you-don't.

References

Jerram, Sophie. 2007. 'Claims on Beauty', *New Zealand Journal of Photography*, no. 65.

Noble, Anne. 2008. Artist's statement for *Ice-blink: Antarctic Photographs*. Centre for Contemporary Photography, Melbourne, in Association with Melbourne International Arts Festival, 9–25 October.

Noble, Anne. 2010. Presentation to Dialogues with Tomorrow forum *Antarctica: Terra Nullius?* Wellington, 22 April.

O Salutaris – Between Here and There

Ralph Hotere

Pacific Highways (*Griffith Review*, 43, Autumn 2014)

1

Pā Henare Tate, the elderly Catholic priest who conducted the requiem mass for the artist Ralph Hotere, did so in Māori, Latin and English, with a bit of French thrown in here and there for good measure. At one point he referred to Ralph as a 'Latinist' as well as an artist. Because of the large crowd assembled on Mātihetihe marae at the end of a gravel road on the remote west coast north of the Hokianga Harbour, the mass was held in the wharenui or meeting house called Tu Moana (At the Ocean) rather than in the small church, called Hato Hemi (St James). The meeting house had room for about 150 mourners, and at least that number spilled out across the marae next to the adjacent church and the whare kai called Nga Ringa Rau o Te Akau (the Hundred Hands of Te Akau).

Ralph was famous, a recipient of New Zealand's highest civil honour, the Order of New Zealand, his work sought after by private collectors and public museums, and so the crowd included many from the art world where he was held in high esteem. But the majority of those paying their respects were Māori. The nearby car park was jammed with vehicles and children played among them. A large marquee had been erected next to the dining room; visitors had slept there and in the wharenui over the four days of the tangi. It was Monday, the last day. Many people had been up all night in the wharenui telling stories and singing. After the mass, Ralph was carried up the hill to Maunga Hione (the Hill of Zion), the urupā of Te Tau Māui, a hapū of Te Rarawa. Ralph's own family was from another affiliated hapū of Te Rarawa, Te Aupōuri. His mother Ana

Maria is buried down by the church, but his father Tangirau and some siblings are buried up there in what locals call 'Hotere Lane'. After lengthy debate on the marae, his grave was dug right out on the promontory affording what his brother Moss described as a million dollar view; the best seat in the house.

Ralph's coffin arrived in a black Air Force NH90 helicopter on Friday afternoon, after what was effectively a state funeral in the Catholic cathedral in Dunedin, but the tangi at Mitimiti was the real one as far as most people there were concerned. The Air Force helicopter, a black New Zealand Army Humvee that conveyed his coffin from the landing pad to the marae, and the large catering tent with army supply trucks and staff, had all been requisitioned by senior Māori politicians. No one, least of all the Minister of Defence, the Chief of the New Zealand Defence Force, or the Governor-General, Lt Gen Rt Hon Sir Jerry Mateparae, himself a former Chief of Defence, had apparently thought twice about turning the request down. The landing pad for the helicopter was in a paddock near the car park. It had been marked out with a large black cross of scorched diesel. Next to Ralph's open coffin in the wharenui were a number of objects associated with him, placed there by members of his family and by friends. They included a customised numberplate: HOTERE; as the black Humvee suggested, he'd loved flash cars as well as the colour black.

However, the first vehicle of Ralph's that I remember was a battered Land Rover in which we used to rattle over the hill to Pūrākanui in Otago to get mussels. I also remember a red Mercedes and an elegant E-Type Jag. Among the objects next to the coffin in Tu Moana were some of Ralph's favourite golf clubs, including his number one wood, Big Bertha. After the burial rites up on Maunga Hione, mourners descending to the marae were invited to take one of Ralph's drivers and belt a golf ball out across the black sand of the beach. Several elderly kuia hitched their black skirts up and confirmed what most people knew already, that Ralph's extended family offered mean odds on the golf course. They'd mowed a nice driving strip just below the urupā, and one after another the white balls arced across the black sand or the oxidised glitter of the creek. A couple of Ralph's hard-case nieces had jacked this up, and they'd got it just right – people were laughing as they went on down the hill, but the flights of the golf balls also drew gestures that, along with the black-cross landing strip, seemed to come from Ralph's own hand.

The last time I saw Ralph alive was a couple of days after his 80th birthday, in the Sacred Heart Home run by the Little Sisters of the Poor high up in Brockville in Dunedin. We had a glass of very good Twin Paddocks pinot noir from Sam Neill's vineyard and a slice of birthday cake. Ralph had never said all that much but now the stroke he'd suffered some years previously meant he said even less. Then it began to snow heavily but slowly outside his window. It was late in the afternoon; the snow fell in thick arcs and loops across the dark foliage of the garden. Ralph put his glass down and began to trace the movement of the falling snow. 'White,' he said. I remembered his smile a year later as the white golf balls drew parabolas across the black sand at Mitimiti.

2

Pā Tate made the requiem mass congregation in Tu Moana titter with a slightly risqué play on what he called 'Sixty-Niners' – those familiar with the pre-1970 Tridentine mass. Then he took the children of Mitimiti School and Te Kura Taumata o Panguru through the Latin phrasing of 'O Salutaris', for which he'd handed out copies marked with the intervals and stresses for us all to follow.

'Again!' he said, rolling his eyes in mock frustration. 'Again!' The Sixty-Niners inside knew their stuff and sang along; they also knew the Latin responses in the liturgy. At one point, Pā Tate suggested that he probably deserved a salary hike on the strength of offering a Latin mass. After a well-judged comedic pause, he added that one of Ralph's paintings would do instead. The congregation laughed – jokes about the market value of Ralph's work had been a feature of the tangi. They laughed again when Pā Tate added, 'So long as I can tell which way up it goes.'

Northland in New Zealand is poor country: unemployment figures are the highest in the country at about ten percent, the unacknowledged cash crop is marijuana, whose 'social harm' costs were estimated at $100 million in 2012, and methamphetamine labs are also causing enormous harm. So the running gags about works of art worth tens or hundreds of thousands of dollars have an edge up there. The edge has been sharpened by a few well-publicised disputes over ownership of Ralph's work, and during the tangi there were mutterings about the Hotere Trust's rumoured intention to dragnet 'gifted' art works. Ralph was famous not only for his alleged wealth, but also for the reasons why he wasn't all that wealthy in the end – he gave a lot of work away, he paid for members of his family to visit his brother's grave at the Sangro River in Italy where Jack had been killed in action during World War II, he gave away cars, he sometimes paid his lawyers, former landlord, dentist and occasional tradesmen with works, he gave works to friends to help with their kids' educations . . . During the dusk-to-dawn storytelling session in the wharenui the night before the funeral mass, one person after another got up and told a story about Ralph's generosity.

These were real stories, not just sentimental wake yarns. The sculptor Chris Booth told the story of leaving Port Chalmers in Otago where he'd had an artist's residency and had built a large work on the promontory where Ralph's studio was situated. Chris and his family were trying and failing to fit everything into their car. Ralph chucked him the keys to his ute and said, 'Take it.' Chris thought he meant borrow it, but he didn't mean that. He considered it a fair swap for the work Chris had made. Or not even an adequate swap – as Chris and his family were leaving, Ralph and his wife then, the poet Cilla McQueen, ran out with paper parcels which they stuffed into the ute. Chris thought these were food, but back home in Northland they discovered the parcels were rolled-up artworks.

Ralph and Cilla's daughter Andrea, who'd sat to one side of the open coffin in the wharenui for three days while Ralph's wife Mary sat on the other, told a story (as I remember it) about the time she and her husband were struggling to make sense of things, and Ralph tossed the keys of the red Mercedes on their kitchen table and told them to keep it, the car would make it easier for them to visit. But, she said, the real reason was that Ralph knew how much she loved the Merc, and that it would cheer her up – it did.

When my son Carlos was about four years old he drew a circle with squiggly bits coming off it, called it 'A Sun With Legs', and gave it to Ralph. A while later, Ralph gave him a painting called 'A Sun With No Legs' – one of his immaculately drawn circles on a mottled ground of black and amber lacquer. Ralph and I collaborated a couple of times, and he always considered an exchange of works was fair enough in return for whatever I'd written. There are hundreds of these stories.

There are also many stories about Ralph's survivalist savvy. Once, after we'd collected a feed of mussels from chilly water at Pūrākanui, he took his soaking pants off, rolled them in the dry sand, and shook them out. It's the kind of thing you'd get used to doing if you'd only had one pair at some time in your life. He helped me to lay a tongue-and-groove floor once. He knew how to do it without fancy tools, just a couple of nails and a four-by-two lever. He stared down the powers-that-be on the Otago Harbour Board and parlayed ownership of a fine old two-storey bluestone bank building on the main street of Port Chalmers when his studio up on the hill was demolished to increase wharf space.

He was an implacable leader of protests at the proposed siting of an aluminium smelter at Aramoana near the Otago Harbour heads. He seldom spoke out, but the works of art he made on that theme became the well-known speaking-objects of the protests. They made use of recycled sheets of rusty corrugated iron with beautifully scumbled and dripped surfaces, the lead-head nails he loved, bits and pieces of scrounged timber, and laconic, stencilled phrases such as 'Aramoana pathway to the sea'. These works were both vernacular and sophisticated – recycled frugally from the kinds of useful stuff you'd hoard in remote, under-resourced places; and at the same time reminiscent of Mark Tobey's white calligraphy, and in particular the *pintura matèrica* of the Catalan artist Antoni Tàpies, whose work Ralph knew well even before spending time in Barcelona in 1988.

3

On Sunday, while some of those attending the tangi were at mass in Hato Hemi, I went up the Moetangi valley with Ralph's brother Robin Hotere (one of five surviving siblings – there were 15 in all), his niece Debbie Martin (Robin's daughter) and the cinematographer Fred Renata. Debbie was recovering from a loud, boozy party on Saturday night. It's a good hour-and-a-bit's hike up the creek to Moetangi where the Hotere house used to be. Ralph and the other kids used to walk to school at Mitimiti and back every day. But first, once they were about eight years old, they'd have to round up the cows and milk them. They'd start about 4 in the morning, in the dark; they milked by hand, in the open. The milk can went down to the road on a sledge behind a horse. The horse had to be rounded up in the scrub too.

Ralph's mother Ana Maria, named for St Anne, was a devout Catholic. His father, Tangirau, was a katekita or catechist; he was also a poet. Robin said there used to be a rosary garden by the house, and that the roses had run wild over the scrub. When we got to the little plateau above the creek where the house used to be there was nothing to see but a clump of self-propagating arum lilies. The severe summer drought of 2012 had killed the roses. Robin pointed out where the vegetable gardens used to be – you could see how the plateau retained the contour of cleared land. There were a couple of lichened, rotting fence posts still sticking up. There's a spring that runs from a cleft in the hillside down to the creek. Once, there had been an orchard of peach trees above the spring's gully. They had apples and pears as well. They grew corn, kūmara, potatoes and greens; they had chickens and sometimes a pig.

The house had one room and a hard earth floor. There was a lean-to for cooking. Another room was added as the family grew larger. There was no lavatory at first – you did your business up in the bush. Later, the Department of Health provided materials for a long-drop. Sometimes Tangirau and Ana would be away at tangi for weeks at a time. The kids knew how to look after themselves. Further up the valley, said Robin, there's a cave with some old canoes, feather cloaks, and other taonga or treasures in it; there were probably human bones. Robin pointed out an old karaka tree where bodies used to be placed until the flesh had gone and the bones could be interred. When heavy rain caused a slip to expose the entrance to the cave and to what was inside it, members of the whānau dynamited it and sealed it off. Now the markers that vectored the entrance are gone, along with most of the big forest trees.

On the way back down the valley we came to a bend in the creek where a natural pool formed. Robin looked at it a bit misty-eyed. This used to be the family's bath. We could all see what he was thinking. We stripped to our undies and hopped in. Fred took a photo of Robin and his daughter Debbie up to their necks in the pond. They have their arms around each other's shoulders and are grinning broadly. It looks like a kind of conjoint baptism, into memory, perhaps – the kind of memory that can never be erased from a place if you know how to read the signs, however minimal.

4

There's a question that begins to form around the circumstances, memories and symbols of Ralph Hotere's tangi. He was one of the most esteemed, successful and celebrated New Zealand artists yet. In the late 1960s, after four years in London and in France, he began to paint what would come to be known generally as 'Hotere's black paintings' – austerely minimal works in which, in three seven-part series from 1968, impeccably black lacquered rectangles were marked by finely drawn crosses, each panel's cross in one of the seven subtractive primary or spectrum colours. At the time they were first exhibited, most critics drew parallels with the black paintings of Ad Reinhardt; Hotere himself was on record as having expressed regret at missing a lecture by Reinhardt at the ICA in London in 1964.

In 1997, after visiting the USA to watch Tiger Woods play at the US Masters Tournament at the Augusta National Golf Club, Hotere gave his dealer Sue Crockford a copy of the 1991 MOMA *Ad*

Reinhardt catalogue. Having skipped 50 pages of plates, he annotated the 18 plates of Reinhardt's 1956–66 black paintings with the names of the Augusta Club's 18 holes, granting each a par of given yards, beginning at 'Amen Corner' with the overall attribution, 'This is Tiger Country' – also the title of one of his own works from 1983. This elegant homage links Hotere's 1968 black paintings to what is in effect a book-end late series of works including large, black lacquered sheets of corrugated aluminium in 1999, again marked by variations on a cross, this time cut out of the metal or formed in part by vertical space between the corrugated sheets.

Ralph managed to combine his love of black with his love of fine cars: the late works were made in collaboration with an artisan car-painter in Dunedin who laid their impeccable mirror-black grounds. A major collaboration with his friend the artist Bill Culbert, *Blackwater* (1999), commissioned by René Block for the Museum Fridericianum in Kassel in Germany, is said to have had its sheets of sleekly reflective corrugated iron painted by Mercedes Benz at Ralph's request. Here, a certain kind of content – a narrative about cars, friendship, and a political claim to pleasure – becomes a kind of deadpan subversion. The minimalism, elegance and sophistication of these works made them favourites with critics and curators wary of narrative content, traces of regionalism, or, god forbid, affective hooks into the kind of cultural memory that might have been laid down in the artist's childhood in tough, self-sufficient conditions in the remotest part of Northland, imbued with Catholic ritual and symbols and Māori mōteatea. Nor were the works' enigmatic subversions noted. They were seen to be aligned with formalist international benchmarks of the time, not with some kind of narrative thick description or backblocks art semiotics. Ralph himself contributed to the laconic austerity associated with his work by famously refusing to talk about it. It was this aura of detachment and coolness that guaranteed the Mitimiti congregation's knowing response to Pā Tate's joke about 'which way up'.

Many in the congregation also knew that Ralph had chosen to live in Otago, a long way from the place of his birth near Mitimiti – a long way from them, his whānau, and a long way from Northland, for that matter. They knew about the time he'd spent in Europe, especially in France, including time at Avignon with Cilla McQueen from 1978, the year Pope Paul VI died; and in Menorca the following year when John Paul I died (a well-known series, *The Pope is Dead*, came from these events). Along with jokes about the value of artworks they might have stashed under the bed in the sleep-out, or whether a collector might now want to fork out a couple of hundred thou' for the corrugated-iron shed down the back, the congregation joked about how they'd got Ralph at last – how he'd 'come home'. The hidden narrative here, of course, is that there was a gap between where Ralph had gone and what he'd come back to in the end.

It's the nature of this gap or the tension between here and there (there and here) that shapes the question that has kept emerging hesitantly over the years in critical discussions of Ralph's work. Sometimes the question has been repressed in exhibitions that privileged the minimal black works and their apparent occlusion of content by form (with much explaining-away of the cross motifs). It's made frequent, dithering appearances in discussions over what to do about the fact that Ralph was Māori but refused to be characterised as a 'Māori artist'. It's associated with Ralph's own annoyance with the reappearance at auctions of his early, genre works including still lifes. The question has sometimes appeared as a full-blown revision, answered when the cross motifs in Ralph's work are sheeted back unambiguously to the religious traditions of the Hāhi Katorika, the syncretic Catholic-Māori devolution of French Society of Mary missionaries via Mill Hill Brothers in the Hokianga; or in which the white-scumbled, rivulet-and-splatter surfaces of corrugated-iron works in the 1980s are read as transliterations of the mudflat landscapes of the Otago Harbour; or in which 'black', both the colour and the metonym, is invariably read as political. But neither formalist avoidance of content, nor modernist squeamishness about the ethnographic, nor their contraries in literal narrative content match-ups, understand the question about the gap between here and there, let alone come up with good enough answers.

All of these options want to answer the question, What's to be done with the apparently contradictory co-presence in Ralph's work of austere understatement and rich content? And by implication: Does urbanity trump provincial narrativity, or can rich content be attributed to even the most minimal forms?

The space between the backblocks and the metropolis is easily – even usually – characterised as one between a simple, probably uneducated, culturally unsophisticated place, and the cultural complexity and sophistication of cities. The urban sophisticate appreciates refinement, including the aesthetic refinements of minimal abstraction. The provincial likes stories. This, at least, was the modernist diagram of progress towards hegemonic art 'centres'. Though the diagram has been contested and redrawn since Ralph first made 'black paintings' in the late 1960s, it still exerts influence, and it still asks the wrong question. Development remains a one-way traffic, apparently. Anything going in the reverse direction from the city to the provinces is on a sentimental trip into the never-never – the jaded sophisticate in search of traditional authenticity, the urbanite looking for the naïvely exotic.

But at Mitimiti for Ralph Hotere's extended requiem, we were reminded of some simple facts. He was brought up and educated in a trilingual culture – Māori, English and Latin. His father, Tangirau, was a noted poet. Ralph himself was well versed in the poetic traditions of Ngāti Ruanui and Te Aupōuri, and could quote at length from memory. The place he grew up in was in the vicinity of old, buried treasures. Baptised Hōne Papita Hotere by the successors of Bishop Jean-Baptiste Pompellier, the French Society of Mary missionary who came to the Hokianga in the 1830s, his name was a reference to both John the Baptist (described by Pā Tate as 'a stirrer') and to the French bishop. I got the impression his French was okay and he read poetry in it, and in Spanish. He was aesthetically at home both with the dark austerities of Reinhardtian minimalism and the poetics of Spanish tenebrists.

Often, however, the character of his work is defined by the radically simple anti-aesthetic of political outrage. His sociability –

the extent of his friendships and associations, his legendary hospitality – was equally well described by the French word *gentillesse* and the Māori manaakitanga. In his garden at Carey's Bay, he used to grow fierce, reddish Provençal garlic. His house contained an astonishing collection of artworks, most of them by friends. And when he travelled, he liked to do so in style – as in the black Air Force NH90 helicopter that brought him back to the marae at Mitimiti, over the hill from Moetangi, the place he'd left in 1946, sponsored by the church to go to school at St Peter's Māori College in the city, Auckland.

The cultural complexity of this metropolis in the 1940s may even have seemed thin by comparison with where he'd come from up north – or, at best, not likely to overawe Hōne Papita Hotere, a kid 'from the sticks'. He went where art took him, which was often a long way from Mitimiti, but it would be a mistake to see that journey as an improving trajectory from the benighted to the accomplished, or his 'return' as a vindication of roots. It's not a question of how he managed to juggle 'there' and 'here', periphery and centre. He closed the gap – he shut the question down.

Decentred

Saskia Beudel, *A Country in Mind*

Review of *Saskia Beudel, A Country in Mind: Memoir with Landscape* (UWA Publishing, 2013), in *Cultural Studies Review* (Vol. 20, No. 1, 2014)

Like many writers, Saskia Beudel included, I need to go for walks in order to think, and therefore in order to write. I believe that walking, observing, thinking and narrating are wired into old biological networks. These days, this has become a commonplace of evolutionary psychology, and seems both theoretically and intuitively right; as well as *sensible*, in that this is how I feel the process working in myself. Our nomadic ancestors used to walk and talk a lot, I'm sure – entertaining each other with stories and songs, kibitzing, socialising, mapping the places and routes they traversed, naming things, commemorating events along the way, commenting on changes, teaching their children how to find their way around the place and how to get home (and maybe sometimes how to get lost). Such old (but also new) business was often, subsequently, codified in elaborate literatures, such as classical Arab poetry whose footprint is nomadic, with its mnemonics of desert trade routes, oases, campsites and campfire stories.

The rhythms of thoughtful language organised as spoken and written narratives are related to the rhythms of physical movement – walking most obviously, but also dancing, travelling in cars (or on camels), and typing at a keyboard, and the visual rhythms of words on pages. The rhetorics of storytelling are also physical and even material, in that they are the embodied and situated vehicles in which narratives move and by which they are articulated. There is a dumb, tum-te-tum margin to this, of course, where 'the foot' as a measure of prosody can reduce rhythmic and narrative subtlety to marching or plodding. But there are also open margins where the *flâneur* subverts and *détournes* habit, where hiphop artists improvise, where Robert Burns's 'Standard Habbie' verse form introduces a jaunty, syncopated dance–step. More complexly, rhetorical structure expands meaning where a tauparapara of Ngāti Whakaue in Rotorua fluidly links and maps waterways, social relations, landmarked narratives and, indeed, the watery human bodies of paddlers in motion through place and time within the chant and the waka. Water, blood, story and navigation circulate in and through each other. You can't tell where waka, chant and the body are distinct. Such fluid rhetorical principles ally with Epeli Hau'ofa's concept of a 'sea of islands', in which the ocean links islands rather than separates them from each other; here, Hau'ofa is both recovering indigenous mapping of relationship, and critiquing the alienating cartographic rhetoric of European voyagers, who saw oceanic spaces as vast wastes with easy–to–sail–past pinpricks of landfall (Hau'ofa, 2008).

There may at a stretch be room for Zygmunt Bauman's concept of 'liquid modernity' here, too, as if we are now, like Beudel, discovering modern ways of doing old imaginative work, where narrative certainty, foreclosure and structure are no longer paramount (Beauman, 2007). Nor is it incongruous to reference liquidity in the context of this book, with its primary focus on the deserts of Australia, since the groundwater, so to speak, of its big narrative arc is water, and the ecological relationships and conflicts that water and its scarcity have produced over time. Indeed, Beudel's account begins with a kind of traumatic baptism. The opening sequence of life–threatening passage through the freezing water of a gorge off the Larapinta Trail is also a narrow rite of passage into the expansive field of the book's main business, the desert. It's a rite of passage characterised by dread and a sense of transgression – I won't second–guess whether this was intended by Beudel, but it's there in her account.

And of course there are delimiting systems and cognitive technologies, whose purpose is to enclose narratives: the Claude glass; the landscape painter's *repoussoir* (sometimes evolutionised as a protective 'lair' perspective); the theodolite followed by its procession of survey pegs; and, among the sublime mountainscapes of New Zealand, the viewing platform designed and located to render as primeval wilderness that which is traversed by processions of creaking campervans. The weakening of the Resource Management Act in New Zealand is symptomatic of a viewpoint shift away from ecology towards the monetising of energy–generating natural resources – not what to look at, but what to look for. Such framing devices are, of course, instrumental as well as rhetorical, as Beudel shows she knows very well. Unlike rhetorics whose effect is to open up decentred viewpoints and expansive narrative fields, the effect and indeed the purpose of delimiting rhetorical strategies is to reduce or even censor the imaginative scope of thought.

I read quite a way into Beudel's book, whose title is in effect a kind of puzzle, with a question nagging at me. It had to do with the rhetorical uncertainty of her narrative, of its viewpoint. Is this book primarily a memoir incorporating her family narrative, beginning with its troubling story of the Dutch in Indonesia under Japanese occupation? A meditation on home, and homelessness? Is it an account of her personal explorations of Australian desert country, with an underlying theme of therapeutic self–discovery? Is it primarily a broad–brush research summary of work done by anthropologists and ecologists, from which a history of Aboriginal alienation can be sifted? An advocacy essay making the case for ecological understanding of the desert and its history? A collection of exquisitely observed landscapes, both grand and miniature? An aesthetic map of country that enlarges our sense of what that might signify? A participant history of desert exploration?

I'm being only slightly disingenuous here – I had an idea of what Beudel was up to from early on. But the text's uncertainty – its shiftings of perspective, rhetorical purpose, content, and even genre – were what affected me most as a reader. There's a sense that country and its complex and chaotic inscriptions have written Beudel's text, and that this text has written her.

Then, not quite halfway through the book, I read this:

> Minoru Hokari argues that 'Gurindji cosmology is based on the networking among many sites, countries and people without a concept of "the centre"'. Because there is no 'authentic centre that guarantees the validity of information, the knowledge naturally creates many variations'. Thus different stories, which may contradict one another, 'do not conflict, but simply co–exist'. (p.154)

A couple of pages later, this:

> As I came across and assembled these references to Indigenous narrative structures, it occurred to me that my own mode of writing, with its crossings between locations, people, and points in time, was being prompted, too, by the very place I was exploring. Perhaps my mode of composition, the seeming disconnections and reconnections, the heterogeneities, was being informed by the landscape's dynamics. (p.156)

Gurindji narrative, then, derives from country – its widely distributed, networked and intercut storylines. Yet Beudel's narrative, given her reflexive position in relation to indigenous narrative, derives not just from country but also from the ways country has already been narrated, not just in accounts like those of Gurindji people but also in the anthropological, explorer, booster, ecological and literary texts that Beudel cites and quotes at length. In fact, this complex patterning of quotation and citation is another aspect of the book's 'heterogeneities'. The 'country' Beudel is exploring, sometimes driving in almost-got-lost circles, is as much textual as physical. The country is deeply inscribed, not just by the narratives of a hundred thousand years of indigenous inhabitation, but by the proliferation of written, video and sound texts that Beudel describes herself poring over in archives and libraries; by the conversations she has at kitchen tables; and not least by the mediating presence of her daughter Olive, who grows from infancy to 'over three' in the course of the book.

Olive's small but hardly insignificant presence in the book – her reappearances at different stages of development, often being given a frugal bath with some of the book's reiterant water – is typical of a far from disconnected meshing of narrative threads throughout. Looked at in big, filmic terms, the opening sequence of terrifying entrapment in and emergence from an icy gorge is bookended by the final emergence of Olive and her mother from another gorge, this one the nocturnal house of Desert Park at Alice Springs, where the dead snake of the icy gorge reappears as a live one in captivity being fed a mouse. The dim chill of the nocturnal house, a place of undead, close–to–extinct species, is contrasted with the sight of a 'large lizard basking in a sunny sheltered spot' as Olive and Saskia emerge into the 'sharp high light of another clear desert day' (p.323).

The breath-stopping chill of the opening gorge has already picked up an echo of the death of Beudel's father in the book's preface, which itself does a narrative throw to the big theme of 'place' and home: 'We waited, not knowing what to do, with no good place to go' (p.xv). Of course, 'what to do' and the 'good place to go' are what the book then explores. The subtle coherence and continuity of Beudel's text don't so much work against the grain of its 'heterogeneity' as unobtrusively compose – or edit into coherence – those 'seeming disconnections and reconnections'. I think Beudel is admitting as much when she uses the word 'seeming', as if she wants both the decentred, open, underdetermined narrative, and structural shapeliness. She manages to have both, and does so gracefully without sentimental or presumptuous mimicking of what might pass for 'songlines'. I confess here to a highly prejudiced relief at not finding Bruce Chatwin referenced in the book, and an equally prejudiced disappointment at not finding Barry Hill's *Broken Song* there, in particular its section on translation (Chatwin, 1986; Hill, 2002). But I was both relieved and moved to find substantial references to Eric Michaels – nearly 30 years after *Francis Jupurrurla Makes TV at Yuendumu*, his work continues to stare down egregious bromides about what constitutes 'Aboriginality' as does the posthumous *Bad Aboriginal Art* (Michaels, 1987, 1994).

Beudel's own explorations of the desert-scapes are informed more often by the wonder that goes with ignorance than by the overconfidence of expertise. There are many storylines whose apparently under–informed discontinuity is, in due course, picked up again – the story of buffel grass being a good example. Beudel describes a conversation with a friend in Alice Springs, Dave, who introduces her to buffel grass: 'I've never heard of buffel grass, and it's through Dave's passion about the subject that I begin to see the local landscape in new ways.' (p.210) The storyline of buffel grass spreads out like a capillary root system from this moment into the remainder of the book, reappearing as the narrative vehicle for descriptions of what it has overgrown and smothered: the fragile groundcovers of indigenous plants; the history of seed distribution and of acclimatisation societies; the story of the Overland Telegraph Line and the camel teams with their 'Afghan' cameleers; the boosters of pastoralism and the ecological disasters of overgrazing; the grass's damaging relationship to desert fire ecology. Towards the end of these 'disconnections and reconnections', Beudel is able to come to a modest but comprehensive conclusion, one that is both particular and metonymic:

> So through my days spent in Alice Springs libraries it was possible to trace in this one exotic grass broader patterns of human desire in the desert landscape: desire for wealth, desire to settle more extensively and comprehensively across the colonised landscape, desire to overcome the perceived limitations of the arid lands, with little comprehension of where those 'improvements' might lead and what unforeseen consequences may result. (p.251)

Typically, however, she doesn't let the matter rest there, on a solemn admonishing note. An old friend, Ian, arrives unexpectedly (as if walking the talk of the book's rhetorical surprisingness) at Beudel's mother's house in Melbourne, where she and Olive are staying while she does research in Museum Victoria, looking at photographs by the biologist and anthropologist Donald Thomson. Ian has a folio of drawings of buffel grass.

> He'd brought some of his recent botanical illustrations to show my mother, in one of those small coincidences or serendipities that occur once you're absorbed in a subject or object, or theme. Suddenly it starts appearing everywhere, in unexpected places and guises. 'I've just finished this,' he said. 'The spikelets and upper flower of buffel grass are extraordinarily beautiful.' He laid his drawing on the table. We bent over his finely drawn illustration, and in that moment buffel grass transformed into an aesthetic object. (p.258)

I'm struck by Beudel's phrase, 'absorbed in a subject or object, or theme'. Its careful distinctions imply the possibility that these categories may get mixed up – as they usually do with aesthetic experience. At this point I could reverse-spool the narrative thread of the aesthetic back through Beudel's text, and bring into view a rich sequence of diverse instances of the aesthetic's shell game, its tricky shuffling of 'subject or object' from her own descriptions of landscape, to accounts of her father's photographs, to a discussion of the aesthetics of Aboriginal knowledge of country, to the visual structure of Francis Jupurrurla's video, to her mother's Sunday painter work, to the paintings of Albert Namatjira, and more. Unobtrusively, in this final appearance of buffel grass, the significance of its aesthetic value is inseparable from the beauty of knowledge about it, including its shapeshifter, destructive capacity. The ambiguity we're left with is at once delicate and disturbing as two stories are permitted to coexist – one about threatening 'unforeseen consequences', the other about beauty – without any final editorial judgement repressing the tension between them.

I've long admired the complex, conflicted literature of country that the Australian situation has generated, if not the history as such. Beudel's book is a fine addition to that engaged discourse. Where I am now in Berlin I can't reach for the books that are on my shelves back in Auckland. Many are in Beudel's bibliography and many have been in conversation with writers in New Zealand. I think in particular of my friend the late Geoff Park's citations of Deborah Bird Rose (Park,

2006, 1995). Geoff's work was increasingly informed by the Māori concept of 'whenua', in which place, home, natural world and human placenta are inseparable. The way the word 'country' has come to be used in Australia resonates with this.

I went walking to think about Saskia Beudel's book in Treptower Park here in Berlin, where the river Spree was frozen over and people were exercising their dogs in the snow among bare deciduous trees. I may have been distant from the minds and locations in her book, and spectacularly remote from the landscape she describes so well, but I didn't feel so. The loosely coupled narratives Beudel weaves into shapely thought could be deployed as a conceptual template where I am – though of course her lovely attentions to the particular and local would be missing. Here, as anywhere, it's not possible to walk around the place without being conscious of an incessant muttering. It comes up out of place, out of country, out of whenua – for example from the little brass plaques embedded in Berlin's pavements, which mark buildings from which Jews were taken by the Nazis.

The park where I was walking and thinking about Beudel's book was bare and pale, the snow marked sporadically by footprints; but it was also dense and garrulous with confluences of human activity and natural forces, the city there because the ancient trade conduit of the river was. And the park, a palimpsest of the natural and the artefactual, was full of the stories that people were repeating in chilly puffs of breath as they walked along together, laughing and bickering. They were mostly speaking the fast, singsongy, slang-rich German of Berliners, not the Plattdüütsch of my Baltic ancestors, but I felt uncertainly connected within a network whose spatial and temporal coordinates were occasionally, unpredictably, clear and present. At such moments, I wasn't thinking about Saskia Beudel's book as an object; it was sympathetically present as a method or practice, a supple bridge between subject and object, and a subtle drawing-together of the thematic terms in her book's puzzling title: 'country', 'mind', 'memoir', 'landscape'. Beautiful.

References

Bauman Zygmunt. 2007. *Liquid Times: Living in an Age of Uncertainty.* Cambridge/Malden, MA: Polity Press.

Chatwin, Bruce. 1986. *The Songlines*, Franklin Centre, PA: Franklin Press.

Hau'ofa, Epeli. 2008. 'Our Sea of Islands' and 'The Ocean in Us', in *We Are the Ocean: Selected Works.* Honolulu: University of Hawai'i Press.

Hill, Barry. 2002. *Broken Song: T.G.H. Strehlow and Aboriginal Possession.* Sydney: Knopf.

Michaels, Eric. 1987. *For a Cultural Future: Francis Jupurrurla Makes TV at Yuendumu.* Art and Criticism Monograph Series, vol. 3, Artspace.

—. 1994. *Bad Aboriginal Art: Tradition, Media, and Technological Horizons.* Minneapolis: University of Minnesota Press.

Park, Geoff. 1995. *Ngā Uruora: The Groves of Life: Ecology & History in a New Zealand Landscape*, Wellington: Victoria University Press.

—. 2006. *Theatre Country: Essays on Landscape and Whenua*, Wellington: Victoria University Press.

Design for Living

Dave Kent

Introductory note, *Into the Mind's Sky: Poems by Dave Kent* (Dave Kent Poetry Society, June 2014)

The Dave Kent I knew before disease began to shut down his speech and movement was an exceptionally expressive man. What's extraordinary is that he remained so as his illness progressed. But is this surprising? His persistence is something to celebrate, and these poems can be read that way, despite the sorrow their narrative generates. It also gives us the opportunity to ask what we mean by 'expressive', a word too easily uttered and therefore too easily made banal.

The Dave Kent who popped his head over the fence at the bottom of the section at 11 Albany Ave, Mount Victoria, a few days after Donna and I moved in with our kids, said a few words of greeting. But his expression of welcome was conveyed also by his smile, which we could see because of the steps he'd made that allowed him to look over the fence and indeed to climb over to our side if he wanted. We could climb over in the other direction, too, to the big house in Brougham Street that backed on to ours. Behind the moment when Dave's smile appeared and his few words were uttered, there was thoughtfulness, and thought, a bit of design, some materials assembled, and some making. The purpose of this sequence was primarily hospitable – to get over the fence – and Dave expressed himself through its entire extent as well as at the moment he popped his head over the fence and said hello. The Kent/Baxter family moved out all too soon for our liking, and was replaced by another one which dismantled the steps and had little to express other than complaints about the music our kids played.

When Dave welcomed us to the ramshackle building and junk-filled yard we'd committed to, he did so from a fine building and orderly back section which themselves owed much to his expressiveness, at once meticulous and improvisatory. The Dave I knew wasn't a garrulous man; like the brass screws with which he secured key sections of the restored tongue-and-groove flooring of the Brougham Street house, his words came as much from the need to listen as from the desire to speak. The old house had a story to tell, such as unevenness in its warping structure, and how to respond required thought, patience, empathy and ingenuity.

I don't think this house metaphor is far-fetched. It comes to mind not just because of my memory of Dave's friendly expression appearing over the fence at number 11, Albany Ave, but because of the kind of expression a house embodies. A house is designed and built to serve those who will live in it. It's a social space within which people are brought close to each other. Within the house, relationships are necessary – people and spaces have to work together, or work out how to. What we've come to know (after Ernst Plischke) as the principle of 'design and living' is the condition and context within which self-expression takes place – takes its place, that is, within the complex circumstances of the social space. A human body is also, of course, a 'design *for* living'.

Dave was a very good designer. What made him so wasn't just his imaginative and creative flair, technical skill and craft ethic. He was a good designer because he worked with an understanding that his self-expression was substantially articulated by the needs of people and causes. Of course we can detect Dave's hand in the large and various body of graphic work he produced, but always in relation to a process that had also been hospitable to the stories, needs and conditions of others. In his example, that impoverished cliché of the creative writing manual – 'find your voice' – has to be read against the grain of its implicit reflexivity, its self-regarding egoism; and not least against the absurd implication that you have somehow lost your voice.

What are we to do, then, with the moment when Dave does literally lose his voice? The first time I met him after that had happened was at a lecture by Polly Cantlon in the Art History Department of Victoria University. Dave was taking a paper in theory, and he sat writing quick conversational notes about the course on the jotter pads that had become his mode of expression, along with an articulate semaphore of thumbs-up, smiles, and other gestures. His ability to express himself was diminished, but the way he now did so retained many of the characteristics of his fully-empowered condition.

The diminishment continued, of course – the 'design for living' that was Dave's body could no longer walk, and finally, completely immobilised, could only dictate to an amanuensis through minimal movements of a thumb to approve or reject a vowel or consonant, thereby building sentences one letter at a time. It was a process that heartbreakingly enacted the intense focus of making poems. The last time I saw Dave he dictated a one-letter-at-a-time version of the message that many others remember as his last words: 'Beneath this wooden Picasso face flows a torrent of love.' His expressive ability, now channelled through the tiniest of apertures, was still characterised by sociability.

Not long after he became bedridden, Dave emailed me a copy of the poems he'd been writing. With characteristic modesty he called them *Clashing Clichés*. They weren't, of course. The anguish and fear in them were clear then. But what's more apparent than ever now that the aperture for self-expression has closed, and the design for living that was Dave Kent has been disassembled, is the presence of a voice articulated by a relational not an egoistic impulse.

> Receiving the embrace of my stalwart lover,
> mopping my mouth as it drips on her shoulder.
>
> Smiling at my loving friends,
> mewing, choking, minutes on end.

Even at this extremity, self-pity and self-expression don't elide. The voice Dave Kent found in the poems that replaced speech was the one he'd always used to express his wish to be attentively with us.

A Real Piece

Available Globally via PostShop, REAL Aotearoa, 0800NZstamps

An autoethnographic essay into the shifty and shifting place of the real on the location and within the set contructed in the mind of an adult with the help of a five-year-old child by the New Zealand Post/MGM marketing campaign for the final instalment of the *Hobbit* trilogy.

Extraordinary Anywhere: Essays on Place from Aotearoa New Zealand, edited by Ingrid Horrocks and Cherie Lacey (Victoria University Press, 2016)

Nostalgic nationalism

While not wanting to re-enter 'Middle-earth', a place that has had most of its discursive oxygen sucked out, I'm going to focus on my encounter with an item of merchandise marketing by New Zealand Post that – like it or not – will return me to that place whose reality is at once jammed with contesting narratives, and strangely hollow.

This involves the ordinary activity of a morning walk to the post office and then on to a café for a cup of coffee. It's something I do most days, usually with my wife Donna. A lot of people do something similar, and we greet some of them, but only occasionally as close friends. As an exercise in autoethnography research it's got to be a low-yield option – a somewhat shallow social regime.

But there are various markers along the way that could at a pinch be mined. There's a large Australian eucalypt whose roots are pushing up the pavement just past our place, and an abundant frangipani tree a bit further up the road. The botanical topography of the inner city and its traces of Australian-Irish and Pacific working-class cultures might be a research option. This could inaugurate a novel-of-ideas – an *essay* – about the dynastic interrelationships of an Irish-Australian and a Pacific Island family as the working-class suburb of Ponsonby underwent its process of *embourgeoisement* and Ponsonby Road became chic. It wasn't chic when I lived here as a student in the 1960s, so there's also a subject position reserved for me in this story.

The morning traffic along the feeder link to the harbour bridge provides a slow-moving portrait gallery of commuter activity and emotion. This could become a fixed-viewpoint camera video essay in which a passing parade of cellphone-checking, nose-picking, hair-fixing and child-pacifying is observed without comment. Much could be made of the morning's joggers; their preferences for black sportswear, the proportion of them who have small dogs running alongside and their disproportionate gender weighting towards women. And so on. But usually, I walk along this familiar route after a short morning stint clearing emails and stuff, my thoughts elsewhere, immersed in rather than observant of what's around me.

This is an urban narrative, but because the city of its location – Auckland – is a small one, it retains vestiges of small-town social and cultural geography. Its intimacy is that of small crowd space rather than big crowd crush. The exuberant woman who runs the post office box service is often sitting outside by the back entrance we use, having a smoke and a cup of tea, and she'll usually greet us cheerfully with a 'Morning, darlings!' It's a neighbourhoody atmosphere. The owner of the café we go to after clearing the mail has a daughter living in Melbourne, where my son Jack also lives – our kids are friends. Nonetheless, there's a perceptible tension between the neighbourhood and the global. Some of the regulars at the café, including my wife Donna, work in film and television and they're involved with international contacts on a regular basis. Unless they're travelling, their small place intersects with big place via Skype calls and the like. These relationships are articulated virtually, for the most part, very often along a north–south axis governed by international time and season zones, as a result of which morning talks to evening, winter to summer, and so on. No doubt there are diurnal and seasonal fluctuations of emotion and thought along this axis – gloomy end of winter day talking to cheerful summer morning, and so forth.

Then there are young tourists from large European, Asian or

American cities who stay at the Brown Kiwi backpackers just down the road and enter the café as visitors from big to small. This relationship is articulated physically – in fact, one often hears comments about how lovely it is to be really *in* an uncrowded place with a beautiful 'unspoiled' landscape, and so forth. This is a mindset that often turns out to have been pre-programmed by the international phenomenon of 'Middle-earth' as promoted by Peter Jackson's *Hobbit* movies. The congested traffic around the café in Three Lamps must be a disappointment for many of these optimists, and I sometimes hear them discussing this.

These are familiar and even banal terms of engagement, and they are haunted by all-too-familiar ghosts of nationalist and/or nostalgic models.

So, one morning I enter the post office in my usual low-attention state and there see a poster inviting me to 'Get a real piece of Middle-earth'. At this point, whether I like it or not, I know that when I get to the café I'm going to write this sentence down in my notebook, and that it will, sooner or later, inaugurate some thinking and writing – an *essay* – that will fold the narrative of my routine together with a list of paradoxical challenges thrown at me by the post office poster; and that this will happen despite my disinclination to be drawn into an already exhausted discussion about whether 'distance looks our way' or not. It's just as likely that what I've jotted down in my notebook will make its way into an essay – that is, the product of some thinking and writing – in the form of a novel, or even a poem. I don't know where this little shock of *noticing* will end up, and I don't really care. The notebook I carry around with me is full of stuff whose final destination is very often uncertain or even unknown. What's important is that I've *noticed,* that my mind has been happily provoked into thought, that my heart is beating a little faster, and that all at once the world seems to be more interesting than it was.

In effect, research involving this folding-together of a personal narrative and a thought-provoking issue has been under way for some time, since its basic fieldwork plan is my regular morning excursion to the post office and across the street to the café. What's now changed is the fact that the accumulated information of this daily routine has been charged with a purpose because of the poster in the post office. In Geertzian terms, I can now begin to unpack an accumulated 'thick description' of the event for material to 'include in the consultable record' (Geertz, 2004, pp.6, 30). I can begin to move from inscription to specification if I want to. And in fact, even without wanting to programme what I might do in the form of a Geertzian autoethnography, I'm pretty much doing so involuntarily.

I'm doing this not just by default, but because I'm a writer, and am therefore the kind of reader who is excited not just by the content of what I read, but by what I might learn from its techniques. Over the years I've read a fair bit of ethnographic literature – and have recently reread the 2000 edition of Clifford Geertz's 1960s essays which were mind-changing for me when I first encountered them in the 1973 Basic Books edition. The personal essay, here, is not simply an effect that is somehow extruded by the pressure of my noticing something that is narrated through my presence – my 'subject position' – within the observed event. It is also a narrative that has another writer's presence at its shoulder or, indeed, 'in mind'. In Georges Poulet's terms, which were roughly contemporaneous with those of Geertz, I find myself in the uncanny situation of thinking another's thoughts (Poulet, 1969). So from quite early in the piece, I may encounter Clifford Geertz and Georges Poulet in conversation with the first-person me whose viewpoint will be directing the narrative, but whose consciousness has been strategically occupied by the thinking of others – an occupation, it has to be added, that has remained provisional, indeed *mobile*, through the 40 years since my first encounter with these writers.

Mobility, migration and place

We are beginning to circle around another of the themes with which this colloquium is concerned – 'How might we talk about the relationships between mobility, migration and place?' Parking, for the time being, the mobility of thoughts jostling in our minds over time, and the mobility of those jostled-in minds in and out of different locations and conditions, this theme is most often deployed around discussions – or 'stories' – of belonging (or not), of 'settling' or 'unsettling', of the problematic, paradoxical nature of 'home'; and will have used and often worn out a vocabulary struggling to be at once forensic and descriptive, for example 'diasporic'.

The discussion has found a productive local terminology in what the late Geoff Park characterised as a disjunction between European concepts of landscape shaped by viewing, and Māori concepts of whenua shaped by embodiment. This language has had useful counterparts elsewhere; for example, in the frequent use over many years of the word 'situated' by both James Clifford and Donna Haraway in the United States, signalling the need for ethnographic work of whatever kind to proceed from an acute awareness of context and conditions and, therefore, of their shifts and shiftinesses.

But I'd like to tackle this theme from a different perspective, albeit one that requires the point of view to be *situated*, to be reflexively aware of 'how it's placed'. Our deepest (thickest) awareness of the mental and spatial mobility of thought – of how our own thoughts and those of others are constantly migrating, visiting, conversing to and fro across borders – will usually derive from our adult relationships (if we are adults). Such relationships will be diasporic, or distanced, only to the extent that their cultural contexts are unsettling. If we are curious about (rather than merely tolerant of) difference we will welcome and even seek out such diasporic unsettlings. They are what we expect of grown-up conversation. But there are other opportunities close to home, situated or embodied in ways we too easily take for granted and therefore overlook.

A couple of days ago Donna came home from visiting our five-year-old granddaughter Bella, to whom she'd delivered a present from her great-grandparents. The present was a blonde doll. Bella, whose part-Samoan parentage has given her a head of lush black curls, was pleased with the doll, but wanted to know where she was from. Fearing that Bella might be anxious about her own identity in relation to the blonde doll's, Donna began a conversation about Bella's question 'Where are you from?' But as it turned out, what

Bella was asking was what movie or TV show the doll was from. Was she a Princess Merida, a Cinderella, an Aurora, a Rapunzel, or – best of all just now – an Elsa, the Snow Queen of the Disney animated feature *Frozen*? Identity is artefactual, but the artefact will come to life through imaginative play that is informed by the character's back-story. The blonde doll will enter Bella's life because her story already has. Bella will put her in play with other toys whose stories she also knows. Then she will mash the stories up and make new identities for the dolls, because that's the most fun thing to do. This mash-up will essay or try out personality; will be a personal essay about the relationships between mobility, migration and place – including the 'place' of the movies. More on this place soon.

Personal and cultural memory

It may also essay and be an essay about personal and cultural memory. However, I'd like to tackle this issue by means of yet another anecdote. I have a twin brother, Dave, who is blessed with an exceptional memory and tremendous equanimity. My memory is unreliable, and I'm given to melodrama. The collective family memory – a cultural memory – has bequeathed both of us a story about the time when, as infants just getting our first teeth, we were taken for a walk in our double pram by our grandmother, Aggie Horne. All at once, so the family memory asserts, the normally happy Dave began to shriek. Nana Horne assumed it was me, but as it turned out it was Dave who was screaming. The reason was that we'd managed to swap thumbs to suck, and I was sucking his – but had also begun to gnash it with a sharp new tooth.

The family liked this story because, over the years, it transmitted their sense of how my devious character was shaping up. But my brother is quite sure that the biting was being done by him, that it was me who was shrieking, and that Aggie got it wrong. But since neither of us can in fact remember what happened, we have only the family's 'cultural memory' to go by, and that was the product of much hilarious repetition of Aggie Horne's eye-witness account. But since all members of the family who might be consulted about this 'eye-witness account' (or essay) have been dead for many years, we are left with a space of uncertainty between the realist Dave's account and that of his fantasist twin. Out of this space a number of potential narrative threads emerge – for example, does either of us accurately remember how the family story went when we first heard it at an age when we could retain it? Did I in effect overwrite the family's version because, back then, I wanted to be the biter? Or was Nana Horne wrong about the biter, but allowed herself to be persuaded that I was he because that fitted her uneasy sense of how the infant Ian was developing?

We will never know. What matters, in terms of the 'personal essay', is that this space of narrative unreliability is probably its greatest asset, and is what by and large distinguishes its kind of epistemology from that of the academic essay, reliant as that usually is on reductive and contestable measures of truth, and on a watchful perimeter of scrupulous citation. The personal essay's narrative unreliability is rich in many ways, but perhaps richest in the destabilising effects it has on first-person presence and on the ambiguities that consequently attend the question of who, exactly, is situated, exactly, where? Yes, I can be clear and forthright about the ways in which I'm embedded – situated – in this or that narrative. But the pleasure this presence might generate in readers is about imaginative truth-values, about play, and about orders of reality that are multi-perspectival, digressive and contradictory. Bella knows this, and enjoys inventing and then subverting identities when we play.

But this is not just kid stuff. The ironic or self-reflexive *style indirect libre* as deployed by Flaubert in *Madame Bovary* is perhaps the most obvious model of what this parsing of first and third person (plus author) presences can accomplish – and *Madame Bovary* has always seemed to me to be an *essay*, an ethnography, about the unstable values of bourgeois reality and of subject positions within that reality; and to be an essay not rather than, but because it is also, a novel. The personal essay's ontology may disclose impeccably observed correspondences between words and facts – but we encounter these truths through subjectivities that invite us to play with the essay's construction of reality. The model is less one of a helpful, perhaps patronising, arm's-length hermeneutics, more one of a deliberately unhelpful seduction, an invitation to get situated by joining in a game whose rules are contingent on us agreeing to play.

'A real piece'

Finally, back to the poster in the Ponsonby post office that got me started on this line of enquiry.

The poster promises us 'a real piece of Middle Earth', but since we know that Middle-earth doesn't 'really' exist, the poster seems to be in flagrant breach of advertising standards. However, as my granddaughter Bella knows, the answer in respect of where the 'real piece' comes from is: from a movie, stupid. But how, then, can the 'piece' be 'real' in a material sense? The answer is in the small print. The exculpatory text reads, '. . . contains real wood from the Hobbiton movie set'.

Harking back for a moment to an ontology that may 'disclose impeccably observed correspondences between words and facts', we can say with confidence that the 'real wood' referred to in the New Zealand Post media small print does, physically, exist. 'Wood' corresponds to wood which exists, in fact, as wood. However, to say that this real wood comes from 'the Hobbiton movie set', which has entered the story here as a small-print advertising standards risk-management gloss on 'Middle-earth', is to nudge reliable but boring ontology in the direction of the game. A minimal amount of research on the New Zealand Post media centre website reveals that the piece of 'real wood' is 'particles' from the 'party tree' which featured on the Hobbiton movie set in both the *Lord of the Rings* and *Hobbit* motion picture trilogies. These minute material fragments are embedded in images of the 'iconic door to Bag End', the home of Bilbo Baggins. These images with their particles of real pieces of Middle-earth feature on commemorative coins and stamps issued by New Zealand Post, produced in a partnership with Peter Jackson's New Line Cinema and Metro-Goldwyn-Mayer (MGM). Their purpose is to promote the final movie in the Middle-earth saga, *The Hobbit: The Battle of the Five Armies*, which opened in December 2014.

The wood is real wood, even if the particles of it are minute. The Hobbiton movie set also exists: while initially packed down after filming, the set was soon rebuilt solely as a tourist destination, complete with the Green Dragon Inn open for business. What gets it across the advertising standards anxiety line is an artful conflation of 'location' and 'set': a location being a place that exists in the 'real world', and a set being an entirely fabricated artefact. The Hobbiton movie set remains a location: a few hectares of farmland near Matamata ('Discover the real Middle-earth at the Hobbiton™ Movie Set near Matamata.' www.hobbitontours.com).

So is this where Middle-earth is located – the Middle-earth of which we are promised a 'real piece'? Not quite, because the location, while a real place, has been production-designed, landscaped, and equipped with props (such as the wooden 'party tree'), and has therefore shifted across to that ambiguous zone between location and set, which can in the end only *really* be situated, embodied, in the film experience of it; in the film where, and only where, Middle-earth exists – *really exists*, according to the truth-values of the cinema. A tantalising stretch remains between location at Matamata and Middle-earth on the screen: the situation of the located set, of the place that is simultaneously here and there, in this truth and in that. I guess you could say that religious relics sometimes have this kind of paradoxical existence, at once manifestly and fictionally real – occupying not a liminal but a magical space in which disciplining edges or thresholds don't count; the space of the movies, for example.

If I purchase the 'presentation pack' of coin and stamp, I go into the prize draw to win a trip for two to the Hobbiton Movie Set and a picnic under the 'party tree'. The products are of course 'available globally' via nzpost.co.nz/thehobbit, or – and this is the bit I like – from PostShop, REAL Aotearoa, 0800NZstamps.

Distance is now looking every which way, and I know which realist granddaughter will be joining me under the party tree when I win the draw. Bella will be satisfied with the answer that the 'real piece of Middle-earth' comes from a movie about a place that never existed, except that she's there having a picnic, what's your problem? And I'll be satisfied with that answer as well, but, because I'm older, will also know that the meaning and value of the 'real piece' of wood have been generated by the global marketing narratives of a major film production consortium, and a national communications delivery system whose job it is to deliver these meanings and values to its customers, who, like the happy picnickers, prefer to believe that there's nothing particularly unusual about this construction of place.

Most of us don't have much trouble feeling at home here. It's pretty much what most of us do, most of the time. Happy (maybe unhappy) picnickers in a paradoxical 'location' that may even constitute a new kind of indigeneity, perhaps situated in something like a set of conditions James Clifford has provisionally defined as 'traditional futures' (Clifford, 2004). This, I hasten to add, is not exclusively a modern situation, though its conditions may have been normalised by the proliferation of virtual realities. Film, if not cinema, is, after all, 125 years old. But then, *Mahābhārata* has its origins somewhere between the 8th and 9th centuries BCE, and movie adaptations have continued to gush spectacularly from this source since 1920; had Bella been born in India rather than New Zealand, she'd very probably be 'situated' in the latest Bollywood retelling of a story out of *Mahābhārata*. There's a Twitter version of *Mahābhārata* that will go on ekeing out its 140 characters through many human generations after Bella's, if Twitter survives. Right now *Mahābhārata* is trending, in multiple languages and places, and continues to reel the future into a present that persists in playing with the past. Bella will soon outgrow the Elsa of *Frozen*, but will continue, let's hope, to essay herself 'on locations', plural.

References

Clifford, James. 2004. 'Traditional Futures'. In *Questions of Tradition,* eds. Mark Phillips and Gordon Schochet. Toronto: University of Toronto Press.

Geertz, Clifford. 2000. 'Thick Description: Towards an Interpretive Theory of Culture'. In *The Interpretation of Cultures.* New York: Basic Books.

Poulet, Georges. 1969. 'Phenomenology of Reading', in *New Literary History,* Vol. 1, No. 1.

Returns

James Clifford

Review of *Returns: Becoming Indigenous in the Twenty-First Century* by James Clifford (Harvard University Press, 2013) in *Museum Worlds* (Berghahn Books, Vol. 3, Issue 1, 2015)

Road map

Returns is the third in a trilogy of books by James Clifford, described succinctly by Clifford Geertz as 'one of the few persons who connects history, literature, and anthropology' (1988, back jacket). The trilogy's titles suggest a narrative trajectory: *The Predicament of Culture* (1988), *Routes* (1997) and now *Returns* (2013). Simply, this three-part narrative could be mapped as moving from an inciting question ('Who has the authority to speak for any group's identity and authenticity?') via journeys and translations ('the transcultural predicaments for the late twentieth century') to the inherently paradoxical condition of 'returning' ('becoming indigenous in the twenty-first century'). The new book's subtitle is typical Clifford. If indigeneity is often understood as an historical, even autochthonous condition, how can its ontology involve contemporary becoming? This question is the intellectual driver of *Returns*. The 'returns' that are mapped here are not to a romanticised pre-modern authenticity, but rather to what Clifford calls traditional futures (another paradox). The agency of the word 'indigenous' is, in this book, deployed to examine the ways, means and meanings of Native persistence. A 'return' might usefully be thought of as a 'comeback' in this context, except that this misses the infolded sense of journey as both physical and existential. 'Returns' thus, from the outset, proposes a set of complications that need to be unpacked.

This Clifford does by assembling his texts in three sections. The first, a nuanced discussion of the historiography of ethnographic theory and practice, consists of three chapters and is set in motion by the first sentence of the first chapter ('Among Histories'): 'Indigenous people have emerged from history's blind spot' (2013, p.13). The second, 'Ishi's Story', is a case study of that emergence. It is a fascinating account of the Yahi 'wild man' Native Californian from Deer Creek who emerged into the modern world in August 1911. Part three consists of three chapters, each of which looks at ways in which indigeneity might now be deployed strategically and practically to establish productive terms and conditions – political, institutional and cultural – for 'traditional futures'.

Returns is thus both an elegant segue and an appropriately open-ended ending – though it completes the narrative arc of the trilogy, it leaves open the question of where the story might go from here. It also raises issues of narrative presence: where and how does Clifford locate himself in this ongoing story? In what follows, I try to map the overall work of the trilogy and the function of *Returns* in it; but I try also to examine the rather more literary question of subject position – a question that I think may, at this juncture, be of overriding interest.

Subject positions

James Clifford's new book begins with a dedication, 'For my students, 1978–2013'. This is modest code for Clifford's long involvement with the UCSC History of Consciousness Department, from which he retired in 2011 as Distinguished Professor Emeritus. The department's famous and even radical PhD programme continues, some 40 years since it was established, to operate (as its website promises) 'at the intersection of established and emergent disciplines and fields, acquainting students with leading intellectual trends in the Humanities, Arts and Social Sciences' – though not, it is safe to suppose, without some constricting intellectual and managerial 'rationalisation', over the past decade, of its foundational planks of interdisciplinarity, dialogic models of discourse, and intellectual experiment. The dedication, in any case, announces an ongoing commitment to the terms of engagement that have shaped Clifford's work over four decades; and is an elegant and generous salute to students who have appeared with increasing frequency in his citation references.

The History of Consciousness programme's refusal of narrow, teleological disciplinary specialisation, its embrace of opportunities for intellectual cross-pollination, and its acknowledgement of the complex, contesting politics of research and fieldwork are of course the products of Clifford's own thought – indeed, of the ethics of his thought – along with that of his senior colleagues such as Donna Haraway. And so the dedicatory code of *Returns* at the front of the book links up with the citation references at the back, characterised as these are by exceptional diversity. And we begin to see the outline of a larger, more quixotic and *literary* venture than the programme announced in the book's table of contents, intriguing though this is.

In a chapter on Michel Leiris in *The Predicament of Culture*, Clifford quotes in full the *prière d'insérer* that Leiris had inserted between the pages of the first edition of *L'Afrique fantôme* (1934). In this apparently capricious positioning of himself as an unreliable narrator, Leiris announces, 'It's up to the reader to discover the germs of a coming to consciousness attained only well after the return, while at the same time following the author among peoples, sites, vicissitudes from the Atlantic to the Red Sea' (p.166). Also in *Predicament*, Clifford opens his first chapter, 'On Ethnographic Authority', with an epigraph from a fellow spirit, the anthropologist Paul Rabinow ('anthropology of reason'): 'Clifford takes as his natives, as well as his informants, . . . anthropologists . . . We are being observed and inscribed' (p.21).

Reading *Returns*, it was the question of Clifford's self – positioned as subject, the how, why and where of his self-inscription – that began to interest me; and, coactively, his self-positioning as object 'being observed and inscribed'. Was I in fact reading the ongoing account of a 'coming to consciousness' (without the egoistic flourish of Leiris) in which Clifford is by turns subject and object – the observer and the observed? Or, more likely – as I will argue – was I reading an account in which the distinction between subject and object was being disputed, subverted, found to be *complexly articulated* or *contingent* (two of Clifford's 'signature' terms)? I had to ask, Is this question a distraction from the real business of the book – its substantial content? In the end I came to the conclusion that it is central to that 'real business'. That real business, inevitably, circulates in one way or another around issues of power and authority, and thus about point of view (therefore narrative control), and knowledge (therefore access and privilege).

With characteristic methodical and methodological lucidity, Clifford's prologue maps his new book's narrative arc – its 'architecture' as he calls it (p.9). It also locates the book as 'the third volume in a series beginning in 1988 with *The Predicament of Culture* and followed in 1997 by *Routes*' (p.1). This larger narrative arc, spanning 25 years, may seem to announce a more determinate project than Clifford's frequent readers are likely either to expect or to believe he intended to write from the outset. For one thing, each book has been a carefully organised edition of existing, which is to say more or less discrete, essays, lectures, reviews, and performance texts such as interviews or question and answer sessions, the provenances of which are listed carefully in all three volumes under Sources. For another, Clifford's characteristic vocabulary has always been richly and suggestively seeded with a number of key words: 'discrepant', 'contested', 'emergent', 'situated', 'complexly', 'rearticulation', 'nonreductive'; 'determinations without determinism', 'partial histories', 'constitutive tensions'; 'the contradictions and paradoxes of postmodernity'; and, of course, 'contingent'. No one whose *mentalité* is expressed in such change-agent terms is going to pretend that these books chart a journey that was comprehensively mapped and provided for about 1980.

That said, the narrative coherence – the ongoing 'coming to consciousness' – of the trilogy is remarkable. And so is the persistence of the issue of Clifford's rhetorical presence. Of course, 'coming to consciousness' and presence (or performance) are complexly related, as Clifford might put it; and this relationship is articulated (a term

Clifford likes from Gramsci via Stuart Hall) or rearticulated also through the agency of his readers. We are talking about varieties of observed performance. In order to track this performative coherence through its various stages, modes, turns and *détournements*, it is useful to refer briefly to the book co-edited by Clifford and George E. Marcus, *Writing Culture: The Poetics and Politics of Ethnography* (1986), and to the aptly branded Prickly Paradigm Press collection of interviews with Clifford, *On the Edges of Anthropology* (2003). In an interview with Alex Coles (1999), Coles pounces on a shift from the way Clifford had discussed museums in the 1980s. In response, Clifford has this to say:

> One of the first things I published after *The Predicament of Culture* was an essay comparing 'Four Northwest Coast Museums' in Vancouver. Two of these were 'tribal' museums/ cultural centres. The essay, reprinted in *Routes*, marked a crucial discovery for me. I began to see the museum, that most stodgy and Eurocentric of institutions, as a dynamic, disseminating institution which could take a diversity of forms in particular local/global conjunctures. (Clifford, 2003, p.36)

It has been varieties of 'crucial discovery' such as this that have opened up pathways for Clifford's ongoing 'coming to consciousness' his 'routes', as one might say; his 'expeditions', even. Such shifts, realignments, or even changes of mind have invariably been marked by candour and, indeed, by the enjoyment, the intellectual and emotional rush, of discovery – including, it must be said, of self-discovery. It is perhaps this exhilaration, decorous though it is by comparison with Leiris, that gives Clifford's writing its literary, almost novelistic character (think Bakhtin): here is a character (the ethnographer) on a journey; here is a series of subtle narrative moves, declensions of a *style indirect libre* in which subject voices and presences are in play with each other and with the reader.

The museum

Of course, Clifford's work is primarily directed at the scholarly analysis and critique of historiographic and ethnographic practices. Scrutinising 'conjunctures' between history, anthropology and ethnography, between the observation of culture and the writing of it, and between participation and sitting-in, the scope of Clifford's diverse attentions has been increasingly defined by museums and by actions initiated or defined by museum agendas. Many of his discoveries have been located in these places. Museums are sites of power, surveillance, and cultural scripting. They are where academic research and thesis-cultivation happen. They are agents of nationalist or imperial hegemonic conformity. Their core business includes hoarding, archiving, conserving and protecting. They are facilitators of complex indigenous identity-building or advocacy, as in the 'tribal' cultural centres mentioned above, or the complex 'interdependencies' of the Centre Culturel Jean-Marie Tjibaou in Nouméa, New Caledonia – the latter the site, I think, of one of Clifford's most significant turns.

Clifford is not, and has never claimed to be, a feverish pith helmet anthropologist fieldworker in the early 20th-century tradition. His doctoral research and first major research publication, *Person and Myth: Maurice Leenhardt in the Melanesian World* (1982), were structured around the history of anthropology, with an emphasis on the 'French tradition'. The 'field' in which he conducts his research would once, in the extended, embedded encounter era (think Michael Jackson's 'existential ethnography' fieldwork with the Kuku Yalangi of Cape York Peninsula in Australia in the early 1990s), have been characterised as the domain of 'secondary' research: museums, publications, archival records. In a key essay, 'Spatial Practices: Fieldwork, Travel, and the Disciplining of Anthropology' (Clifford, 1997, pp.52–91), Clifford uses Michel de Certeau's term 'spatial practices' to subvert the hierarchical implications of 'primary' and 'secondary' research. He suggests that a 'multiplicity of practices blurs any sharp, referential meaning for '"fieldwork"' (p.54). But lest this result in a sedentary characterisation of 'fieldwork' as comfortable academic commuting, Clifford also suggests a 'disciplining' of fieldwork that requires the 'postexoticist' researcher to, at very least, 'get out of the house' (p.88) – to 'travel'. He suggests that 'there is truth in the cliché, "Travel broadens"'.

> Sojourning somewhere else, learning a language, putting oneself in odd situations and trying to figure them out can be a good way to learn something new, simultaneously about oneself and about the people and places one visits. (p.91)

'Travel broadens' is, with a characteristically well-timed narrative flourish, shifted past backpacker cliché in the following chapter, 'White Ethnicity', in which Clifford intercuts his youthful expeditions around New York City neighbourhoods with quotations from John Wesley Powell's *The Exploration of the Colorado River* (1895) and Audre Lorde's *Zami: A New Spelling of My Name* (1982). Clifford was (and remains) a lover of folk music. Writing his young self in the third person, Clifford's mature field notes record that, 'He went into the subway at 116th Street and traveled, a hundred blocks south, to Kentucky [in Washington Square]' (93). The 'folkies' who assembled at Washington Square in New York City on Sundays constituted a 'somewhere else'; but also a kind of museum.

The descriptor 'museum' has, in Clifford's wide field of interest, come to include by implication the written texts and other kinds of records such as photographs and sound recordings with which ethnography has stored and displayed its presence and history. 'Text' performs as cultural artefact, ceremonial or performance script, thought-map – and, indeed, within a wider perimeter of cultural performance such as art and poetry. These sites of the museum's instrumentality include its built environments for display and performance, and therefore also the tangled social, cultural, political and economic (which is to say institutional) environments that both facilitate and delimit performance. They encompass the museum's textual and graphic objects and their infrastructures. They are the theatres of discussion and debate in symposia and public consultations or meetings, as well as the imaginative fields of art and literature. They function as exchange networks that resemble the material semiotics of Actor Network Theory (and the complex valencies of Donna Haraway's feminist analyses). And all are comprehensively where Clifford's fieldwork takes place. Indeed, his fieldwork also takes place in the course of 'a wonderful French lunch' near the Kodiak Launch Complex on Kodiak Island in Alaska (Clifford, 2013, p.312). In this, his method and attitude exceed even the extension mooted by Paul Rabinow (anthropologists as 'natives'), though his most ubiquitous 'fields' (museums, texts, symposia) might still be considered 'secondary' in some quarters.

In his introduction to *Writing Culture*, Clifford shows us this expanded frontier:

> Ethnography is an emergent interdisciplinary phenomenon. Its authority and rhetoric have spread to many fields where 'culture' is a newly problematic object of description and critique. . . . [the writers collected here] see ethnographic writing as changing, inventive: 'History,' in William Carlos Williams's words, 'that should be a left hand to us, as of a violinist.'
> (Clifford and Marcus, 1986: p.3)

And, a few pages on, after a careful history of change and invention presided over by the poet Williams's violinist figure, her left hand organising on the fret what the bow hand will produce on the strings, we read this:

> Dialogical modes are not, in principle, autobiographical; they need not lead to hyper self-consciousness or self-absorption. As Bakhtin (1981) has shown, dialogical processes proliferate in any complexly represented discursive space (that of ethnography, or, in his case, a realist novel). Many voices clamour for expression. Polyvocality was restrained and orchestrated in traditional ethnographies by giving to one voice a pervasive authorial

> function and to others the role of sources, 'informants', to be quoted or paraphrased. Once dialogism and polyphony are recognized as modes of textual production, monophonic authority is questioned, revealed to be characteristic of a science that has claimed to *represent* cultures. (p.15)

'Coming to consciousness'

This editorial note was published in 1986. It announces with considerable political confidence a kind of manifesto, a commitment to multivalent points of view, even to a subversive code-switching along the lines of Bakhtin's heteroglossia. It constitutes a supple methodology that informs Clifford's 'coming to consciousness' (learning 'something new') of which the history has been written in the three books inaugurated by *The Predicament of Culture* in 1988. Which is why, on the first page of Clifford's new book *Returns*, we shouldn't be surprised to read the following:

> Rereading my words in *The Predicament of Culture*, I feel most acutely their distance. They belong to another world. There is no 'globalization' in the book's index, no 'Internet', no 'postcolonial'. Searching for a historical narrative to make sense of what has changed, I now recognize a profound shift of power relations and discursive locations. Call this change, for short, the decentering of the West. (Clifford, 2013, p.1)

Tracking the coherence of Clifford's 'coming to consciousness' through the trilogy involves simultaneous experiences of persistent convictions and ongoing revisions and, indeed, doubts. Structurally, the three books have much in common. Each starts with a prologue (or, in the case of *Predicament*, an introduction, 'The Pure Products Go Crazy' – which draws again on the poet William Carlos Williams). These opening texts are all uttered emphatically in the first person, and all contain embedded credos or statements of intent: 'My primary goal is to open space for cultural futures, for the recognition of emergence

. . .' (1988, pp.15–16); 'The kind of situated analysis I have in mind . . . assumes that all broadly meaningful concepts, terms such as "travel", are translations, built from imperfect equivalences' (1997, p.11); 'In *Returns* I argue for an ethnographic and historical realism – recognising that ideas of history and the real are currently contested and also inventively translated in power-charged sites from land-claims courtrooms to museums and universities . . .' (2013, p.7).

These early-seeded ideas – cultural emergence, travel as translation, ethnographic and historical realism – are as much rhetorical provocations as organising theses. They provoke us, the readers; but they also have acted as provocations or challenges to Clifford himself. What follows in each volume are varieties of ways (and voicings or presences/performances) in which he rises to his own challenges, or contests them. In an epilogue to *Returns*, Clifford returns to the rhetorical challenge of a statement by Barbara Shangin, an Alutiiq elder whom he quotes first in *Routes* (p.343) and again, twice, in *Returns* (pp.253, 315): 'Our people have made it through lots of storms and disasters for thousands of years. All the troubles since the Russians are like one long stretch of bad weather. Like everything else, this storm will pass over some day.'

Revisiting this statement at the end of his extended deployment of the principle of 'ethnographic and historical realism', Clifford closes the book with a disclaimer:

> I have tried to take seriously Shangin's view of historical possibility, not just as a story of indigenous survival, but as a way of living in modernity, and a way through to something else. How could such a vision be realistic, in a world of industrializing nation-states and global capitalism? *Returns* has offered not so much an answer as a deepening of the question. (p.315)

Read one way, the stretch between early challenge and late disclaimer is entirely consistent with Clifford's methodology and politics – he is a resourceful and principled critic of hegemonic, essentialist, top-down authority and control, his own potential included. His politics are identifiably left, with loyalty lines to Raymond Williams and Stuart Hall, among others. His hermeneutics are, to a fault, informed and shaped not just by reference to academic epistemologies, but also by inclusive citations of Native voices such as Barbara Shangin's.

But there is another way of reading (or experiencing) this stretch. Each of the trilogy's three volumes contains one or more extended, and trenchant, readings and critiques of professional texts and activities. In *Predicament*, such an extended review of ethnographic literature and practice begins, in 'Part One: Discourses', with a chapter on 'Ethnographic Authority' and moves via a chapter on Marcel Griaule to 'On Ethnographic Self-Fashioning: Conrad and Malinowski'. In this chapter, Clifford implicitly introduces another, or parallel, way of reading that stretch between confident challenge or assertion, and self-deprecating disclaimer. With the presences of Bakhtin (heteroglossia) and Flaubert (*style indirect libre*) not far from his text, Clifford channels Henry James's concept of a 'controlling intelligence' and writes of Malinowski that: 'The literary problem of authorial point of view, the Jamesian requirement that every novel reflect a "controlling intelligence", was a painful, personal problem for the Trobriand diarist. The ample, multiperspectival, meandering structure of *Argonauts* resolves this crisis of sincerity' (1988, p.104). *Returns* opens with an often autobiographical, first-person 'Prologue'; moves to an extended review ('Among Histories') of theoretical and terminological approaches to the historical-ethnographic, from which the first-person pronoun is largely withheld, and from which a carefully functional set of tools is derived: 'Articulation, Performance, Translation'. To these must be added the 'realism' mooted in the book's 'Prologue'. Pronominal presence henceforth prefers 'we': 'We have already seen . . .' etc. The fascinating and substantial section, 'Ishi's Story', a history not just of 'the wild man of Oroville' but also of the tellings of that story (not least within the writings of Ursula K. Le Guin), rarely enters Clifford's personal time and place, except where he attends meetings at which the repatriation and burial of Ishi's remains are discussed. This attendance constitutes a kind of fieldwork – yet the by-now unexpected appearance of 'I' on the page comes as a small shock. Reading, 'I sensed here . . . a strong feeling of reconnection with a lost relative' (p.148) I was aware both of Clifford's presence, and of a kind of modesty, a self-effacement or partial withdrawal, as if he didn't want to make too much of his attendance at or participation in these meetings.

In the next chapter, 'Hau'ofa's Hope', the mode of address is that of an intimate, casual lecture in which Clifford unambiguously speaks as 'I', even naming one of his students, Teresia Teaiwa (now Senior lecturer in Pacific Studies at Victoria University in Wellington) by her first name: 'It was Teresia who gave me Hau'ofa's 'Sea of Islands' essay not long after its first publication' (p.199). Such modalities of presence continue throughout the book, in variously marked degrees. Contrapuntally, Clifford asserts in chapter 6, 'Looking Several Ways', that: 'Gone are the days when cultural anthropologists could, without contradiction, present "the native point of view . . ." (p.213). And it is at moments like this that the gap between subject and object presence becomes one of tension rather than distinction: as if Clifford is in effect wary of writing his own point of view, of objectifying his experience, of presuming first-hand knowledge – wary, even, of ontological certainty. It's at such points that subject and object presences seem to drift together, or across each other. And so the other – or an other – way of reading and experiencing the stretch between assertive challenge and self-deprecating disclaimer is as a kind of self-imposed hesitancy, paranoid about Jamesian 'controlling intelligence', withdrawing authority when or if it seems about to become peremptory or presumptuous.

But there is a profusion of idiosyncratic instances such as 'a wonderful French lunch' near the Kodiak Launch Complex on Kodiak Island. There are the attentions paid to poets such as William Carlos Williams and Aimé Césaire, and to artists such as Susan Hiller. There's Clifford's own 'Year of the Ram' section in *Routes* and 'The Jardin des Plantes: Postcards' in *Predicament*, among many other such non-academic, literary subversions of narrative coercion. And so my preferred option is to bypass the need to make a clear distinction between Clifford's firm, somewhat politicised rejection of hegemonic authority (including the authority of a confident self) and an over-anxious *amour propre* (a hesitancy to appear or perform as an over-confident self).

Clifford's unwillingness to mark the distinction between a confidently observing, analysing, recording subject committed to certain clear political and theoretical standpoints, and an observed, objectified, reflexive self wary of overconfident closure is in the end what constitutes the unusual, literary character or tone of his shape-shifter ethnography. His prodigious scholarship is of course the reliable armature on which this slidey narrative rhetoric of unreliable narrator is *articulated*, along with his acutely employed terms such as articulation and interpellation: he not only refreshes and problematises the narrative rhetoric of ethnographic writing, he also invariably sharpens the practical applications of its vocabulary.

'Crisis of sincerity'

Having come down in appreciative favour of Clifford's complex narrative ethics, I should add, as a kind of postscript, that I sense a build-up and even repression of political indignation in this latest book. I sense what Clifford has called a 'crisis of sincerity'. His hankerings for utopian outcomes, and the *realpolitik* of his readings of *discrepant, complexly articulated* dystopian forces at work in global capitalism, may perhaps lead at some point to him losing patience with his own self-deprecating accommodations of diverse points of view. This leftist political attitude has roots in Clifford's childhood, as the autobiographical fragments in 'White Ethnicity' reveal. It has been deeply cultivated during his years as a highly principled teacher committed to the multivalent programme at the History of Consciousness Department. It has, needless to say, been repeatedly informed and enriched by his own scrupulously *realist* approaches to fieldwork.

But maybe now's the time to cut loose. We may one day read an assertion of forthright narrative control – an expression of personal outrage that exceeds the generous, accommodating optimism of

Returns. Such outrage might demand cutting through the kind of pragmatic and strategic 'realism' expressed in what has long been one of Clifford's mantras, Jean-Marie Tjibaou's statement that, 'L'indépendence, c'est de bien calculer les interdépendences.' If and when that cut-through happens, it will have been well prepared for.

Among the preparations one could include Clifford's sympathetic and paradigm-changing discussion in *Returns* of 'Native art' – relocating it in a wider and more complexly articulated cultural field than that of the hypercapitalist art market, with its inescapable collusions of dealers, curators, collectors and institutions. I think back to Clifford's exemplary dissection of the 1984–85 MOMA exhibition *'Primitivism' in 20th Century Art: Affinity of the Tribal and the Modern*, first published as 'Histories of the Tribal and the Modern' in *Art in America* (April 1985). Such preparation, goaded by outrage, could and perhaps should also prompt an investigation into where, within what demographic, and in what cultural conditions, voluntary or inescapable, are the marginalised communities and individuals for whom the complex rearticulations of Native art (and identity) are either irrelevant or out of reach?

A similar challenge might devolve from Clifford's paradigm-shifting analysis of 'museums' as sites of Native cultural and social 'return' – a noun whose companion verb suggests not just coming back but recirculating and reinventing. So – what about the fieldwork that would describe comparatively the conditions, lifeways and predelictions of communities and individuals for whom such museums are inaccessible and/or of no interest?

In *Returns,* Clifford is in effect writing a distinctly politicised socio-historical ethnography. A sub-section like 'Entangled Agencies' in the chapter 'Second Life: The Return of the Masks' (pp.306–12) is a canny, pragmatic analysis of *realist* conditions, in this case of the Alutiiq Museum's support strategies and networks. The museum, concludes Clifford, shares with the US Strategic Defense Initiative 'improved connectivity, joining local, regional, and global worlds' (p.314). The Kodiak Launch Complex essential role in the United States's missile defence system is also bundled with its facilitation of 'remotely guided emergency surgery at the Kodiak hospital' – and was the site of Clifford's 'wonderful French lunch'. An ironic allegory lurks about this conjuncture.

'How to understand this tangle of different histories, separately and together?' (p.314), Clifford asks on the occasion of his 'wonderful French lunch' – seeming to leave open the possibility that it might be time to 'get out of the house', to act on a 'crisis of sincerity', to move past or cut through the decorum of a 'spatial practice' perimeter that has begun to frustrate him. Clifford has been a great teacher, as the dedication to his students at the start of *Returns* indicates – not least because he has encouraged them and us to listen to and make speaking space for many discrepant voices. So none of us will begrudge Jim the opportunity, now, to speak and write in his own straightforwardly articulated, unmediated, self-centred voice, about those who remain marginalised by even his immensely hospitable 'museum'. I have enjoyed and admired *Returns*; but I would like to read *that* book next.

References

Clifford, James. 1985. 'Histories of the Tribal and Modern.' *Art in America* 73 (4): pp.164–77, 211, 215.

Clifford, James, and George E. Marcus. 1986. *Writing Culture: The Poetics and Politics of Ethnography – A School of American Research Advanced Seminar.* Berkeley: University of California Press.

Clifford, James. 1988. *The Predicament of Culture: Twentieth-century Ethnography, Literature, and Art.* Cambridge, MA: Harvard University Press.

Clifford, James. 1997. *Routes: Travel and Translation in the Late Twentieth Century.* Cambridge, MA: Harvard University Press.

Clifford, James. 2001. 'Indigenous Articulations.' *The Contemporary Pacific* (13 (2): pp.468–90.

Clifford, James. 2003. *On the Edges of Anthropology: Interviews.* Chicago: Prickly Paradigm Press.

Clifford, James. 2013. *Returns: Becoming Indigenous in the Twenty-First Century.* Cambridge MA: Harvard University Press.

University of California Santa Cruz (UCSC). 2015. *History of Consciousness.* http://histcon.ucsc.edu/ (accessed 31 October 2015).

Russell Haley 1934–2016

for Jean and Ian Haley

thespinoff.co.nz/books (31 August 2016)

Russell Haley died in the morning on Monday 4 July this year. It may seem inappropriate to follow this by saying that he was the funniest man I've ever met, but it feels right. You can't be as funny as Russell was without being clever; but you can't be as clever and funny as he was if there isn't darkness somewhere in or under the humour. Early in Russell's last published novel, *The Spaces Between*, his male protagonist Jervis Kraik notes (in the third person), 'He detested jokes of any type.' I think Russell did, too. There had to be more to humour than an easy gag. The world's a funny old place, a terrible funny old place.

I met Jean and Russell in Auckland in 1967 – they'd moved to Auckland from Australia with their kids Ian and Kathy a year earlier, having gone to Australia with Ian in 1961 as ten quid migrants from the north of England. They laughed together a lot and pulled each other's legs, often adopting Yorkshire accents, and Jean would say, 'You daft bugger!' The deadpan decorum of Russell's scrupulously elegant and correct sentences is constantly subverted by varieties of daft (or daftly arcane) counterfactualities. Off the page, Jean and Russell were a great double act. On the page, Russell's nimble wit always has the character of social yarn-spinning. The yarns are those of migrants from tough times.

I remember a routine Russell improvised at the massive wedding party for Alan Brunton and Sally Rodwell at their place in Tinakori Road, Wellington, in June 1975. Russell transformed himself into a gliding, obsequious salesman whose obscure wares were, without doubt, rubbish. He'd manifested an oozy oil gland on his shoulder into which he dipped lips that had become a kind of beak with which he preened his chest in between purring his salespitch. His ad-lib patter, as he toured the room with an entourage of weeping-with-laughter followers, lasted a good half-hour. I remember, too, a minibus trip from Auckland to Wellington in 1969 which was dubbed *Za'oud Over the Mountains* and included Russell's play *The Adoration of Za'oud.* On the way back it was Russell's turn to drive when the van was enveloped in fog on a ridgeback road with precipices on both sides. Where were we? In a Haley story? Russell jammed on the brakes in the middle of the road. He was laughing his head off, but we had to unclench his hands from the steering wheel. At *Cabaret Paris Spleen* in Wellington in 1975, Russell beat clouds of talcum powder out of his hair and wore a toppling *boutonnière* of arum lilies. He had them in fits.

Earlier this year, a performance of *Turtle Time*, Jack Body's setting of a poem by Russell, was advertised by Auckland University Music School's Karlheinz Company. Dismayed that Russell hadn't been invited (he and Jean had just moved from Mangawhai to Whangārei), I arranged to go up, spend a night with them, and drive back with Russell in time for the performance on Saturday 15 May. Russell's recent emails had been odd, with occasional keystroke mistakes and even wrong words, but it was a shock to find he was having trouble matching perfectly clear thoughts to the right word. He was laughing about it, and typically was also enjoying and laughing at the subversive oddness of the thought-to-word process, as if a kind of spoken psychography or automatic writing, or a surrealist or OULIPO djinn had commandeered his language. In the morning we drove down to Auckland talking the whole way. Clearly Russell was anxious to find out what was wrong, but that evening at the performance of *Turtle Time* he received a round of applause and talked to a number of people. At 82 he was in very good physical shape, lean and agile, in fact matching Moira's description of Jervis Kraik in his novel *The Spaces Between*: 'Jarvis's skin was smooth and tanned. He was in remarkably good nick for his age. Probably an exercise freak.' He caught the bus back to Whangārei the next morning.

A month later Donna and I went up to spend the weekend in a bach out by Whangārei Heads, visit a newish grandson at Parua Bay, and see the Haleys. Russell had been diagnosed with cancer and they were planning a week of treatments at Auckland City Hospital. We had lunch – Russell was thinner and was having more difficulty with his speech, but he and Jean were both optimistic and determined.

But later in June, Jean phoned to tell us Russell was having more difficulty. I went up on Tuesday 28th to lend a hand for a few days, expecting to come back the following Friday. Murray Edmond said he'd take over at the weekend. Russell's speech was worse, and his balance was affected. He needed help to stand up and walk. On Friday we went for a meeting with Russell's oncologist at Whangārei hospital. Russell learned that his brain cancer was terminal but that he could win some time with a course of radiotherapy. He and Jean committed to doing this. They both seemed buoyed by the decision and by the impetus of doing something.

In the afternoon, an old delight-in-laughter friend, David Kisler, came to visit. Russell's good cheer seemed to dissipate after David left, as if a flow of social energy had stopped. He went to bed and, early on Saturday morning, had become unable to move or speak. The hospice nurse came and fitted him with an analgesic drip. Russell and his and Jean's border collie Pip exchanged a long look across the bed and Pip lay down beside it and refused to move. Then Russell lost consciousness – whatever that means. Ian Haley and Russell and Jean's grandson Kei arrived, and so did his sister Caryl. On Sunday, Murray Edmond came up. We took turns reading Russell's favourite Beckett novel, *Murphy,* to him; Ian and Murray were also reading him his story 'Fog', from the 1984 book of stories *Real Illusions.* None of us doubted that, despite appearances, Russell was aware of the words being read aloud.

Russell died on Monday morning and, after another long look, Pip left the room. Jean knew what Russell wanted to happen: no undertaker, no embalming, no religion; she never wavered. A Haleyesque sequence of events began, at once sad and funny. Ian and I drove out to the crematorium and met Dennis, who had a packet of smokes in his shirt pocket and emerged from behind the furnace. He gave us a wad of forms to fill in and we made a booking for 10.30 am the next day. Donna arrived from Auckland and helped Jean fill out the forms. I located a coffin-maker north of Whangārei at Hikurangi. His name was Iain. And so Ian and Ian Haley drove up there to meet Iain, whose signage on the road frontage read, 'Quotes for trespassers free and so's the first bullet', or words to that effect. Russell's last wishes began to resemble a conflation of two writers he loved, Samuel Beckett and Ronald Hugh Morrieson.

Back at the house, we moved Russell into the coffin in the front room. Jean and Russell's old German friends Hubert and Ria arrived, as well as some neighbours from next door, and we all raised glasses to Russell Haley – and to Harry Lurber, Commissioner Gerder, Simon Fesk, Harry Rejekt and Jervis Kraik, among other persona of the man we loved. We wrote messages on the coffin. On Tuesday morning, Jean and Russell's old mate Barry Read arrived with his ute, Hubert and Ria came back, and we loaded Russell into the ute and drove very slowly in a small convoy to where Dennis was waiting at the crematorium. We said goodbye to Russell in his richly inscribed coffin. Then we went back to Jean and Russell's place and drank a Laphroaig or two. Ian Haley remembered a favourite final paragraph from Russell's story 'Looping the Loop', in *Real Illusions*:

> We are all composed of such tenuous substance. Mother and father call to you through blood and genes but time stretches us in every way until we are a thin vibrating membrane. And how delicately then the mind is poised like a spider skimming over an elastic skin of water. How easy to collapse inwards with the pressure of an event or touch against others in affinity and merge.

The following Saturday there was a party at Jean and Russell's place. A lot of people came, including David and Mary Kisler, Greer and Dee Twiss, and many others. A great many very good stories were told.

The first paragraph of *Moonshine Eggs* (not yet published), the last novel Russell Haley finished (or perhaps the last one was *Inside the Black Clock*?) and which I recently read in manuscript, begins like this: 'Harry Rejekt listened to his friend but he found it hard to pay proper attention to Joseph. Somehow he couldn't get a clear focus on what Bartleby was saying.' There's an immediate – deliberate? – wedge driven between 'Joseph' and 'Bartleby', as if this 'friend' we soon come to know as singular could also, at some level, be a conjoined double, a 'Joseph' and a 'Bartleby'.

Knowing Russell, the name 'Bartleby' almost certainly gestures towards 'Bartleby, the Scrivener', Herman Melville's ambiguous allegory of a copy-editor who, having been driven out of a job at the Dead Letter Office in New York City, ends his days staring at a blank wall from the office of a Wall Street lawyer and, finally, dying beside another blank wall at the Tombs, the municipal jail in Lower Manhatten. The droll Beckettian quality of this plot synopsis is probably not coincidental – Beckett was perhaps Russell's favourite writer. Jean tells me he read 'Bartleby' many times – 'He couldn't get enough of it' – and, says Jean, 'almost drove me crackers by using Bartleby's answer, "I would prefer not to," for days afterwards'.

One inevitable effect of reading Russell's work is the sense that the most factual and even banal components of it, such as the names of people and places, are stretched thinly over layers of alternative reality and identity, a kind of subversive, deadpan, comedic surrealism informed as much by arcane scholarship as by Russell's extremely fertile subconscious – a sub- or unconscious in which the narrative components of Russell's own life coexist as both phantasmagoric and deadpan-factual stories. I first encountered this in his often very funny poems in *The Walled Garden*, published by the aptly named Mandrake Root press in Auckland in 1972 (I quote one here in full):

the balloon factory

Before we presented him with his coronary
the Boss had a few last requests to make:

Keep the cyanide machine working:
Don't lean on the two new boys,
Jesus and Mohammed in the basement:
no more tricks with small-bore washers
or pressured air-hoses up the anus:
and fix me a statue
in the roofgarden,
something vulgar to remember me by.

Mahan, the foreman, made the dies,
Koenig, a onetime Doctor of Thanatology,
pumped up and blew
the extrusion machine.
Dedo, the finger, hauled the thing up
in the threeway lift,
and in amongst the beetlegrass,
the frangipani and the
sesame tree,
between the eggplant and the artichoke,
we put it up
we put it up:
Seven plastic cowboys
and a statue of new England.

(Please to notice the lower-case 'n' on 'new England'.)

But back to Harry. The first paragraph of Russell's second-to-last published book, *Tomorrow Tastes Better*, opens, 'Harry Rejekt glanced up the road and saw there were no empty parking spaces outside Joseph Bartleby's shop.' Did Harry begin to notice the doubling effect in his friend after writing this book? *Tomorrow Tastes Better*, published by Harper Collins in 2001, has a subtitle on the cover: 'A Harry Rejekt novel'. Was Russell planning a series of Harry Rejekts? Harry Rejekt is one of several character names (Harry Lurber, Commissioner Gerder, Simon Fesk, others) that seem to elide with their author, Harry Russell Haley. An earlier novel, *Beside Myself* (Penguin, 1990), doesn't feature Harry Rejekt but its first chapter opens with a brilliant account of the personality that might, at any moment, generate (or degenerate) a doppelgänger version of itself:

> I'm an actor and I'm my own audience rolled into one . . . I was aware of this person who'd been nicknamed Midge but I didn't know what to make of him. I was puzzled about myself . . . We were a family of four. Mum and Dad and Midge lived in an old weatherboard villa in a Wellington suburb and I lived inside me. It was this relationship with myself that was difficult. I was never sure which one of me people might be seeing so the pair of us always backed off . . .
>
> 'What do you want to be when you grow up?'
>
> Every child is asked this question by uncles and aunties. I bogged down on 'want' and 'be' and 'growing up'. I once said I wanted to be *me* and everyone in our living room laughed . . .
>
> . . . I'm talking to myself and speaking to you. Whoever and wherever you are. And when you listen – surely you too are split without a visible division. Aren't you? Consciousness is a wedge of words.

In *The Spaces Between* (2012), the last novel Russell published, Harry Rejekt is parked in favour of a character called Jervis Kraik, who throughout the book is referred to interchangeably as either 'Kraik', 'Jervis' or 'Jervis Kraik'. Sometimes it seems that 'Kraik' is the third-person subject of the narrative, and 'Jervis' the third-person object: sometimes the 'he' that is 'Kraik' commands the point of view, and sometimes the 'Jervis' is observed or discussed, mostly by Moira, his caregiver or nurse in the facility where he's in recovery from a mysterious, near-fatal accident in the novel's early stages. But the wedge between 'Jervis' and 'Kraik' is never entirely clear: sometimes Moira refers to him as 'Kraik'. It's as though this consciousness-as-a-wedge-of-words is prising Jerviskraik's presence apart – and since 'Jervis Kraik' is, at first, largely incapable of speech as a result of his accident, and communicates through writing, the wedge may also be prising apart the persons who might either write or speak, but only with traumatic difficulty both; especially as the few words the recovering Jerviskraik manages to say come out in a thick South African accent that he loathes (as did Russell). But then, too, '. . . his writing was undecipherable, even to himself, and Moira had turned away'.

Academic descendants of the founding father of narratology, the Russian Vladimir Propp (a perfectly Haley-ish name!), would love this stuff. I also loved the writer, and so am struck more than anything by the honesty, subversion, playfulness and intelligence of Russell's lifelong game of selves. His fictions, his comedies at the expense of reality, grew in the spaces opened up by these personality and person games.

Russell's comedies were subversively heteroglossic (after Bakhtin) and darkly serious as well as funny, and after his and Jean's daughter Kathy died in an accident in March 1986 the comedy went away for a long time, or retreated into deep, hidden places. His book of stories after Kathy's death, *The Transfer Station* (1989), is one of the most extraordinary reflections on grief that I've read, though not announced as such. Russell wrote it in France while he and Jean were in Menton; Russell had the Katherine Mansfield Fellowship there in 1987. Within it, consciously I believe, is a reflection on the kind of person one might be before and after grief, how they might be separate, how they might be reconciled. The stories circulate in one way or another around the facility known as the Transfer Station, a sinister place that had appeared earlier in one of the *Real Illusions* stories, 'Dogmaster'. In *The Transfer Station* it's where the city's rubbish is ground up and pumped out to sea, where it poisons the fish. Sometimes people jump into it. The first-person protagonist in the story grieves for his wife Helen, and for the native forests that have been replaced by pine. It was Helen who made gardens and knew about trees.

In real life it's Jean Haley who knows a lot about trees and other plants, and who has always made gardens. Russell loved trees, especially natives, and had an encyclopedic knowledge of their Māori names, and Jean and he planted a great many of them; but I think it was Jean who taught him their botanical, Latin names. Ian describes his mother as 'an unsung horticultural genius'. Russell also loved birds, and there are many in his stories. They both loved dogs and had lots of them. Back at their place in Whangārei, there's now a montage of photographs of Russell, often with Jean and the kids and with friends in different parts of the world – Russell is often playing with a dog. In the story 'Dogmaster', the protagonist pawns his dog Zero every day. Then, one day, he liberates Zero from 'the broker' early. The story ends like this:

> You sleep with the prospect of a dream of waking to another world where such facility will be granted that even Zero will hold conversations with the light.
>
> I can see that dream in the half-open moving eye of the black dog.
>
> And the broker will play his evening flute from his blockhouse at the farthest end of the narrow bridge. Not one of us will be inclined to respond except Zero with his dark note of derision.

I remember the long look that passed between Russell and their border collie Pip the day before Russell died. On the morning he died, Pip rested her chin on the bed near Russell's head. Then she made a sound like a growl and left the room. He'd gone, and Pip's 'dark note of derision' said it was time to go for a walk among trees and birds.

How Not to Be at Home

Home: New Writing, edited by Thom Conroy (Massey University Press, 2017)

1

I'm writing this in a hotel in Wan Chai, Hong Kong. This isn't my home in a conventional sense. The 'place I call home' is a modest, inner-city, body corp-managed unit in Auckland that I share with my wife Donna and, often, with a couple of our grandchildren, or with one or another of our adult kids who regard our place as an occasionally convenient 'home away from home'. Those people aren't with me in the Wan Chai hotel, and this is the biggest point of difference between where I am and where I'll be when I 'get home'. Is home 'where the heart is'? Are these people 'the heart'? If so, would my hotel room in Wan Chai be home if they were here with me?

I'm here to install an exhibition of photographs of 'Asia' by the late Brian Brake, a New Zealander, and Steve McCurry, an American. A key question raised by the exhibition is: what does it mean to stage pictures of Asia by non-Asian image-makers, for an 'Asian' audience, in 'Asia'? Wherever exactly that is when it's your home. The question rather obviously sheets back to Edward Said's 1985 commentary on his book *Orientalism* (1978) and his restatement of that book's core theme: 'the representation of other cultures, societies, histories; the relationship between power and knowledge'. If I can't in any conventional sense be 'at home' in a foreign place, then how do – can – I represent myself as feeling that way, at home, there; in fact *here*?

We've been working very hard and Hong Kong is a busy, noisy city, so to get a couple of quiet hours to myself this morning I went to a favourite place, the open air aviary in Hong Kong Park. Here I encountered the enchanting chestnut-backed scimitar babbler

(*Pomatorhinus montanus*); its home is on the Malay Peninsula, Greater Sundas, and its habitat is Montane Forest. There were lots of sociable Bali myna (*Lencopsar rothschildi*), from Bali, Indonesia. These and a myriad other many-tongued refugees – internees? – migrants? – were obvious inhabitants of Said's orientalist regime. The domination of representation by the exertion of power over knowledge is clear from the names of these birds (*rothschildi*?) as they appear on the aviary's labels. The birds have been rendered homeless by relocation, perhaps, but also by how they are uttered and represented, by how we *know* them; but then, perhaps they have their families with them, or have raised families in the aviary, which is a bit like a hotel, somewhat sealed off from the world around it, with people coming and going to clean the place up; with room service, even.

Where I am now, the location and the languages most people are speaking are also obviously different from the home where my heart is. But in some way that I need to think about, location and language don't seem to matter that much – not as much as the absence of a small core of people 'back home'. Nor does it matter that the hotel, which is located near the Wan Chai MTR station, will be my home away from home for a couple of weeks at most. Would it matter if I was going to be 'away from home' longer? I'm not sure. It doesn't matter now and may not matter for a while, despite home being where the heart is. The fact is, I like my home away from home in the present. This is partly because, if I walk by the MTR station around 7.30 in the morning on my way to get breakfast, I'm likely to be engulfed by a crowd of workers disgorging into the street. Most are smartly dressed office workers and they fan out from the station exit in a dense, determined pack, tracking towards destinations according to a schedule that I cut across as if invisible.

This invisibility interests me. The sense that I am visible and can, as it were, see or represent myself in a place I know intimately within a crowd of people whose general sense of purpose I share – as would often be the case in my home neighbourhood in Auckland – amounts to a kind of self-recognition. Not having that self-recognition and that environment here in Hong Kong, in a place that is somewhat familiar but not intimately so, among people who don't, in a general way, reflect my sense of myself back to me – this sense of disconnected anonymity, of being somewhat invisible, unrecognisable, even unrepresentable to myself, is quite pleasant and even liberating, for a while. The pleasant sensation is as much about being in a strange person as it is about being in a strange place. I'm free of the sometimes claustrophobic sense of being defined and uttered within a social hive.

It's possible that language is the key here. In Anglophone countries, and to some extent in France and Germany, I'd feel less invisible to myself because I'd be hearing languages I understand. I'd be hearing myself. In Hong Kong, not speaking Cantonese, the language of the streets, I become inaudible and therefore, in some way, invisible – not materialised through speech, not represented, not known.

2

This is a narrow, personal, circumscribed place to start thinking about where I am when I'm 'at home'. What about a wider cultural or even spiritual context, such as the one conveyed by the Māori word tūrangawaewae? The place where I feel I can stand, that I belong to and that belongs to me and many others? My homeland? Can this kind of place be transported? Could I have brought it with me to Hong Kong? Internalised it?

Not, for me at any rate, in the encompassing sense of indigeneity, which I neither feel nor claim, but perhaps in a personal, symbolic or talismanic way? In 'My Lady's Parlour', a slightly nasty sketch in his 1922 collection *On a Chinese Screen*, Somerset Maugham describes an expat woman's efforts in an unspecified location in China to transform 'an old temple, a small one, in the city' into her home away from home. 'She was obliged to buy her carpet in China, but she managed to get one that looked so like an Axminster that you could hardly know the difference.' And, a few sentences on, 'She needed a screen and there was no help for it, she had to buy a Chinese one, but as she very cleverly said, you might perfectly well have a Chinese screen in England.' Maugham's expat has managed both to appropriate the foreign to her sense of what it took to make her place homely, and to recognise that the foreign had already been incorporated into the décor, so to speak, of her homeland – either a colonialist or transcultural trope, depending on your point of view. By contrast, my plain white modern boutique Hong Kong hotel room is entirely anonymous and free of transcultural exchange, with Wi-Fi but no 'Chinese screen', and might be anywhere.

The Comfort Hotel in Cuba Street, Wellington, has almost identical rooms to the one in Hong Kong. So do most of the Nordic Choice chain, which includes the Comfort and Quality range. A couple of years ago, Donna and I stayed in an especially modest one in Kiel, a small German city on the south-west shore of the Baltic where my great-grandmother Maria Josephine Catharina Reepen came from. The plain Nordic styling of the Comfort's rooms was no longer culturally specific. I didn't feel haunted by Maria Reepen in the Kiel version of the Nordic hotel room, though I wanted to and had gone to my ancestor's homeland hoping to encounter her presence in some way; and I don't feel the unease of Maugham's culturally displaced Englishwoman in my Hong Kong room. It's not quite true to say that these more or less uniformly styled rooms are 'nowhere'. It makes more sense to say they are 'anywhere'. Where they are not is wherever tūrangawaewae is, whether substantially or emblematically.

3

The Maugham sketch reminds me of my mother Linda. Until we were seven, my twin brother and I were brought up by our mother and father in our maternal grandmother's house in Blenheim. The house was a modest California bungalow with a large back section where my mother had seasonal flowerbeds. Then, when we were seven, the family went to East Pakistan, now Bangladesh. We lived a long way up the Karnaphuli River from the port city of Chittagong, near the Chandraghona paper mill, where my father was the accountant. We lived at first in a semi-detached concrete house with no garden, but a balcony that Linda soon filled somewhat desperately with planters of parched-looking geraniums. Inside, she replaced the bamboo blinds with curtains. She shopped in the bazaar for fabrics with which to cover the bamboo furniture and the beds. The place never resembled the house back in Blenheim, but you could see that she was trying to make it more homely along the lines of the California bungalow. When we moved to another house on a scraped-bare hilltop, Linda laid out a garden of flowering shrubs and planted a bougainvillea and a number of shade trees. This exotic garden couldn't be a copy of the one 'back home', but you might say, in Maugham's terms, that it did an Axminster. I still have her botanical guide to the flowering trees and shrubs of South Asia – the book that allowed her to translate the garden 'back home' into the one under the Assam hills. In this translated garden, I think she could see and hear herself enough to feel represented and at home.

Over the years that she and my father lived and worked in many different parts of the world, this process of transcultural translation steadily shifted its axis towards the places where they were actually living. My brother Dave and I visited them every two or three years and saw their homes – which were not 'family homes' – in Khulna and Seoul. I saw their home in Amman while working there in 1969–70. By the time they returned to New Zealand for the last few years of their lives, they'd accumulated a great many things that were not of New Zealand – fabrics from Bangladesh, ornate silver tea sets from Egypt, black cast-iron pug dogs from Korea, mother-of-pearl inlay furniture from Damascus, carved hardwood bowls from Zambia, and more – and trunks full of my father's 35mm slides. The house they bought in St Heliers, Auckland, became their home away from the homes in which they'd lived elsewhere for close on 40 years. Or, it became a museum of homes.

A couple of years after my father died, my mother bought a round-the-world plane ticket and spent a year visiting friends in many of the places where she and my father had lived. She wasn't well, and knew this trip would probably kill her. She came off the plane back in Auckland in a wheelchair, and died only days after. She didn't unpack. It was as if she'd wanted to go home to die, and did, progressively, in a succession of joined-up places where she'd been 'at home' with people she loved.

4

Recently, my cousin John Wedde, whose father was my uncle Paul, and my second cousin Peter Wedde, whose father was my great uncle Wilhelm Friedrich 'Bill' Wedde, organised a Wedde family reunion in Wellington. The reunion brought together a couple of hundred descendants of Heinrich August Wedde and Maria Josephine Catharina Wedde (née Reepen). Great uncle Bill, a blacksmith, was the second of Maria and Heinrich's eight children. His brother, Herman Conrad 'Monty' Wedde, was the seventh child. In about 1908, Bill and Monty went into the remote Kaitīeke valley in the King Country to establish adjoining Land Settlement farms as pioneer farmers. Bill walked off with his family during the 1930s Depression when wool prices collapsed, but Monty stayed and became a successful apiarist. He's remembered for the apple trees he cultivated – 'Monty's Surprise' – which are said to have levels of quercetin flavonoids and procyanidins capable of fighting cancer; there's a sense in which these Montys utter or represent my great uncle. I like to think my great grandmother Maria, who went up to the remote Kaitīeke without her husband in about 1910 to join Bill and Monty and her daughter Bertha, enjoyed eating this apple.

Peter remembers going out to his uncle Monty's farm and beehives as a kid, for the Christmas holidays, and after the family reunion in Wellington he agreed to drive back up to Auckland with me via Maria's grave at Raurimu. On the way, he told me stories about his grandmother (my great grandmother) and about what his father Bill and his uncle Monty had to do to cut roads, build bridges and clear land for pasture. Maria died in 1927, a decade before Peter was born, but was remembered in the region for the care she took with her clothes and appearance, which must have been hard given that her sons were burning off and clearing forest on the slopes.

She was also remembered for her fine needlework. From the

Danish town of Haderslev on the South Jutland peninsula, her last known place of residence in the Baltic states, she'd brought to the King Country in New Zealand what became a legendary piece of linen in which she'd documented all the many stitches she knew. This marvellous object was displayed at the family reunion. I think of this sampler as an archive, as perhaps the only object from her homeland that, as a talisman, was able to mark where she was *as* home. She was at home where the sampler was. It represented her, and uttered her. The stitches would have had German names. Perhaps it was through the sampler that she could see herself. She also loved poetry, and is said to have been reciting poems in German or Danish when she died. Perhaps these poems constituted the language in which she could hear herself.

It wasn't easy to hold fast to the idea of Maria seeing and hearing herself through these charged mediums as Peter and I stood by her dilapidated grave in the little graveyard high above the long Kaitīeke Valley, with a yard of sweltering sheep bleating beside a nearby shearing shed, and a vista of the steep, eroding land from which Bill and Monty had taken the timber with which they'd built a house for their mother. But then, it wasn't easy, either, to imagine her arriving in Wellington in 1879, almost certainly speaking little or no English. This must have been hard.

But the possibility occurs to me that she may have liked being invisible and inaudible – freed for a time from the social claustrophobia and cramped horizons of a small trading port into which, however, had sailed ships with suntanned sailors wearing Polynesian tattoos and with fabulous objects in their kit bags (a giant conch shell, a whalebone patu); freed also from the political claustrophobia of a country suffering the aftermaths of the two Schleswig Wars of 1848 and 1864 and, in Kiel, the garrisoning of Prussian forces and *die adelige Preussen Offizieren*, the noble Prussian officers in their pomp by Kieler Schloss.

5

And now, too glibly, the thought arises that all New Zealanders are descended from immigrants – including tangata whenua who whakapapa to the waka in which they came south to these islands. This is a feeble cliché that doesn't distinguish motives for becoming an immigrant – or migrant – nor the distinction between immigrant and refugee that has become dangerously politicised in the last decade; nor does it interrogate the motives and attitudes of the receiving society; nor does it distinguish between those humans who came first, whose 'receiving society' was the land and its non-human creatures, and those who came subsequently and were received by people. Why did Maria come to New Zealand? What were the conditions of her reception? How did she meet her future husband, Heinrich August Wedde, a runaway sailor who'd jumped ship in Wellington a year earlier? How did their children feel about being in New Zealand in a German-speaking household? How did their children's children feel?

While I was working at Te Papa Tongarewa, the Museum of New Zealand between 1994 and 2004, we commissioned research into immigrant histories, for example into the Dutch who came to New Zealand in large numbers as assisted immigrants during the 1950s. A pattern emerged. The arriving generation, despite being dispersed by the government's 'pepper-potting' assimilationist policy, tended eventually to congregate around economic and social opportunities, and worked to sustain at least some elements of their 'home' culture. Their children, on the other hand, were keen to integrate and tended to shy away from the 'traditions' sustained by their parents. But *their* children – the third generation – tended to have a resurgent interest in the cultures of origin and language of their grandparents. However, this third generation found that the cultural practices and traditions their immigrant grandparents had tried to sustain and that their parents had avoided had become provincial anachronisms, sentimental and quaint, and no longer bore much relation to the contemporary world back in the ancestral home of the Netherlands. How did these 'traditions' represent and utter this generation? Did they in fact do this? Or did these preserved traditions alienate the third generation immigrants from their contemporaries in their ancestral homeland?

6

I am Maria Josephine Catharina's great-grandson and I'm interested not only in what her home was like in the Germany she left, and not only in the home she made for herself and her family when she came to New Zealand, but in the space between – the immigrant's space of transit, the stateless space. From the age of ten, I lived away from any traditional family home while my mother and father travelled and worked. As an adult, I've lived in several different countries. Most of the books I've written have had the question, 'Where and what is home?' as a theme at some level. I've been attached to most of the places I've lived in, in one way or another, especially after I had children. But I always like the 'Hong Kong' experience of not being at home in a conventional sense, or of being at home with or in a different self, invisible and inaudible to some degree, free to some degree, lonely perhaps, but content.

In this lonely but somewhat contented adult self I think I can recognise vestiges of the child-in-transit self, free both of the anxiety of not being fully at home with the people who minded us during the school holidays, and of the sorrow of not being fully at home in the parental homes we visited – or, if you like, of not being at home in a foreign place, nor in the home that had become inauthentic. But this sense of home as a state of anxiety-free transit between homes derives also from my enjoyment of a solitary imaginative world – a fantasy world when I was a kid, perhaps, in which I could invent secret, alternative identities for myself. Or, let's say that the adult fantasist is free to indulge his anonymous self in a stateless condition that isn't beholden to either a domestic or a national 'home'.

This condition of being at home in homelessness reminds me of the thought that seems to push up against the surface of the text in Hannah Arendt's great, bitter, 1943 essay on exile, 'We Refugees' – a thought that is never explicitly uttered. In a sense it's a thought that could not be uttered, not by Arendt, anyway; or that it would have been improper for her to utter, because the stateless condition she was writing about was not that of the voluntary immigrant, but of the involuntary or forced refugee – the Jewish refugee from Nazi persecution. Nonetheless, her sarcastic distaste for the assimilationist compliance required of, and often enough displayed by, those rendered stateless by persecution or forced homelessness does make itself heard in her essay; and so, by inference, does the unstated freedom of identity that noncompliance might offer. 'Refugees driven from country to country represent the vanguard of their peoples – if they keep their identity.' Not, then, the statist identities of the countries to and from which they are 'driven'. The last, scornful sentence of her essay comes close to being a declaration of that stateless freedom. 'The comity of European peoples went to pieces when, and because, it allowed its weakest member to be excluded and persecuted.' Arendt's wariness of and even distaste for 'homelands' founded on xenophobia, indeed for overmantling *Weltanschauungen* of any kind, was hinted at subsequently in her controversial 1963 account of the trial of Adolf Eichmann, *Eichmann in Jerusalem: The Banality of Evil.*

7

In 1969 I went to Amman in Jordan with the naïve hope of being a scoop journalist, and to visit my parents whom I hadn't seen for a few years. As well as visiting refugee and Fedayeen training camps, hanging around the edges of drinking sessions with cynical journalists in the Red Lion tavern on Djebel Amman, and attending briefing sessions by various Fedayeen organisations, I ended up teaching English in a long-established Palestinian refugee township near Russeifa. The first wave of refugees to settle there had arrived, mostly from Lydda and the Galilee region, after the expulsions of Palestinians in 1948 – the *Yawm al-Nakba* or Day of Catastrophe. I was teaching young adults, second generation refugees, several of whom had children of their own: the third generation. Some of my students also had grandparents in their households, so there were homes in Russeifa with four generations of refugees living in them.

For these people, however, 'home' was not in Russeifeh. In the Red Crescent hospital in Amman I saw young, camp-born Fedayeen whose feet had been blown off by Israeli claymore mines along the border with the occupied territories. Many Palestinians I talked to were bitter about what they saw as King Hussein of Jordan's appeasement of Israel. They did not think of themselves as 'stateless', since their state or homeland – in Lydda and Ramla, for example – was about four hours drive away in what they continued to call Palestine.

I left Jordan in mid-June 1970 during a lull in the fighting between the Jordanian army and Palestinian militias, which had broken out when Hussein attempted to remove the armed Fedayeen cadres from Amman. The refugee camp massacres of Black September followed later that year, and the subsequent expulsion of Fedayeen to Lebanon. Collusion between the Israeli Defence Forces and Lebanese Phalangist militias led to the subsequent massacres of Palestinians in the Sabra and Shatila camps in Beirut in September 1982. One might say that, 'The comity of Middle Eastern peoples went to pieces when, and because, it allowed its weakest member to be excluded and persecuted.'

8

My indulgent and even selfish pleasure in a temporary state of 'homelessness' in a hotel in Hong Kong may seem to bear no meaningful relation to the complex, paradoxical, and often dissonant narratives of home in the lives of my great-grandparents, let alone in the diasporic lives of Jews and Palestinians. Nor can any comparison be made with the disgraceful stories that continue to emerge from Manus Island and the Nauru detention centre, most recently in 'The Nauru Files', 2000 leaked incident reports assembled by Nick Evershed, Ri Liu, Paul Farrell and Helen Davidson and made available by the *Guardian*; or in Eva Orner's horrifying documentary film about Nauru, *Chasing Asylum*. 'The comity of humanity went to pieces when, and because, it allowed its weakest members to be excluded and persecuted,' we might say.

Who are these 'weakest members'? Are they people who have no choice? Not necessarily, because many have chosen to be homeless rather than risk death or enslavement 'at home'. Are they people who can no longer remain at home in whatever sense we use the word, because the condition of 'being at home' has become intolerable? Not necessarily, because plenty of people choose to remain in intolerable homes; for example, the heartbreakingly brave 'white helmet' civil defence forces in Aleppo who refuse to leave, and often die, because if they don't stay who will continue to sustain and utter their homeland? Are these people who choose to leave, or stay, victims? Not necessarily, because many have made brave decisions to leave their homes in the hope of finding better ones; many have left their homes simply because the grass was greener on the other side of some fence or, indeed, wall.

Are those who leave people for whom the possibility of imaginative statelessness is grotesquely inappropriate – the self-reflective luxury of a globalised elite? Not necessarily, because, surely, the imaginative possibility of living elsewhere, as someone else, or as a speechless nobody making their way within 'their identity' anywhere across the grain of society's collective purpose, may be a better and more subversive option than remaining at home in, being compliant with, assimilating to, appeasing totalitarianism. Such totalitarianism will be political; it will also, inevitably, be social and cultural, and therefore historical. It may demand to regulate what we are permitted to nominate as 'home'. As Salman Rushdie wrote in *Shame*, 'I, too, like all migrants, am a fantasist . . . I, too, face the problem of history: what to retain, what to dump . . .' The homeless 'vanguard' Arendt wrote about in 1943 is now, more than ever, the prospect that terrifies the resurgent border guards of gated homelands, since what they are shutting out is imagined futures and future homes, and not least homes 'in the world' that, increasingly, in its contracting condition of crisis, is the only one we all have and have to share.

References

Arendt, Hannah. 1943. 'We Refugees'. In *Altogether Elsewhere: Writers on Exile, edited by* Marc Robinson. Boston/London: Faber & Faber, 1994.

Maugham, Somerset. 1992. *On a Chinese Screen.* Start Publishing LLC, 2012.

Rushdie, Salman. 1983. *Shame.* London: Jonathan Cape.

Said, Edward. 1985. 'Orientalish Reconsidered'. In *Cultural Critique,* No.1. Minneapolis: University of Minnesota Press. Available at http://www.jstor.org/stable/1354282.

Get a Move On

Refer Judy Millar

Wunderblock (2017)

'It's very interesting that your work refers to painting,' is what Judy Millar told me a German critic or artist said to her after looking at her work in her studio in Wedding, Berlin.

Millar also remarked that it was a German kind of thing to say – refreshing because it forthrightly confronted and described an oblique quality in her work.

Though the remark is wide open to interpretation, it is also simple and direct: Does Millar's work turn rather more towards painting, or rather more away from it?

*

When I visited Millar's Berlin studio in the summer of 2014 and heard the story with the phrase *refers to painting* in it, I saw painted works there as well as works that derived from painting – enlarged photographic vinyl prints of painted works laminated on variously shaped supports.

It's not *very interesting* to suggest that these photographic enlargements *refer to painting*, and I don't think this is what the German critic meant. Or if it was, then let's ignore the statement of the obvious that a photographic print taken from a painting *refers to painting*, and take the idea that Millar's work refers to painting at face value.

If we do that, then every action and material property associated with the work – indeed, including immaterial consequences such as negative space – can be thought about by using the idea that it's very interesting that Millar's work *refers to painting*.

*

In the Berlin studio, some of the supports themselves extrapolated the apparent three-dimensionality of sweeping, gestural brushstrokes. These shapes, themselves, could be said to *refer to painting*, and especially to painting as both the product of action, and the action itself.

What is also interesting, and what had perhaps interested the succinct German critic, is that the paintings themselves could be said to *refer to painting*, even though they are, themselves, paintings. In their materiality – their painterly substance, if you like – they seem to *refer to painting* rather more than being paintings. This despite the fact than some of them either have already, or might soon, become derivatives of themselves as paintings – might become those photographic skins stretched over supports. They might become surfaces that refer to painting as surface, on supports that refer to the physicality of painting as performance or gesture.

Another way of putting it might be to suggest that the paintings convey ongoing thinking about painting as much as, or even rather more than they appear to be conclusive – to be thought materialised and immobilised: completed.

They do not appear to be in the least immobilised or, in some sense, completed. They seem to be active. They continue to resemble thinking rather than thought.

At this stage it gets hard to avoid putting 'painting' in quotation marks – but to do so would miss the point.

*

The word 'gesture' also becomes hard to avoid at this stage. Overworked and almost redundant in the toolkit of art historical commentary, it gets a strange new life when I use it in the sentence I can't avoid:

'This painting gestures at painting.'

Which immediately bifurcates into two ideas:

This painted object (a painting) gestures at painting (the activity that makes objects).

Or:

This activity of painting gestures at painting (a generic materiality).

Or even (not quite a third idea):

This performance of painting gestures at painting.

Or even – letting the *ad infinitum* unspool for a while – This performance of painting gestures at painting as gesture.

Painting as theatre for gestures at and of painting.

*

But of course all paintings are gestures, even those apostate paintings that deny gesture, depth and even colour; for example, Kazimir Malevic's suprematist painting *White on White* from 1918.

In effect, Malevic's gesture was a grandiose and even metaphysical one, in that his white painting gestured at infinite possibility, at an essence, at all colour; and even, perhaps, at all meaning. Perhaps at the sublime longing for annihilation, including the annihilation of meaning, or so it's been suggested – though I, for one, don't see that.

Perhaps Malevic's *White on White* gestures at a mystical infinity that lies beyond or behind it, in or through the depth that it seems to deny. I like this paradox, which even seems to resemble the paradoxical suggestion that Millar's paintings gesture at painting.

*

More recently, the American artist Patricia Johanson relocated the old apostasy of minimalism to the natural environment. Her major public works demand of art the capacity to perform as civil engineering – challenging Malevic's encompassing mysticism to make environment-specific meaning, to find a location, grounds, for infinitely possible depth.

A rigorous functionality characterises Johanson's big civil engineering projects. In referring to art, they demand that art defer to nature. A space of negotiation opens up. What the German critic said to Millar makes a lot of sense in the context of Johanson's negotiations.

Unlike the work of her near contemporaries Nancy Holt and Holt's sometime collaborator Robert Smithson, Johanson's public works almost disappear into the environment they refer to. They refer to this environment by being part of it, but also by maintaining a space of negotiation. Referral or reference may, in this context, become a kind of incorporation that is constantly renegotiated by the movements of people within and around the work.

What the work is, where it is, what referrals or references are being negotiated, how we might perform the work by moving with and in it, all seem possible along the trajectory of the German critic's statement, 'It's very interesting that your work refers to painting.'

*

One of the reasons for not using quotation marks to distinguish 'painting' as something that isn't really that, from painting as something that is, is simply to avoid making the distinction.

Not making the distinction frees up certain other possibilities.

One is to complicate the distinction between performance and object. Doing this allows me, a viewer, to perform the painting by moving around it. I can *move around* the painting by standing still in front of it and moving my eyes *around* its surface. Or, indeed, I can *move through* the painting by standing still and *looking through* its surface – by simultaneously seeing and 'seeing through' the painting's surface.

By 'seeing through' the painting's performance of surface as well as its performance of depth. By both accepting the optical truth of the experience by *looking through* the surface of the painting into its perspectival depth; and *seeing through* it in the sceptical sense of knowing that depth is an illusion.

*

But, if the painting has been wrapped around a freestanding support, I can move around it by walking as well as by moving my eyes. If I do this, something else happens.

The surface of the painting becomes coterminous with my movement. The surface both follows me and goes before me, until I end up where I started. There will have been no negative space.

But sometimes the surface of the painting is planar and singular not coterminous, so that when I move around it I'll encounter what's behind the surface of the painting. This *behind* won't be depth, it will just be a different plane.

Will it be the back of the painting? No – how can it be the back of the painting when the painting is all singular surface?

What if the all-surface of the painting is organised as a Möbius strip? Then, when I go all the way around the painting I end up where I started but on the other side. But this 'other side' isn't the back of the painting. Except it is.

This kind of paradox seems to be anticipated in the German critic's suggestion.

*

In the late 1980s and early 90s, Rob McLeod, known now for his exuberant, cartoonish, cut-out paintings, made a number of almost minimal (albeit impasto), conventionally square paintings on stretched canvas, around the edges of which peeped little fragments of what appeared to be anarchic, colourful underpainting, or perhaps brightly coloured 'backs'.

McLeod's minimalist paintings referred to minimal painting, but at the same time conveyed a mischievous awareness of the ongoing discussion about surface. Where was surface, what was it, and was the puncturing of surface by pictorial perspective in early Renaissance painting associated with the rise of commodity capitalism and banking? Was it the trick moment in art history when it became possible for art to be a representational illusion materialised as a transportable, tradable window?

What were these perspectival window paintings referring to? Not to painting, anyway – as allegories they were referring to depth; but also to narratives: to deep, embedded meanings that receded through perspectival depth towards some vanishing point past the back of the painting. If you ran around to the back of the painting's window, you wouldn't find the meanings there. You'd find nothing. Or, rather, at least, you'd find confirmation of a conjuring trick.

If you run around Millar's free-standing paintings you don't find conjuring tricks. You find that the work refers to the question of what a surface is and where it begins and ends.

*

I notice that a few paragraphs ago I allowed an implicit synonymy to pass unchallenged: that involving *referral* and *reference*. But no synonym is a simple ontological substitute for its companion.

It seems to me that a *referral* passes the major burden of responsibility for meaning to another term. A referral defers to the other term's agency in making meaning; defers to how that other term represents its conditions of existence.

But a *reference* seems to me to impose a lesser burden of agency on its counterpart. It implies an exchange rather than a delegation or devolution.

Obviously, both derive from the same root verb, *refer*. However, unlike *referral*, *reference* can be both a verb and a noun: x can reference y, and it can also be or embody a reference to y. This small, pedantic distinction seems disproportionately significant to me as I think about Millar's art. The more implicitly active word *reference* is appropriate in the context of active works such as Millar's.

*

The dynamism of the word *reference* has to do with it being both a noun and a verb. It will usually be one or the other, an action or an object. But its singular use as one will always imply the other: the object will always seem dynamic, and the action will always have substance.

Something that is at once an object and an action, that is simultaneously substantial and dynamic, that is at once ontologically singular and capable of referring to other ways of being – this begins to read like a description of Millar's work.

*

In addition, a *reference* can be at once a subject and an object. When x references y or when x is a reference to y it is in some way both the subject of the verb *reference* and in some way also the verb's object: the subject projects itself into the object of its action. It transfers something of its existence and meaning from one self to another. *Its* meaning and existence become *their* meaning and existence. Or, their meaning and existence become reciprocal.

Theirs is a dynamic, unstable, shape-shifter ontology. Nothing is settled.

When you walk around x (something) expecting to find y (something different), you may find what x *becomes* when you walk around it expecting to find something different. You find that x had already referenced y in the first place, but you had to go around the back, so to speak, to find that out.

Or, in some of Millar's work, when you *go around the back*, you'll find what appears to be a blank: what the work becomes when it's no longer a surface that refers to painting. Except that the apparent blank was always and remains inherent in the surface that refers to painting. You can't have one without the other.

*

The children's pop-up book *Swell,* made by Millar in collaboration with the children's book writer Trish Gribben and the paper engineer Phillip Fickling, begins with a poem by Gribben that includes several very dynamic verbs: *rolled, twisted, looped, swelled, heaved, stretched, flee, dipped, dived*, and more.

In her statement just inside the book, Millar concludes, 'Sometimes I am terrified by the storms at Anawhata [where she lives when in New Zealand]. In Berlin, I am disturbed by being on the edge of a deep dark tragic history. Things push and shove at me. That's good for art-making.'

The title of Millar's work *be do/ be do/ be do/* deserves to be written as intended:

be do
be do
be do

That old bebop scat doubles as dynamic rhythm (how to perform or articulate rhythm) and as a kind of koan about the rhythmic tension between being and doing (how to be what we do but also do what we are). This is the intrinsic *push and shove*, the *rolling, twisting, looping, swelling, heaving, stretching, fleeing, dipping* and *diving.*

*

Writing about

be do
be do
be do

at the Institute of Modern Art in Brisbane, Rosemary Hawker found the word *haptic* useful. It reinforces the importance of bodily movement as the activator of the art work and the artwork. *Haptic* also marks the exchange or transfer or reciprocity – the referencing – that makes being and doing inseparable.

*

Haptic also helps us to understand and appreciate the feedback loop that links thought and action, especially when the feedback loop is paradoxical, like a Möbius strip.

Paradox is a key dynamic in Millar's work. Often it provokes the materialisation of subversive thought. One of the targets of Millar's subversion is the sublime. The large scale of the work doesn't dimish us. Rather, it allows us to feel that we can be what we do. It allows us to enlarge our sense of reference.

*

One of the subversions produced by enlarging our sense of reference in the case of

be do
be do
be do

is that the work's originating painted mark has *be-do'd* into a half-tone dot file – the DNA of print – which has then been enlarged, as well as *rolled, looped, swelled, heaved, stretched, twisted, dipped* and *dived.*

When we refer ourselves to the printed mark, when we stretch ourselves around it, when we objectify our sense of subjecthood and subjectify our sense of objecthood, it is no longer clear whether we are in the land of Lilliput or that of Brobdingnag.

Like Jonathan Swift's satire in which these parodies of scale, power and significance were printed, the impact of Millar's print-outs is both serious and playful.

*

Millar's 2010 installation at Hamish Morrison Galerie, Berlin, *A Better Life*, appeared to rush through the gap between a wall and a partition. An allegory seemed to be implied, of escape perhaps.

Was this in some way an allegorical enactment of Millar's sense of the *push and shove* of a *deep dark tragic history*? If so (in some way), then the drama was also somewhat carnivalesque.

On the other side of the partition an even greater mass of similar material appeared to bunch up and press towards the gap.

But then, depending on which side of the partition you started from, the great mass on the 'other' side could equally be the escaping body.

Viewed side-on with the partitioning wall between the two masses, a kind of contest seemed to be under way.

It's tempting to read this ambiguity about effort and direction back into the work's title. Whether that ambiguity (of *A Better Life*) might accommodate a *deep dark tragic history* is an open question.

*

Viewed front-on, Millar's large outdoor work for the 2015 Christchurch public art project SCAPE, *Call Me Snake,* rears up, a credible representation (of a snake). Viewed from other directions it ceases to represent. It does something more oblique.

Let's say that it *refers.*

But clearly, what it *refers to* isn't simple, unless you choose to stand in only one place. But then you'd miss the point.

It refers – to its solid self, perhaps, but also to a haptic dynamic of what it might displace, what depth might be displaced by flatness, what surface by whatever happens when you get a move on.

It refers to what it might become, but hasn't yet, and might not.

*

In an installation shot taken of *The Model World* (2015) – a work that relates to

be do
be do

be do

– when installed at Te Uru in Titirangi near Millar's home on the west coast of Auckland, a child's feet and legs can be seen scooting under and through one of the large suspended sections of the work. She knows what to be-do.

Nearby, the feet and legs of some adults appear immobilised. They need to *get a move on.*

*

Frederic Jameson recently suggested that, 'in the late 19th century, writers became aware that the world of newly emergent capitalism was an unrepresentable totality which it was nonetheless their duty and vocation to represent'.

This may be an interesting overstatement.

More interestingly, Jameson went on to suggest that the 'great moderns' (by implication including artists) dealt with this paradox by 'representing their inability to represent'.

Artists of Millar's generation have moved a long way from this anxious and even neurotic impasse.

There were anxiety-free exceptions among the 'great moderns'; for example, Barbara Hepworth's 1930s photomontages and double exposures. By transposing three-dimensional sculptures into layered, over-layered and multi-perspectival film, she not only played with the representational paradox, she also played with surface, dimensionality, materiality and perspective.

Hepworth's photographs that relocate sculptures in architectural environments *refer us to* the conditions in which our haptic engagement with the location might be-do how the sculpture takes up space, empties space, realigns the relationships of spaces, directs visual and physical movement (the little girl scooting under the work at Te Uru) . . .

. . . and seems also to direct or conduct time.

*

Speaking about *Giraffe-Bottle-Gun*, the large installation she showed at the 2009 Venice Biennale, Millar said that a work doesn't really exist until it is placed in a context. It depends on what you do with it. She suggested that the work could make us feel bigger and that this is also what grand religious architectures and interiors can do.

Giraffe-Bottle-Gun was installed in Santa Maria Maddalena, a small church in Venice. Its architecture, which *refers to* architecture (the Pantheon in Rome), bends and foregrounds our relationship to the paintings Millar installed there.

Millar's paintings in the church did not seek an accommodation with the space. They altered it (and us) by being what and where they were.

*

Paintings are simple things, says Millar. They are usually made on material stretched over a support.

This is neither an understatement nor an overstatement.

*

It seems to me that these *simple things* also refer to time.

In *Dissensus: On Politics and Aesthetics* (2010), Jacques Rancière proposed that, 'Art has lived for two centuries from the very tension by which it is at once itself and beyond itself, and by which it promises a future destined to remain unaccomplished.'

Or, as before: Millar's work does not appear to be in the least immobilised or, in some sense, completed. It seems to be active. It continues to resemble thinking rather than thought; to be in a state of *tension*.

*

It's very interesting that Millar's work *refers to painting* as a gesture representing the time in which it is simply present; but also as a gesture towards the time in which it is always becoming what we make of it.

Judy Millar, *The Model World* (detail), 2015 – mixed media, collection of the artist. Photograph Simon Devitt.

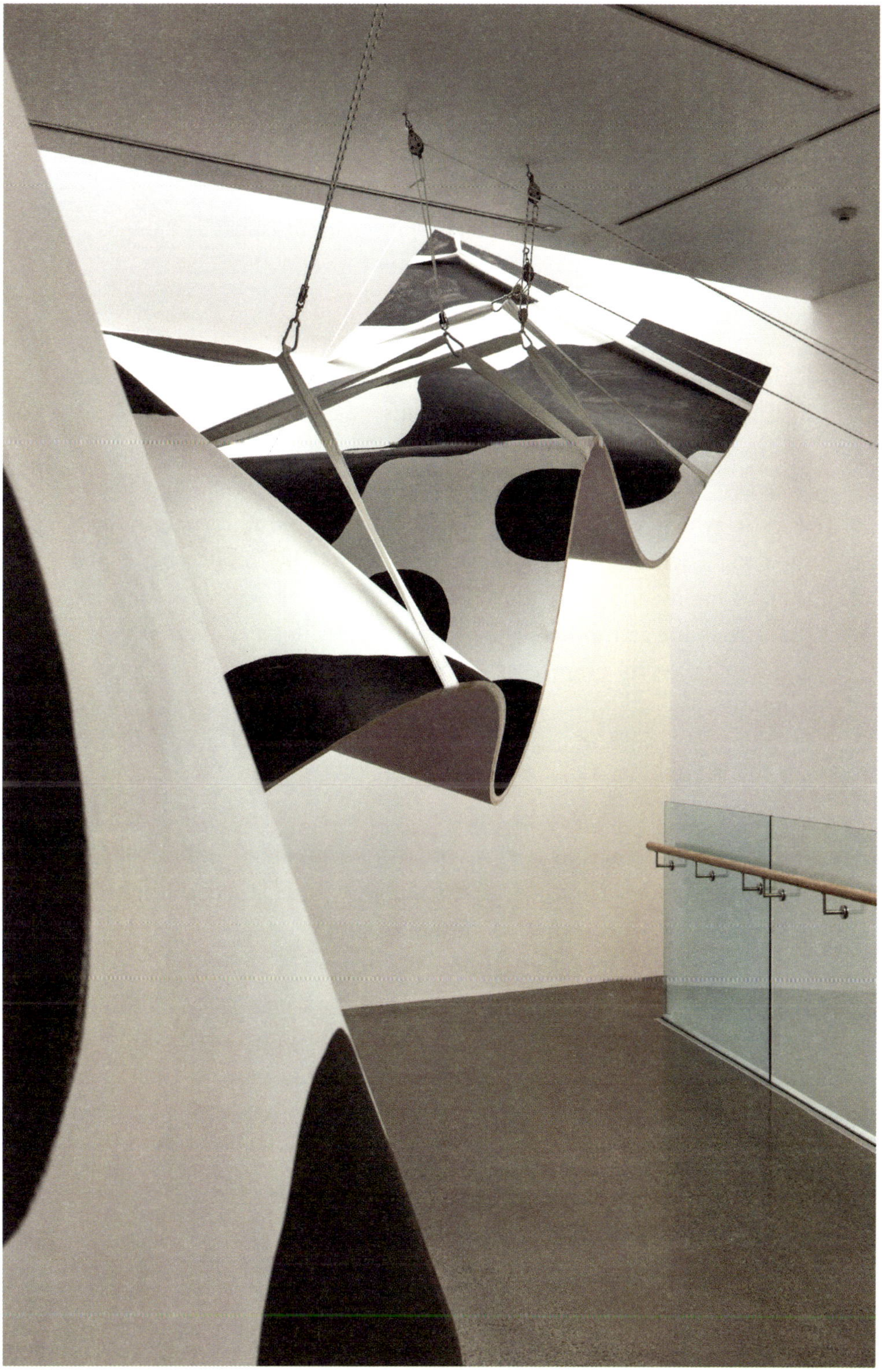

Curating Time

In *Curatopia: Museums and the Future of Curatorship*, edited by Philipp Schorch and Conal McCarthy (Manchester University Press, 2019)

Reading the essays in this book I was struck by how often issues of time were critical to the discussions. 'Time', of course, is a very complex word, which James Clifford parses with great economy in his essay 'The Times of the Curator'; but I was interested also in the ways in which issues of time were present as a kind of haunting in the texts assembled here, present (so to speak) by implication rather than by intent; and sometimes it was the absence of reflection on time that struck me as another kind of haunting, as if issues of temporality could be taken for granted as givens within the framing concept of a 'curatopia'.

The neologism 'curatopia' around which this book is organised is, of course, a temporal portmanteau within which *progress* – in the form of an evolving trajectory of curating practices or an ideal curatorial future – is proffered as a conceptual lure; or, more optimistically, as a *present* in which an ideal state of affairs has, finally, reached a destination in which current curatorial practices can be framed in utopian time. But then we all know that utopia by its nature does not exist except as an emergent or, as it may be, aspirational condition, and that what Clifford calls 'the times' are always at once fixed in an historical context and 'a-changing'; and a-changing for the better in the curatopian scenario. There may be, or may have been, utopian pasts – 'golden ages', etc. – but these are clearly not relevant to the current project, except as reminders of the slippery nature of the temporalities variously under discussion here.

Among several key passages in which Clifford probes and case studies these issues, the following are critical:

> In what follows I evoke two senses of temporality: 1. 'The Times': as in the historical moment or context, 'the life and times of x' 2. 'Times' plural: a sense of the curator's task as enmeshed in multiple, overlapping, sometimes conflicting times.

And:

> My primary concern is the discrepant temporalities (sometimes I want to say 'histories,' or even 'futures') that are integral to the task of the curator today.

What this formula allows for is the possibility that an historically fixed instance of 'the times' in the past might be folded into an apparently 'discrepant' temporality: the present. This happens routinely when a museum object continues to be displayed within what we deem to be an outmoded or even inappropriate interpretative narrative – for example, a colonialist one. A progressive curatopian impulse may want to remove or rescue this object from degrading anachronism. Left in this anachronistic state, the object will however yield knowledge not only about 'the [historical] times' from which it can or should be liberated, but also about 'the [present] times' in terms of which we now believe it should be understood. And, I want to add, even if this object is re-presented in 'the [revisionist] times' of a progressive present, it will still continue to bear witness to its past or, indeed, pasts.

Curators themselves are likely to embody such over- or in-foldings of times: the curator's temporal presence and consciousness will be furnished not just by contemporary theories and beliefs and their associated practices, but also by accumulated evolutionary and developmental steps along the way – by co-present temporalities and instances of 'the times'. The progressive and improving impulse of curatopia may seem to be linear but it will also, inevitably, be accumulative; and, we should expect, accumulative in a critically dialogic way. The curator will be the repository of these critical accumulations and even of sheddings and disavowals of them, and will move through time *with*, not just despite or on from or beyond, such accumulations, sheddings, and disavowals.

As well as thinking about things as historicised subjects 'with stories to tell', and about curators as subjects with accumulated knowledge about ways of telling those stories or enabling them to be told, we need to think about participating subjects in the form of diverse communities of interest, as many writers in this book do: traditional or customary owners of things, including their stories, general as well as scholarly audiences, and even future audiences, as Sharon Macdonald and Jennie Morgan suggest in their essay 'What not to collect? Post-connoisseurial Dystopia and the Profusion of Things': 'But at the same time, we have a duty to future generations to actually try and show the way things are today.'

What is suggested here is a curatorial duty to project a model of 'the [today] times' into the future. Macdonald and Morgan are not quite talking about 'the times' in Clifford's sense, but about the embodiment of 'the times' in their historically specific material cultures: in things – objects, images, texts, sounds, technologies, archives – that curators will have to make decisions about collecting or not collecting *today*. However, these things cannot be detached from collection development policies and priorities for the accumulation of things. Equally, such policies cannot be detached from 'the times' of curatorial practices 'at the time' of collection; nor from 'the [accumulated historical] times' of past practices known to the curator; nor from the accumulated stories the things-as-subjects have told and will be able to tell to 'future generations', including stories about the ways in which curators have treated them 'over time'. This at once overarching and cumulative time might best be characterised as archival or memory time – and as such, time that will inevitably be political, in as much as it will have encompassed ongoing contests and negotiations over ownership, including ownership of truth and truth values, and therefore over power and knowledge; over class, taste and privilege; and, indeed, over contesting knowledge systems or epistemologies.

In their essay 'Concerning Curatorial Practice in Ethnological

Museums: An Epistemology of Postcolonial Debates', Larissa Förster and Friedrich von Bose cite several writers, including Macdonald, and introduce the challenging term 'memory politics'. Paul Tapsell's statement that, 'in a Māori sense, we are our ancestors', is a political framing of embodied memory. Memory, of course, is not inert: in their essay 'The Figure of the Kaitiaki: Learning from Māori Curatorship Past and Present', Philipp Schorch, Conal McCarthy and Arapata Hakiwai refer to Awhina Tamarapa's statement that 'the display of the *pātaka* (food storehouse) called *Te Tākinga* in the exhibition *Mana Whenua*' at the Museum of New Zealand Te Papa Tongarewa 'did not talk only about the tribal *past*, but their *present and future*'. A Polynesian concept of time predicated on facing the past in order to move into and understand the future is mentioned several times in this book. The epistemologies of memory and of time have long, fractious histories in metaphysics and, more recently, in cognitive science, with the question of whether memory can ever be disconnected from systems of belief a persistent point of contention (e.g. Frise, 2017). In addition, as well as the problem of truth values in relation to memory and belief, the factual reliability of individual memory is hardly certain in matters of public record. How memory functions is also, then, an inherently political issue, a provocation or irritant at the juncture of social/cultural and political histories since the cultural turn of the mid-1970s (e.g. Pincus and Novak, 2011).

The question of how memory may inform or shape the future is also, currently, reshaping how we might think about conservation – a word that has a rapidly expanding and urgent remit. The UK Arts and Humanities Research Council's project *Heritage Futures* (with which both Sharon Macdonald and Jennie Morgan are involved) is a good example of work that challenges 'heritage' to take legacy responsibility for impacts of 'the [today] times' on the future. *Heritage Futures* asserts in its oxymoronic name and in its mission statements that the work of 'designing the future' goes well beyond conserving cultural memory for consumption by future audiences. The project's multidisciplinary goals are expressed in activist terms; memory is given explicit agency in a future imagined as potentially dystopian.

> Current global crises and transformations (from climate change to mass migration) highlight the need to develop more sustainable and resilient future-making practices, and encourage different areas of interest to pursue common goals and learn from one another.

'The [political] times' of the curator is, it seems to me, the prevailing theme of this book, and the context within which variously improving, revisionist and critical curatopian scenarios are discussed, analysed, critiqued and played out. A majority of these scenarios are concerned in one way or another with aspects of decolonisation, which of course involves a folding of time: interventions in the present on 'the times' of past or persisting colonialist practices, belief systems or mind-sets; and all scenarios gathered in this book draw to some extent on memory resources with, inevitably, varying degrees of politicised belief-system affiliations.

Inevitably and appropriately, the scenarios cluster around museum work and discourse, both curatorial and academic. As I began to draw together the themes and scenarios of the essays collected here, I increasingly felt the need to move outside points of view determined and contained to greater or lesser extents by the politics of museum practices and, indeed, by the locations and institutions that conventionally or unconventionally constitute museums. When teaching curatorial practice, I used to remind my students that an audience's museum experience begins some time before they enter the museum as such, and will not end the moment they leave: all museums are, so to speak, 'museums without walls'. The affective, cognitive and psychomotor components of a visitor's pre-visit time, not to mention the latest news item they read or heard, the varieties of excitement or indifference with which they approach the visit over preceding hours or days, their existing knowledge, interest or indifference – their cultural capital, if you will – the weather, the ease or difficulty of transportation, the company they are in: all of these (and more) times, temporalities and conditioning experiences come in to the museum with them. What they encounter in the museum will probably add to, challenge or affirm aspects of this pre-loaded mélange of times, moods, beliefs and memories. What they encounter and *perceive* may also influence how existing memories are stored, prioritised and framed: the museum visit may 're-mind' the visitor of something that happened in their past and may draw that 'long-term' memory into 'short-term', front-of-consciousness awareness – awareness based on sense and perception. From there, the 'short-term' memory will soon retire once again to its 'long-term' brain-space, but may do so in an altered or edited state.

To state the obvious in this way is only to remind ourselves that the temporalities of the museum experience exist within and in relation to the expanded field of the diverse subjectivities, including memories, of subjects-as-audiences. Despite the generous and diverse reach of curatopian thinking in these essays, I found myself wanting to reorient my point of view outside 'the [institutional] times' of the curator, to find a subjective view-shaft on the urgent issues discussed under the heading *Curatopia*.

There is a personal story that I have shared a few times over the years in essays and occasional writing, and this may be a way of pivoting from the museum-centric focus of *Curatopia*. But first, some preparatory thoughts. Looking back across the occasions on which I have told the story and the motivations for returning somewhat obsessively to it, I now notice a predictable set of conditions. These include the fact that I am usually trying to find a point of departure from which to understand and discuss the apparently paradoxical relationship of memory to a present, and at the same time trying to understand why abjection – an anxiety about self-identity or authenticity – also seems to be in play; this comes down to a self-doubting question: 'Am I telling the truth?' Or, to put it another way, does a narrative based in memory do credit to my consciousness, which I believe to be responsible not only for representing who I am, but how I got to be this way – how I got to be *present*?

The issue of whether or not the presence of memory is paradoxical will always be both a phenomenological and an epistemological one: what and how do I perceive, how do remembered perceptions inform the constitution of a present, and what and how do I learn from this? And what, indeed, do I learn from being conscious of – perceiving – the phenomenon of memory as a reticulation of the past in the present?

The German writer W.G. Sebald has made this paradoxical dynamic the basis of much of his work, in particular his 1992 novels *Die Ausgewanderten*, published in English as *The Emigrants* in 1996, and *Austerlitz* (German and English translation, 2001). In *Austerlitz* the eponymous character, obsessed with memory and how he came to be who he is in a time he cannot fully comprehend as 'present', addresses a long disquisition on time to his unnamed companion (who resembles Sebald himself). In the course of this monologue, the ageing art historian Austerlitz, who was the emigrant child of Jewish parents murdered during the Holocaust, says this:

> I shall find that all moments of time have co-existed simultaneously, in which case none of what history tells us would be true, past events have not yet occurred but are waiting to do so at the moment when we think of them.

Despite its tragic and traumatic historical context, the experience of time that Sebald describes through Austerlitz will be familiar to many of us. In my own case, I remember a particular moment in which a set of vivid sensory experiences caused a hallucinatory flashback to a time in my childhood, a kind of experience shared by many people I have spoken to about it, and made famous, of course, in volume one, *Swann's Way*, of Marcel Proust's *À la recherche du temps perdu*. The experience is phenomenological in as much as, *pace* Merleau-Ponty, it consists of an apparently empirical record of perceptions, where memory is the recording agent. It is epistemological in as much as it discloses knowledge about the past that I have no reason to doubt, though that rationality is subverted to some extent by abjection; and it also shows me a kind of neurological or mentality experiment whose yield is how sensory perceptions such as smell can directly access knowledge we call 'memory' – can, in fact, recall the past into the present, producing that apparently paradoxical palimpsest.

So, the story. In 1969, I was 23 and recently married. Rose and I were travelling out of Colombo in what was then still known as Ceylon, to stay overnight in Kandy up in the mountains. We were in a battered, dark green Austin Cambridge with a driver whose name I cannot remember, though I am sure I have in the past. Let's call him Ricardo, a plausible Portuguese name, since our driver told us that he was a Roman Catholic whose family could be traced back to the Portuguese who had once colonised much of Ceylon in the 16th and 17th centuries. We made a deal with him to drive us up to Kandy and back that would cost a bit more than the bus, but that would return us in time for our flight out the next day. The deal included us staying in his cousin's hotel in Kandy and having a pre-departure meal in his brother's restaurant in Colombo.

It's odd that I can remember the car because I am not interested in them, but this banal detail seems to be the key with which to open the time capsule of memory. As part of his sales pitch, 'Ricardo' smacked the bonnet of his Austin Cambridge and assured us that English cars were the best, assuming that we were English or at least Anglophile. Entering the superior English car and driving out of Colombo on the left-hand side of the road, we were conveyed by colonial history as well as by Ricardo – at that time as New Zealanders we shared the same Commonwealth monarch and rules of the road, despite Ricardo's Portuguese ancestors and my German ones. In 1969, I belonged to a generation of New Zealanders that increasingly rejected traces of colonialism in our society, such as the designation of England as 'home', varieties of settler privilege, and imperialisms marked for us by the war in Vietnam; and so I felt somewhat ashamed of having a private car with a driver, a shame evidenced by our willing concessions to Ricardo's bargaining on behalf of his extended family.

However, part of my childhood had been spent within the Austin Cambridge, as it were, of colonialist protocols and privileges: when my twin brother and I were between the ages of seven and ten, our family lived in a remote part of East Pakistan, now Bangladesh. Despite coming from the frugal, post-Depression small-town home of our maternal grandmother in the South Island of Aotearoa New Zealand, we became accustomed to a household with servants and clear demarcations between the 'us' of a management elite and a 'them' of Bengali people living in the township by the paper mill where our father worked in one of the start-up projects planned to accelerate the country into industrial modernity. This was a past that, in 'the times' of 1969, I wished to banish or at least repudiate – but could not forget.

In 1954, the township of Chandraghona near the paper mill, the banks of the Karnaphuli River and the dusty roads through the surrounding countryside were filled with a rich variety of pungent smells: dust, wood-smoke and the smoke of dried cow dung, drying fish, jasmine and frangipani flowers, shit. Fifteen or so years later, as we were driven in the green Austin Cambridge through villages and countryside on the road to Kandy, these same smells blew into the car and triggered a hallucinatory memory of the floral patterning of my mother Linda's frock when I was about seven. I turned to look at Rose and was momentarily shocked to see not my dark-haired mother Linda in her patterned frock but a slight, fair-haired young woman wearing jeans. This disconcerting effect came and went for the duration of our stay in Ceylon and only dissipated once we got back on the plane. The place and time I was in for about 48 hours, the senses and phenomena I encountered there, even the person I was with, all seemed to be shifting back and forth across another set of conditions that were at once vividly present and from the past. The effect, though, was not of separation but of a kind of simultaneity.

Were I now to curate this simultaneity as a Sebald-like social and political history project, its key artefact might well be the battered green Austin Cambridge driven in the late 1960s by the Sinhalese descendant of a 16th-century Portuguese trader or soldier or colonial administrator. The car's passenger narratives would fold together a childhood in small-town New Zealand during the late 1940s and early 1950s, the experience of colonialist expatriate privilege in post-partition East Bengal during the mid to late 1950s, a counter-narrative of youthful radicalisation and postcolonial chagrin in the late 1960s, and a 'present' rather like that described by Sebald's character Austerlitz, in which 'the moment when we think of them' is when events happen.

This contingent and uncertain 'moment' is, of course, profoundly and unassailably subjective, and easily dismissed as such. But it is also, I suggest, the kind of juncture at which any credible 'curatopia' occupies time and opens up the possibility of agency in the task of 'designing the future'. The juncture is not just a critically inert one between an individual consciousness and 'the times'. I think of it, rather, as the battered, inevitably anachronistic vehicle of thought that must be kept circulating through many 'presents' that will be at once hallucinatory and cognitively secure, abject and confident, expedient and speculative, anarchic and programmatic, ephemeral and obdurate. We will have a lot of fun in this vehicle, and we will probably be scared and uncertain sometimes, fearful of what may be about to happen and where we are going. As part of our trip we may visit a museum or historic site, such as the Sri Dalada Maligawa or Temple of the Tooth in Kandy, where one of Gautama Buddha's teeth is kept. We may receive the gift of healing holy water from the tooth's weekly bathing. The water will be scented with flowers called *nanumura mangalaya*. We remember the name of the flower. Then we catch our plane to the time when we remember this moment, and it happens.

References

Frise, M. 2016. 'Preservationism in the Epistemology of Memory'. In *Philos Q. Heritage Futures*. AHRC. https://heritage-futures.org.

Merleau-Ponty, M. 1965. *Phenomenology of Perception*, trans. C. Smith. London: Routledge & Kegan Paul.

Pincus, S. and W. Novak. 2011. 'Political History after the Cultural Turn'. In *Perspectives on History*. Washington DC: American Historical Association.

Sebald, W.G. 1996 *The Emigrants*, trans. M. Hulse. New York: New Directions.

—. 2001. *Austerlitz*, trans. A. Bell. New York: Random House.

Losing It
'Watchful archaeology'

The Murray Talk, Mildura Writers Festival (10 July 2019)

I'll start, by way of paying my respects, with a poem I wrote after visiting Les Murray at Bunyah in 1990.

Ode to Unsealed Roads

Lone bird on a wire, the hills
misty and far. Waking there
I should have been pleased with space.
As well, I found myself
fleeing into the solitude of travel.

And so now I speak up
in praise of unsealed roads.
Not the slick turnpike
plunging its destination into orthodoxy.

We travel in words and shed them
along our tracks. They are names that dry
and crack into the mosaics of towns,
reticulations of roads, the homely
enclosures of the power-grid.

And through them meanders
the unsealed road. Desire
transgressing as it must
the maps that say, this name is near.

Flying into Newcastle
I looked down at the distant
Nepalese turquoise of swimming pools.
In every one, I imagined
the fair limbs of my love.

Later, at a place called Teagardens,
sipping from a can on a
wormy jetty, I ate mullet tasting
of the brown tide. Out across khaki water
the pelicans grandly sailed into mudbanks,
jarring their heads open.

I thought, this is the exact taste
of an inexact word. A colour
desire transforms into food.
Or desire shoaling, agape and hungry,
On nomad alluvia.

Trailing my bushy tail of dust
I advanced by an unsealed road
towards Bunyah.

You were my hospitable destination, Les,
but you'll understand if I say
I was driven more towards
those turquoise sky-chinks above the Bingham Divide.

Departing like Bingham's Ghost,
there when you think you can see him, then
nothing but a pair of empty boots,
one a huge stride from the other.

I'll explain about the boots in a moment. But first, it's an honour to be asked to give what is now known as the Murray Talk following the death of Les Murray in April this year. I was invited to give a talk here at Mildura before Murray's death and before the talk was named after him, so I feel as though you've been ambushed by the circumstance that has a Kiwi writer giving the inaugural Murray Talk rather than an Aussie one. However, of course Les Murray's work has a wide reach, and so I can claim if nothing else to represent that audience.

I was also lucky to visit Les and his family at Bunyah and spend a night there back in 1990, whence the unsealed roads poem. I'd been shouted a trip to Australia by the Foundation for Australia and New Zealand Arts. I was asked to nominate a number of people I'd like to meet. Les Murray was one of those people. I'd read his poems, especially *Walking to the Cattle Place: a Meditation*, which I carried around with me like a kind of talisman for several years while I tried to understand the impact those poems had on me.

I thought it would be interesting to meet Murray on his home patch, and so on good advice I bought a bottle of single malt whisky, caught a flight from Sydney to Newcastle and then drove a rental car to Bunyah. When I got there I was greeted hospitably by Les and Valerie and was soon taken for a walk around the place by their young son Peter. Along the way, we came across a single very large boot and, a bit further on, as if at the span of a giant stride, a second one. Ah, said Peter, clearly the boots belonged to Bingham's Ghost, who inhabited the hills over there, and the reason the boots were left behind was because Bingham was in a hurry to get back to the hills, and the reason one boot was such a long way from the other was because he was taking such huge strides in his hurry to get to the hills.

Peter's wonderful story about Bingham's Ghost seems to me to be a good way to introduce the idea that forgetting or abandoning the means to get somewhere may be a good way of finding the story you think you're hurrying towards.

*

The story of the lost and forgotten empty boots allows me to take a giant stride from Bunyah and Bingham's Ghost to the short title of this talk, 'Losing It'. On Friday 18 January this year I 'lost it', as we say. I shared four pizzas with two of my granddaughters, the younger called Cara and the older called Bella, their father, called Mischa, and my wife, who is called Donna, and went happily to bed a bit drunk at half past 11 o'clock. I'm being pedantic about names and times and details such as the number and type of pizzas – mine was a medium-sized seafood pizza on a thin crust – because during the night I was extremely sick, though not in the way I think most of us are familiar with and might normally blame on the seafood pizza and the wine. It was more like a whole-body reaction to something that was happening in my head, and in the morning I found I had not so much forgotten as stepped past the names of close family members as well as the passwords for my computer, iPad, bank accounts, gate access code to our apartment units; nor could I locate my cell or landline phone numbers, nor many other codes that we all take for granted. I was unsure about where our place was located in the city of Auckland. I could not locate where neighbouring suburbs were. I could not find my birthdate when I tried to do so as a kind of thought experiment.

I set about rediscovering these codes from a variety of negligently maintained notebooks and found that after about a week I'd begun to relocate most of this wiped-out information – partly I think by prompting my brain to retrace its steps, but also because my brain was doing that anyway.

Five months later I know where everything is, including the right keys on my computer keyboard, and am hardly aware of what happened back in January, except that *I remember something happened.* It's as though the deep memory *that something* happened, which is not quite the same as the shallow memory of what happened *as a consequence*, has been the key instruction issued by my consciousness. The details could get filled in later by one means or another. What seemed to matter most at the time was what could perhaps be called the meta-narrative of 'losing it' – of overstepping or missing out what I knew.

My GP referred me to the public hospital for an examination and a couple of months later a young registrar training to be a neurologist took me through a programme of tests that I later looked up on the internet and remembered having done at the hospital. The tests revealed that I was pretty much OK but that I couldn't quickly draw a picture of the hands of a clock to show ten minutes past eleven. I have limited practical graphic skills, but anyway it seemed that I was somewhere about five and ten percent downside of normal – whether my own normal or a statistical normal for white males aged 72 was of course an open question, since no benchmark existed for my own personal normal except what I remembered of it. My self-examining sense on the basis of the tests was that I was indeed a couple of notches short, and that a CT scan as recommended by the young registrar's supervisor was a good idea.

Once, when my dad was just a couple of years older than I am now, he twice brought my mother and me a nice lunch of sandwiches down in the garden, joining us for both lunches but taking the dishes back up to the kitchen after the first one and repeating the exercise, having forgotten that he'd already made and delivered a lunch. My mother didn't comment on the repetition but ate her sandwiches and continued our conversation involving my father – unlike the forgotten and repeated lunch, the conversation was normally continuous, moving on from where it had left off while another lunch was being prepared. I found this extremely sad and disturbing, but my mother was unperturbed – after all, she said when I asked if she was worried, look at everything Chickie had accomplished in his life and all the complicated situations he'd been in, what did a superfluous lunch matter?

But I lacked her equanimity and was thinking about my dad's serial sandwiches when I went for the CT scan recommended by the young registrar who'd watched me fail to draw a clock-face with the hands pointing at ten past eleven. I was pretty much shitting myself as I lay on the platform and heard the machine above my head make a deep groaning sound that was like a memory of the sound I had made when I strode past my memory during the post-seafood pizza night –

and indeed stepped out of my memory as if it were an uncomfortable old boot.

A few days later my GP sent me an email to say that the CT scan had found nothing wrong with my brain – no sign of a stroke or bleeding. I bought a bottle of excellent champagne that Donna and I polished off pretty quickly. In the privacy of my own thoughts I raised my glass to my serial-sandwich father Chick Wedde and to the equanimity of his wife my mother, whom he called Lindy, sometimes with a tipsy tear in his eye. The next morning it occurred to me that I had not gone out and bought other bottles of champagne, having forgotten that we'd just drunk one, though I remembered having wanted to.

*

At the time in January when this *something happened* happened I was heading into the final stages of the first draft of a large novel called *The Reed Warbler*, in which a young woman from the north of Germany leaves that country in the late 1870s, as did my great grandmother, and travels to New Zealand with her illegitimate daughter. The story of this young, fictional woman is only very tangentially and circumstantially connected to the historical narrative of my great grandmother, who did not have an illegitimate daughter when she came to New Zealand, nor many of the experiences that my fictional woman has in the book. However, the ghosts or traces of almost-forgotten histories do haunt the fiction I've now finished writing a second draft of.

In writing this haunted fiction over the past couple of years I've been aware that I was constantly putting my mind and imagination to work in a place where the distinctions between what was remembered, what was fabricated as memory, and what layered or ambiguously located chronologies or time-zones were occupied by these memories both real and fabricated, were uncertain at best and in any case deliberately thought about and written as being constantly on the verge of being forgotten.

I apologise for the convoluted structure of that sentence, but its hard-pressed turns may be the best articulation of a mind attempting to do what mine was back then. In the course of the novel, the voices and presences of characters as well as the events in their lives fade away and in many cases disappear as the text moves on past their moment in it.

What might be called immigrant amnesia is a factor here – the remorseless fading-away of family memory and connections when, in the 19th century, people undertook long sea voyages to 'the other side of the world'. Return exchanges of letters between New Zealand and Germany, for example, could take between five and eight months. In addition, many immigrants, including my great-grandfather Heinrich August Wedde, preferred to be forgotten about back in the place, or situation, he'd left as a sailor who jumped ship and made himself scarce for a few months after arriving in New Zealand, where, like a number of other settlers no doubt, he preferred to have no past and therefore in a sense no memory of it.

What was unexpected at that time in January when I got crook was that only a few days after I forgot a bunch of stuff such as my phone number I was able, despite being physically tired and sick, to get on with finishing the last bit of a first draft of the book, which I completed in mid-March. I had only occasional trouble remembering – if that's the right word under the circumstances – what the book was about and who the characters were. I finished a second draft of about 650 pages at the beginning of May, by which time I could hold together the book's complex details.

These details included the family tree I'd constructed for what became a cascade of descendants from the young woman I'd named Josephina. The tree came to have about 30 individuals in it, covering six generations, and in addition back in Germany and Denmark there were Josephina's grandmother, mother and father, aunt and uncle, her two sisters and the husband and children of one of them, not to mention the grandfather and two uncles who had perished at Dybbøl during the Second Schleswig War of 1864 between Germany and Denmark.

In addition, the novel has two contemporary characters, second-cousins Beth and Frank, who are living in the present time of the book. Beth is approaching 60 years of age and her cuzzie Frank is in his early 70s. Frank has lived in Queensland for most of his adult life. They had spent parts of their childhood holidays together at the remote farm in rugged, inaccessible back country in the central North Island where Josephina (their great- or great-great-grandmother) had ended her days about a decade before Frank was born. Now, they are driving back up to Auckland from a family reunion in Wellington and make a detour to visit the ruined grave of their common ancestor Josephina Wenczel née Hansen who had also been off-the-record Josephina Bloch along the way, having had a child called Wolf to the radical Social Democrat Wolf Bloch, himself based somewhat on my shit-stirring ancestor Johannes Wedde, the author of a long, windbaggy poem about the Paris Commune of 1871. Beth's and Frank's ongoing, somewhat quarrelsome investigations of family history provide a kind of real-time narrative about how the present and imperfect family records fail to explain much of what had happened in Josephina's life and the lives of her descendants, but do, in a sense, help and provoke her great- and great-great-grandchildren Frank and Beth to examine their own lives in relation to the woman whose headstone they had found toppled over in a remote back-country graveyard near a place called Kaitīeke. The name is Māori and translates as food of the tīeke or saddleback bird, a denizen of the dense forests that were felled and burned off by pioneer settlers to make way for sheep. Not many tīeke are to be found in that country these days – in a sense the environment has forgotten them.

Was it the pizza, my brain, or the novel that caused the convulsions of that Friday night in January? Probably all three, but I suspect it was the novel that had a lot to do with producing the effect and subsequent result of fragmented and unreliable historical narrative and memory. Serve me right, and I wish future readers of the novel all the best and good luck.

*

Now I want to take another stride, this time to the tagline of this talk, 'watchful archaeology'. The phrase was used by the French art critic Jérôme Sans and borrowed I think from Paul Virilio's classic book *Bunker Archaeology*. Sans used the phrase when writing about the work of the New Zealand artist Bill Culbert, who died aged 84 on 28 March this year at his home in the Vaucluse region of Provence. It's a home that he and his wife Pip began to establish in 1961 from dilapidated farm buildings on a small hilltop at a deserted hamlet called Croagnes. From Croagnes, the view rose northward towards the slopes of a steep escarpment near Sault on the high Plateau d'Albion down which spilled the discarded rubbish of a *décharge* or tip. Culbert regarded the tips as historic sites with links back to neolithic culture. In a vital sense, what he was recycling in the process of fixing up and furnishing the dilapidated roofless house at Croagnes were also the fragmentary traces of stories that had passed out of meaningful use in the midden – he was recycling their meaningfulness as well as their usefulness.

The recycling of materials in Culbert's art implies a kind of return journey, not in any literal sense but rather, as Jérôme Sans wrote in his catalogue essay for *À Charge de Décharges*, quoting Paul Virilio, as watchful archaeology, as being on the lookout for 'whatever has been silent that will now speak, whatever was shut that will now open up'.

In 1978, having left New Zealand for London in 1957, Culbert returned to Christchurch as a Visiting Fellow. Among the several works he made during his tenure are *Blackball to Roa*, an old kerosene tin pierced by a fluorescent tube. There's a familiar tension in the kero-tin *Blackball to Roa* between the work as a stand-alone art object the significance of which is found principally within art-historical discourse ('found object' or bricolage etc), and the 'watchful archaeology' identified by Paul Virilio that might locate the work's signification within a complex of recovered or reconstituted memories activated by an old kero tin. Bill seems to be inviting us to share these ghostly companions of the rubbish tip we call memory – a congenial approach to making art in their company.

They are among us, these ghosts – these Binghams – and if we allow our brains to become deranged enough, or accept the fact that they have become so, the Binghams may even consent to talk to us.

*

I'll conclude with a ghostly reading from the novel I talked about earlier, *The Reed Warbler*. The inaugurating character of this heavily populated narrative is Josephina Hansen. Her mother Agatha and father Adam recognise that she is a gifted seamstress at an early age, and she is given an old sewing sampler that has been added to over many years and that may have originated from her great-great-grandmother. The sampler, which Josephina calls the 'Oma', as if it was in fact a grandmother, has small scenes sewn or embroidered into it, such as a little house with a smoking chimney next to a blue lake with white ducks on it. Each of the sewn or embroidered stories as well as the sampler's edging shows how certain stitches are made – the sampler is a complex mnemonic text, if you like, an aide-memoire, a graphic teaching aid and encyclopedia, as well as the repository of old family connections. It is worn and dirty because it cannot be washed without damaging the stitches, which is to say without damaging its memory. Josephina regards it as a magical object, one that will allow her to access memories and secrets and the powers they may transmit.

At the age of 17 she is raped by a Prussian officer garrisoned at Kiel when delivering a lying-in nightgown to his pregnant wife. Her mother and father turn against her when it becomes clear she is pregnant to the Prussian officer, and send her to have the baby at her older sister Greta's place in Sønderborg across the border in Denmark, on the understanding that she will leave the baby in Greta's and her husband Danne's care. She refuses to leave her baby daughter, whose name is Catharina, eventually travelling to New Zealand with her, by then aged four. Josephina is now pregnant again, this time to the radical Social Democrat Wolf Bloch, author of the windbaggy panegyric to the Paris Commune. Wolf dies on the voyage and Josephina arrives in New Zealand a widow with two children.

Winding the clock back, though: Prior to her going to her sister's place in Sønderborg, Josephina's mother and father have confiscated the sampler or Oma from her as punishment for her disgrace, but her older sister Elke pinches it and brings it to Josephina at their sister Greta's place.

I'll read a short section from the time when Josephina has had the sampler taken from her by her mother and father after revealing that she is pregnant to the Prussian officer. Her father is a craftsman carpenter whose stock includes coffins for the wealthy townsfolk of Kiel, and Josephina and her mother often sew the special decorative shrouds. Since her parents took the sampler or Oma from her, she and her mother are refusing to speak to each other. They are sitting on opposite sides of the table with a shroud between them, and sewing in silence.

*

> Outside by the main door, Papa's journeyman Franz was planing coffin planks. The regular panting sound of the plane came into the house and as far as the back where Josephina and her mother sat at opposite ends of the big table with the shroud between them. It was one of the fresh new linens and smelled of sunlight. They were doing a border of blue crosses. Because they were not talking to each other any more, the sound of Franz planing was like words going back and forth, mixed up with the clucking of hens looking for grains near the fodder stall. Now Mathilde had Josephina's old linen scrap treasure with the picture of Puck Puck the special chicken she'd embroidered on it, but she sometimes told herself Puck Puck stories in the silence of her work with Mutti, and remembered the warmth of her special chicken against her chest when she was little, and its occasional pecks. When Mutti wanted to move her section of the border she rapped with her knuckles on the table. Soon it would snow and Papa and Franz would keep their work inside for winter. Then they would all be there together, the two cows and old Gunnar in

their stalls, the chickens, Franz or whichever worker stayed long enough, Josephina and Elke in their little loft, the trestles with unfinished coffins and tabletops on them in the space between the stalls, and her papa and mutti by the fire arguing about how to get established in the town.

But ‘the Oma’ wasn’t there – her grandmother’s sampler that was Josephina’s now, covered all over with little stitches making pictures of flowers and houses and animals in different coloured threads, and a snowy mountain with a little deer on top, that spoke the names of the stitches and also had Oma’s voice in them, in the stories that each stitch told, little words for big stories that Oma told over and over and especially in winter, starting when Josephina was too small for sewing anything but Strikkelise, and when the birds made footprints that were like stitches on the snow by the big door and told the stories of the birds’ songs, how they were cold now, not like those lucky ones that knew how to fly away somewhere nice and warm. Oma died after her husband was killed in the Danish war at Dybbøl Mill – he was buried over there somewhere by the marshes along with the other ‘fools’, including two of his sons who thought it was a great thing to shoot at Danes with wonderful Prussian rifles because otherwise they would take all the farms and smallholdings like theirs. Josephina was seven when Oma fell down dead after making a sweep of her arm to scatter grain for the hens outside in the yard – she heard the old lady shout ‘Hein!’, which is what she called her husband, and then she fell down flat on her face like a plank. She was too angry was what Mutti thought, angry with the ‘fools’ who marched off to get blown to pieces for the Prussians, it was anger that killed her. But Josephina could remember Oma’s stories, which were not angry; and when she was twelve Mutti gave her ‘the Oma’ to look after so she could properly learn the stitches that told the stories that told the stitches and that, after a while, began telling Josephina who she was: that she was a young woman now, that she could be proud of her skill, that she had value. But now the Oma was locked away in the big dark chest in her papa's and mutti's room, and Josephina couldn't have it back until she began to talk again.

Mutti rapped her knuckles on the table and then gave the shroud cloth a yank. Josephina was snipping a thread and the yank made her hand slip; the scissors pierced her thumb and some blood flicked on to the white linen.

It wasn't her fault, and when her mother said, 'Now look what you've done you stupid girl,' Josephina stood up and walked down between the stalls and out the big door past Franz who stopped planing to smile at her and make a little bow – it was going to rain, he'd be coming inside, he said – and down the hill as far as the gate. An inky black storm cloud quivering with lightning was stalled out over the sea. She stopped and let the great sobs burst out.

*

And now to finish I'll return briefly to the artist Bill Culbert and his way with 'watchful archaeology', and how stories and even memories can be unearthed from cast-off objects such as a pair of discarded boots – to return also to where I started with Bingham's Ghost.

One evening in 1979, Bill was sitting at the kitchen table at his place in Croagnes with some friends, drinking brandy out of shot glasses. He noticed that the light from an electric lightbulb was being refracted through the glass and on to the table. The next day he took a glass of wine outside and put it on a stone slab in strong sunlight. It cast the paradoxical shadow of what looked like a lightbulb. He took a photograph of it and called the work *Small Glass Pouring Light.*

Subsequently, in 1983, he developed this phenomenon into an installation also called *Small Glass Pouring Light*, in which 25 bistro wine glasses filled with red wine are set out on a white table under three white industrial-style lamps. All the glasses are casting the same kinds of shadows as in the 1979 photograph.

This installation has been exhibited widely and now resides as part of the French National Collection at the Château d'Oiron in western

France. Here, the artist's instruction is that the wine in the glasses may be drunk and that the glasses must be replenished regularly. It seems that both parts of the instruction have continued to be followed for some 30 years, and so I close with this toast to the hospitably anarchic ghosts of the imagination and the watchful archaeology that will bring them to light.

And a toast also to the Ghost of the Bingham Divide, Les Murray.

Walking and Swimming to Venice
Bill Culbert

In *Bill Culbert: Front Door Out Back, Venice Biennale 1 June – 24 November 2013*, exhibition catalogue edited by Justin Paton and Heather Galbraith (Christchurch Art Gallery & Creative New Zealand, 2013)

1

It's a brilliantly sunny day in midsummer in Auckland, New Zealand. High tide on the Waitemata Harbour is at 10am. I walk from my place down the hill to a small beach at the bottom of Hamilton Road for a swim. Most days when I do this I have a rather contradictory purpose in mind. Walking is good for thinking, so I'm hoping that some of that will happen, especially when (as today) I've stalled in front of the admonishing luminescence of my empty computer screen. I even have a little notebook in my bag along with my towel. But while the grounded rhythm of walking is good for mindful thinking, the suspended motion of swimming is good for not thinking – for mindlessness – and I'm hoping for some of that as well. After swimming for a while back and forth between the boatsheds at either side of the bay my mind seems to empty: neurotransmitters, endorphin release, muscle bliss, that kind of thing no doubt. In any case, thought is suspended, like my body in the water, somewhat weightless, in touch with a medium but not grounded on anything solid. The mind 'drifts', as we say, perhaps in a state of liquid consciousness.

Walking down the hill to the beach, I'm trying to think about Bill Culbert's installations and how to describe the distinctive ways in which they co-opt and subvert perception: how they fix or capture perception in material effects at the same time as they seem to dematerialise those effects. It's enjoyable, visualising the works, recalling what Culbert has had to say about them; and both imagining, and resisting the urge to speculate about, what Culbert might make of the opportunity at Venice. But this thinking is also somewhat anxious: I want clarity, precision, an argument or generative idea that can become writing – that will project thought in the form of words. I want something substantial, material almost, not something fluid. I want the process of thinking and writing to have concluded at a result. I'm impatient for this result, partly because I need it, but also because I look forward to the pleasure it will give me when I can look at it in one place: dark words fixed on the bright screen of my computer. I want to arrive where these emphatic marks aren't drifting away or changing shape. I want the result to be unambiguously on message.

In the water, though, after a while, that anxious desire for conclusive thought dissolves, as it were. My head is sometimes in the water and sometimes half out of it. One eye glances sideways as my mouth turns to breathe. Across the glittering surface of the bay in one direction I can see the practical parabola of the Harbour Bridge; lines of flashing car windscreens flicker across it. In another direction I can see the outrageously whimsical pink Chelsea Sugar refinery, lit by hot sunshine, an opulent palazzo. If I stop and look around, the surface of the water appears to be moving along as the receding tide pushes little waves up against the breeze. The darker greenish patterns in this surface look solid, like floating islands; the refractive glitter of sunlight is interlaced across the bay.

When I get out of the water, these two states of mind seem to merge happily. The anxious desire for clarity encounters the endorphic bliss of suspended thought; hard-edged practicality enters the same field of perception as whimsy; movement and fixity change places promiscuously; surface and depth cease to be distinct from each other; patterns of light and shade generate the appearance of floating islands, which at one moment are masses of brightness and at another of darkness. It's a condition very like the one produced by looking at Culbert's work: a perceptual immersion at once simple and paradoxical. Is this perhaps like the Copenhagen principle used by physicists to explain why light appears to act like a wave when we think of it that way, and like a particle when that is what we ask of it? Is there a strategy for collapsing that binary; and could it be art?

A similar question might be asked concerning the stretch between what Culbert has already done, and what he might do next: how might he make fluid what was once materialised, how might the work continue to move? And how might it contain within itself, at the moment of its arrival *somewhere else*, a sense of its own continuing potential, its ability to transplant memory into a set of fresh conditions? How is it that the work can appear at once so simple and specific, and so fluid?

I now have a place to start – not with indeterminacy or hesitation but with Culbert's deliberate production of such laminated, tensioned effects as paradoxical simplicity. Weightless mass, solid mass dematerialised and pierced by light; light that is space, not just space's delineator; light that casts dark shadows of itself; the rigorously practical, used and homely, whose other profile is extravagant splendour.

And now it seems I'm also thinking about Venice, a place that fits the description, as we say. Culbert's large installations have always been phenomenally responsive to their sites. How brilliantly *site specific*, then, is this opportunity to make work in a place where light, space, horizons, reflections, the solid and the fluid (the particle and the wave), the grandiose and the homely, the new and the recovered are always in play, and were so in Venetian art 400 years before impressionism. Giorgione, Titian, Tintoretto, Veronese – the magnificence of this Venetian Renaissance history may give Culbert cause to push back sceptically, as his previous deadpan rational subversions of framing and perspective suggest he could; but it will also locate him in the art capital of light, and for that matter along the trajectory of Venetian art's relish for life and pleasure. Even where the subject matter is religious (a thematic Culbert has no interest in), as in Giorgione's *The Adoration of the Shepherds* (1505/1510, Samuel H. Kress Collection, 1939.1.289, National Gallery of Art, Washington, DC), the painting's chief effects are sensuous and celebratory, and even homely; subversive of the kind of pomp associated with patronage: the newborn baby lying outside on the ground, the shepherds in rough working clothes, and, following the glittering track of a rivulet of water, a subtly lit vista of sea coast, city and sky.

Is it preposterous, then, to suggest that Venice itself is already a site-work merely waiting for Culbert's presence? Of course it's an excessive claim. But Culbert's previous occupations of what seem to have been ready-made sites, situations, and even histories have raised the same unlikely question before. *Ebb and Flow* or *Light Splash* by the great windows and harbour vista at the Musée des Beaux Arts André Malraux in 1990, for example, seem to have been *inevitable*; to have existed already as perception projected by thought . . . needing only the right moment for that concept to materialise, which it duly did when Culbert saw that the time *was* right; but materialised in a form one of whose chief characteristics was a kind of evanescence, the light tubes on the reflective floor surface seeming always to be on the point of reverting to a condition more conceptual than material, more fluid than grounded; and yet 'for now' *here*, completely in the presence of the moment.

2

For now: another day, another swim. Today it's cloudy; the surface of the sea is dull, the pink of the sugar works is muted, and the industrial tiara of the Harbour Bridge isn't glittering. How do I perceive this? Partly through remembering how different the experience was yesterday. I'm now walking and swimming towards a Venice that is a palimpsest. Walking back up the hill under trees that, today, hardly cast any shadows (while remembering yesterday's Moorish filigrees), I'm also reminded that the purpose of words is not just in their use (and usefulness) – for example, their use to narrate meaning. What words 'mean', what their 'use' consists of, is inextricably entangled in their circumstances. 'Site specific' they may be; but the site may also be as much a product of memory as of present use.

In 1986, Bill Culbert staged a major two-part installation, *Light Vessels, Jars and Plains*, at Salford and Newcastle upon Tyne. One section, *Lampfloat I and II* at Zone Gallery, Newcastle, appeared to remember – to be analogous to – the *nymphéa* waterlilies made familiar by Monet's paintings in which the refractive surface glitter of water, its implicit depth, and the materiality of the plants seem to drift together across an ambiguous plane tilted up against the logic of perspective. In Culbert's version, the light source that dapples the shiny surface is a number of white lampshades ('*nymphéa*') 'floating' on a floor where electrical cables resemble tangled plant stems in a pond. And yet, of course, the 'use' or meaning of the artwork isn't limited to any kind of banal mimicry, either of nature or of art. A component of the larger project, *Light Plain*, installed a ceiling of lampshades tilted in a *trompe l'oeil* subversion of perspective made possible by the severe gallery architecture. Unlike *Ebb and Flow* or *Light Splash* at Le Havre, however, the 'site-specificity' of the complete suite of 1986 Newcastle upon Tyne works seemed to have as much if not more to do with memory as with the physical conditions of the place and its architecture.

The French artist and critic Yves Abrioux has used the term 'paradoxical literalism' to describe Bill Culbert's work. Abrioux is one of Culbert's close friends as well as a close analytical reader of his work. Abrioux's elegant formulation was applied to the *Light Vessels, Jars and Plains* installations. It captures not just the adroit physical play of the works, but also their play as palimpsests in which memory – including the memory of other works of art including Culbert's own – allows the work to drift across time and place. It's where it is; but it's also *somewhere else.*

3

When I speak, the words don't appear. If I don't hear what others are saying, their words are gone; they are immaterial, like light without matter on which to make colour register. But when I write words they do appear, on my computer screen or on paper. There they are like dark shadows or projections. Seeing them, reading them, I want to know how they come to be there. Where, so to speak, does the light come from that casts them, these shadowy projections? What is its source? It's thought. And where does thought come from – what projects thought?

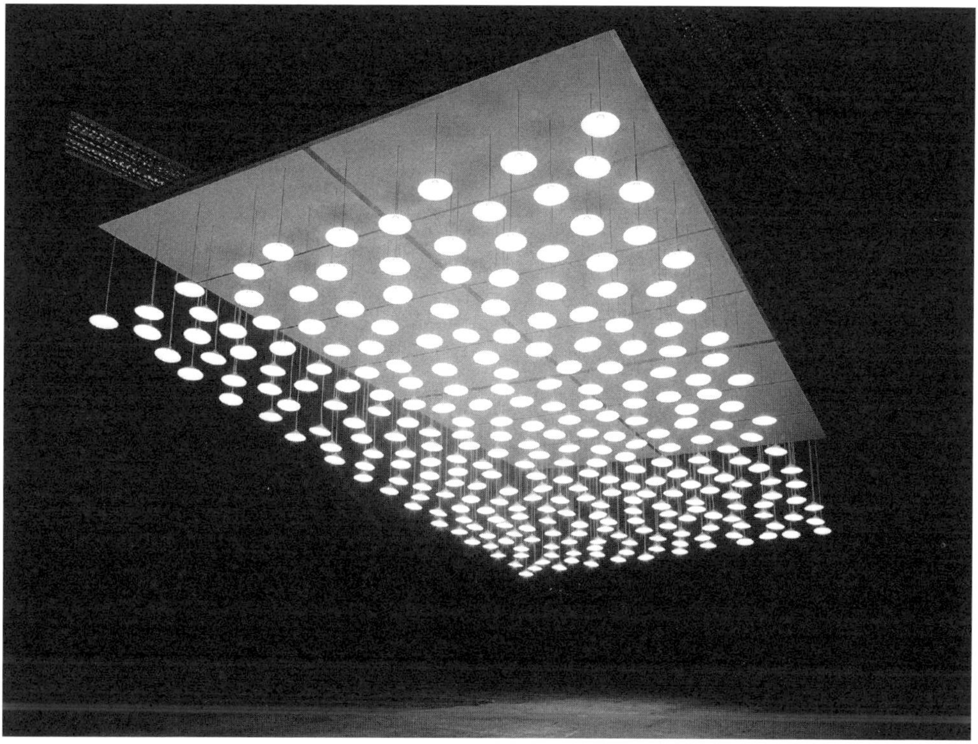

Bill Culbert, *Light Plain*, 1996 – lamp shades, lightbulbs and fittings, 2250 x 8540 x 4880 mm. Chartwell Collection, Auckland Art Gallery Toi o Tāmaki. Photograph Bryan James, Govett-Brewster Art Gallery. Courtesy of The Bill and Pip Culbert Family Trust.

It's consciousness. And what projects consciousness? Perception; the incomingness of the world I'm alive in. I perceive: neurotransmitters go to work. My consciousness lights up: I begin to process perception. Now, I'm thinking: language begins to codify and organise thought. And now I'm writing: the large structures of language are projected as details: as words, as the letters that constitute words, and also as the white spaces between letters and words. Now I'm looking at a complex patterning, a web or filigreed network of projections.

This complex surface, a matrix of dark marks and light spaces, seems to have stopped. It seems to be all surface and no depth. It's motionless: it neither moves onward in time, nor does its surface alter in the present. It seems that when I return to this surface at any time in the future it will be the same as when I left it in the past. In this way it seems to contain its own future, which is the future in which others will look at it, read it, become conscious of it, begin to think about it, speak about it, and perhaps even write about it; they may make copies of it. In this sense, though it may not seem to move or to have depth, it always contains in its unchanging surface the capacity to be in a future, and to be itself a future moment when it extends itself into the depth of another's consciousness.

But wait – isn't this inherent future like memory: that function of consciousness whereby events (some words perhaps) travel in time becoming always present again far from their time of origin and perhaps far from their place of origin as well? How ephemeral, then, are unwritten words? Their immateriality may deny writing, but not inscription. We can describe remembered words as inscribed in the consciousness of someone who has heard them; in a sense they have bypassed or vaulted over the intermediary projection of thought as writing. But there's a difference: while writing is an unchanging materialisation of thought, having become solid, memory is subject to change: it retains the mutability of thought's processes and reformulations; it remains fluid. There are powerful tensions between the material solidity of writing and the conceptual fluidity of memory.

It seems to me, walking and swimming, on days that are sometimes sunny and sometimes overcast, that it's a tension like this between solid writing and fluid memory that is one source of the 'paradoxical literalism' of Culbert's work. It's simultaneously 'written' in a site-specific present, and 'inscribed' in a time and place that might, even now, be moving somewhere else, taking its presentness with it. It's at once particle and wave.

In 1997 at Avignon, in a complex suite of installations called *Incident in Marlowe's Office*, Culbert staged an occupation (or *dérangement*) of both a physical and an historical site at the Musée Calvert, with its inscribed memories of medieval princes of church and commerce; and in an abandoned urban ghetto across town in the cité Guillaume-Apollinaire housing complex, with its contemporary memory of the marginalisation of poor immigrant communities and the physical detritus their evictions had left behind. The total work was a vast complex of tensions between the literal and the paradoxical, between site-specificities both immediate and remembered. Distinctions between different registers of thinking and drifting (walking and swimming), material and concept, seemed to be suspended.

Suspended *now*, that is, in the material record Culbert kept of this event, his own archive, his *memory*; since the physical, *literal* complex of installations at Avignon ceased to exist in the autumn of 1997. Might we expect this memory or archive to become, in turn, an aspect of the site-specific presence of Culbert's occupation of time and space at Venice? Might this be where wave and particle are thought together? For example, what might be the relationship between the simple, chandelier-like *Lustre with 2 Chairs* suspended in the grand stairwell of the Musée Calvet at Avignon in 1997, and the sketched hints that reach me of a vast in-pouring of suspended *lustres* at Venice 16 years later?

4

Today as I walk and swim to Venice brief humid showers of rain pass across the city. Steam rises off the hot black asphalt; the surface of the sea is stippled; then, suddenly, the sun glares. It's too much – too much *condition*. I want to retreat from this excess towards something unconditional and singular. An all too familiar current is dragging my words towards metaphor, the seductions of the word 'like'; towards *likenessing*, analogy, parallelism, substitution-for. A similar current drags art towards representation; even a pure white fluorescent tube can be likened to 'illumination'; illumination to an affect, 'lucidity', for example; or to a mythopoetic 'enlightenment'. Culbert's resistance to such undertows has always been unconditional.

But now, if I succumb to the metaphorical *flow* and go with it, and if I continue to *write* rather than just think about Culbert's installations, my writing will itself begin to represent and even stand in for Culbert's art. How can I resist this?

A few years ago I asked Culbert which of his works he considered the most rigorous. He nominated *Black Box* (1969); he also hinted that it remained his favourite, even a benchmark against which he could measure where his work was going. The work is indeed a plain wooden 1220 mm^3 black box, nothing more as far as anyone can *see*. However, the square black box contains a different system of lighting on each of the six interior surfaces. A time switch lights up each unseen system in turn: we perceive (become conscious of, think about, utter or write words about) this inner light through the sounds of switching and the shifting warmth of the interior lit surfaces: we hear and touch light. A kind of camera obscura, *Black Box* is at once a rigorous denial of likeness, and a reminder that there may always be more to such rigour than meets the eye; that perception is never singular.

The sun comes out. Across the steamy water, the pink Chelsea Sugar Refinery is opulently lit, Byzantine, excessive. Can I describe it as 'Venetian Gothic'? My sight may be a little blurred with salt, my thoughts are pleasantly adrift, and it's not hard to imagine I've arrived at a Venice projected in effects I'll remember when I get there, when I'm in their site-specific moment.

Note on *Time Tables*

Bill Culbert

Time Tables, exhibition catalogue, Roslyn Oxley9 Gallery, Sydney (11 April – 5 May 2018)

Bill Culbert is up to his old tricks again. One of them is his way with deadpan puns. 'Time tables' are how we travel on as well as in time; they are how we calculate the passing of time; they may also be what we make of time as an assemblage of things that locate it materially. These things could include tables, as well as other objects, that can be dated and that may also become dated with the passing of time.

In 1992, Culbert made an assemblage called *Hotel Sydney* consisting of a wood and metal table, a suitcase plastered with travel stickers (places that time tables got him to in time), fluorescent tubes and electrical cable. The table looked back in time to Culbert's favourite low-cost post-war designers such as Clive Latimer, Robin Day and Jean Prouvé. The whole assemblage also remembered the utility of the *décharge* near his and Pip's home in Provence, the source of much of Culbert's bricolage material as well as useful stuff for the house. When scavenging the tip, it was only a matter of time before some of the recycles became household items or art – or, in another kind of pun, both.

The Culbert house in London has a standard lamp with a plastic bucket as its shade. It looks like 'a Culbert'. There are wall-mounted assemblages of plastic containers pierced by fluorescent tubes that came to be known as 'bottle combinations', beginning in 1985 with *Long White Cloud* – some of these can be found lighting domestic spaces. There are works that have travelled in time: the punning *Table Lamp II* (1982) consisted of what looks like a genuine Robin Day table pierced by a fluorescent tube. The work was 'lost' but 'remade' in 2004, thus becoming a time-traveller.

In the current exhibition there are elegant variations on the 'bottle combinations' that extend the lifetime of a series yet to time out after more than 20 years. There is also an assemblage, *Time Tables* (2018, furniture, fluorescent tubes, dimensions variable), of a time-worn Latimeresque wood and metal desk providing the foundation for a stacked chrome table and a plastic seat-table-lamp combo that read like fresh-faced reissues of post-war moderne. They are pierced, or united perhaps, by a neon tube. The tube might even be seen as an archaeological measuring device, calibrating and illuminating a vertical timeline of things recovered from the midden or *décharge* of discarded objects. Culbert has reunited these 'objects of my affection', as Man Ray called his versions of Duchampian readymades, in time for their performance of his time-tested wit.

Raising a Glass
Remembering Bill Culbert

Christchurch Art Gallery Te Puna o Waiwhetū Bulletin 197 (Spring 2019)

Bill Culbert, whom the French critic Yves Abrioux called Master of Light, died aged 84 on 28 March this year at his home in the Vaucluse region of Provence. Built from dilapidated farm buildings on a small hilltop at a deserted hamlet called Croagnes, it's a home that he and his wife Pip began to establish in 1961. Then, the region was a sparsely populated economic backwater – the Culberts bought the hilltop buildings for just £100. In the valleys and on the surrounding slopes were a few small vineyards and farms. A 1962 painting, *Gerard Going to Work*, shows their neighbour, the farmer Félix Gérard, trudging off down the stony hillside wearing a wide-brimmed hat like the one worn by Vincent van Gogh at Arles.

From Croagnes, the view rose northward towards the slopes of a steep escarpment near Sault on the high Plateau d'Albion, down which spilled the discarded rubbish of a *décharge* or tip – there's a triptych colour photograph of the site in the collection of Christchurch Art Gallery, *Décharge, Sault* (1991). This tip and many like it were cleared away after 1992 when a landfill tax finally doomed the rural *décharges* and the region became fashionable – and very expensive. But when the frugal Culbert family began to fix up the tumbledown buildings at Croagnes the tip was a vital source of recycled materials.

Culbert himself also regarded the tips as historic sites with links back to Neolithic culture. In a vital sense, what he was recycling in the process of fixing up and furnishing the house at Croagnes were also the fragmentary traces of stories that had passed out of meaningful use in the midden – he was recycling their meaningfulness as well as their usefulness.

The tip also became a source of materials for many of the artworks he would make over the next 30 years, such as the melon-harvest box of *Box 1* (1974). These works combine the sense of recovered stories with the idea of the found object, whose origins are often sourced to Pablo Picasso's *Still Life with Chair Caning* (1912). In that work a printed image of chair caning is pasted on the surface of the painting, becoming integral to the work's governing topic. More pertinent in Culbert's case, however, is Marcel Duchamp's entirely autonomous *Bicycle Wheel* of 1913, which announced itself as a work of art by being mounted blithely on a plinth. Culbert's strategy – engaging and even affectionate compared to Duchamp's critical irony – has often been to light the object with electric bulbs, fluorescent tubes, direct sunlight or natural light reflected in various ways. Sometimes his interest has been as much in the effects of shadows as of light itself. These strategies are often very simple, as for example in *Bucket, Croagnes* (2012), in which a plastic bucket is filled with sunlight. They can also be complex and jazzy, as in *Bebop* (2013), part of *Front Door Out Back,* Culbert's large, multi-component work for the 2013 Venice Biennale. The mid-century chrome and Formica tables and chairs that seem to be dancing pell-mell towards some unknown destination were Culbert's design favourites, but their provenance as narrative recoveries and the brand-name 'Bebop' also coincide with the arrival in Provence of many Algerian pied-noirs – people with French settler origins who fled or were expelled from the colonial territories after the end of French rule. The brand-name references bebop jazz, a Culbert favourite, and the recycled Bebop table implicitly puts back into circulation or at least embeds a fragment of the lost story of the pied-noir family that had owned it.

In 1991, as if anticipating the demise of the tips, Culbert held an exhibition at the Galerie Froment & Putman in Paris with the title *À Charge de Décharges*. The title can be understood in a variety of ways. Culbert himself enjoyed the possibility that he was 'charged up' (like a battery) by the tip, and also the meaning 'on condition of', implying that in using the resources of the tip he was repaying its largesse. The recycling of materials in Culbert's art implies a kind of return journey, not in any literal sense but rather, as Jérôme Sans wrote in his catalogue essay for *À Charge de Décharges*, quoting Paul Virilio, as

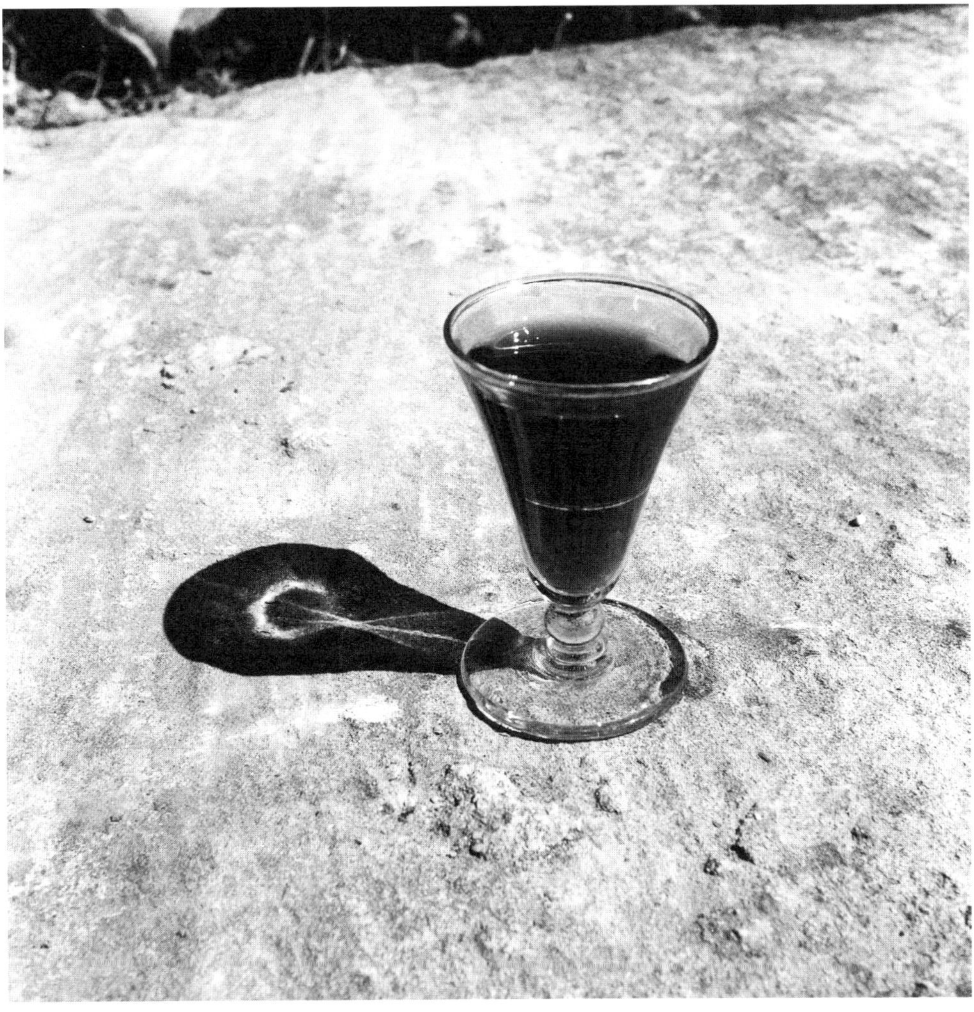

Bill Culbert, *Small Glass Pouring Light*, 1979 – black-and-white photograph, silver gelatin print, 190 x 190 mm. University of Auckland Collection. Courtesy of the Bill and Pip Culbert Family Trust.

watchful archaeology, as being on the lookout for 'whatever has been silent that will now speak, whatever was shut that will now open up' (Virilio, 1994).

Though it would be an excessive stretch to see the jostling queue of *Bebop* as representing at some level the arrivals of refugee pied-noirs from Algeria, other works by Culbert – not least his collaborations with Ralph Hotere – have clear political narratives in respect of 'whatever has been silent that will now speak'. The gallery collection contains a number of lithograph drawings referencing his large floor-based collaboration with Hotere, *Pathway to the Sea – Aramoana* (1991), protesting at the proposed aluminium smelter at the Otago Harbour heads. Another example of Culbert giving voice to silent or silenced subjects is *Stand Still* (1987), a selection of seven mundane objects, such as a plastic bucket, mounted on upright neon tubes, which represent ordinary citizens commanded to halt and 'stand still' on the Protestant and British firing lines in the town of Derry during the Troubles. The ordinariness of the found objects is poignant, but also wryly subversive given the kind of simple splendour they have had bestowed on them by the neon tubes. The front window of the Culberts' house in Putney, London, has a standard lamp in it made of a lamp stand with a plastic bucket instead of a lampshade. Though not declared as a work of art, like the self-deprecating objects in *Stand Still* the bucket glows with a kind of emancipated dignity.

In 1978, having left New Zealand in 1957 after four years at the Canterbury University College School of Art, Culbert returned to Christchurch as a visiting fellow. Among the several works he made during his tenure are *Blackball to Roa* (1978), a kerosene tin pierced by a fluorescent tube. This type of tin would certainly have been familiar from his childhood in Port Chalmers on the Otago Harbour. The family home was near the Carey's Bay graveyard where Culbert's maternal great-grandfather, Captain Alexander Rae, is buried; Bill and Pip Culbert's son Rae is named after this ancestor. In the Culberts' Putney house is a maritime painting by Nicholas Cammillieri of the brigs *Aurora* and *Dasher* entering Malta Harbour. Both vessels were from Kirkcudbright in Scotland, and miniature buoys from them used to hang in Culbert's grandparents' house.

There is a tension in *Blackball to Roa*, between the work as a stand-alone art object, the significance of which is found principally within art-historical discourse, and Virilio's 'watchful archaeology' that might locate the work's signification within a complex of recovered or reconstituted memories activated by an old kero tin. Of course few if any of these memories will be accessible to most viewers of the work. And yet the presence of narrative haunts the old tin of *Blackball to Roa* – perhaps the memory of the rubbish that used to spill down the slope to the 'Back Beach' at Port Chalmers. Or, to locate the work's geographical provenance and narrative more exactly, somewhere on the West Coast road between Blackball and Roa where, in 1978, there were a number of old coal mines and, no doubt, plenty of tips with empty kero tins on them (if they hadn't already been recycled with the tops cut off and wire handles fitted, like the ones I remember from childhood).

The word 'redolent' seems stuffy and old-fashioned when used to describe Culbert's work, and yet it usefully subverts a narrative-averse account of the aesthetic impact of artworks. The marvellous and even dazzling aesthetic presence of many of his major works is undeniable – they delight and amaze in ways that seem largely self-sufficient. And yet an installation such as *Voie lactée* (Milky Way) at Tournus in 1990, even with its inbuilt art-historical reference to the erotic Milky Way element in the upper part of Marcel Duchamp's *The Large Glass (The Bride Stripped Bare by Her Bachelors, Even)*, is redolent of what Culbert called *conditions*. Such conditions at Tournus might include the fact that the location was the refectory of the Abbaye Saint-Philibert, to which the blue enamel milk jugs might well have belonged. Because of the fluorescent tubes, milky light seems to pour over the flagstones from the jugs. At night, the Milky Way seen through the arched windows might pour its star light on to the floor. The installation as a whole becomes a night sky flooded with milky stars and projected into the refectory through its windows.

Another major floor-based installation of neon tubes and containers is *Pacific Flotsam* (2007), originally made for Brisbane's Institute of Modern Art, subsequently exhibited at the Govett-Brewster Art Gallery in New Plymouth, and acquired for the gallery collection in 2008. The image of this work on the gallery's website shows a topographic view – not the one experienced by viewers in a gallery, who would look at it laterally as if from the margins of an expanse of water. But the top-down viewpoint of the museum's photograph is *redolent* in several ways: it conveys the density of a floating island of plastic rubbish on jostling crosscurrents of light; and it matches the detailed topographic installation map drawn by Culbert, which is in itself a calligraphic narrative or storyboard.

There's a story behind one of Culbert's best-known images, a glass of red wine lit by sunlight and casting what appears to be the paradoxical shadow of a lightbulb. Culbert made many versions of this, both as photographs like the one at the beginning of this text, and as a major installation. But all reflect to some degree the moment when, sharing an evening glass of eau-de-vie with friends at Croagnes, he noticed that his glass was refracting an image of the overhead lightbulb on to the table. This small congenial narrative detail is perhaps the most appropriate to recover from the *décharge* of memories associated with Bill Culbert, and with which to salute a great artist whose work was always hospitable to its conditions and their narrative traces.

Reference

Virillio, Paul. 1994. *L'Horizon Négatif: Essaie de Dromoscopie.* Paris: Editions Galilee.

‘The thing we hold up between us’
Acknowledging the relationships between fiction, family storytelling, and what tends to get immunised as the ‘historical record’

Keynote talk at the Encounters and Exchanges Conference, Blenheim (3 December 2019)

A Ballad for Worser Heberley
for the Heberley Family Reunion,
Pipitea marae, Easter 1990

1

I remember the pōhutukawa’s summer crimson
and the smell of two-stroke fuel
and the sandflies above the Waikawa mudflats
whose bites as a kid I found cruel.

At night and with gunny-sack muffled oars
when the sandflies were asleep
with a hissing Tilley lamp we’d go fishing
above the seagrass deep

– a-netting for the garfish there
where the nodding seahorses graze
and the startled flounders all take fright
stirring the muddy haze.

And who cared about the hungry sandflies
when a-codding we would go
my blue-eyed old man Chick Wedde and me
where the Whekenui tides do flow.

It's swift they run by Arapawa's flanks,
and they run strong and deep,
and the cod-lines that cut the kauri gunwale
reach down to a whaler's sleep.

When the tide was right and the sea was clear
you could see the lines go down
and each line had a bend in it
that told how time turns round.

The line of time bends round my friends
it bends the warp we're in
and where the daylight meets the deep
a whaler's yarns begin.

I feel a weight upon my line
no hāpuku is here
but a weight of history swimming up
into the summer air.

Oil about the outboard motor
bedazzles the water's skin
and through the surge of the inward tide
James Heberley's story does begin.

2

In 1830 with a bad southerly abaft
soon after April Fool's Day
on big John Guard's *Waterloo* schooner
through Kura-te-au I made my way.

And I was just a sad young bloke
with a sad history at my back
when I ran in on the tide with mad John Guard
to find my life's deep lack.

Seaspray blew over the seaward bluffs
the black rocks ate the foam
my father and my mother were both dead
and I was looking for home.

But what could I see on those saltburned slopes
but the ghosts of my career:
my father a German prisoner from Wittenburg
my grand-dad a privateer

my mother a Dorset woman from Weymouth,
I her first-born child,
and my first master was called Samuel Chilton
whose hard mouth never smiled.

He gave me such a rope-end thrashing
that I left him a second time,
I joined the *Montagu* brig for Newfoundland,
though desertion was reckoned a crime –

and me just a kid with my hands made thick
from the North Sea’s icy net,
eyes full of freezing fog off the haddock banks
and the North Sea’s bitter sunset.

And master Chilton that said when your mother dies
you can’t see her coffin sink
you can only blink at the salt mist
about the far land’s brink.

And in the fo’c’sle’s seasick haven
where a lamp lit the bulkhead’s leak
you’d share your yarn with the foremast crew
your haven you would seek.

Where you came from the rich ate kippers
or if they chose, devilled eggs.
They didn't blow on their freezing paws
they favoured their gouty legs.

And if you pinched an unripe greengage from their tree
they'd see you in the gallows
or if you were dead lucky
wading ashore through Botany Bay shallows.

But I was even luckier, as they say,
those who tell my tale:
they tell how my tale was spliced and bent
about the right whale's tail.

And how poor young James Heberley
fresh from South Ocean's stench
and the foretop's winching burden of blubber
his great good fortune did wrench.

In autumn I came ashore at Te Awaiti
on Arapawa Island.
'Tangata Whata' the Māori called me –
now 'Worser' Heberley I stand.

'Ai! Tangata whata, haere mai,
haere mai mōu te kai!'
Food they gave me, and a name,
in the pātaka up high.

My name and my life I owe that place
which soon I made my home.
From that time, when Worser Heberley went forth,
I didn't go alone.

I raised a considerable family there,
with Ngarewa I made my pact:
from him I got my summer place at Anaho,
my home from the bush I hacked.

I summered there in the mild weather
and in autumn I went a-whaling
from the boneyard beach we called Tarwhite
where Colonel Wakefield's *Tory* came sailing.

And I guessed from the moment I saw their rig
that we had best take care:
not the Māori, nor Worser Heberley's mob
stood to gain from this affair.

With fat Dick Barrett I went as pilot
on the *Tory* to Taranaki.
From Pukerangiora and Ngāmotu descended
Te Āti Awa's history –

a history already made bitter once
in the bloody musket wars,
that might be made bitter yet again
for Colonel Wakefield's cause.

Worser Heberley was never a fool
else I'd not have lived that long:
I could see the Colonel meant to do business,
I could hear the gist of his song.

He was singing about the clever cuckoo
that lays her egg elsewhere
and fosters there a monstrous chick
too big for the nest to bear

so the other chicks must be all cast out
for the greedy cuckoo's sake.
The Colonel sang this song I heard
as he watched the *Tory*'s wake

tack up the South Taranaki Bight
with Kāpiti falling astern,
and I, James Heberley, stayed close
to see what I could learn.

And what I learned has since been written
in many a history book:
that you'll find little enough of our record there
however hard you look.

3

And now Worser Heberley's story ceases,
I hear his voice no more
though my line still bends by the notched gunwale
as it had done before

when I was just a kid gone fishing
in my old man's clinker boat
and hadn't learned that it's history's tide
that keeps our craft afloat.

And now I see as I look about
in Pipitea marae
at the multitude here assembled
that your line didn't die –

and though old Worser Heberley was right
to fear Colonel Wakefield's song,
he didn't have to worry about the family
which multiplies and grows strong.

I thank you for your kind attention
the while my yarn has run.
I wish you all prosperity and peace.
Now my poem is done.

The published version of the poem I've just read has a dedication: *For the Heberley Family Reunion, Pipitea Marae, Easter 1990*. There's a reason for this. In 1986 my novel *Symmes Hole* was launched at Unity Books in Wellington. Much of the book's debt to history is owed to the whaler James 'Worser' Heberley, who came ashore in Tōtaranui Queen Charlotte Sound in 1829. After the formalities of the book launch were complete, two young Māori men and another elderly one came forward and introduced themselves as tuhanga of James Heberley. They had been interested to hear about the novel's fictional account of their ancestor, though they were not aware of any approaches made by me to the family. That was a pity, they suggested, but never mind, there was going to be a Heberley family reunion so perhaps I could donate some copies of the book to the event. Of course, it was the least I could do, I told the Heberley tuhanga. Yes, it was perhaps 'the least', because the descendants of James 'Worser' Heberley then suggested I could as well write something for the family reunion hui on Pipitea Marae in Wellington, and I should come to the hui and share what I had written in honour of their respected tupuna.

I did pick up the wero and write 'A Ballad for Worser Heberley' and read it at the family reunion – but I still owe the Heberley whānau a significant debt. It has to do with the family's firmly uttered lesson in the importance of acknowledging the value of the relationships between fiction, family storytelling, and what tends to get immunised as the 'historical record'.

How does my meeting with the Heberleys connect to the photograph you see here? In the photograph my twin brother Dave and I are in the place where 'I remember the pōhutukawa's summer crimson/ and the smell of two-stroke fuel/ and the sandflies above the Waikawa mudflats/ whose bites as a kid I found cruel' – the place in which my story and the story of James Worser Heberley meet across the century that separates our arrivals in this place with its pōhutukawa and sandflies.

The snapshot and its connection to the place haunted by Worser Heberley generated a poem that plays with the relationship of story and historical record. It's from a sequence called 'The Commonplace Odes'. An ode is usually addressed to something deemed worthy of lofty celebration, such as John Keats's 'Ode to a Grecian Urn'. To call something commonplace, though, suggests that the object of veneration belongs in the world of ordinary things. This subverts the hierarchy that might privilege the truth of an 'official history' against the truth of an ambiguous family story.

1.4 To my twin brother

There are some things I still need to know:
How can I talk to you when we have forgotten our language?
 Where
Can we meet now that our mother is long dead?
How can I bring you gifts when you
Are bringing me gifts? How could our father

Be in the picture when he was always taking it? What
Is this we hold up between us – is it a trophy,
Did we compete for it, is it alive or dead? And how can
My sons speak to your daughters
When they have never learned our language? Where

Can they meet now that their fathers have no place
To meet? How can they share what they have when they have
Nothing in common? And what is this they hold
Up between them? Is it their grandmother's wedding band,
That gateway through which their fathers entered

Life, through which their grandfather left it?
Why are you left handed while I am right handed?
Why did you have daughters while I had sons?
Which of us could have been the other's sister?
And what is this we hold up between us?

Is it perhaps a mirror? Or a moon trail
On the placid ocean where the reflections of our mother and father
Are not disturbed, sitting under royal palms
On the Picton foreshore, tinkle of jazz from the ferry,
Sons unborn, cheek by cheek under Gemini?

The question 'And what is this we hold up between us?' is given several answers in the ode: that this thing is perhaps a trophy we may have competed for, that may be alive or dead, or a mirror, or 'a moon trail/ On the placid ocean where the reflections of our mother and father/ Are not disturbed, sitting under royal palms/ On the Picton foreshore, tinkle of jazz from the ferry,/ Sons unborn, cheek by cheek under Gemini?'

So as well as the fish, the 'thing we hold up between us' could refer to the ghostly presence of another family photograph. Both photographs are at once factual and filled with the presence of story. In this second one, the one that is not seen here, our mother and father are sitting under a palm on the Picton foreshore and exchanging an adoring look; in the one you see here my twin brother and I are holding between us the ends of a stick passed through a loop of green flax piercing the gills of a large blue cod. We're standing on the beach at Waikawa Bay over the hill from Picton and it was there that our family had a bach. The cod in the photograph would have been caught further down the Sound towards the old whaling station at Te Awaiti Bay on Arapawa Island in Tory Channel Kura-te-Au, close to where James 'Worser' Heberley came ashore. The 'smell of two-stroke fuel' in my ballad honouring James Worser Heberley would have been sniffed up from the trusty Johnson outboard motor during a fishing trip in the family's old clinker dinghy, with the incised grooves of hauled-in fishing lines along the gunwales.

One of the men I met at the book launch of *Symmes Hole* was an elderly chap known as Uncle Arthur. Uncle Arthur's Waikawa Bay whānau was connected to the descendants of Worser Heberley through Worser's marriage to Māta Te Naehe, also known as Te Wai Nahi, and more widely to the hapū of Tōtaranui. He worked as a messenger at Parliament, and after the book launch we used to meet from time to time for a beer at De Brett's on Lambton Quay near Parliament. He remembered my mother as a young woman in the Sounds, helping her one-armed father Bert Horne to launch his clinker dinghy at Waikawa Bay.

Here's a short extract from my account of these family stories, from my book *The Grass Catcher.*

> A sad phantom comes part-way into view at this stage in my hesitant return to Dieffenbach Point – the place I know I have to get back to in order to leave again on this journey home. My maternal grandfather, Herbert Stacey Horne, known as Bertie, was born in Blenhein in 1877. Among the many memories Uncle Arthur had of my mother at Waikawa Bay, the most central was of helping to launch Bertie's heavy clinker dinghy down the beach on the mainland side of the bay – the same dinghy whose wet, cod-line grooved gunwales were central to my childhood world. The help was needed not just because the boat was heavy but because what I came to know as our family bach was built on the Snout peninsula, across the bay from the road and the boatsheds, on land provided to Bertie Horne by Uncle Arthur's hapū. Uncle Arthur's help was also needed because Bertie had only one arm. According to my mother, he'd lost the other one as the result of an accident at a farm-equipment trade show where he'd volunteered to demonstrate a new harvesting machine. One coat sleeve got caught in the conveyor, and his left arm was dragged through the sprockets.
>
> . . .

Uncle Arthur remembered that one-armed Bertie sculled the dinghy expertly with a single oar over the stern once it was in the water. My father taught us how to do that, using kid-sized oars. I remember how the seawater ran along the oars and on to my hands when I rowed – me on one side, Dave on the other, an oar each, and also with two oars, ‘putting our backs into it’. Chick knew a few stirring poems by heart, one of which he’d adapted as a rowing chant – John Masefield’s ‘Cargoes’.

> Dirty British coaster with a salt-caked smoke stack
> Butting through the Channel in the mad March days,
> With a cargo of Tyne coal,
> Road-rail, pig-lead,
> Fire-wood, iron-ware, and cheap tin trays.

He’d haul back on the stress syllables and reach forward in between: ‘*Dir*-ty British *coas*-ter with a *salt*-caked *smoke*-stack . . .’ He didn’t so much love poetry as respond fervently to hearts-of-oak jingoism amplified by meter. But I’ve remembered the Mansfield poem; and I remember how to row.

Chick also showed us how to line up a marker astern and keep it in place as we rowed so as not to have to look over our shoulders at where we were going. Looking into those astern viewfinders, still sharp in my memory, it’s the scrubby bush of the Snout that I can still see, a fold where the creek ran down, the yellow stain of clay in the sea by the creek mouth, a little pebbly beach. When I go back to Waikawa now I can still spot the place as if I’m rowing across the bay with my back to the little store by the road, the old boatsheds, the big Arthur house on the hill with the royal palm in front. These days there’s a marina, the town of Picton has extended its suburb all the way out past Waikawa, and there are expensive holiday homes overlooking the Sound. But from the foreshore on the mainland side, standing on familiar pebbles, sticky yellow clay and wave-smoothed broken glass, I can return without effort to the place across the murky bay from which we'd have set off early in the morning to Dieffenbach Point.

The somewhat ambiguous account of Bertie's bach at Waikawa Bay being on land provided by Uncle Arthur's hapū has another equally shifty backstory, this time involving the man known as 'the colonial doctor of Dillon's Point', my mother's paternal grandfather and my one-armed grandfather Herbert 'Bertie' Horne's father, Dr Lewis Keele Horne, an English ship's doctor born in 1832 or 33. Horne Place in Springlands, Blenheim, is named after the good doctor, who, however, has a scandalous story associated with his disappearance from Blenheim, a disappearance that the official record attributes to the burning down of the Criterion Hotel in Blenheim in 1887. In the official version of the story, the good doctor had run back into the burning hotel to rescue his son Leonard and had perished in the attempt – his body was never found and was thought to have been consumed by the inferno. However, Leonard had already been taken care of, and the unofficial version of the good doctor's disappearance is that he had left the burning hotel by a back door, taking his mistress with him; the following day they are thought to have caught a river vessel down the Ōpawa River and disappeared to Christchurch and after that to exotic options elsewhere.

Whether the good doctor decamped by a back door of the hotel – the unofficial story – or perished heroically – the official story – he had for many years earned a stipend from the New Zealand government in his official position as (quote) 'Vaccinator of the Natives of the Wairau'. My mother told me that Dr Horne was however mostly paid in kind with vegetables and fish. The link seems to have been sustained 'in respect of' the doctor's children, or at least in respect of the family of my one-armed grandfather Bertie and my nana Aggie. When my brother Dave and I were kids in Francis Street, Blenheim, Māori from Wairau used to come round with kerosene tins of whitebait, and Bertie's widow, our Nana Horne, would dip mugs of it out into a big bowl. It's likely that the family connection reached across to Waikawa Bay, where Aggie Horne's husband, one-armed Bertie, built the bach on what the family used to describe as 'Māori land'.

These days, Waikawa Bay over the hill from Picton is a built-up residential and holiday zone. When my brother Dave and I were there and holding up a big blue cod between us in about 1950, there was just one general store and a marae. To get to the family bach the heavy clinker dinghy would be hauled down from a boatshed, loaded up with supplies and family members, usually including our grandmother Aggie Horne, the trusty outboard motor would be jerked into smoky life, and we would putter across the bay to where a creek ran out at the edge of a pebbly beach. Waikawa could be translated as 'bitter water' or 'acid water', perhaps a reference to the leaf-mouldy taste of the creek water that ran into the bay. I still remember the taste of that water, and of the garfish that were netted by the light of a hissing tilley lamp above the seagrass shallows in a neighbouring bay. Our Nana Aggie or our mother would cook the garfish for breakfast. The taste as much as the memory as much as the historical factuality of this commonplace breakfast are what are recorded in 'A Ballad for Worser Heberley'; the poem's 'truth value' or perhaps even 'Bayesian probability' is rich in uncertainty, in its relation to highly subjective and possibly unreliable (or untestable) information.

These often vivid but subjective fragments of personal information exist alongside other, let's call them *official,* items of information. Many of these are preserved in place names with various kinds of historical resonance. 'Waikawa', of course, has a different kind of resonance from Dieffenbach Point, Tory Channel or Endeavour Inlet, all three of which have contributed to what became 'the official history', though this imposition of imperial and colonialist epistemology has been challenged in more recent times. The narrative work of the placename 'Waikawa' is more commonplace, recording the fact that the water in that place is somewhat acidic.

Endeavour Inlet is of course named after the vessel that brought James Cook to Tōtaranui in 1770, and Tory Channel, Te Kura-te-Au in Māori, is named after the New Zealand Company ship *Tory* that in 1839 brought Colonel William Wakefield, charged with making preparations for the arrival of colonists. Also on board the *Tory* was the German political refugee and naturalist Ernst Dieffenbach – Dieffenbach Point at the head of Tory Channel Te Kura-te-Au is named after him. These namings fix their occasions firmly in the colonial historical record, and link to the records kept by those named – for example, the scrupulously detailed accounts by Dieffenbach in the two volumes of his *Travels in New Zealand,* not least his analysis of te reo Māori.

However, what is mostly hidden behind Dieffenbach's scrupulous account is another one, the *Journal* of James 'Worser' Heberley, the manuscript of which is kept in the Alexander Turnbull Library in Wellington. 'Worser' was taken on as pilot and interpreter by the master of the *Tory*, Captain E.M. Chaffers (hence, of course, Chaffers Marina in Wellington). Worser's *Journal* is a fascinating document, not least because, in order to identify where advantages or threats might be found for his own people, the extended Te Āti Awa whānau he belonged to as a result of his marriage to Māta Te Naehe, he was closely observing the colonising activities of the *Tory's* New Zealand Company contingent. Worser Heberley's *Journal* is substantial at 77 pages. Key sections deal with his experiences after coming ashore and marrying Māta Te Naehe, also known as Te Wai Nahi – they were married under Māori kawa in about 1831, and according to Christian kawa by the Reverend Ironside in 1841. Three of their children were baptised at the same time as the Ironside marriage; they had two daughters and six sons.

There's a section of the *Journal* that describes Worser's time accompanying Ernst Dieffenbach while the *Tory* was on the Taranaki coast. They climbed Mt Taranaki – named Mt Egmont by James Cook in 1770 – together in December 1839, and reading Worser's *Journal* account as a counterpoint to Dieffenbach's is like encountering a ghost. Dieffenbach's scrupulously observant and factual record of the expedition introduces Heberley in a perfunctory sentence: 'The companions of my last trip again accompanied me, and our party was joined by Mr. Heberley, a European, who had come with us from Te-awa-iti, where he had lived for several years as a whaler and who was most expert in finding his way through all the difficulties attending such an expedition as this.' Thereafter, 'Mr. Heberley' disappears into the pronoun 'we', as when 'We prepared to rest among the stunted and dwarfish shrubs, amongst which I observed the *Dracophyllum rosemarinifolium*, *Solidago arborescens*, and several other *compositus* plants.' This eerie haunting by the presence of Worser Heberley among the carefully taxonomised botanical specimens, while not detracting from the marvellous richness of Dieffenbach's observations, is in its way a dramatic enactment of the tensions between what becomes enshrined as an 'official record' with its regulation taxonomic markers, and the unofficial narrative, detailed and vivid in its own terms, of what is a kind of family history.

In my novel *Symmes Hole* there's a lengthy section in which Worser Heberley hangs out with Ernst Dieffenbach in a variety of situations, including a visit to Worser's home at Anaho. Anaho means something commonplace like deep bay; the name given it by James Cook in 1770 was Cannibal Cove after human bones were found in the remains of a meal. Here is an edited and shortened section where I've played with a conjunction between Dieffenbach's account and Heberley's journal.

> But then he did go – they took a gaff-rig whaleboat that was too leaky to put to work, and went around into East Bay, and the Doctor sat and baled a good part of *that* trip too. Then they fetched across to Anaho, running north between Long Island and Motuara, the sou'wester brought some fine clear cool weather . . . he let the gaff set square and they ran along with a good sight way up toward Kāpiti and the distant half-imagined curve of the Bight. Then they'd made a brisk reach into Anaho, and the Doctor had baled away pretty cheerfully.
>
> The house was full of Ngarewa's mob, they'd met the Doctor and the rest when the *Tory* came in and so the house filled up fast . . . and the Doctor sat quietly watching and drinking a brew of scrub tea while the old boy told Heberley that things were getting hot up the coast at Ōtaki, and he didn't like what he heard about that mob hanging about again down by Kaikōura . . . grumbling away and why wasn't Heberley back at work around there

catching the whales! . . . and why was he here, didn't he trust the people to mind the place for him? . . . was he checking up on them, hadn't they helped him to build the house, didn't they mind his fences during the winter . . . ?

Heberley handed over the tobacco before the old man could finish his show of anger. It was getting on in the afternoon and he and the Doctor walked up the back past the gardens with their stave and brush fences. Under his breath the Doctor was keeping up a steady mutter – *Veronica ligustrifolia, Myrtus bullata*, oho a *Solanum laciniatum, Coriaria sarmentosa* . . . and what's this? He stopped at the edge of the gardens where Heberley had terraced the slope above the gully with nīkau trunks. In a corner where the mould and humus had washed away grew a tallish thick plant with small green prickly fruits, succulent-looking leaf-stems and an oak-shaped leaf . . . it had long pale, lily-like flowers, and a faintly vomitous odour came off it.

'That's, why that's a *Datura stramonium*, that's a thorn apple we call it, it's quite poisonous you know, how came that here, that's not a native of the place?'

And Heberley replied that it was all over the show this part of the Sounds, there was some with a bigger trumpet flower that smelled strong at night, they grew where the people that was here before had cleared the ground, Rangitāne people, and Ngāti Kuia, the same that ate some of that Captain Cook's crew near here . . .'

'Ah, the *Adventure*, Captain Furneaux . . .'

. . .

And Heberley watched him survey the place, taking it in stages . . . he began with the forest floor of ferns, the great mossed-over up-heapings of surface roots . . . he next took a lateral sweep of the crazy interwoven dangle of supplejack . . . with an expression of delight and another of those churchy movements of the hands he looked at the ponga tree-ferns, the lovely symmetry of their sectioned trunks and irradiating fronds . . . the intermediate canopy of young growth, five-finger and lancewoods and young green big-leaved karaka. And then his head tilted slowly back, and he followed the great trunks up again to where they seemed to be toppling forever across the moving clouds which they almost reached . . . the daft flights of canopy-playing kākā parrots crashing about way up there . . . dense high clotting of orchids . . .

And while it was true that Heberley didn't know how to trust the man, he could see that harm wasn't going to come from *him.* And because he'd remembered old Ngarewa telling him, and because he'd begun to feel abashed by the Doctor's silent delight, he flipped out that comment about the stinky lily, and then watched the man's blissful face alter – first a look of doubt, then an expression of sick horror . . . !

'. . . unmöglich . . . das ist . . . ach, *nein* . . . !'

And he saw that Dieffenbach would never again look at the bush with that first expression of ecstasy.

This *fiction* makes a subversive intervention in the space between the official (Dieffenbach) and the personal (Heberley) record. This is the proposition that the poisonous datura noticed with horror by Ernst Dieffenbach was introduced to avenge the killing by Māori in Wharehunga Bay (or Grass Cove) in December 1773 of 11 crew of *Adventure* under Captain Furneaux on Cook's second voyage. The wider corollary of the naturalist Dieffenbach's horror is that the introduction of exotic plant species amounts to a kind of revenge on a people or ecosystem identified as different and hostile.

Of course there is no documented evidence that the introduction of poisonous datura was a deliberately malicious act. Cook's own habits of restraint and respect are well documented, as are his careful responses to the tragedy at Wharehunga Bay – though his admonition to 'cultivate friendship and alliance' was not always observed, and would certainly have been thwarted on the first voyage without the interventions of the Tahitian arioi and navigator Tupaia. And of course, to get back to the datura story, the recording by the Russian doctor Galkin on the Bellingshausen expedition of 1820, of stupefaction and swollen joints among the people of Anaho, could be put down to local conditions rather than a maliciously introduced poisonous plant.

And yet the paranoid revenge *fiction* could contain a kind of truth: that the introductions of foreign plant and animal species were revenges on the unacceptable strangeness or hostility of an environment that had to be subdued as if by the pacifying effects of datura; just as Christianity might be characterised as an intervention against the perceived hostility of indigenous beliefs that, like the environment, also had to be pacified rather than negotiated with as they were by James Worser Heberley, the 'whaler-Māori' who made his pact with Ngarewa, married Te Wai Nahi of Te Āti Awa according to both Māori and Christian belief systems, and established his summer place at Anaho, which means deep bay, or, in the alternative, parallel version of reality (or of truth) at Cannibal Cove, a composite or folded place some of you will have visited on the tour of Tōtaranui Queen Charlotte Sound.

Over half of all wild plant species in New Zealand are exotics. Datura was naturalised in New Zealand in 1867 but would have been introduced before that date. To insist that such plant introductions – not to mention Christianity, penal systems, and many other exotic naturalisations – were all acts of revenge on hostile difference is surely asking too much of what I've called 'relationships between fiction, family storytelling, and what tends to get immunised as the "historical record"'.

And yet, and yet . . .

A couple of weeks ago on a Sunday morning national radio programme about Britain joining the European Common Market on 1st January 1973, I heard England referred to as 'the Mother Country'. Even 200 years after the naming of Cannibal Cove on the site known to Māori as Anaho, that term 'Mother Country' still casts some shade, and a bit of subversive fictional weighing of 'the thing we hold up between us' may not be a complete waste of time. Nor will it be a waste of time to hold up and weigh the fact that when the United Nations General Assembly adopted the Declaration of the Rights of

Indigenous Peoples by a vote of 143 to four in 2007 – a mere 12 years ago – the four nations that voted against were the US, Canada, Australia – and New Zealand.

I will end where I began, with the photograph of two kids holding up a large blue cod. Some questions arise from this commonplace image:

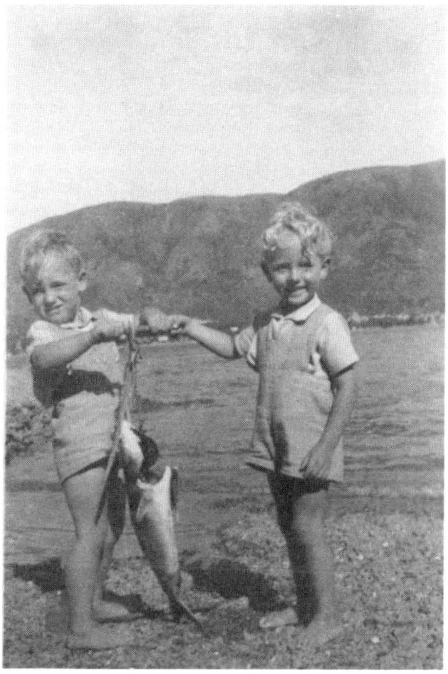

David and Ian Wedde at Waikawa Bay, c. 1950. Black-and-white photograph, (?) Frederick Albert Wedde (father).

Which of the two is doing the heavy lifting and which one is mugging for the camera, or, if you like, for the 'historical record'?
What kind of claim on the catch is represented by this joint holding-up of the fish?
What kind of history endorses this joint but rather skewed ownership of the fish?
Where was the fish caught and what was it called; what was the place called, and how did it come to be known to the person who caught it?
Who's taking the photograph, which is to say who's controlling the narrative?

This photo of me and my brother Dave is not intended as a convenient simplification of how cultures work. Rather, its location in the complex and haunted location of Waikawa Bay shows how the subversive interplays of fiction, family stories and historical records can usefully trouble the mentalities of entrenched official histories.

I enjoyed troubling the mind of the excellent Ernst Dieffenbach with my paranoid fiction in *Symmes Hole,* and I hope you've been able to share my enjoyment. I hope you get to enjoy some blue cod too, from somewhere down around Anaho perhaps, though sadly I doubt it will be as big as the one my brother Dave and I got to show off back in about 1950.

Imagine Libraries

Centennial Lecture, National Library of New Zealand Te Puna Mātauranga o Aotearoa (26 February 2021)

> E ngā mana, e ngā reo, e ngā pātaka o ngā taonga tuku iho
> Tēnā koutou katoa, ngā mihi aroha.
>
> Ko te Parinui o Whiti te māunga
> Ko te Kura-te-au te moana
> Ko Curtis Ogilvie Wedde tōku hapū
> Nō Blenheim ahau
> Ko Ian Wedde tōku ingoa
> Nō reira, tēnā koutou, tēnā koutou, tēnā koutou katoa

It is a great privilege to be invited to talk at the National Library of New Zealand Te Puna Mātauranga o Aotearoa and also to have been asked to say a few words yesterday evening at the opening of the marvellous exhibition *Mīharo Wonder: 100 Years of the Alexander Turnbull Library*. This exhibition is a rich example of what the treasure houses we call libraries can do, ngā pātaka o ngā taonga tuku iho, which is collect and take care of a wonder-full variety of objects whose relationships to each other or differences from each other are among the most valuable pleasures and learnings we will encounter anywhere.

These relationships (this is *like* what I know) and differences (this is *unlike* anything I know) are also critical. Our encounters with them train our imaginations to coach our intelligence to understand and cherish the complexity of the world we live in.

In her essay for the *Mīharo Wonder* catalogue, Fiona Oliver begins with a translated quotation from the French poet Paul Valéry:

It depends on those who enter
That I become tomb or treasure
That I speak or remain silent.
You alone must decide.
Friend, enter not unless filled with desire.

Soon after this challenge or wero we encounter the image you see now, which dates from around the mid-1800s when Eruera Te Uremutu, a chief of Ngāti Whakaue, wrote a history of Te Arawa. The image shows 'the ancestral people and canoes that sailed across the Pacific Ocean to Aotearoa. It was a perilous journey. The voyagers were almost swallowed by a sea creature, Te Parata, but were saved by a mythical shark, and the people renamed the canoe and themselves Te Arawa in its honour.' Fiona's note adds that, 'The volume, *Some Arawa Legends*, is one of many in the collection of ethnological manuscripts that are part of the Polynesian Society records; a rich and fascinating resource of largely unpublished material about Māori and Pacific cultures.'

Let's begin by imagining the library as a place in which the story of resourceful but also, surely, imaginative Pacific explorers is kept, a place that thanks to Fiona has at its entrance a challenge by a French poet celebrating the spirit of adventurous, desire-filled imagination; and in which the preservation of this fragment of the Pacific story has been taken care of by a diversely multinational, bicultural scholarly organisation. A place, furthermore, that the contemporary descendants of those and many other imaginative and desire-filled explorers can enter and be challenged by the stimulants of relationship and difference.

Before going on with this theme, however, it's important to acknowledge the presence here of the desire-filled explorer after whom this library is named, Alexander Turnbull. The exhibition *Miharo* that some of you will already have visited is a wonderful testament to the curiosity and inclusiveness of his desire, and it's an honour to salute him and his legacy on the occasion of this centennial.

A warning: my talk from here on may seem to part company

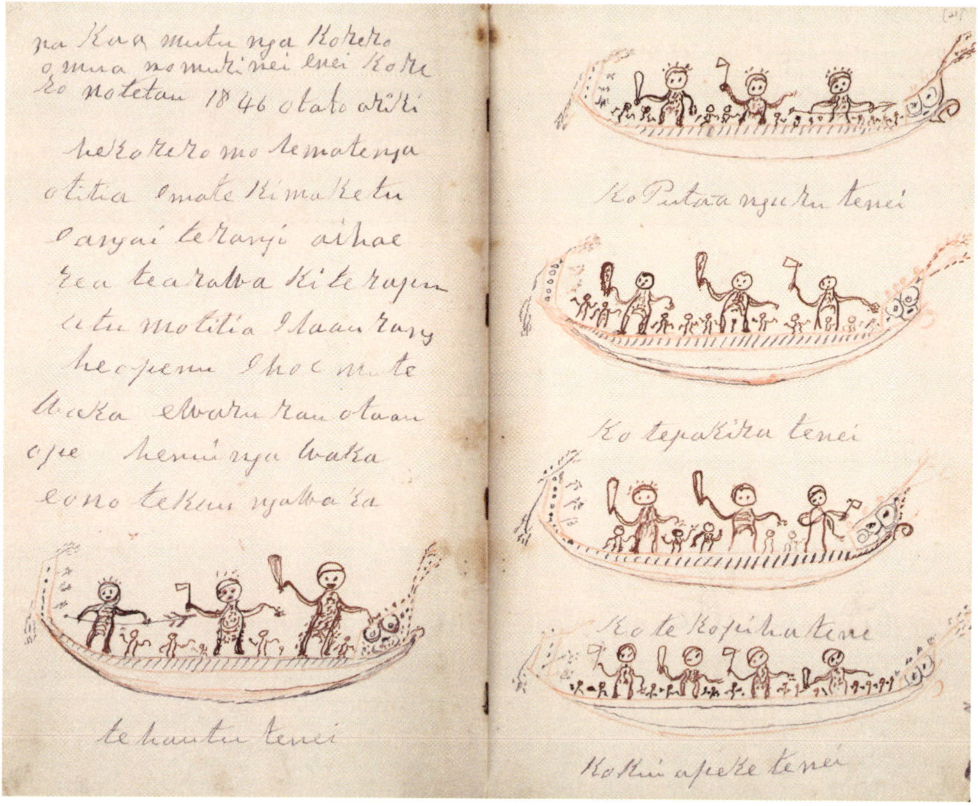

Eruera Te Uremutu, Diary entries and sketches. Polynesian Society: Records. Ref: MS-Papers-1187-191-20. Alexander Turnbull Library, Wellington. /records/22442715

with Alexander Turnbull and his inclusive and curious legacy, but I believe that his kind of curiosity would have found much to wonder at and about in our contemporary world of digital information archives and the wider world of vast, seemingly unmoderated public archives constituted by Facebook and Instagram, and software such as Photoshop and Meitu – all of which have, in addition, brought about a redefinition of what we mean by the word 'object'. And, as Turnbull had 'agents' who informed, provided for, activated and probably second-guessed and reinforced his curiosity and his desire, so contemporary digital archives have algorithms that remember our likes and explorations, and our social networks will not only feed these 'likes' but will often lead them.

I'll begin with a bad dream.

1. Introduction: Bad Dream

There's a well-known image by the English tag artist known as Banksy, it's called *Instagram video, 'If you don't mask you don't get it'*, London Underground, July 2020. It shows a still from the video of Banksy tagging the interior wall and window of the Underground with an image of a creature associated with the plague, a rat, which has just sneezed across the window next to it. The tag was removed soon after but the video survives in the archive that is Banksy's immense territory on Instagram, as well as in a vast number of social media postings and links. Last time I checked in November last year there were close on 11 million followers of the Banksy archive and related sites. The Getty Instagram archive by contrast has 109,000 followers.

The image is a useful prompt to think aloud about the Covid-19 information mass that accumulates and repeats itself at an incredible rate – the predominantly unofficial or non-institutional virtual pandemic Covid archive if you like. As I'm making notes for this talk, a quick log-in Covid check on Safari reveals a running total of 6,250,000,000 hits in the space of less than a minute. This gets me thinking about the nature and function of a national library –

and most obviously about what the term 'national' means in these circumstances.

A few weeks ago I was lying awake thinking about what this talk on imagining libraries could tackle – and then I went to sleep and woke looking into the dark at the fading traces of a dream about a pandemic of contagious butterflies (rather than rats), terrifying because their beauty was in proportion to their sinister danger – and then went back to sleep and woke in the morning with a sense that I'd been given the best way to approach a talk about imagining (but not imaginary) libraries.

Very easy to dismiss as delusional over breakfast coffee.

However, at the time I had this dream in mid-November last year Auckland had just been gripped by anxiety about a fresh community coronavirus outbreak involving an employee in a downtown Auckland recycled fashion clothing shop on High Street. This person had gone to work after becoming sick with coronavirus symptoms. One of the production crew on a TV series for which my wife Donna is a producer had been to that shop within its potentially contagious time, and Donna had been in close contact with that crew member before news of the possible contagion broke. Donna came home after I'd caught up with the news about the recycled fashion shop employee on National Radio and social media and told me what had happened to the crew member, and I told her that I had that same day been downtown in High Street, though not in the recycled clothing shop. So we were both within the potential contagion area. We ate dinner together but at the approved distance from each other and then watched a couple of episodes of a grim dystopian Spanish-language TV series about a pandemic called *La Valla* or *The Barrier* that we were following, only this time while seated at regulation distances from each other, a situation at once absurd and necessary. Then we slept in different rooms, having watched TV in a subtitled foreign language, and I had the dream I've described as involving a plague of beautiful but malignant butterflies.

This scenario seems weird when you highlight its coincidental details – but then seems normal in terms of the complex world we negotiate on a daily basis, a world in which viruses and foreign language TV series are not unusual, any more than strange dreams are. But I found myself wondering where in all this were the borders or links between imagination, dreaming, real life events, the factual narratives of present-time reportage, and narratives that imagined future events and even consequences? There was a real time limit to the situation we were in, it would be when Donna's colleague tested okay in terms of the potential Covid-19 contact. But meanwhile a normally complex reality ran together what could be imagined and what could be given the closure of official record. And in the end – though there isn't really an *end* to this process – much of this vast, variously moderated or if you like curated body of digital objects continues to exist in various kinds of what can be thought of as libraries.

2. Plague catalogue

We are living in a time of plague, the Covid-19 plague, that's a fact of which the records will be kept in databases and libraries of various kinds; but the ways in which this plague is remembered as narrative and visual representation will take many forms, including dreams; even, eventually, perhaps in literature as fiction – think Albert Camus' novel *La Peste* (more on this in a moment). Our Covid-19 plague won't be the first to generate records and narratives – 'we' in our contemporary situation are not the first to have lived in a time of plague.

Back to Camus and *La Peste*, known in English as *The Plague* – we are not in 2021 referring to Covid-19 as 'the plague' but as 'the virus' and 'the epidemic', which is a contemporary linguistic readjustment of historical narrative from vengeful act of god to medical or epidemiological condition. Camus' 1947 deployment of the term 'plague' itself reached back to a cholera outbreak in Oran in 1849, referred to as a 'plague' in its time, which he used as the basis of his novel, and he almost certainly knew about outbreaks of bubonic plague in the region in the 16th and 17th centuries, and so his 20th-century narrative also contains traces of what might be called archival narrative. The library of which we imagine Camus' novel is a part – this library, for example – will be haunted by dreams or dream memories and even by the texts in which those dreams and dream memories were recorded.

So: imagine a library in which every imaginable kind of plague record is kept. One record will be the plague catalogue; but this once-only thing will also be a list-*ing*, a *kind of* list – a sample of what we mean by 'catalogue' – and as such a type of cultural object that shows how the list makers think about their categories and priorities as ways of understanding the, or a, world by using a thing called a catalogue. The catalogue will be simultaneously and discretely an historical object (that is, a thing called a 'catalogue' with a date on it), a taxonomic specimen (that is, one example of many of what we might mean by the category 'catalogue'); it will be the record of a methodology (that is, of the organising principles of *this* catalogue); it will be a thesaurus of terms and a grammar of descriptions (that is, an implicit guide to the semantics and vocabulary of *this* catalogue); and it will be a typology of narrative and representational forms (that is, a record of how the catalogue's contents and vocabularies will function as a guide to how it tells its stories).

In simple terms, we know that a library that exists in a time of plague will include, or will be capable of including in its 'plague catalogue' – that is, in the database resource activated by a search for 'plague' – medical records of plagues (or epidemics), reportage of them, biographical accounts, novels, poetry, very probably sound recordings, including songs, and visual material such as recorded video interviews, newsclips, and works of art or reproductions of them in books and exhibition catalogues. A favourite example of mine: Boccaccio's 14th-century *Decameron* deals with the Black Death of 1346–53, which caused 75–200 million deaths across Europe alone – his characters entertain themselves with sexy stories while in exile (or isolation) from the plague. The book itself will exist in a great many libraries and in many languages; it also exists as a 1971 film by Pier Paolo Pasolini, and so will be found in film libraries as well as digital online repositories.

'Danse macabre' or 'dance of death' works of art recorded the plague – there's a Pinterest site on which Michelle Graves has assembled 468 images of *Danse Macabre,* including a reference to the film director Ingmar Bergman's 1957 film *The Seventh Seal* in which Jof the Juggler witnesses the dance of death and tells his wife that the dead 'dance away from the dawn and it's a solemn dance towards the dark lands, while the rain washes their faces and cleans the salt of the tears from their cheeks'.

As I noted earlier, in July 2020 the artist Banksy posted an Instagram video of himself tagging a train in the London Underground with a work urging passengers to wear masks – it featured a sneezing 'plague rat'; which is, of course, an anachronism since it is associated with the bubonic plague not with Covid-19.

The tag was removed within a few days, but the Instagram video exists in a kind of library or archive, accessible through the 'catalogue' activated by a search engine – the accumulated database of Banksy Instagram material that, as mentioned earlier, had 11 million followers last time I checked. So in effect those 11 million viewers are looking at an anachronistic anomaly (the rat) that is also a narrative linking their contemporary virus situation to an historical plague one (same but different) and implicitly implying a continuum. Which is the kind of historiographic and even serial narrative effect found rather often in libraries.

3. The library: open or shut?

To return to the catalogue or pūtea korero or ngā upoko tukutuku in the environment of the library: it will have categories that in Māori organise its contents around a world view in which aspects of taha tinana/the people, taha wairua/the spiritual and taha hinengaro/the mind are intrinsically connected and related to each other; and in the 'Enlightenment' European-derived system probably into taxonomic disciplines such as medicine, law, justice, art, literature, politics, religion; and topics such as famous people, catastrophes, fashions; and cascades of sub-categories, many of them the ephemeral products of their 'times' and locations, and as such destined to become esoteric in the futures, including 'post-Enlightenment' or postmodern futures, in which they too will become quaintly anachronistic catalogue items about historical classification systems.

The catalogue will reveal, or try to conceal, hierarchies of knowledge and the access to or denial of access to knowledge. The territorial and discipline limits of the catalogue will say much about the world view of its organising society and belief system, and especially of those in power for whom the library's catalogue may be a means of controlling who knows what – as a way of managing a world view, if you like.

Some catalogues will be private, as in the case of catalogues identifying the contents of private collections and the tastes of their owners. But let's concentrate on what we think of and describe as 'public collections', such as those of public libraries. In the public library to which the catalogue offers implicit passcodes, there will be an even more complex assembly of potentially weighted, privileged or under-represented, or anachronistic, categories of objects constituted – since this is a library – as *texts*.

These *texts* will potentially include visual and sound materials that we will use or consume as readers of meanings and narratives – of stories, if you like. The National Library of New Zealand Te Puna Mātauranga o Aotearoa has three catalogue subsections. Under the second of these, INNZ (Index New Zealand), we will find 'Descriptions for articles from a wide range of magazines, journals and newspapers related to New Zealand and the South Pacific. Some full-text online content available.'

The Index New Zealand catalogue is vast and comprehensive. It is also overwhelmingly a national New Zealand text with some regional Pacific and Australasian material. The archive's title (Index New Zealand) and the name of the library (National Library of New Zealand) may make this a no-surprises discovery; but it does raise the question, Does this designation imply the deliberate introversion of a world view? A world view limited for practical reasons of economy (how much space is there in the library) or restricted for political reasons (as a way of controlling national identity)?

5. A case study: Hong Kong

In 2016–18 I was involved as curator and catalogue editor in an exhibition of photographs of Asia by the New Zealand photographer Brian Brake and the American Steve McCurry. Brake's work was available from the comprehensive and exhaustively catalogued archive of it at Te Papa, much of it gifted by his partner Wai-man Lau in 2001. McCurry's vast archive includes both film and digital materials; his website and blog are in themselves curated collections; a photograph published on Instagram of 'An office clerk reads at Chhatrapati Maharaj Terminus in Mumbai' had 50,000 likes when I looked at it a week after it was published.

The Brake/McCurry exhibition was called *Picturing Asia – Double Take* and was shown at the Asia Society Hong Kong from September 2016 through into January 2017, and subsequently at the Shanghai Centre of Photography from June through into September 2018. The exhibition showed two non-Asian points of view of Asia to Chinese-Asian audiences in what were then rather more than now two distinct political constituencies – although frictions in this distinction had become overt, as in the Umbrella Movement protests that broke out in Hong Kong in September 2014.

The exhibition and catalogue included a section titled (in quotation marks) 'Exotic, Enticing Hong Kong'. This had been the title of a Steve McCurry photo-essay in *National Geographic Traveller* (Winter 1986/87). Brian Brake settled in Hong Kong in 1962 and made it his base until 1976. Many of his Hong Kong photographs were collected in the book he made with the writer Robert Elegant, *Hong Kong: Great Cities*, published by Time-Life Books in 1977. The quote-marked title of the catalogue and exhibition section, 'Exotic, Enticing Hong Kong', was meant to flag the potentially exoticised, outsider viewpoint of the photographers – a kind of protective irony with which to frame a small selection of nine photographs. These were discussed without significant worry on the part of the Hong Kong team in September 2016 and the records of them made their way into the Asia Society archive, along with the exhibition catalogue which, as well as reproducing the complete set of exhibition photographs, included three contextualising essays that clearly marked Hong Kong's independence. One of these, 'Picturing Asia' by the film director Evans Chan, notes carefully that, 'The photos on view represent the visual sense of curiosity and benign cosmopolitanism of two gifted photographers.'

What Evans Chan also does, however, is include the famous 1989 Tiananmen Square protests 'Tank Man' photograph by Jeff Widener, in which a lone individual stands in front of four advancing tanks of the People's Republic; and also the Spanish-born and Hong Kong resident Xaume Olleros's photograph 'The Umbrella Man', taken during the 28 September 2014 tear-gassing of protesters in Hong Kong.

As the exhibition curator and editor of the catalogue I was confident that the inclusion of these images within the catalogue text was a useful and even necessary complement to what Evans described as the 'benign cosmopolitanism of two gifted photographers' – a characterisation that, in itself, was implicitly critiqued by the inclusion of images such as Brian Brake's 1957 *Walls of the Forbidden City, Beijing, China*, an image not published in a mass-market magazine but included almost 40 years after being taken in the publication *Brian Brake: China, the 1950s*. In the photograph a forbidding sense of enclosure and overpowering darkness is captured beneath the free expanse of blue sky, an image whose political impact is as powerful as its stylistic simplicity.

The inclusion of images such as this in the exhibition extended the scope of the material defined purely by its historical use in 'mass-market magazines'. Their inclusion stretched the limits of what a published record allowed us to understand. And the more contemporary context provided by Evans Chan in his selection of catalogue images for his essay simply complements and invites into a dialogue what he called Brake's 'benign cosmopolitanism'.

Another catalogue essay, this one written collaboratively by the exhibition's two young assistant curators at the Asia Society Hong Kong, Kristy Soo and Ashley Nga-sai Wu, was titled 'Selfies First'. It further extended the archival record not just of the exhibition and its catalogue, but of 'the times', that is the times of what became known as the 'Umbrella Movement' and widespread emergence of personal digital cameras, especially those incorporated in cellphones from about 2004 – these were widely available and used in Hong Kong by 2014. Kristy and Ashley are members of an inaugural generation of digital, online networkers, and they note that, given the ubiquity of phone cameras and the emergence of Instagram and software such as Photoshop and Meitu, the 'easy dissemination of photographs, and the potential to generate misleading content, collided during the Umbrella Movement in Hong Kong'.

They note further that the cellphone photographic records that accumulated in huge quantities during the Umbrella Movement were circulated through social networks and social media – generating a virtual archive and digital library at odds with those retained or excluded by Hong Kong's conservative print media and TV stations.

These images and the texts that accompanied them have now become part of the library of record, since the physical exhibition catalogue has made its way into libraries. And, of course, the vast, cellphone-generated visual record continues to exist as an expanded library augmenting the small moment of the *Picturing Asia* exhibition. However, when the exhibition went to the Shanghai Centre of Photography the following year the catalogue was banned.

Recently, as reported in the international press, there has been a culling and censorship of libraries in Hong Kong, including school libraries. Our own National Library's Services to Schools has an instructive page headed 'Weeding your school library collection'. Among the useful tips and instructions for weeding these libraries is one that suggests 'You can offer pre-1940 children's books to the National Library for the Dorothy Neal White Historical Collection'. I rather hope my grandchildren at school can develop a sense of history that doesn't stop around the time their grandfather was born.

Back in 1998 when I was head of art at Te Papa the museum became involved in a major public controversy over an artwork included in the *Pictura Britannica* exhibition, the *Virgin in a Condom* piece by Tania

Kovats. I supported the decision not to censor the work. In October last year there was a furore over the exhibition *People of Colour* in Mercy Pictures' new space on Karangahape Road in Auckland. Currently, a controversy is raging over the lamentable decision to postpone the *Philip Guston Now* retrospective exhibition due to anxieties expressed by the National Gallery of Art, Washington, the Museum of Fine Arts in Houston and in Boston, and the Tate Modern in London about Guston's iconic Ku Klux Klan hoody figures, despite Guston's lifelong critique of white supremacy.

I don't wish to enter into the controversy that surrounded the National Library's decision to cull a substantial quantity of what are termed 'overseas collections', but I hope the National Library of New Zealand Te Puna Mātauranga o Aotearoa will preserve and sustain such across-time-and-space dialogues as that between Albert Camus in Oran, Algeria, in 1947, Banksy in the London Underground in 2020, and our own Covid-19 stories as they emerge in Aotearoa New Zealand and find their way into the wider world catalogue where our stories will always enrich each other and our understandings of both difference and shared experience.

If I have veered off the theme with which I began, that of plagues and viruses, it's because I worry that the exponential global expansion of varieties of virtual, shared, online databases and archives combined with the introspection brought about by a global pandemic will encourage a protective contraction of world views, with resulting xenophobia and insularity, an unimaginative and unadventurous mindset that is, as Sarah Hopkinson pithily described it in writing about the Mercy Pictures *People of Colour* exhibition, 'phobic to difference and change'. The xenophobic politicising of the 'China virus' by Donald Trump is only the most egregiously obvious and stupid example recently.

Which brings me finally and with pleasure to a counterexample of how to imagine libraries here within the world of the National Library of New Zealand Te Puna Mātauranga o Aotearoa and the Alexander Turnbull Library. This is the Alexander Turnbull centenary exhibition, *Mīharo Wonder: 100 Years of the Alexander Turnbull Library*. The image with which I began is of Eruera Te Uremutu's representation of Te Arawa waka, in itself a representation of 'resourceful, adventurous, desire-filled imagination'.

There's another image with which I'd like to finish what I've had to say. This, as Fiona Oliver writes in her catalogue for *Miharo Wonder*, is 'a representation of New Zealand history, inscribed on the trunk of a kauri tree, almost 2.5 metres high and 1.5 metres wide, drawn with a pen by a Mr James Meek' in 1876. Fiona suggests that, 'Whether his emphasis on certain historical events is his own, or reflects the thinking of his time, his world view is very different to ours now.'

This *difference* between then and now, between his and ours, between relationship and stranger-ness, like and unlike, is why Mr James Meek's presence in this marvellous exhibition and in this library matters and is a necessary challenge to us to imagine libraries as places to enter as adventurous explorers 'filled with desire', as Paul Valéry urged; the desire to encounter the unlike and the unknown – as I said when beginning this talk, to enter into 'these relationships (this is *like* what I know) and differences (this is *unlike* anything I know).' These relationships are also critical. Our encounters with them train our imagining intelligence to understand and cherish the complexity of the world we live in.

Nō reira, tēnā koutou, tēnā koutou, tēnā koutou katoa

Meek, James McKain, 1815–1899: *Chronological Tree of New Zealand History*, 1876. Ref: F-009. Alexander Turnbull Library, Wellington. /records/22709054

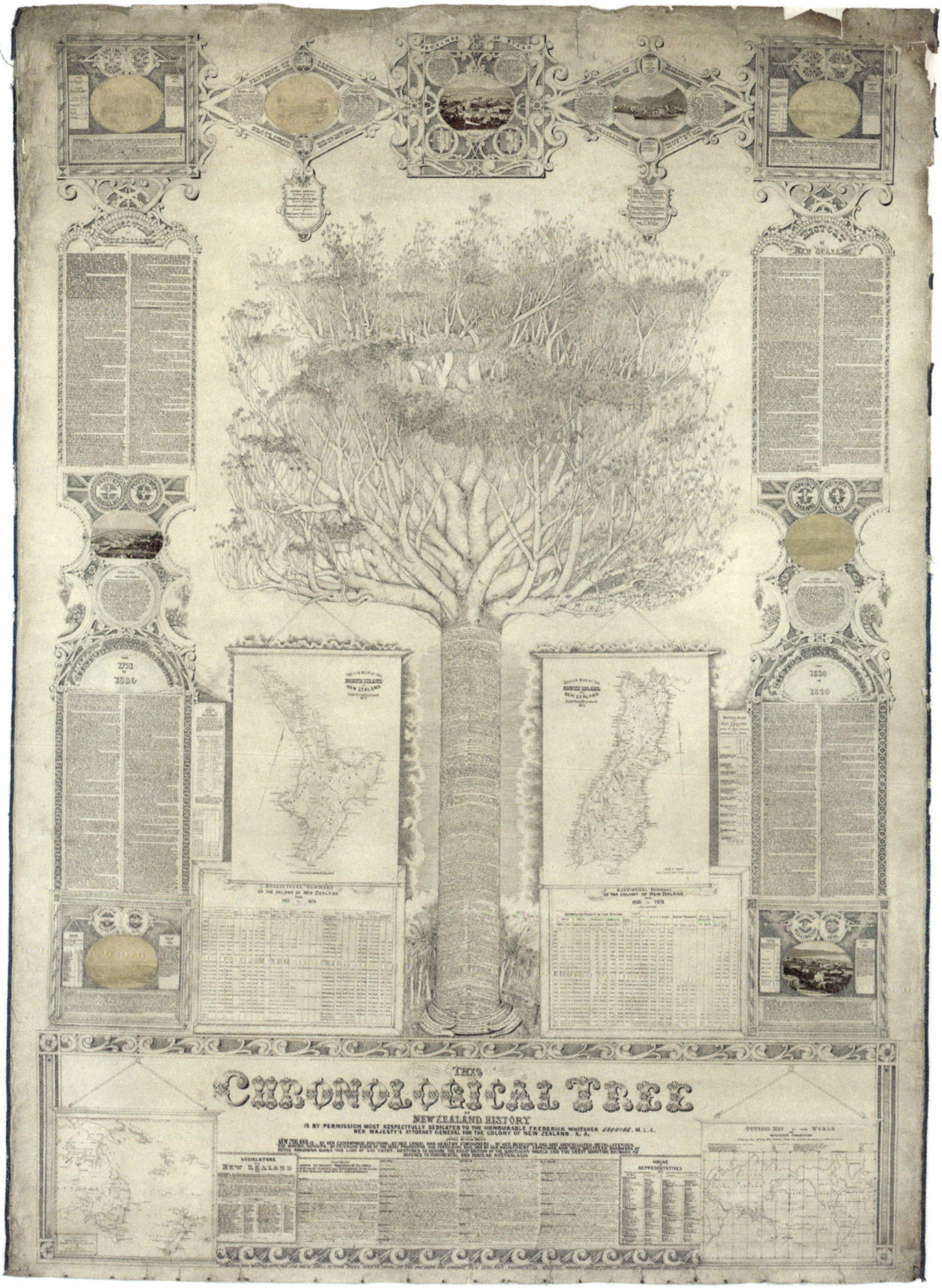
THIS
CHRONOLOGICAL TREE
OF
NEW ZEALAND HISTORY
IS BY PERMISSION MOST RESPECTFULLY DEDICATED TO THE HONOURABLE FREDERICK WHITAKER ESQUIRE, M.L.C.
HER MAJESTY'S ATTORNEY GENERAL FOR THE COLONY OF NEW ZEALAND &c &c
LEGISLATURE OF NEW ZEALAND
HOUSE OF REPRESENTATIVES
STATISTICAL SUMMARY OF THE COLONY OF NEW ZEALAND
HISTORY OF NEW ZEALAND

'We're stuffed . . .' But then, also we're not

In memory of Bill Hammond

Art News Aotearoa (May 2021)

Bill Hammond was a marvellous, imaginatively daring and scrupulously self-honest artist, and a gentle and lovely person, and I can't start to write about him and his work without saying first up that like a great many other people I mourn his passing while thanking him for the work he made and with it his immense and unique contribution to our culture.

I wrote a review of one of Bill Hammond's first exhibitions at Peter McLeavey's gallery in Wellington in March 1987 – rereading it now, the pleasure and admiration I felt still come across. What I also get is the sense of relief I felt then, a sense that, 'The ways in which [Bill Hammond] switches signals in his paintings have more to do with a world view than with a narrow view of the art scene and its conventions.' If there's a trace of reviewer art-world weariness in that comment, it's counterbalanced by the review's celebration of the work's unique qualities, its smearing and distorting of perspectives, subversions of material propriety, and incorporations of popular culture, especially music (T. Rex – *Get it On, Bang a Gong, Get it On, T. Rex*, 1986; two paintings called *Country and Western Song Book* I & II; and Bob Dylan – possibly *Bobby's Alright*, 1986).

A vital part of the pleasure I felt back in 1987 was the work's sardonic but not self-congratulatory I-know-better humour, displayed in part by its grotesque distortions of scale and perspective, but also by the underlying sense of a morally satirical intelligence. That 1987 exhibition had an epigraph taken from Orson Welles' *The Lady from Shanghai*: 'An empty amusement park makes a great hideout.' What was hiding out in Bill's amusement parks was a tone rather than just a representation or 'message' of social scrutiny.

Commentaries on Bill's development as, or into, an artist have often referenced his earlier work as a toymaker. Toys are fun playthings for children; they can also be sinister (think Chucky-the-killer-doll movie franchise); and they are often, let's face it, stuffed animals whose cuteness a disenchanted view might see counterbalanced by taxidermied trophies. There's an earlier painting of Bill's, *Well I Never Felt Better in My Life* (1983), in which a grotesque, sinisterly grinning, bulgy, potato-headed, Santa-capped toy is urging us to applaud while in the distance, on what looks like a disproportionately large back-draped stage, a tiny human figure seems to be performing (Bill drumming?) at a table. If 'All the world's a stage, and all the men and women merely players', as the melancholy and disenchanted Jaques has it in *As You Like It*, then Bill's take on this, or *the* human, situation, is at once mordant and compassionate.

Connections have been suggested between Bill's work and that of the post-World War II Chicago Monster Roster or Chicago Monster School. But to me Bill's bent world views are more about perception than representation, despite the graphic content of works like *Get it On, Bang a Gong, Get it On, T. Rex* (1986) in which the classic Fender Telecaster comes monstrously to life. The Roster's work as a 'moment' has been read as a reaction against the influence of post-war New York School abstract expressionists. Be that as it may, and though Bill was certainly aware of both the New York and the Chicago 'moments', his own brand of figurative monsters seems mostly indifferent to these art historical contexts, let alone influences or contra-influences.

The toymaker's lovable animal doubling as a stuffed trophy made a significant appearance in Bill's work after 1989 following time spent with a small group of other artists and photographers in the subantarctic Auckland Islands. It's been suggested that this moving experience of a primordial environment populated by unthreatened birds was a kind of road-to-Damascus moment for Bill, when he woke up to the need for an urgent message about the devastating effects of human occupation on natural environments and creatures. In 2020 he was quoted in Christchurch Art Gallery's *Te Wheke: Pathways Across Oceania* exhibition publication: 'It's bird land. You feel like a time-traveller, as if you have just stumbled upon it . . . It's a beautiful place, but it's also full of ghosts, shipwrecks, death . . .'

While paintings such as the now iconic *Watching for Buller. 2* (1993) have understandably been read as evidence of this awakening, I see them more as extensions of the pre-1989 works' satirical sensibility, only now conveyed by more unambiguous representation – of birds, especially. In *Watching for Buller. 2* the confluence of moral satire (Bill referred to the ornithologist and specimen-collector Walter Lawry Buller as 'Buller the Bird Stuffer') and the representations of bird-figures – part bird, part human, both watchful and apprehensive – is marked by Bill's by now familiar, even trademark, sardonic humour. The not-quite 'untouched' landscape has already been cleared of forests of which some fallen tree trunks survive; there are already a few scattered tower blocks. In *Waiting for Buller. Bar* (1993), the bird-people are playing pool in a pub. Are they about to be stuffed? Passing the waiting time as best they can, hanging out with friends, enjoying a drink? The painting is at once affectionately rueful and, as we've come to expect, critically mordant.

'We're stuffed . . .'

But then, also we're not. Who knows what schemes the birds are hatching? Give them the benefit of the doubt. For all the pessimism and dismay in these last paintings by Bill Hammond, what I've called their maker's morally satirical intelligence may be the tonic we need. I thank him for that, and the special pleasure that comes with it.

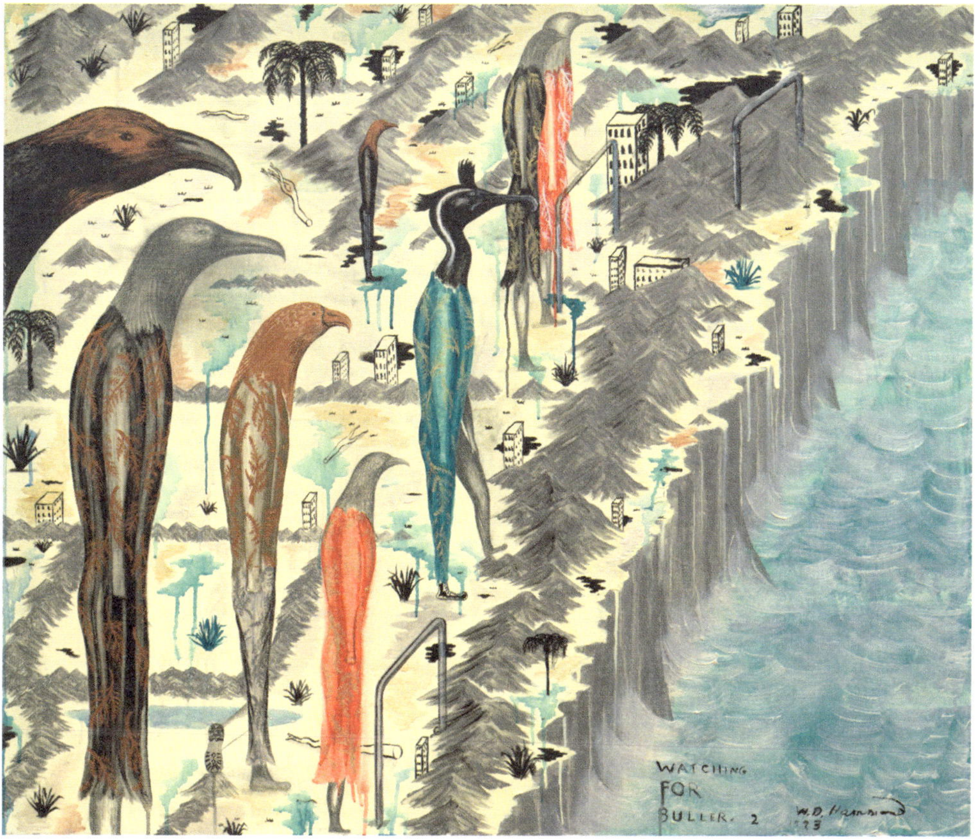

Bill Hammond, *Watching for Buller 2*, 1993.
Acrylic on canvas. On loan to Christchurch
Art Gallery Te Puna o Waiwhetū

The Dark Is Light Enough

Ralph Hotere: A Biographical Portrait, by Vincent O'Sullivan

Academy of New Zealand Literature Te Whare Mātātuhi o Aotearoa (anzliterature.com, 31 March 2021)

Vincent O'Sullivan has written a comprehensive and intimate biography – not an art history monograph. It's necessary to state this up front because, although a separation between a 'life' of Ralph Hotere and an account of his work as an artist would be absurd, the generous biographical scope, depth and detail of this book both exceed, and provide critical insights into, the conditions from which Hotere made his art. It provides the kind of rich personal detail that a more academic art-historical perspective might have skimped – or might not have sought nor gained access to.

In a lengthy, in-depth interview with O'Sullivan by Bruce Munro in the *Otago Daily Times* (19 October 2020), O'Sullivan says that his and Hotere's relationship, '. . . was a congenial friendship – but we weren't what you'd call intimate friends'. In 2004, Hotere asked his friend to write his biography. O'Sullivan makes it clear that Hotere didn't want 'anyone with an agenda', which is possibly a careful way of saying anyone from the art world – nor, possibly, anyone co-opting or stereotyping Hotere as a 'Māori artist'.

The latter was something the artist resisted more by silence than by explicit denial, most obviously to counter the restriction of what he and his art could be, and (the silence suggests) to protect the privacy of those vital aspects of his life and upbringing that were informed by his relationships within Te Aupōuri culture and history. O'Sullivan says, 'I think my ignorance might have been to my advantage. He realised I wouldn't be pushing any particular line.' O'Sullivan's modesty and Hotere's self-protective caution constitute a laconic brief for a book that could be written from a distanced and watchful viewpoint (albeit a trusting one) rather than one narrowly defined as Māori, or immersed in the 'art world' and over-determined by art history – O'Sullivan records that Hotere often preferred to meet at the pub rather than go to his own exhibition openings.

At this point an elephant enters the room – not art history as such, but its necessary corollary. There are no reproductions of art works by Hotere in this book. This was clearly not the artist's wish, as noted by O'Sullivan in his understated Introduction to the book; nor was it O'Sullivan's own decision in what would have been a bizarre contradiction of his friend's wishes. The result is a detailed narrative referencing numerous artworks that we cannot see while reading about them. The reasons for reproductions of works by Hotere being excluded, as well as the reasons why the book was temporarily halted and, in fact, never continued past the time when O'Sullivan was barred from meeting with the artist, are not discussed by him in his Introduction.

The Introduction ends with a forthright and generous disclaimer: 'I see what I have written as an incomplete portrait, rather than the more desired account of one of this country's great artists and compelling personalities. Future scholarship will attend to so much more. But as Ralph himself asked me to write on him, and I assured him I would do so, it now seems a personal debt I owe to him, and to his constantly encouraging whānau.' The subtitle that O'Sullivan has given his book, *A Biographical Portrait*, with its elision of text and picture, is surely deliberate, even (if I may guess) a challenge or wero.

The question of why this state of affairs came to exist and had the anomalous consequence of an artist biography without illustrations is best put aside at this point; no doubt discussions about it will continue to find their way into the public domain. To date, such discussions include an in-depth article by Mark White in *Stuff* ('Bitter feud over Ralph Hotere's legacy', 15 November 2020). But for me, one unintended consequence is the book's weighting towards a biographical overview with the rich and sympathetic presence of 'constantly encouraging whānau', friends and colleagues; not to mention the exceptionally scholarly, detailed and generous Notes,

Further Reading and Index that complement the book's research and manaakitanga. Far from being irretrievably impoverished, the book offers a great many ways in which to find images of works by Hotere, as well as a rich resource of secondary sources, catalogues and discussions of his oeuvre in a wide variety of publications.

A quick online check-in at Auckland Art Gallery reveals 40 works available for viewing on the collection site, as well as collaborative works with Bill Culbert and photographic portraits of the artist by Marti Friedlander and John Miller. A similarly perfunctory search at Te Papa finds in excess of 60 works, including major collaborations with Bill Culbert and the monumental *Black Phoenix* (1984–88); the Alexander Turnbull Library archive has 732 'results', including many publications, catalogues and journals with illustrations; and so on. O'Sullivan's book with its numerous detailed, carefully chosen but comprehensive references can certainly be read as a guide to the substantial complementary resource of unrestricted public archives.

There's another respect in which the absence of images feels at times like an unintended bonus. Early in the book's biographical timeline we read accounts of the Hotere family's life when Ralph was a child. Their first house on land at Taikarawa, north of the Hokianga Harbour near Mitimiti, didn't have electricity; working days began about 4am – before dawn – when older children rounded up the cows for milking. This story, rather than, or as well as, art-historical models of tenebrism in art, is a sympathetic situation from which to look ahead to Hotere's mature work, in which darkness, sometimes in combination with white streaks or splatters, came to be a signature effect. In one of the book's most sympathetic accounts of originating or contributing factors to the darkness in Hotere's work, O'Sullivan notes that the artist grew up:

> . . . in a household where after sunset, darkness was the norm, a home of candles and lamps and open fires, of golden streaks reflected in expanses of glass, of refractions and shadows and pools of light. The darkness was not only those gradations of te pō that variously carried in Māori thought deepening notions of

vacancy and loss, the notions of what preceded life and followed death. It was also home.

While this and other biographical sketches cannot replace images of artworks, they are vivid and complex and contribute significantly to the 'portrait' components of this biography. Also significant, as O'Sullivan notes with careful understatement, is the origin of the artist's Te Aupōuri tribal name, in which 'au' refers to smoke or a current, and 'pōuri' to darkness, the pall under cover of which the tribe escaped an attack. Such contributing narratives need to be read in association with clear evidence of Hotere's knowledge of and admiration for the American Ad Reinhardt's minimalist 'black paintings' from the 1960s.

Similarly, the frugality and make-do skills of Hotere's use of recycled materials, such as rusty corrugated iron sheets, lead-head nails and recycled timber, reflect the kind of useful stuff you'd hoard frugally in remote, under-resourced places, not to mention where I saw such careful stores while living near and visiting Hotere's studio at Port Chalmers and home at Carey's Bay between 1972 and 1975. At the same time, their markings are often reminiscent of Mark Tobey's white calligraphy or 'white writing', with which Hotere was familiar by the early 1960s, having spent time in England and Europe between 1961 and 1965, including time in Vence in the south of France at the Korolyi Foundation; and their materiality recalls the *pitura matèrica* of the Catalan artist Antoni Tàpies whose work Hotere knew well before spending time in Barcelona in 1988.

O'Sullivan, in his detailed and respectful account of Catholicism in Northland, notes that the Hotere family lived intimately with the legacy of Bishop Pompellier, the French Society of Mary missionary, during the formative years of the artist's childhood and youth. The environment in which Hotere grew up was trilingual: Māori, English and the Latin of the Catholic church. It was rich in the images and symbols of both Catholicism and Māoritanga. What becomes clear while reading O'Sullivan's 'biographical portrait' is that it implicitly resists and confounds an all too predictable model of art history programmed to a greater or lesser degree by distinctions or weighted tension between the benighted, 'primitive', narrative art of remote or provincial cultures, and the sophisticated, evolved art of metropolitan centres.

Hotere grew up in a visually and symbolically complex, linguistically rich and environmentally distinctive environment; his subsequent political activism in works such as the Aramoana protest panels was seeded by Te Aupōuri history, as well as by experiences of protest and resistance in London and Europe in the 1960s; the symbolic complexity of his early environment met with and in many respects complemented what he encountered during the Karolyi International Fellowship that enabled him to work and exhibit in France and Europe for several years, and view works, including Matisse's final masterpiece in the nearby Chapel of the Rosary at Vence. O'Sullivan writes that this was one of Hotere's favourite places to visit, and his careful account of what grew in the space between Matisse's Stations of the Cross and 'those fourteen scenes Ralph had looked at for years at Hato Hemi in Mitimiti, and as a schoolboy at St Peter's' pretty much closes the false gap between province and metropole.

This rich section is followed by one that folds Hotere's family story into a time of vital transformation. Hotere's brother Jack was killed while fighting with the Māori Battalion at the Sangro River in eastern central Italy in 1943, and Hotere and his wife Bet went to visit Jack's grave at the Sangro River War Cemetery. The biography includes a family photograph of Ralph 'kneeling, one arm resting along the top of his brother's grave, holding against the tombstone the rosary his mother had given him to take from home'.

This, writes O'Sullivan, a 'deeply personal event, a compelling idea, a dominating public or political occasion, a resonant arrangement of words, would propel him to work on a series of paintings that expanded and diversified until their impelling drive was resolved.' This was the *Sangro* series, made, with what would be Hotere's typical recycling economy, 'on the dismantled sides of small packing cases', and marked with 'the kind of stencilling familiar to young men who had worked on farms or in freezing works or wool-stores'. O'Sullivan notes that, 'For the first time Hotere used extensive areas of black, mostly in the wide framing borders. It was also, perhaps, the first occasion that he drew on the specific Māori resonances of what was meant by te pō.' This series, O'Sullivan suggests, 'that the visit to Jack initiated was the beginning of what te pō both declares and contains, what it takes to itself, what it allows to be revealed'.

O'Sullivan's account continues for a further 230-something pages from this moment; but it remains the pivot around which this rich 'biographical portrait' turns into something substantially more than a bare or mere text.

Rāwaho/The Completed Poems
David Howard

Academy of New Zealand Literature Te Whare Mātātuhi o Aotearoa (anzliterature.com, 4 September 2022)

This substantial book (329 pages including notes and indexes) was preceded by *the in-complete poems* in 2011 (274 pages with notes etc.). The poems in both volumes are scrupulously dated and, in many cases, accompanied by detailed endnotes, and in these ways as in others differ from a by-now familiar contemporary style or even culture of poetry-book, which is if anything under-presented, intimate, and unpretentiously personal. Alex Grace's review on *Goodreads* of James Brown's latest book, *The Tip Shop* (Te Herenga Waka University Press, June 2022), set a typical tone: 'Funny, dark, insightful and nothing close to a chore to read. Poetry, but it doesn't suck.' – 'Poetry sucks' being an insider poetry-reader quote, of course.

The first poem in each of Howard's collected volumes is 'Judy is a punk', dated 1976 (an endnote tells us 'The title echoes The Ramones' 1976 song'); in the second, recent volume this title from 1976 is in addition reprised as the last poem on 20.8.2020 but with subtle echoic changes; for example, the last word in the 1976 version, 'Perfect', has become 'abject' 44 years later. What's implied – and encountered by a close reader – is not only overarching control of the whole corpus across a wide span of time and material, including all poems being scrupulously numbered, dated and many annotated, but an implicit subtext that in itself comprises a controlling narrative of order-as-meaning, of a consciousness or character at once fastidious and cartouche-like, detailed and overarching; this implicitly expects a degree of 'chore' in the reader's approach.

In both volumes, this conscientious, *engrossing* character begins on the book's cover. The lower-case cover title of the earlier book separates 'in-complete' on different lines, forcibly emphasising '**in**complete' (my emphasis) but also introducing a sense of paradox, of deliberate, even playful ambiguity. The title of the second book, *Rāwaho/The Complet***ed** (my emphasis) *Poems*, gestures at the historically conventional type of title, *The Complete Poems*, meaning 'this is a wrap'; but amends the meaning to 'these are all that were finished' – while also adding the te reo term rāwaho for unrelated or outsider individuals who could potentially become insider ahi kā with decision-making rights by returning to the appropriate tribal area.

This is a lot of deliberate and deliberated business to encounter before even opening the book, where, on the inside cover-flap, there's a note by David Howard where he records that 'many uncollected pieces served as preparatory studies for these 150 titles', and concludes, 'This book has thousands of lines but in making it I am drawing one line. Another decade has gone, I'm done. This is the best I can do.' Further in are two epigraphs, one from Hahi Wilson (2019) that explains the book's title, *Rāwaho*: 'we are not from here'; and a second from Samuel Butler (1872), a gloss on the subtle instability of the word 'exploring'. The dating on the four-line poem *Rāwaho* (poem 93, p.148) indicates it was explored in one way or degree over fifteen years, 6.7.2006–19.4.2021. Under an epigraph from Albert Camus *L'Étranger* – 'Aujourd'hui, maman est morte' – is the following enigmatic yet precise gloss on 'not from here' – snatches of foreign language, solitariness, a sense of being distanced from what defined the location, a sense, even, of 'appropriate' tikanga in that alienation:

> Occasionally there was a sentence
> in French. You felt it appropriate
>
> to languish on the *chaise longue.*
> You loved the sea from the shore.

And also in the book's foreword material is a dedication to the poet's father Reginald William Howard, 'who taught me how to read' – with very close attention I would add, as a grateful if sometimes exercised reader of the result.

My attention to what comes before the poems themselves might seem pedantic were it not for Howard's matching detail, precision, and critical commitment to the poems themselves which, far from being dry or pedantic are fine-tuned, imaginatively inventive, often elegantly lyrical, and often – opening a random page – witty. On page 156 we encounter poem 99, 'Originality'. Sample verse:

> Freighters destabilised by their cargo,
> poets nose into the bar
> and take on water.
> The resigned smile of a lemon slice;
> the parasol that drags like an anchor.
> What a to-do
> now there's nothing to be done.

And another random pick, using an adroit line-turn, from poem 11, 'Morning' (p.18):

> My candle pales as dawn breaks
> down the door. Let's get up
> . . .

The term 'aphoristic' can easily be applied to many of the poems in this book, but it misses a range of linguistic and formal complications, including several poems that use a two-column format, for example poem 45, 'You say it's your birthday' / 'Well it's my birthday too', four columns across pp.58–59, where the reader's experience is of echoic or overheard voices speaking simultaneously. The critical value of terms such as 'laconic' and its natural companion 'droll', along with stripped-back lineation, sometimes recall the formal and tonal economies of Robert Creeley. In the opening paragraph of his ten pages of detailed 'Notes' in the book's final sections, Howard references the jazz pianist Paul Bley and quotes from an interview he, Howard, did with Lynley Edmeades and Catherine Dale in 2013: 'I heard someone who was not afraid to activate silence . . . I'm amazed by Bley's ability to let you hear the melody he's *not* playing and that's what I brought over to my poetry . . . I want that complex song from my poems.'

What 'complex song' refers to includes a substantial amount of rhyme and line schemes, especially in the latter sections of the book, for example in the ten-page poem 'The Ghost of James Williamson (1814–2014)', dated 19.11.2014–5.1.2015, which is also a voiced set of two dramatic monologues. Among the substantial long works, also dramatic, are libretti such as poem 144, 'Water Globe: A Libretto for Brina Jeź Brezavšček', which proceeds over 26 pages of closely rhymed lyrics sung by characters including the teenagers Martina and Martin, Veles ('the first tormentor of Martin'), Giant Water Snake ('the second tormentor of Martin'), Dragon ('the third tormentor of Martin'), Lucifer ('the fourth . . .') and Šembilja ('a projection of Martina . . .'). The short note to this work describes it as a 'libretto for young adults commissioned by the Slovene composer Brina Jeź Brezavšček for performance at Ljubljana town hall in December 2019'. These works enlarge and complicate the scope of what I described earlier as 'laconic' and 'droll' ('Water Globe' is neither of these), and it's fair to say my enjoyment and appreciation of the book's idiosyncratic substance as a whole had to take on its 'chore' expectations. I'm glad I did.

This is an appropriate place to revisit the book's closing poem, 'Judy is a Punk (Reprise)' and to check out the substantial note that annotates this small poem – the final note in that section of the book. The note includes the following quote from the Croatian Daša Drndić's novel *Belladonna* as translated by Celia Hawkesworth, which I take the liberty of quoting in full, since I couldn't have described Howard's own book better:

> He has already thought out everything in his life. In little heaps, small piles, he has laid days, years, births and deaths, loves, the few there were, journeys many, acquaintances, many, family dramas, his senseless chases and even more senseless small battles, on the whole lost, languages, foreign and local, landscapes, he

has tidily classified it all, and tidied up that baggage, that now unheeded burden, and arranged it in the corners of the spacious rooms as though yet another great removal awaited him.

‘There was no Met here’
The art scene in 1980s Wellington

The Bank of New Zealand Art Collection (Webb’s auction catalogue, 19 December 2022)

How to contribute to Webb’s book-catalogue on the BNZ collection of art with a text ‘contextualising the collection in terms of the Wellington art scene of the 1980s’? At a basic level this brief involves applying a spirit-level to 40-ear-old memories of where the art crowd partied in dealer galleries on opening nights, crucially between 1982 and 1987 – the years when the collection was assembled, so some memory overhaul required. The overall memory, though, is that we were having fun. The parties were happening around a mostly younger, new-kids-on-the-block crowd of artists; there was a sense of change and excitement in the work we were looking at and in the places where it was being shown, and in the talk and writing that was generated.

In addition, an evolving international cultural discourse diagnosing the changing conditions of art in the later stages of the postmodern informed how I and others interpreted what was going on in ‘the Wellington art scene of the 1980s’. Its precursor was Clement Greenberg (who lectured in New Zealand in 1968, thanks to Peter McLeavey), and the argumentative post-Greenberg consensus was that art during the 1980s was in a phase of reaccelerated change; what I now reread of my own commentary on the times reflects this. Postmodern discontent and impatience through the 1960s and 70s had opened up possibilities for performance, installation, conceptual and intermedia art practices, among other reactions against restrictive Greenbergian modernist ‘standards’. But as the postmodern began to settle down into its own conformities, what were the Aotearoa New Zealand manifestations of new, turbulent energy?

I wrote a lot about art during the 1980s, so I have a memory preserved in real-time text. I also have some documentary resources, including auction catalogues in one of which I find a Barry Linton cover illustration for the comic magazine *Strips*, Issue No. 2, c.1977 (Bowerbank Ninnow, Auction No. 6, 9 August 2017); in the same catalogue are six Bill Hammond drawings, 1980–82, with titles like *Waiting for the Pain to Piss Off* (ink on paper c.1980–82), which modernist art-historical convention might call 'primitivist', but which read as entirely contemporary back then, owed much to comics (art?) and also included a stylised Māori kōruru mask (primitive?). Art's crossovers with a Kiwi vernacular began to announce some kind of post-postmodern shift.

A sample of what was showing on opening nights in the 80s dealer galleries can start with the late Peter McLeavey's at 147 Cuba Street. McLeavey was the arts advisor to and effectively a lead curator of the Bank of New Zealand collection, and any retrospection on that collection has to begin with what influence the gallery culture – including McLeavey's – had on its development. The gallery's first Cuba Street listings in 1968 seemed a clear statement of intent: as well as McCahon and Woollaston they included Gordon Walters, Michael Illingworth, Milan Mrkusich, Michael Smither, Ian Scott, Pat Hanly, Ray Thorburn, Don Driver and Barry Brickell. A majority of these male artists were still with McLeavey in 1980, and so my memory of the 80s inevitably carries with it what came 12 years before.

In his 1998 show *What We Do Here* McLeavey made it clear that he was committed from the start to 'selling my dream of New Zealand. I have my reading of New Zealand culture, and I frame everything I sell within that . . . there wasn't any Prado in this neck of the woods. There wasn't any Bayreuth on the other side of the Hutt Valley. There was no Met here'. A key installation in 1980 was Richard Killeen cut-outs; I remember that the absence of obvious 'dream of New Zealand' nationalist introversion (boomerangs? A hippo? Anonymous tree branches?) seemed to bookmark an enlargement from McLeavey's McCahon/Woollaston opening address, perhaps to the I-told-you-so satisfaction of Petar Vuletić in Auckland: Vuletić's denunciation of what he saw as Wellington's self-centred chauvinism in the 1970s didn't include Killeen, nor Gordon Walters, Milan Mrkusich or Ian Scott, all of whom were included in the 2003 Gus Fisher Gallery *Vuletić and his Circle* tribute to the Petar/James Gallery, but all of whom were also founding artists at McLeavey's.

Even my unreliable memory of what emerges from the long view of McLeavey's from the late 70s through the 80s is not xenophobic listings. It's useful now to look at the 2018 Peter McLeavey tribute exhibition *50 Years, 50 Knockout Works,* which included, among others, Billy Apple, Laurence Aberhart, Nick Austin, Mark Braunias, Octavia Cook, Derek Cowie, Julian Dashper, Veronika Djoulai, Darryn George, Bill Hammond, Jeffrey Harris, Matt Hunt, Michael Illingworth, Richard Killeen, Zahra Killeen-Chance, Andrew McLeod, Oleg Polounine, John Reynolds, Peter Robinson, Ava Seymour, Michael Smither, Yvonne Todd, Barbara Tuck, Warren Viscoe, Robin White and Brendon Wilkinson. Of the 30 artists, seven were women.

This list reads like a straightforward enlargement of my memory of the gallery in the 1980s: an excited sense of what's happening, a continuous engagement with new artists. By my count of the BNZ collection website listing there were 117 artists in the collection in 1987. Of these, 24 were in the McLeavey stable of 32 – that is, 75% of the gallery's 'reading of New Zealand culture' and a bit over 20% of the BNZ collection.

Other dealers during this crucial time included the Bett–Duncan Gallery, established in Cuba Street by Elva Bett and Catherine Duncan in 1968. Bett was the curator in 1964 of the exhibition *A Room of One's Own: Women in New Zealand Art* at the then National Art Gallery – a signpost to her future agenda as a dealer committed to addressing imbalances in the representation of women artists in the dealer gallery economy. Duncan left the gallery in 1976 and it became the Elva Bett Gallery. Bett's stable (subsequently Louise Beale's) in the 80s had a substantial headcount of male artists, including many acquired for the BNZ Collection. But the Bett/Beale stable also included Kathryn Madill, Mary McIntyre, Sylvia Siddell, Dilys Rees, Andrea Robinson, Hariata Ropata-Tangahoe, Carole

Shepheard, Barbara Strathdee, Robin Swanney-Macpherson and Jane Zusters; gallery works by Gretchen Albrecht, Glenda Randerson, Pauline Thompson and Robin White were acquired for the BNZ collection. In 1980 when the gallery and implicitly its stable were passed to Louise Beale it was renamed the Louise Beale Gallery. Julia Morison and Claudia Pond Eyley joined the gallery; a work by Pond Eyley, *Kiribati Window* (1984), was acquired for the BNZ collection.

The slow but cumulative increase in a head count of women artists within the dealer gallery economy through the 1980s was further advanced by the Janne Land Gallery and Bowen Galleries (Jenny Neligan and Penny Moir), both established in 1981; and from 1980 the Women's Gallery. As well as Philip Clairmont, Gordon Crook, Terry Stringer and Dick Frizzell, the Land stable contributed Louise Henderson and Philippa Blair to the BNZ collection. Jenny Neligan and Penny Moir (Bowen) opened with Debra Bustin, whose work was also included. Lindsay Park's *33 1/3* gallery in Martin Square opened in 1987 and was just past the active acquisition time of the BNZ. Christina Conrad's marvellous *A Survey of Works 1970–1987* at Wellington City Art Gallery in June 1987 also falls just beyond the reach of the BNZ project, as does the gallery's installation series in 1986. Merylyn Tweedie at New Artists Gallery in upper Willis Street (1986) caught my reviewer's eye back then, but not the BNZ scout's; ditto Jane Pountney a bit late at Southern Cross in April 1987. However, Joanna Paul's 1983 *Stanza* series was, I think, included in Kay Roberts' Kelburn-based Brooker Gallery's 1987 exhibition. *Imposing Narratives: Beyond the Documentary in New Zealand Photography* at Wellington City Art Gallery in December 1989 fell beyond the scope of the BNZ project, but its curator Greg Burke reflected some of the shifts that were gaining momentum through the 1980s. Of the nine photographers in the exhibition, six were women, of whom four are included in the BNZ collection: Marie Shannon, Megan Jenkinson, Margaret Dawson and Fiona Pardington.

I'll close with two key memories: the New Zealand-born but US-naturalised citizen and New York-based sculptor and film-maker Len Lye's bequest of major works and archives to the Govett-Brewster Art

Gallery in New Zealand on his death in 1980; and the opening of the Women's Gallery below Photoforum in Harris Street, Wellington, also in 1980.

The Women's Gallery opening exhibition included Juliet Batten, Allie Eagle, Keri Hulme, Bridie Lonie, Heather McPherson, Nancy Peterson, Helen Rockel, Carole Stewart and Tiffany Thornley. Joanna Paul and Claudia Pond Eyley (see also Louise Beale above) were included in the BNZ collection, but the gallery's decade-long influence contributed momentum to an ongoing shift in dealer economies and demographics. It's instructive to look at a recent sample of this momentum: established in 2009, Bartley and Company Art's current listing includes 21 artists ,of whom 13 are women. The BNZ Collection as a whole includes works by 117 artists – 83 men and 34 women. The collection is both 'of its time' and on the cusp of what was changing in the tiring years of the postmodern.

The other key memory is of Len Lye's bequest to the country of his birth. Lye's interest during the 1920s and '30s in what was characterised as 'the primitive' in modernist terms was the outward sign of his complex and sympathetic engagement with indigenous cultures, and in many respects the impetus for his subsequent turning away from the modernist art centres of gravity in London and New York – he'd became a naturalised citizen of the United States in 1950. It's possible to read his posthumous New Zealand bequest in 1980 as a recognition that the metropolitan, anti-provincial modernist forces that had drawn him to London and New York had become anachronous, that vital energies and transformative shifts were to be found in what had once been characterised as provincial.

In many respects the BNZ collection of art is an endorsement of this realignment's opening moves, and even perhaps of Peter McLeavey's challenge back in 1998: '. . . there wasn't any Prado in this neck of the woods. There wasn't any Bayreuth on the other side of the Hutt Valley. There was no Met here.'

Shapeshifter

Tony Fomison

The Bank of New Zealand Art Collection (Webb's auction catalogue, 19 December 2022)

There is an extraordinary photographic diptych of Tony Fomison made by Shirley Grace in 1989, the year before the artist's death. It is simply and descriptively titled, *Double Portrait of Tony Fomison*. On the left side of the composition, Fomison faces us with his legs bared to reveal the lower sections of the prestigious Samoan pe'a administered by his friend, the tufuga ta tatau Sulu'ape Paulo II. On the right side of the artwork, Fomison is portrayed in the guise of an artist with outstretched brush in hand, facing his posed, tattooed self; he appears to be painting himself.

A self-narrative dramatising Fomison's commitment to inhabit as well as represent a complex reality incorporating Māori and Pasifika worlds is pictured in this image. Its implicit narrative theme, of esteemed privilege and its potential entrapments or conflicts, informs many of his paintings. It reads alongside the artist's early relationship with Māori in the vicinity of Lake Waiwera in the 1950s, and his archaeological interest in rock-shelter drawings and the punctilious tracings and notes he made of them. This complex convergence of personal identity, anthropology, and the quest for alternative, postcolonial national narratives are what make Tony Fomison's work unique.

A major work in this convergence, in which Fomison's self and that of an anthropologised subject come together, is the large painting *The Fugitive* (1980–82). In the foreground of a menacing, anthropomorphic landscape, in which the roots of trees gripping giant boulders resemble the talons of huge birds, a small, naked human figure is running – we assume fleeing. An interpretive background to this narrative is that the fugitive is a young woman of high birth, a

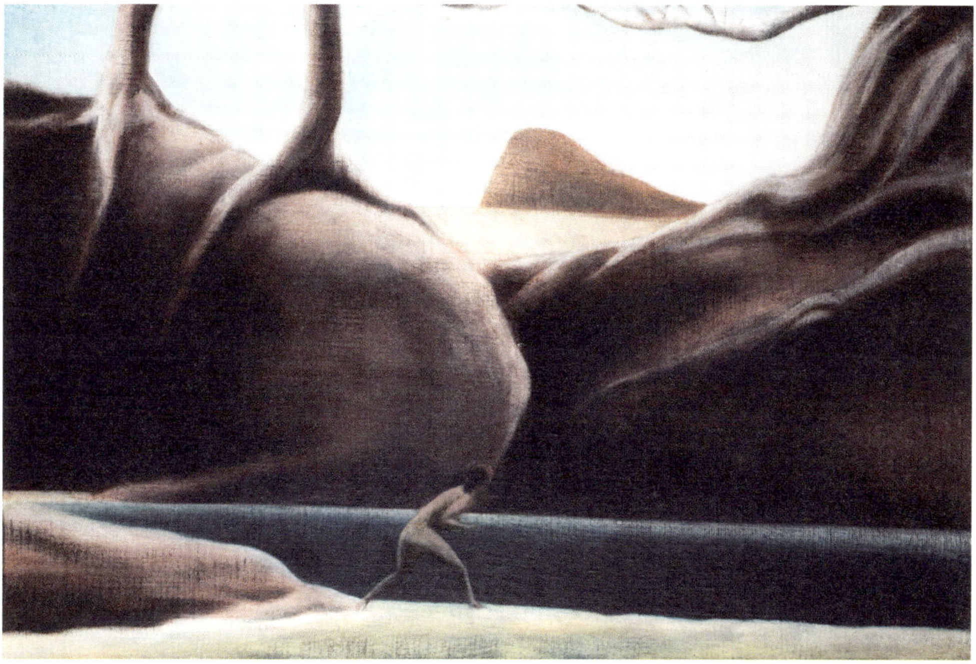

Tony Fomison, *The Fugitive*, 1982–83.
oil on jute on board, 1230 x 1830 mm.
Image courtesy of Webb's. Private Collection, New Zealand. Courtesy of the Fomison Family.

puhi destined for a significant prearranged and probably diplomatic marriage, whose life is controlled and managed according to strict tikanga. She is pictured fleeing captivity – either that of her own iwi or the one she has been gifted to for political reasons.

In Fomison's other treatments of puhi, for example *He Puhi (as Tribal Ancestress)* (1981), a dark shadowed mask-like face is portrayed against the light blue of an outside world – entrapment or restraint is implied. In *Te Puhi o te Tai Haruru* (1985), the small head and shoulders of a puhi with a topknot puhipuhi is loomed over by a giant face in the shadow of a cave-like overhang, with open sky beyond. In an earlier painting, *Open Window* (#193, n.d. 1977), a small naked figure confronted by a giant menacing head is looking towards the blue outside sky in a section of open window. Other images of entrapment include *In the Maze: Whose Mask Is This?* (#197, 1977), in which a pair of hands are holding a mask-like face up towards the outside light entering from above; in *Study from a 'Time' Cover* (#46, 1971), a face peers out towards a light source from behind bars; in *Untitled (Self-portrait)* (#196, 1977), the artist himself peers out past the restraining barred frame of a window; there's a photograph by Des Helmore of Fomison's front door at Beveridge Street, Christchurch, c.1971, in which the dimly perceptible artist's face peers out from the dark interior.

In these and other compositions featuring forms of enclosure, the caves and rock-shelters with petroglyphs that the youthful Fomison explored and documented in the vicinity of Lake Waiwera provide a background that is at once literal and symbolic. Stints in prison in Paris, in Banstead Hospital in London for a drug overdose in the 1960s, and subsequently in Rolleston and Paparua prison for drug offences also inform these narrative framings. In them, Fomison's self-identity as an esteemed artist-outsider in flight from restrictive social conventions is implied, as it was in the Militant Artists Union formed with fellow artists Philip Clairmont and Allen Maddox in the 1970s. In 1983, Fomison visited Western Samoa with a film crew making a documentary about pe'a. There, the conflicted, reception/rejection ambiguities of his outsider status as a sogaimiti or untitled tattooed Palagi were also significant.

Christ in the Desert: Crossing the Pass (1982), bears a structural resemblance to *The Fugitive* (1980–82) – a lone figure is diminished by a brooding, moonlit landscape as it makes its way towards a liberating opening or passage. In the New Testament gospels, Jesus Christ spends 40 days and nights in the wilderness being tempted by the devil. During the temptations, the devil takes Jesus to a 'high place' from which all the kingdoms of the world can be seen and tempts him with dominion over them.

Fomison would have seen art depicting this story during his time in Paris and London. His version of the Gospel story developed from another painting, *A Pass in the Limestone Country* (1980), and echoes several others involving moonlit tracks leading out to open space. These structural and symbolic repetitions of entrapment and escape in Fomison's work often involve rites of passage in various forms: mazes, windows opening to a lit world, caves and birth passages. The dramatic and even filmic lighting and narrative drive of these and other paintings reflect the artist's fascination with late Victorian children's books, which he collected. And again, the conflict theme of esteemed and outcast identities is key to the drama of *Christ in the Desert: Crossing the Pass.*

Untitled (Icon by Fra Angelico No. 1) (#78, n.d. 1973) is a copy of the cover of *Man, Myth and Magic* magazine (No. 88), from Fomison's collection. The second-hand copy probably also reaches back to Fomison's time in Paris and London, when he'd have seen Early Renaissance works by Fra Angelico in the Louvre and London's National Gallery – the magazine copy is in a sense a work of prompted memory. The crafted jute-on-wood support with its curved top echoes the frame shapes of 'windowed' Early Renaissance icons, a device repeated in other 'icon' paintings by Fomison, for example *Christ* (#121, 1976). In both #78 and #121 there's a sense of mirror image, of the phantom self-portrait the *Man, Myth and Magic* magazine cover may have suggested, along with its reflection of a time in the 60s when Fomison would have seen icons such as the one by Fra Angelico. Fomison did paint a literal self-portrait in 1975, *Self Portrait* (#98), an image that seems complicit in the company of the icon memories.

'I am painting the one picture all the time'

Gordon Walters by Francis Pound

Landfall, 2024

I'll start with some short samples of Francis Pound's text selected from many options in this immense book. They allow me to identify a few of its key qualities. Just over halfway through, in Chapter Eleven, 'Development of the Koru Series', a heading most readers, myself included, may assume announces the book's core moment, we read this under one of the chapter's subheadings, 'Sudden spasms and the reserve':

> However, there is an irregularity amidst all this regularity that cries out to be mentioned. In a sudden spasm, the top register's lowest red ochre bar turns down at right angles to itself, as if bent back in collision with the frame, defying the by now well-established law of the horizontality of the koru bars. A similar paroxysm seizes the fourth stripe down of *Koru Study: White/Grey/Yellow/Black* (1966/73), again disrupting the smooth, continuous, expected flow of the bars, but this time jerking the bar's end up rather than down.

A couple of pages earlier, in a chapter subsection titled 'Brutality and the return to colour', I encounter the phrase 'the sheer hardness and vehemence of what remains', and a little further on, in Pound's discussion of the influence on Walters of American minimalists, especially Frank Stella, during the 1950s and early 60s, there's the following: 'Walters was surely encouraged to stick with his pitiless stringency . . .' And, a not entirely fortuitous coincidence, in one of the great many lengthy marginal notes that enrich this book's discursive layers, a distinctly sarcastic reference to the likelihood that

Colin McCahon was influenced by Walters' 'pitiless stringency': '. . . though this is something no one will ever admit, since everything that McCahon does must always be entirely unprecedented.'

So: we're informed by implication that everything Walters did may have developed to greater or lesser extents from precedents that encouraged him in his 'pitiless stringency' and 'sheer hardness and vehemence', resulting for example in a 'sudden spasm' and a 'paroxysm . . . jerking the bar's end up'. This is language that dramatises the author's experience of dynamic and even sensational artworks that many, myself included, have read as cool and restrained – minimal both in their subtle impacts and in terms of their art-historical moment as associated for example with what 'has been called the first minimalist show: *Black, White and Grey*, at the Wadsworth Atheneum, Hartford, Connecticut, in 1964'.

Pound's language is immensely stylish, surprising, and infectiously eloquent. It's a great pleasure to read in itself, but also because what at first seemed hyperbolic ('cries out') startled me into a fresh way of looking at Walters' work. Here, then, are two of the book's key qualities: its stylish language and that language's provocation of a revitalised response to the dynamism of the work being described.

A third quality is found in the reference to McCahon (45 out of 55 substantial marginal notes in this chapter, 'Development of the Koru Series') which, as well as representing the highly unusual quantity and length of such notes throughout the book as a whole – a demanding and even eccentric book-within-a-book component – points to one of its major themes and accomplishments. This is the scrupulously and exhaustively documented in-depth scholarly account of Walters' search for and explorations of international models for his practice outside the claustrophobic confines of the New Zealand art scene from the time of his early experiments in the 1940s with what the Auckland City Art Gallery director Peter Tomory called the 'cliché' in which 'burnt forests and tortured tree roots writhed about the hills'. As Pound writes in Chapter One, 'Beginnings', '[H]e was demanding more of himself than a small, provincial culture demanded: setting himself an inward standard of excellence, based on distant European models.'

A key encounter within this thematic was with the Dutch/East Indian émigré Theo Schoon, who introduced Walters not only to aspects of contemporary European art, but also to what should be learned from the art and thought of non-European cultures; and that one could learn too from 'such groups as children, the mad, and the "primitive".' Walters' relationship with Schoon was not unproblematic, but the consequences of Schoon introducing him to Māori rock art, for example, would be long lasting and profound. The influence of Schoon's own artwork (which Pound describes as 'really rather dreadful') was unimportant; Pound quotes Walters as saying, 'I never actually liked his painting very much. In fact, I didn't like it at all.' Pound suggests that the young Walters 'prefers to immerse himself in reading rather than look at Schoon's paintings'. And the book goes on to document in great detail the quantity and persistence of Walters' lifelong research through art books and catalogues, as well as (eventually) through travel to Britain and Europe.

The outbreak of war in 1939 delayed Walters' planned journey to Europe. But in 1950, as Pound dramatises the moment in Chapter Four, 'The Journey to Europe: London and Paris', 'He was thrust into a state of impassioned receptivity, in which he was enabled to absorb sufficient to last him for the rest of his life.' A characteristic Poundian marginal note both qualifies and expands on this drama: Pound records that he heard Walters identify two pre-Europe moments as critical to his development, the first being his study of academic drawing under Schoon, the second the wartime discussions of modernism among 'the European refugees at the Ministry of Supply' (where Walters worked during the war). In this chapter we read both an account of the hostility to abstract art in New Zealand, for example where A.R.D. Fairburn wrote of 'the falseness of all abstract art' and 'the death-corpse-stinking falseness and utter dishonesty of Picasso'; and a scrupulously researched and documented record of what Walters saw and heard – a lot! – during his travel.

Critically, as well as benchmark encounters with the actual rather than reproduced work of Mondrian and other European abstract artists, Walters also saw 'examples of tribal art sensitively displayed in galleries as works of art'. And, 'I understood too how much of the vitality of twentieth-century European art came from the discovery by artists of this material.' And, '[It] was only by coming to terms with my being a New Zealander that I could go on to paint', Walters said in a lecture at the Auckland Art Gallery in 1983.

He was 31 when he went to England and Europe and, as Pound emphasises in the Chapter Four subsection 'Walters' Pre-journey Reputation', had already honed an accomplished figurative style and was on the edge of a successful career as an artist. But as a consequence of seeing the abstract work of artists including Mondrian, and the presentation of 'primitive' art in museums, he built 'a conception of his art as, in essence, a constructive operation with elementary, non-mimetic forms'. Here Pound quotes the great American art historian Meyer Schapiro, who was in fact writing about the 'astonishing conversion' of Mondrian, 'an accomplished painter of nature at the age of forty'.

This is one of the most illuminating revelations in Pound's book, an expansion of the third quality noted earlier, the scrupulously documented in-depth scholarly account of Walters' search for and explorations of international models. What's striking about the companioning with Mondrian, however, is a fundamental difference in Walters' situation: the intimate proximity in his own country of Māori art, as first pointed out to him by Theo Schoon but reinforced by his encounters with tribal art in the museums of Europe.

His 'conversion' when confronted with works by Mondrian, and several others including (up to a point) the geometricism of Auguste Herbin at the Denise René gallery in Paris, was complete enough, given the hostility towards 'abstract' painting in New Zealand in the 1950s, to lock him out of a local art world in which, as Pound notes acidly of artists including Toss Woollaston, the nineteenth-century example of Paul Cézanne was the innovative limit. And even Cézanne, Pound notes, was too much for 'the New Zealand Academy and the arts society painters, those middle-aged amateurs for whom Cézanne seemed utterly beyond the pale'. Let alone the work of the 1950s Americans that Walters looked at, including Ellsworth Kelly.

Among the abstract works to which Walters began to develop approaches following his return to New Zealand, Pound includes a gouache on paper, *Study for Grey/Pink* (1955), a fully abstract, geometric work of rectangles with a central pinkish square. Other works of gouache on paper using rectangles include *Untitled [Four Vertical Men (Red, Green, Yellow, Blue)]* (1955) – the square-bracketed titles are Pound's intervention, fully accounted for in his early methodological notes. The hint of figuration these works introduce is consistent with other works yet to be encountered, and also with Walters' omissions of descriptive titles. No such intervention was found necessary in the case of Fig. 90 on page 101, which is the first full-page koru-based work illustrated in the book, *Untitled No. 4* (1956, ink on paper, 278 x 218mm). It consists of what will become the black/white, figure/ground ambiguity composition of subsequent koru-based works, in this early surviving example incorporating a koru shape as yet unrefined and retaining an upcurved bulb and sinuous stem.

It's at this point in his career that Walters' rigorous pursuit of a methodology for an abstract art that would eventually become capable of incorporating the geometric potential of the koru resulted in his exclusion from the art world for almost 20 years. It also resulted in his destruction of almost all the gouache (and gouache and ink) on paper works of the 1950s – years during which he was working full time with little to spare for his art, little or no time to develop the gouaches into paintings, and no gallerists or collectors willing to support his practice.

Then came a breakthrough. Pound begins Chapter Twelve, 'Te Whiti', with a marvellous quote from Walters from 1966:

> I am painting the one picture all the time . . . It doesn't matter what the subject matter is, I am trying to perfect the one thing I was meant to do. To perfect it to my satisfaction. It is an unattainable thing, but you have it there right in front of you, all the time. (Quoted in Keith Stewart, 'Following a Straight Line', part 1, *Quote Unquote* 18, December 1994)

Pound goes on to ask, rhetorically, 'Why did he choose to abandon seventeen years of silence by letting a solitary and undefended single work out into so unmistakably hostile a world?' The occasion was the exhibition *Abstract Paintings by Forty New Zealand Artists* in early March 1966, preceded by the Hay's Prize competition exhibition. The painting was entered in the Hay's Prize with the title Painting 1965 and in the *Abstract Paintings* exhibition as *Te Whiti* – a kind of progressive coming out that also marked the first major sale of a painting by Walters, significantly a koru painting. The exhibition organiser, funder and curated was Baron Ralph von Kohorn, a German-born American businessman living in Wellington and the first purchaser of *Te Whiti*. With a hint of timely melodrama, Pound notes of this moment that '*Te Whiti* comes as a rising up from a dark reserve. Its parts seem incomparably placed and held.'

His book goes on in the following chapter to document Walters' solo exhibition at Kees Hos' New Vision Gallery in Auckland in March 1966, from which fewer than half of the 12 paintings survive, but which marked his entry into the active art world; and moves on through four further chapters to cover the varieties of ways in which Walters continued to explore 'the one painting'. Pound's account of the rigour of these explorations, especially in the 1980s and 1990s *Transparency* paintings (Chapter Sixteen), reads like a reaching back through the impulses and unflinching denials of the preceding 40 years, a narrative that has required a complementary and appropriately admiring homage in Pound's scrupulous account. *The late Untitled [Transparency with Shadow]* (1995) and *Untitled [Transparency with Light]* (1994) are, like the majority of Walters' works, not based on the koru but consist of twin rectangles, of which the left one is overlaid on its left side by a delicately diaphanous top-to-bottom stripe that modulates the colour of the rectangle beneath.

To complement Pound's salute to the artist's vitality ('sheer hardness and vehemence') I want to add this viewer's encounter with works of great refinement and subtlety that have a stillness that reflects an arrival or accomplishment, reaching back to works begun in the mid-1950s, abandoned in the 60s when the koru works predominated, and retaining the trace of Walters' encounters with the overlay works of Josef Albers. As Pound notes, '*The Transparencies* became a major part of Walters' painting of the '80s and '90s, issuing in an unbroken procession ended only by the artist's death.'

The fourth key quality revealed in the text is the book's debt to its several editors; and to the lucid overview of one in particular, Leonard Bell, who has contributed excellent Fore- and Afterwords, and also managed Pound's unabashed and generous use of and homages to the scholarly work of Michael Dunn.

This is without doubt one of the most important art books written in New Zealand, not just about the artist of its title, but also the complex international art history of which Gordon Walters has been a part. Dr Francis Newport Pound, who died in October 2017, made the turning of these pages into an experience of innovative, scrupulous and immensely detailed scholarship, regularly laced with dry humour.

The Clothesline

Canvas, New Zealand Herald (4 April 2020)

My mother and I were sitting on the back lawn in the fluttery shade of the rotary clothesline – its orderly pegging-out of the household's frugal wash was transformed into a disorderly flutter of light and shade across her face where a smile at once wistful and amused shaped the story she was telling me. My father appeared in the kitchen window above us. He was preparing our lunch sandwiches there and made a show of waving one and popping it into his mouth. My mother waved back and blew him a kiss but didn't interrupt her story. Her father Bert had lost one arm in a tipsy accident when she was a girl and she'd often helped him to launch his dinghy at Waikawa Bay. She'd always wanted to tell me what Bertie invariably said to her once the dinghy was afloat. Then my father arrived with a tray of sandwiches and a pot of tea and the dinghy remained half afloat for a while as we ate and drank. When we'd finished, he cleared our plates and cups away and took them up to be washed. My mother resumed her story, which extended past the launching of the dinghy – I sensed there was something important waiting to be revealed as Bertie sculled across the bay. Then my father appeared with another tray of sandwiches and another pot of tea. Oh dear, my mother said to me, he's done it again. But she gave him a kiss. Thank you darling they're delicious she said, and my father's eyes glistened as he looked at her with an expression I often saw. The shadows of the fluttering wash on the clothesline were like the patterns of light and shade on the surface of the bay as her one-armed father Bertie sculled towards the point of the story she was telling me. She reached across for my father's hand when she got to the moment halfway across the bay when Bertie always shipped his oar and always said, 'Love you, treasure,' and let the dinghy drift for a while on the flickering water.

Illustrations

Index

Page numbers in bold indicate illustrations. Footnotes are described by a page number followed by 'n'.